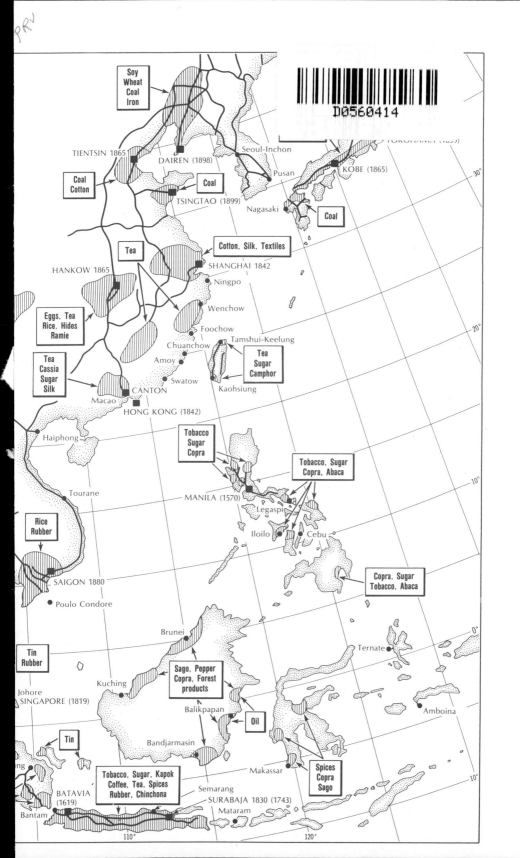

PRv

10

D0560414

Soy
Wheat
Coal
Iron

TIENTSIN 1865

DAIREN (1898)

Seoul-Inchon

Coal
Cotton

Coal

TSINGTAO (1899)

Pusan

KOBE (1865)

Nagasaki

Coal

Tea

Cotton, Silk, Textiles

HANKOW 1865

SHANGHAI 1842

Ningpo

Wenchow

Eggs, Tea
Rice, Hides
Ramie

Foochow

Tamshui-Keelung

Chuanchow

Tea
Sugar
Camphor

Tea
Cassia
Sugar
Silk

Amoy

Swatow

Kaohsiung

CANTON

Macao

HONG KONG (1842)

Haiphong

Tobacco
Sugar
Copra

Tobacco, Sugar
Copra, Abaca

Tourane

MANILA (1570)

Legaspi

Rice
Rubber

Iloilo

Cebu

SAIGON 1880

Copra, Sugar
Tobacco, Abaca

Poulo Condore

Brunei

Ternate

Tin
Rubber

Kuching

Sago, Pepper
Copra, Forest
products

Amboina

Johore
SINGAPORE (1819)

Balikpapan

Oil

Tin

Bandjarmasin

Makassar

Spices
Copra
Sago

Tobacco, Sugar, Kapok
Coffee, Tea, Spices
Rubber, Chinchona

Semarang

BATAVIA
(1619)

SURABAJA 1830 (1743)

Mataram

Bantam

110°

120°

30°

20°

10°

0°

10°

Notes to the Front Endpaper Map

Names in all capital letters are the major ports as they developed to a position of dominance in the nineteenth century. Those in initial capital letters are the most important of the lesser ports, many of them in existence before the arrival of the Westerners, some early Western-founded trading bases, but all eclipsed by the rise of the dominant centers. Dates for the major ports indicate the beginning of significant development under Western influence or control; dates in parentheses show the year of actual founding where this was wholly or partially a foreign initiative (which was the case with nearly all of them outside of China). Note the wide and more or less even dispersal of the smaller (and generally earlier) ports, and the locational advantages suggested by the map for each of those shown in capital letters. Canton is left here without a date, since it was a major port for many centuries before the Westerners arrived. Unlike Shanghai, Tientsin, and Hankow, which had also been important ports earlier, Canton's size and functions were not fundamentally altered by the Western impact, or at least not as much so. Rivers shown are only those on which power-driven vessels carried a significant amount of traffic.

It is extremely difficult to obtain accurate, meaningful, or comparable figures on the volume of trade through the various ports, especially before about 1900. The only widely (though by no means uniformly) available data, generally between about 1880 and 1938, are those listing gross registered tons of shipping entered and cleared (sometimes, especially in earlier years, only the total number of ships). This does not of course have any necessary relationship to actual cargo passing in or out, and tends misleadingly to exaggerate the importance of ports of call, e.g., Colombo, where much of the shipping using the port was in fact carrying cargo to and from elsewhere and might do minimal loading and unloading. For these reasons, no attempt is made to show here any rankings or any indication of trade volume.

An effort is made to indicate the most important goods produced in each shaded area for export, although of course not all goods were produced simultaneously. Rubber, oil, and tin, for example, did not become of major importance until the twentieth century, tea in Assam, Ceylon, and Japan, not until after about 1860, while indigo, opium, coffee, and spices became relatively unimportant or disappeared. The best and simplest single guide to the importance of these and other areas as markets for imported goods is probably a population map. It is very difficult to select and show appropriately both the chief commercially productive areas and the most important commodities. The solution, necessarily gross and arbitrary, is based on detailed analysis of trade figures and on more general economic history for each country and for each major port.

Volumes previously published by the University of California Press, Berkeley, Los Angeles, London, for the Center for Chinese Studies of The University of Michigan:

MICHIGAN STUDIES ON CHINA

THE OUTSIDERS

Michigan Studies on China
Published for the Center for Chinese Studies
of The University of Michigan

MICHIGAN STUDIES ON CHINA

The research on which these books are based was supported by the Center for Chinese Studies of The University of Michigan.

The Outsiders

THE WESTERN EXPERIENCE IN INDIA AND CHINA

RHOADS MURPHEY

Ann Arbor   The University of Michigan Press

Library of Congress Cataloging in Publication Data

Murphey, Rhoads, 1919–
   The outsiders.

   (Michigan studies on China)
   Bibliography: p.
   Includes index.
   1. India–History–British occupation, 1765–1947.
2. India–History–1500–1765.   3. India–Relations
(general) with Europe.   4. Europe–Relations (general)
with India.   5. China–Relations (general) with Europe.
6. Europe–Relations (general) with China.   7. East and
West.   I. Title.   II. Series.
DS463.M84   954.03   76-27279
ISBN 0-472-08679-0

For my teacher and friend, John Fairbank,
in gratitude

Acknowledgments

This book has been overly long in the making, but not for want of encouragement and support from many sources. No one really writes alone, and I have been helped directly and indirectly by many people, including those whom I know only through what they have written. It is a particular pleasure to be at last able to offer this concrete form of thanks to the John Simon Guggenheim Foundation and the American Council of Learned Societies for their support during 1966–67 when I began the bulk of the research for this book in London and Cambridge, where I was also assisted by the friendly hospitality of St. Johns College and the Centre for South Asian Studies. Among many others during that year, B. H. Farmer and Mark Elvin provided friendship, support, and invaluable critical reactions over many informal sessions as I was working out what I was trying to do. Mark Elvin played the same role in a subsequent setting, as a friend and also fellow participant in the conference organized by the Sub-Committee on Chinese Society of the Social Science Research Council at St. Croix in December and January, 1968–69, and then as coeditor of the volume in which the revised conference papers appeared, published in 1974 by the Stanford University Press as *The Chinese City Between Two Worlds*. He has been a genuinely tireless critic as well as a source of materials, documents, ideas, and continual encouragement. I owe him more than I can ever repay. G. W. Skinner, the organizer of the St. Croix conference and coeditor of the published papers, combined meticulous attention to many details of my data and arguments with imaginative ideas about the general approach.

I benefited more recently, in 1972–73, from a grant from the National Endowment for the Humanities and also again from the American Council of Learned Societies during a year of sabbatical leave in which I completed the draft manuscript; it is a pleasure to thank them too for their support. I owe a more particular debt to Wan Wei-ying and others at the Asia Library of The University of Michigan, and to the ingeniously and graciously helpful librarians at the British Museum, the Public Record Office in London, and the Libraries of Cambridge University, as well as to Om Sharma of the South Asia Library at Michigan. Successive staff of the Center for Chinese Studies have provided cheerful assistance in endless ways; I am especially grateful to Gay McDonald for her highly competent help with last-minute mechanics.

Morris D. Morris read in draft the chapters on India with the kind of imaginative care one rarely elicits even from an old friend. He has been my tutor in matters Indian and other for nearly a quarter of a century, and his example long ago encouraged me to think comparatively. Karl de Schweinitz Jr., who has served me well as a constructive reader of my work over even more years, gave the same kind of care to a reading of the entire draft. From him too I have long taken encouragement to pursue the comparative approach, and have come to depend on him as a superb critic. Irene Eber read a first draft and supplied important suggestions and welcome support. My friend and colleague Albert Feuerwerker gave the final draft the meticulous and expert reading of which only he is capable; his many penetrating criticisms have given me major help, and I owe him a heavy debt. Finally my teacher, John Fairbank, who gave me my original training and sense of excitement about the study of China, has continued through the many subsequent years to encourage, prod, inspire, inform, and follow my work. It is typical of him to have sent me detailed criticisms and suggestions, as well as support, as I was working out the final version of the present effort. Whatever I am able to do with the study of China I owe largely to him; this book rests more than anything else on what he has given me over more than thirty years.

Although so many people have helped me, the faults of this book are exclusively my own. I have persisted, sometimes against advice, in pursuing the big picture to the occasional neglect of finer tuning; but my conception of what I wanted to attempt made it necessary, I felt, to sacrifice some detail and some amassing of evidence on many points in order to make a series of larger points, and to look more at the forest than at individual trees. For similar reasons, but also because one book can do only so much, I have dealt no more than tangentially at best with Japan, and only slightly less so with Southeast Asia. It seemed preferable to concentrate in the space afforded by a single book on the two major Western experiences, in India and China, and to use each to throw light on the other. The forest here thus encompasses only a part of Asia, albeit a majority, although I have also tried to set this part to some extent in the larger Asian context, which I believe is useful if not essential.

Some of the material, including large sections of the actual text, of chapters 7 through 12 has appeared in print twice before in different forms: first in Rhoads Murphey, *The Treaty Ports and China's Modernization: What Went Wrong?,* Michigan Papers in Chinese Studies, no. 7, Center for Chinese Studies, University of Michigan, 1970 (as a slightly revised version of the paper prepared for the St. Croix Conference mentioned previously), and then in "The Treaty Ports and China's Modernization" in G. W. Skinner and Mark Elvin, eds., *The Chinese City Between Two Worlds* (Stanford University Press, 1974), pp. 17–71. I am grateful to the many people concerned with both publications. My study of the treaty port system was intended from the beginning as part of the larger effort represented in this book, but as a result of the St. Croix conference it was written up separately and in advance of the rest. When I came to put it to its originally intended use, I found that, thanks in part to the help which so many critics and editors had already given me with it in this earlier form, it seemed both arbitrary and unnecessary to start over again; much of it has therefore been retained, in pieces scattered through those chapters, although a good deal has been added and much of the earlier material and text reworked as well as presented in a different sequence.

The epigraph is from the *Journal of Ralph Fitch, 1583–1591,* reprinted in William Foster, *Early Travels in India,* London, 1921, pages 41 to 42.

Last, my thanks to my family, who have borne cheerfully the burdens which the writing of this book imposed on them.

March, 1975   RHOADS MURPHEY

Contents

Maps

When the Portugalls come to Canton in China to trafficke they must remain there but certaine dayes. And when they come in at the gate of the city they must enter their names in a booke, and when they go out at night they must put out their names. They may not lie in the towne all night, but must lie in their boats without the towne. The Chinians are very suspitious (sic) and doe not trust strangers.

−Journal of Ralph Fitch, 1583−1591

Chapter 1

Introduction

For a brief two or three centuries the West dominated the center of the world historical stage. That period came to a close with World War II, capping a century of unbridled industrialization, urbanization, and techno-logical explosion whose destructive aspects are only now beginning to be realized. As usual, it has taken most of another generation since 1945 to realize exactly what had happened and what it meant. The world stage is now increasingly shared, especially with Asia and most notably of all with China. This growing realization helps to provide a new viewpoint for understanding the preceding two or three centuries, for example, a clearer vision of the truism that the West has been the aberrant in the modern world and Asia more nearly the norm. The ascendancy of the West in Asia is over; it is possible now to see it in perspective and to begin to understand it. The threads which bound the treaty ports, in R. H. Tawney's luminous phrase, as "a fringe stitched along the hem of an ancient garment"[1] have been cut. Asia has reclaimed itself with pride. We are no longer participants, at least not in the same way. We can begin to be students of something past.

This does not make it easy, partly because it has become past too recently and we are still, despite efforts, caught up in it, still reaching for and disputing about even its outlines let alone its meaning and the relative important of this, that, or the other of its aspects. Because it is still recent, there is also still too much material around; attempts to see the forest are hampered by the luxuriant undergrowth. It is important, however, to keep the forest in view. No one book can hope to survey, interpret, or even acknowledge all aspects of any large problem. I have had to be selective because I wanted in this book to look at the modern Western experience in Asia in the large, and within that macrosetting to distinguish in particular the Indian and Chinese cases, as the two major samples of the Western effort at transformation. To deal with both, and to keep the wider context also in mind, has meant that I have often had to depend on broad generalizations and to avoid the presentation of detailed data or argumentation. I have relied on samples rather than on exhaustive coverage for the most part in order to make a number of general points, but have tried to ensure that my general statements do not misrepresent or extend unacceptably beyond existing evidence or reasonable presumption.

I do have a point of view to urge, which I regard as both valid and overdue: the effectiveness and staying power of the traditional Chinese system of production and exchange and its management, and the extent to which this helped to keep the Western effort from making the kind or degree of impact in China which it made in India and most of the rest of Asia where the indigenous context was fundamentally different. My focus is therefore largely, although not exclusively, on the economic scene (values and attitudes were also an important and regionally or culturally distinctive part of this interaction), and specifically on the role and influences of the colonial and treaty ports. These port cities were the early foreign footholds and became the centers of the Western drive to dominate and remake each country. The network which centered on the colonial ports in India came to encompass and substantially to shape the evolution of modern India. The parallel effort based in the China treaty ports largely failed to penetrate the indigenous system, and produced very little change. The revolutionary change which did come to China came through an indigenous movement which explicitly rejected the treaty ports and the model they represented.

The parochialism which has accompanied the growth of scholarly specialization has tended to concentrate attention on the separate regional contexts and has neglected comparative study. Most China specialists know relatively little about India, for example, and probably know more about Europe or Japan in the mistaken belief that such knowledge is somehow more relevant, or that knowledge of India is marginally so. India was the chief base from which the Western assault on China was launched, and their Indian experience remained in the Western mind the model for their ambitions in China. One can learn much about the distinctive nature and evolution of both areas, their cultures, and economies by comparing their responses to the Western effort and the extent to which that effort succeeded or failed to succeed.

The field of Chinese studies is overwhelming in its vastness and richness. In a way it mirrors the traditional Chinese view of the Celestial Kingdom as the Great Imperium; there is no time (and hence no need?) to study other things. Materials for the study of India, especially since the sixteenth century, are also dismayingly extensive, and many of them are readily accessible in the colonial records and in a growing mountain of other primary and secondary accounts in English. Both countries are vast, their experiences complex, their internal regional variety great. Those who try to combine study of both with a look at the larger context do so at their peril, the peril which keeps specialists specialized. But the very abundance of materials on China and India, the scope of Western ambitions and efforts in both, and their rank as the two major components of Asia make a comparison of them in these terms especially compelling, and especially practicable.

India, China, Southeast Asia, and Japan were exposed to the same West at the same time. The Westerners saw their effort, for all its variety, as a single system; at any one period their ambitions and motives in their attempt to penetrate Asia were essentially uniform. There were national differences in colonial policy and in techniques, but the consistent common goal was economic control even if the means varied. Asians as a whole also saw this effort as collective and uniform, although the several Asian responses and the nature of the Western impact differed sharply. There was indeed a grand colonial or imperial design for Asia, a model in the minds of Western expansionists.

The design can be seen clearly in the consistent character and intended roles shared by all of the many port cities established or controlled by Westerners in every Asian area or country which touched the sea. The setting, the local circumstances, the physical appearance, the institutions, the iconography, and the ambitions of colonial Calcutta or Batavia were widely duplicated in two or three score foreign-dominated ports throughout South and East Asia. Westerners (not only Joseph Conrad, Somerset Maugham, and their genre) could and did feel to some degree at home in any of these cities, and only a few superficial aspects changed as one moved among the ports across national or colonial boundaries and from one major Asian cultural area to another fundamentally different one. It was the same set of foreigners in each successive period, often the same firms or even individuals, who helped to plant these cities, to dominate their material and nonmaterial landscapes, and to shape their ambitions. India was the first Asian area to be reached and penetrated by an expanding West for obvious reasons of geography. Originally Indian terms or linguistic corruptions (bund, shroff,[2] chit, tiffin, peg), Anglo-Indian institutions and styles, and Indian-based groups such as the Parsees (one must not forget opium) were widely disseminated by the Westerners throughout colonial and semicolonial Asia to help underline their uniform concept of the grand design.

However, uniformity stopped with the ports, the foreign bastions, and of course did not encompass them entirely. If one can tune out, with an effort made easier by the passing of the colonial era, the noise put up by the foreigners while they remained aggressive actors and can thus examine more carefully the total context in each area, differences immediately dominate over uniformity. Here the Western self-image has been seriously misleading. Western success in India, and in parts of the Southeast Asia, not only in imposing colonial rule but in helping (with Indian collaborators) to transform a major civilization, was not representative of the subsequent experience in China. Everybody knew about the India experience, or took it for granted, if only because India's conquerors and arbiters were the British, or if only because of Disraeli, Kipling, and E. M. Forster. India had in effect been part of Western history since at least the battle of Plassey in 1757. Why should not the eastward extension of the Western wave have produced similar results in China?

Many Westerners indeed kept saying that they were doing so. What was more, their technological and hence, presumably, political power continued to increase enormously, by quantum leaps after Plassey, both relatively and absolutely. Why should they not inevitably and swiftly have prevailed, as they aimed to do and kept saying they were doing, in "opening," "civilizing," and "transforming" China, which remained throughout the whole period the great challenge and the great prize? It was Cathay which Columbus and his contemporaries sought. Dreams of the wealth of China and of the trade profits to be had from access to its immense market shaped the ambitions and the specific plans of Westerners in Asia from da Gama's time to the present, through a series of schemes referred to later in this book. Why did such persistent efforts by overwhelmingly powerful Westerners fail to produce in China the kinds of results produced in India?

The Westerners of the nineteenth and early twentieth centuries built a cumulative self-image of their own power, effectiveness, "development," and "modernity." Other cultures may grudgingly have been given some marks for achievements in art, religion, folk wisdom, or quaintness, but not in the qualities which make for success, status, and survival in the modern world. "Modernization," still a vigorous gospel among many Western scholars, has never, explicitly or implicitly, been distinguished adequately from Westernization. "Be like us," the West has continued to say, "and you will succeed. Persist in your own (i.e., backward) ways and you will fail." The rhetoric of imperialism has continued to blind us to many truths, as it has kept us from seeing the falseness of Western assumptions that Asia was somehow wrong because it did not uniformly react to Western assertions in a Western way.

In many respects the West did attain a rising level of effectiveness, beginning perhaps in the late seventeenth or early eighteenth centuries, and this tended to coincide in time with a falling level of effectiveness on the part of most of the traditional Asian orders. Both the Western rise and the Eastern decline were absolute, and their temporal coincidence shaped the pattern of the great confrontation. One might even attempt to chart this roughly as follows, where the curves represent a combination of military strength, economic prosperity or expansion, technological growth, and political cohesion (fig. 1). The dates are of course more or less educated guesses and should properly be different for each Asian area, e.g., perhaps for India the curves should cross about or before 1750, for China

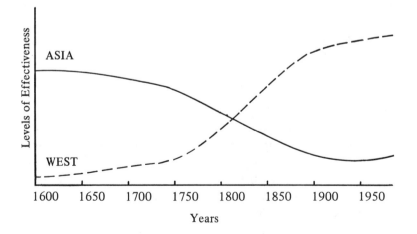

Fig. 1. Western Rise and Eastern Decline

about a century later. In any case, Westerners did prevail, far from uniformly or completely so, but more than enough to feed the illusion that the entire Western system was not only superior but had become the norm of norms for all mankind. The past was dead ("backward," developing, not developed) and the modern West, which had definitively created civilization, would lead the way for the rest of the slower-witted world into a bright future, Western style.

If, as Joseph Levenson has shown, the Chinese confused *meum* (what is my own idiosyncratic culture and valuable to me because it is mine) and *verum* (what is universally and unvaryingly true and valuable for all men), so Westerners have been, I believe, even more profoundly caught up in the *meum-verum* confusion. Material success in competition with other cultures and states as the West rode the wave of its own industrialization fostered enormous confidence in its own particular set of ideas and institutions. The West became convinced that what had proved to be apparently so valuable for it must be valuable for all other cultures, who in their own interests must be transformed into a Western likeness. This was not simply a matter of technology, but of the entire institutional, ideological, and moral system which had, or so it seemed, produced and managed the technology with such impressive results in the achievement of wealth and power. Western morality, Western law, religion, social convention, music, painting, architecture, literature, diet and cuisine, education systems, tastes, clothing, language, and all other cultural traits must be not merely superior to those of other cultures because of their association with material success but must be the universal standard—*verum*—for mankind.

So powerful was this belief that Westerners assumed the spread of their system ("modernization") need not rest on conquest but would take place as other cultures recognized the superiority and the universal truth of the model they had created. Railways should be their own all-sufficient advertisement, and knowledge of their source should similarly convince all "lesser breeds without the law" to adopt the values, mores, and institutions of that source. Surely no people would choose to remain "backward" once it had been shown the example of "progress," Western style. There was indeed a millenarian aspect to this conviction that the modern West had finally solved the universal human problem and that in time the rest of the world would hasten to fall into line, marching into a bright tomorrow as common converts to a gospel which was all things to all men, whatever their original differences.

The West is no longer so confident about its own success, the sufficiency of its answers to its own or others' problems, or the extent to which its model could or should prevail elsewhere; *meum* and *verum* are beginning to be distinguished again. We have now a new and valuable perspective from which to reexamine the recent past, and to distinguish Western ambitions and assertions from Western accomplishments at home and abroad. We can be better historians in part because we have escaped from the illusion which the West succumbed to, "the confusion," in Levenson's words, "one fosters when one judges other times by his own criteria without acknowledging that he himself, not the culminator of history, but the latest comer, has only what his subjects have—ideas, aesthetics, morality that may be reasonable, pleasing, commendable in his own day and age but not surely rational, beautiful, or mandatory as historical absolutes. No one has the norm of norms."[3] Chinese civilization, which had its own perdurable norms, proved both willing and able even in its own decline to resist the Western gospel, however compelling the Westerners saw it as being and however much it may have prevailed in India. We can better see ourselves now as the outsiders we have always been in China, playing for a brief period a role of some importance but never remaking Asia in our image.

The wider setting is presented in chapter 2 which surveys the early and the later periods of Western expansion in Asia as a whole through the planting of coastal footholds and the evolution of a few of them into major urban centers under Western domination which acted as real or intended nuclei for the Westernization of wider areas. This was essentially the Indian model, which was not only the earliest but from the Western perspective the success story which shaped and fed Western expectations and ambitions in China. The gospels of progress and modernization which in the nineteenth century these Asian coastal cities enshrined and advocated are critically examined as a leading aspect of the Western effort. The Western experience in India is then analyzed in detail in chapters 3, 4, and 5, against the setting of the idiosyncratic Indian polity, economy, and society. The Indian response, especially on the part of intellectuals, is presented, and contrasted with the Chinese response, from the totally different Chinese context. The British effort to establish a forward position for an economic assault on China, the persistent goal, by means of an approach through Southeast Asia is surveyed in chapter 6, and a detailed analysis of the Chinese context and response is given in chapters 7 through 12.

In China a culturally based coherence persisted despite political decay at the national level, as did a relatively productive and well-managed traditional economic system. The foreigners were kept on the fringes, in contrast to the inroads which they made in India not only in controlling the economic landscape and setting the pattern for national development along Western lines, but in seeing Indian intellectuals and nationalists admire and follow their ideological and institutional as well as practical or material models. Whereas foreign-founded and foreign-ruled Calcutta, Bombay, and Madras became centers for the transformation of modern India, their treaty port equivalents in China remained to a large extent enclave economies and enclave worlds ideologically and institutionally. The relations between the treaty ports and their supposed hinterlands, in contrast to the Indian experience, were severely limited. They were confined for the most part to the extraction via Chinese agents of a few predominantly agricultural goods for export and the distribution, again through Chinese agents, of relatively small amounts of imported or treaty port manufactured goods. There was some increase in commercialization of some sectors of the economy through the indirect agency of the treaty ports, and a substantial increase in foreign trade, but none of these changes bulked large in the context of the Chinese economy as a whole. In addition, Chinese merchants and entrepreneurs remained in control of the economy in general beyond the treaty ports and maintained a strong position even in the ports themselves despite the persistence of most of them in adhering to their traditional Chinese methods. Most were not followers but rivals of the Westerners, and successful rivals even within the supposed foreign domain.

Trading with foreign firms based in treaty ports, selling Chinese goods, and buying for resale a few Western imports or manufactures were not in themselves innovative or transforming phenomena for the Chinese, but rather the continuation of an old pattern. The Chinese remained in control. The foreigners were never free to invest in the production process outside the ports; they continued to deal with the economy at one remove, through Chinese agents. There was nothing remotely paralleling British, or even Indian, investment in new commercial production, marketing, and processing of jute, tea, wheat, cotton, and other commodities for which a large new national and overseas market was created, nor were there the large-scale nineteenth- and twentieth-century projects in irrigation, road and railway building, and mining. Steamships and later railways were genuine innovations of great potential for basic change, but during the treaty port period in China, for a variety of reasons, their effects were at best marginal. A few of the imports or manufactures—kerosene, machine-spun yarn, and, later, machinery—found a significant place and made a difference toward modernization, but the net results fell far short of transformation. Despite Western faith in commerce as a sufficient agent of transformation, trade alone produced little change, especially since most foreigners (apart from some of the missionaries) remained ignorant of the language and seldom ranged beyond the separate worlds of the treaty ports into the real China. *New* trade created as a result of foreign enterprise toward widening the market was decidedly modest and probably never exceeded, or perhaps even reached, 5 percent of China's net domestic product. This was in itself a measure of the nature and extent of the Western impact.

Ideologically and institutionally, there was also far greater resistance in China than in India to the Western model of self-styled success and progress. Given the disintegrating Indian context, it is understandable that even patriotic and nationalist-minded Indians were willing to recognize the British alternative as attractive, and attempted to replicate its institutions and values. Chinese cultural identity, national pride, coherence, and sense of self-sufficiency were by contrast incomparably stronger. Even though they might recognize the utility of various Western techniques, few Chinese urged a Western solution to China's problems. But no matter how willing to follow a Western model some intellectuals became in their despair over China's weakness, China as an entity did not respond positively to the Western example as displayed in the treaty ports, but negatively. The intellectuals who saw elements of potential strength for China in Western institutions remained a tiny and powerless group on the fringes of the country until after the treaty port era was over. The treaty port model did not spread economically, institutionally, culturally, and ideologically as the equivalent model in India had done and continued to do.

This is not to say however that there was no foreign impact, nor even that it was in the end less than in India. It was not, except on a limited scale, a material impact, but the effect on the Chinese mind was profound. Its profound character can best be seen in the nature and the violence of the Chinese response. The response was long delayed, and perhaps in part for that reason the more revolutionary. A century of national humiliation, as most politically conscious Chinese came to see it, and of rivalry and

challenge by outsiders and their system provoked in the end a new
national reaction. But it was aimed against, not parallel to, the treaty port
model, precisely opposite to the Indian response. The treaty ports remained peripheral, clearly alien, and hence the more easily rejected.
Calcutta and Bombay did indeed transform India, and did so with willing
Indian collaboration. They became a basic part of the Indian fabric,
something with which Indians happily, even proudly, came to identify,
for the good reason that they themselves had helped to build these
new vehicles of India's modernization, and had helped to spread their
impact. The foreign residents of Shanghai called it "The Model Settlement," meaning that its relative order, cleanliness, and "progress" contrasted with their opposites in China outside the treaty ports, but also that
the example of Shanghai would serve to transform the rest of the country
in its path. That never happened, and in the end the treaty port model,
having provoked at last a Chinese response, was rejected as a temporary,
resented, resisted, alien excrescence. The treaty ports had fostered change,
but it became a revolutionary change which in the end swept away both
them and the alternative they offered.

> The products of China are abundant; what need have we for the
> small and insignificant goods of the distant barbarians? Just because
> you wanted to trade we have had compassion for men from afar and
> did not prohibit [you from coming]. Now you are not able to keep
> your place and obey the laws.... The law will be upheld and
> feelings will be pacified. Everyone will return to harmonious co-
> operation.[4]

This conventional and somewhat complacent Imperial statement of the
Chinese position was issued in 1759. Very similar Chinese statements were
made again, notably at the time of the Macartney Mission in 1793, during
the ensuing eight decades while Chinese power and prestige were still
uppermost. For a century after 1842 the tables seemed to have been
turned. In fact, however, the edict of 1759 now seems more prophetic
than pathetic, and more accurate than pretentious. What did the foreigners
achieve in their brief heyday of apparent ascendancy in China? The
Chinese reaction suggests that something did indeed happen; all that noise,
and all the assertions of foreign exploitation, must have had some solid
basis. But it was not the basis which the foreigners strove for. However

successful or at least different the Western record appears to have been in India, China was not the same—as indeed why should one expect it to have been? The rest of this book will try to examine the dimensions of such differences, and the reasons for them, in an effort to see the great confrontation in context.

Chapter 2

The Grand Colonial Design:
The Indian Model of
Western Penetration

One must recognize at the outset the impossibility of dealing with the four and one-half centuries of the Western impact on Asia as if it were a smooth continuum. The obvious differences from one Asian area to another have already been mentioned, but there is at least as important a temporal distinction. The West which first encountered Asia, at the beginning of the great confrontation following Vasco da Gama's arrival in Calicut in 1498, was a vastly different system from that which was attempting to penetrate and transform China after the Treaty of Nanking in 1842. The change was mainly one in power and consequent ambition or confidence; motives and goals changed too, but less so, and in a broader sense remained reasonably consistent, the principal change here being the addition after about 1800 to earlier strictly commercial aims of the still only half-understood mixture of profitable conquest and destructive irrationalities we now label imperialism.

The interaction with Asia was not one way, in the sense that the West was at least as much affected by it as was the East. The European countries were newer and smaller than the great empires and traditions of Asia. Their interaction began just as modern Europe was emerging from its medieval and wholly different past, rapidly changing, eagerly seeking, and easily influenced by new stimuli, of which the Western experience in Asia was an important part. Trade with the East helped to create modern Europe's wealth, and colonial-imperial success to build Europe's ambition and confidence. Even in technology, the push for sea routes to Asia and their development formed the basis for Western superiority in ships, navigation, and naval power which were the necessary foundation for imperialism. Appetite fed on success. Power corrupts, and in this sense the

12

power which grew in part out of the Western experience in Asia produced the corruption of imperialism.

For nearly three centuries after da Gama's voyage to Calicut, however, Westerners remained confined in most of Asia to precarious footholds on the tidal margins. Whatever their strength at sea, they could not hope successfully to challenge the Asian powers on land and were generally content to function as marginal merchants in port settlements scattered thinly along the coasts, on the fringes of a system still dominated by indigenous entrepreneurs as well as by indigenous political powers. They competed not only with local traders in each place (and with one another, as rival European nationals) but with Arab, Malay, Chinese, Gujerati, and other Asian groups who had for many centuries been engaged in maritime commerce. Nor were the Europeans necessarily primus inter pares in this competition, at least not until well into the third century of their presence in most places. The period of relative Western insignificance in Asia, from 1498 to the end of the eighteenth century more or less, lasted a good deal longer than Western dominance, which came to an end in 1941, or at the latest in the 1950s. This point needs to be stressed now that the period concerned is part of the receding past; it may help us to understand a little better what actually happened during the brief high tide of the West in Asia, and why it happened as it did in different places.

It is, for example, startling to realize that Babur's victory at the battle of Panipat, which *began* the period of Mughal rule in India, took place only in 1526, more than a generation *after* the Portuguese had arrived in India and fifteen years after the founding of Goa as a European enclave. At least equally striking, the Portuguese were established at Macao by 1519, while the Ming dynasty (1368–1644) had still well over a century to run. The English East India Company began trading at Canton in 1637 and established a factory there in 1684, six years before the founding of Calcutta. Clearly, the Mughal and Ch'ing (1644) conquests, and the more general shape of events of the succeeding centuries in mainland Asia, were essentially unaffected by the presence of the Europeans; it was as if they had never been there at all. Their ships and their naval gunnery were the greatest single forces along the ocean trade routes soon after A.D. 1500, and as a result they could make some impact in some of the smaller thalassic insular and peninsular outliers of southeast Asia, notably west Java, Malacca, Makassar, and individual city-state kingdoms such as Bantam or Bencoolen (on Sumatra). But they had no power or influence, militarily, economically, or in any other way to create more than the most trivial ripple on the fringes of the great mainland empires in India and China.

European navigational and naval skills were, as suggested above, acquired in large part from their experience in developing the sea routes to Asia. At the beginning of the great confrontation, however, both Chinese and Indian ships were much bigger, at least as able, and far more experienced carriers of sea-borne trade. Asian achievements in this respect were part of a long tradition of technical leadership, especially in China, where by Sung times (tenth to twelfth centuries A.D.) ocean-going junks with separate water-tight compartments, multiple masts, sternpost rudders, and cargo capacities far larger than those of the Portuguese, Dutch, or English ships of the sixteenth century were ranging over great distances by sea. On the west coast of India too, certainly by the fourteenth century, Gujerati traders were sailing to and from East African and Red Sea ports while they and south Indian merchants and shippers were voyaging as far eastward as Malaya, in ships bigger and at least as seaworthy for these routes as those of da Gama or Albequerque. Ironically, when da Gama left the east coast of Africa to strike out for India, he first picked up at Malindi a Gujerati pilot who had sailed the route to Calicut many times before. A little earlier, he might equally well have picked up a Chinese pilot with the same experience, someone who had sailed to East Africa with one of the great Ming expeditions of the early fifteenth century in their ships several hundred feet long.[1]

What gave Europeans the advantage was their success in adapting guns for use at sea, mounting cannon on shipboard, and developing techniques for their effective manipulation in naval warfare. With the experience of the long trip around Africa and the need to beat into the wind (a problem already familiar to them in the Atlantic) they also developed a hull and rig which could function under boisterous and adverse conditions. Traditional Asian ships, sailing mainly before the wind following the monsoonal system, did not need to be designed to cope with these conditions. Western ships thus became faster on long east-west hauls, and rapidly improved on the navigational techniques whose development had been especially accelerated in fifteenth-century Portugal. Again it is ironical that Westerners forced their way into Asia with the aid of innovations originally Chinese—the compass and gunpowder—and used ships whose ability had been greatly enhanced by the adoption of the Chinese-developed techniques of multiple masts and the sternpost rudder. Admittedly, they used these things, and their other maritime and naval skills, with great dash and aggressiveness, true to the character of the modern West, and hence were able to extract additional advantage. They successively reduced Asian naval forces to an inferior position from which Asians rarely dared, after several early and disastrous attempts, to challenge the Europeans at sea.[2]

The principal exception was Asian pirates, who continued hit and run attacks even into the twentieth century. Piracy was endemic in the Bay of Bengal, along most of the coasts of Malaya and adjacent areas, and along the south China coast, where important trade routes ran close to wooded coasts with ample harbors of concealment beyond the effective reach of state power. This was one reason for the avoidance of coastal sites for cities before the advent of the Westerners.[3] In Ming and Ch'ing China the problem was severe enough during the height of Japanese pirate deprada-tions that the government attempted to evacuate all settlements from the coastal zone below Hangchow.[4] But it is instructive that, as Parkinson reports, Asian shipbuilders, especially along the Indian west coast, began soon after the Portuguese arrival to adopt for many of their ships a Western-looking rig in the hope of scaring off pirates, and often added dummy gun ports with the same object.[5] The Portuguese themselves, especially as they increasingly lost their hold on legitimate sea trade in the face of Dutch, English and other competition, became professional if not fulltime pirates, preying mainly on Asian coastal shipping in many areas, particularly in the Bay of Bengal approaches to Calcutta and Dacca, where in the delta there are still several tidal creeks called "Rogues' River."

It is certainly ahistorical to read back into the patterns and events of the sixteenth, seventeenth, and eighteenth centuries a prefiguring of what was to happen in the nineteenth and twentieth, or to regard (as many have done) the arrival of the first Europeans by sea as heralding a new Asian era of "Western dominance."[6] There are obvious risks in trying to discover in the past the seeds of the present; they are there of course, but they rarely dominate the past, which one must make an effort to see in its own terms. In at least the one respect of maritime and naval power, however, what was to prove a crucial Western advantage was apparent almost from the beginning. *They* were the seekers and probers, not the Asians, for the Westerners realized, accurately enough, that they had much to gain, as relatively small, poor, and less developed states, from trade and contact with what they themselves referred to as "the riches of Asia." All early

Western accounts of Asia, from Marco Polo on and in many cases into the late eighteenth century (in China well into the nineteenth) are full of admiring and envious descriptions of the sophistication and grandeur as well as the wealth of the East. Westerners had consequently to develop the techniques which made contact possible, and to become masters of the sea routes. This strength kept them viable, despite their relative weakness in other terms, in their shared or fortified trade bases on the coasts. Over the ensuing three centuries, the land-centered Asian empires, which largely ignored the few Europeans as marginal men of little account, along with other foreigners, went through their own cycles of growth, stagnation, and decline. During the same period European strength at home and abroad gradually and then more quickly increased, in part as a result of the infusion of their Asian commercial ventures. Some of their originally late-medieval trading "factories" spotted thinly along Asian coasts began in India to grow into genuine cities increasingly under Western management and even Western control.

As I have described it in somewhat more detail elsewhere, most of the early European trading posts remained small and never became real cities.[7] European attention was directed from the beginning to sites where maritime trade was already centered, or could be made to center, and which could be linked to sea routes westward. This led them of course to the coasts, the only places where their naval power enabled them to maintain themselves in any event, and to points where Asian goods for export could easily be assembled. While hardly a new development—Asian groups had been in the inter-Asian export trade for centuries—this emphasis was the sole objective of the Westerners, to place themselves where they could tap supplies of Asian goods and from which they could transport them by sea to the West. This contrasted strongly with the traditional Asian emphasis, in trade patterns and in urban locations, especially so for the great land-based cultures whose domestic trade was so very much larger than their foreign trade. Traditional Asian cities were designed to serve the needs of land-based empires whose principal source of wealth was agriculture.

Asian states and empires were predominantly inward facing; the great cities, and nearly all important urban centers, were inland, related to internal rather than external concerns. Without exception, the largest city in each state or empire was the political capital, whose cosmic role was paramount but which also served as administrator of a relatively homogenous and particularistic culture, to which the market towns and peasant villages of the Little Tradition belonged as well as the urban pinnacles of the Great Tradition. Even in insular Ceylon and Java, as in peninsular Burma and Siam with their long seacoasts, the political capitals and most other important cities remained consistently inland until the period of Western colonial dominance. In Japan too, for all its striking maritime configuration and the concentration of its population in a belt which hugs the sea, the capital was retained at inland Kyoto until 1869. Traditional Asian cities, especially the political capitals, were monumentally planned constructs, microcosms of the national or imperial polity, and symbolizations of legitimate authority. Trade and manufacturing, of course, took place in and through urban bases. Although the absolute amount of trade was high, especially by prenineteenth century standards, and almost certainly higher than in Europe, its relative importance rarely if ever rivaled that of administration as an urban function (including the administration of state-controlled trade and the management of revenue systems). Nor did revenue derived from trade ever constitute more than a small fraction of that provided by the land. The Asian states and empires were in most cases enormously larger, more populous, and more productive than any European states. Cities were much larger and more numerous in most of Asia than in the West until perhaps the early nineteenth century, when industrialization accelerated the growth of Western urbanization. But coastal cities designed for or engaged in overseas or even in coastal commerce were comparatively fewer and smaller.

Nearly all of the sites chosen by Europeans for their early ventures (i.e., outside of China) were thus either wholly nonurban or little developed, or were adjuncts to preexisting towns engaged in relatively small-scale local or even smaller-scale long-distance sea trade. Many of these early Western bases were entirely new; not only did they occupy previously unused sites but they represented a new kind of city exclusively centered on trade. With the Western mastery of the sea the Europeans sought out and established themselves at sites heretofore little valued by Asians in response to situational advantages for long-distance oceanic trade which until then had been relatively neglected. As I have put it earlier,

> European attention to the maritime fringes of each country was rewarded by the discovery of plentiful opportunities for a commercially-minded and determined West to establish trade centers on

its own models. . . . It was the seaman and the merchant, usually in the same person, who sought out, from the deck of a ship, the most promising places for the establishment of settlements best calculated to serve the interests of external trade. . . . This was urban development from the exclusive point of view of the maritime commercial entrepreneur, in contrast to the urban patterns of the Great Asian Traditions.[8]

As transport technology improved with larger ships, later with railways and river or coastal steamers, and as the market for Asian goods expanded in the West, the familiar process of urban concentration evolved, as it has under similar circumstances everywhere else. The literally hundreds of small port towns which shared the fragmented trade of early modern Asia were increasingly overshadowed and many of them in the end extinguished, as the Western impact reoriented economic spatial patterns, by the snowballing growth of a few urban giants at the most favorable locations where maximum accessibility to sources of export goods and to the sea routes was combined. The major export goods changed over time, and accordingly so did the areas which were commercially important. The early English base in India prompted efforts to expand trade connections into adjacent southeast Asia, an enterprise administered from India and regarded as an integral part of the East India Company's operations, as were the persistent efforts to penetrate the China market. New transport technology also altered access, both internally and externally. Until the nineteenth century, access to and from the sea was more or less equally possible at a great variety of small ports, each with its own restricted hinterland to landward. Steel and steam, and the rapid increase in the most economic size of ships, made many of these earlier ports physically inaccessible, nor could many of them provide suffcent cargoes or markets. Rising production of many export goods, and rising Western demand, also tended to promote regional specialization. Economies of scale furthered the concentration of production in certain areas, while new mechanized transport made selected areas most accessible and hence most able to specialize. Goods for export were increasingly funneled into a few major ports where internal and external (sea) transport access were maximized.

Paradoxically, many of these major ports had poor natural harbors, in large part because so many of them were deltaic, reached by way of narrow, winding, and silted rivers.[9] This is, however, a common phenomenon among world ports as a whole; harbors are improved or even created ex nihilo where other factors combine to produce trade flows and the need for land-sea exchange. Mechanized dredgers, cement and steel for artificial harbors, and better techniques for managing hydrologic problems on a large scale became available as ship sizes increased and port volumes rose. Deltas, especially in Asia, are exceptionally productive and hence potentially trade-generating places. They also have excellent internal access, via the river that created the delta or along its valley, which tends also to be densely populated and highly productive. Exceptions were few; Bombay, Singapore, Manila, and later Hong Kong, Dairen, Tsingtao, Kobe, and Yokohama had good natural harbors, but most of them had the handicap of more difficult landward access. Some were able to make up for this handicap by access to their hinterlands via easy coastal routes, as did nearly all the ports in the Indonesian and Philippine archipelagos, in addition to Singapore and Hong Kong.

The gradual process of concentration, and some of the reasons for it, are suggested in the front endpaper map and in the notes to the map. [10] The process of concentration took place over several centuries, and the pattern of the Western colonial city in Asia and the treaty port phenomenon did not fully emerge until the second half of the nineteenth century as a result of a combination of changes taking place at both the Western and the Asian ends, including the development referred to earlier as "the crossing of the curves" but centering in the consequences of the Western industrial revolution.

That shift in relative power and effectiveness began to make it possible for Westerners to extend their influence in a landward direction for the first time, and hence to become involved in inland production and transport as they had not been before when they acted only as marginal merchants at the fringes, competing for what already existed. This change began to take place, as it happened, on the eve of the invention of railways and the expanded use of steam power and at the time of industrialization, of which they were a part, with its enormously increased appetite for goods and raw materials which could be produced inter alia in Asia. Western industrialization and the heightened emphasis on trade and markets also increased interest in Asians as potential consumers. The opening of the Suez Canal in 1869 accelerated the force of Western-managed commercialization and penetration of Asia. It marked a significant turning point in Western effectiveness on the Asian scene and in the processes suggested in the front endpaper map. The high tide of the West in the East began its flood only with the opening of the Suez. Westerners were no longer cap-in-hand in the vestibule, but could enter the house and attempt to rearrange it to suit their own interests. Their entry was never complete, in large part because they did not really want to supplant all of the existing Asian systems, even if they could have managed to do it. Their goals could be realized by a combination of investment in selected production, preservation of order where necessary, and provision of transport so that the desired goods would flow in and out through the port cities where the Western presence and power began and where it continued to center.

Although as already suggested we have tended to overemphasize the historical significance of that role, for a century after about 1850 it looked impressive. The center of all important changes taking place in each Asian country seemed to be in the port cities where outsiders called the tune or had set the pattern. These port cities were the links between Asia and the rest of the world (notably the West itself) which was now impinging so effectively on the East. The docks and the forest of masts (later smoke stacks) surrounding each of these cities appropriately symbolized Western success, not only technologically but as a total system which had established itself on coastal beachheads that eventually widened into major entry ports for the transforming infusion of new alien vigor. Indians in particular appeared to be responding, by producing a growing group of "Westernizing" and often enthusiastic collaborators, intellectual and ideological as well as commercial, and in any case by voting with their feet. In the relatively short space of a hundred years—especially on an Asian time scale—longstanding patterns of urban location and hierarchy and of internal movement and ordering were not just fundamentally changed but turned inside out. The new Western-founded or Western-dominated coastal ports became by far the biggest cities in each area and each national unit. These cities appeared increasingly to shape and preside over the national life, and despite their peripheral locations became overwhelmingly the major centers of extra-local spatial interaction patterns in each country. Practically all of the largest coastal or near-coastal cities in contemporary Asia owe the bulk of their growth, their economic character, and in many cases even their origin to Western traders since the seventeenth century. They have always been Asian cities, in the sense that Westerners have never formed more than the tiniest handful of their populations; they grew because Asians flocked to them, as they still do. But they were Asian cities of a revolutionary new kind with revolutionary potential to transform each indigenous system as a whole.

The nineteenth-century Westerners and their Asian collaborators saw themselves as apostles of progress in part because their values and institutions as well as their technology had shaped a new kind of city on the fringes of the great Asian empires which contrasted in nearly every respect with traditional Asian models. As city-based merchants and industrialists had transformed the modern West, so would they transform an Asia which often reminded them of their own premodern roots; its indigenous cities struck them as more like ancient Rome or medieval Paris than like contemporary Manchester. They succeeded in planting little islands of modern Europe on the Asian coasts, some of which in time grew to become the cities which still dominate each Asian country.[11] Their urban skylines came to be punctuated by larger buildings in almost purely European and American style, replacing earlier architectural styles which were a blend of local and Western modes adapted to local climate and materials, referred to variously as "Calcutta Corinthian" and "Compradoric," and reflecting an earlier period of a much lesser Western role in Asia.

Physically, the cities looked like the alien transplants they were, a circumstance underlined by their orientation to the sea and, wherever possible, to surrounding waterways, originally designed for defense against the more powerful Asian orders. Most of these cities had navigable water on two, three, or even four sides, often in artificially created or deepened channels. As late as 1843, this point was explicitly made by George Balfour, first British consul in the water-surrounded treaty port of Shanghai: "By our ships our power can be seen, and if necessary felt."[12] It was indeed by their ships that the power of the Westerners could be seen, as alien intruders from overseas who had developed the means to maintain themselves on these beachheads and then to use them as funnels for the extraction of wealth. They remained peripheral, but nevertheless played a revolutionary role.[13]

Although they did not directly involve more than the tiniest fraction of the area or the population of any Asian country, what went on within them indirectly set in motion changes which spread over Asia like ripples covering a pond from the casting of a single stone. As transplants from nineteenth-century Europe, they enshrined the Protestant ethic, the sanctity and freedom of private property, the virtues of individual enterprise, the power and self-satisfaction of private capital, and the battery of techniques which had burgeoned in the West to carry on the business of this new kind of world: stock companies, agency houses, trading firms, banking and insurance facilities, legal safeguards for the protection of enterprise and property, steam and steel, and the revolution in transport which underlay the new economic growth. Part of the driving power of this mushrooming development was modern Western nationalism, a new and revolutionary concept to Asia. In all these respects, the active working models were displayed in the port cities, and their demonstration effects were powerful.

India was the earliest and clearest case. Like the rest of Asia, it lacked the economic and institutional infrastructure for the new kind of commercial-industrial enterprise which Westerners introduced. Once initiated in the port cities, or once they acquired momentum, such developments attracted and helped to create Indian participants, mainly as workers and hangers-on in an expanding urban economy, but also as partners in Western-style roles such as traders, managers, entrepreneurs, investors, and eventually technicians, civil servants, professionals, and industrialists. This was a key aspect of the Western impact as these cities drew to them certain groups of Asians, exposed them to the demonstration model, and transmitted to them either Western values and techniques, or reactions against them, usually of course both. Modern Asian nationalism clearly grew from such roots, in the long run perhaps a more important transmission even than Western technological developments. Nationalism had been irrelevant in the traditional setting, where each culture and imperium had existed in and of itself and was relatively little involved in interaction with other cultures. Only as each area became more closely connected with other areas and other traditions, primarily through the agency of the colonial ports, did distinctions become apparent. This was especially true in relations with the West, whose model of vigor and effectiveness suggested that Western-style nationalism was an important source of strength.

Different Asian groups of course reacted differently. There was also an unplanned selection process which brought certain groups, such as the Parsees, Marwaris, Tamils, Cantonese, or Ningpo men disproportionately into the booming port cities all over Asia, or in other cases—Bengalis, Shanghainese—deposited a Western-type city in their midst. Some of the groups which achieved new success under these circumstances, as compradores or as independent entrepreneurs responding to radically changed opportunities, appear to have been parvenus, not prominent at least in the commercial landscape of traditional Asia. In any case they were limited to their home areas before but now could expand their commercial activities over large sections of each country and even beyond, as did the Parsees. The Marwaris in India may be the best example, coming originally as a relatively minor group of traders from the marginal and arid area of Rajasthan to acquire commercial dominance in booming Calcutta and a strong position in the other new Indian and some southeast Asian port cities. To a degree, the expansion of Cantonese commercial power throughout the nineteenth-century Chinese treaty ports and beyond into the expanding urban-based economy of southeast Asia was similar, although the change from traditional Cantonese activities was not so radical. But many of the compradores, in China and elsewhere in Asia, people who used their connections with and services to Westerners as a means to wealth and status in the colonial ports, were not representative of the top drawer in traditional commercial circles, let alone in overall status terms. The location of the colonial ports also concentrated new opportunities for advancement in certain areas, commonly not those where advancement was traditionally most available, and hence profited certain regional groups at the expense of others which had been better situated earlier.[14]

Whatever the patterns, these cities produced a new kind and degree of ferment, including new patterns of migration. A further result was the development of cosmopolitan and dynamic urban settings which proved to be romantically and temptingly attractive to both Asians and Westerners, despite the harsher realities involved in the struggle for advancement and wealth. They were stimulating, colorful, and fascinating places not just in Somerset Maugham terms or to merchants, but to Asian peasants and workers as well as entrepreneurs. One can see the attraction at work even in contemporary Calcutta which continues to draw migrants, however dreadful material living conditions and however limited actual employment opportunities may be there. Surely a large part of the reason, aside from the presence of actual economic opportunity (which was and remains real), is the fascination of the center of action, the very heterogeneity, cosmopolitanism, and excitement of these cities which grew so largely on varied migration and supported increasingly the bulk of new cultural ferment at every level. They also offered an escape from structured roles and the constraints of membership in smaller kin, rural, regional, and traditional groups. Thus, it was and remains more attractive to take one's chances of ending up unemployed in an exciting urban setting where there is at least the chance of both handouts and circuses, than to continue an at least equally difficult, and less exciting, struggle for existence in the countryside. Much of the port cities' growth has probably always consisted of hangers on as in many cases it seems to do now. But growth did take place on a truly phenomenal scale, suggesting that there was a solid share of expanding economic and professional opportunity, much of it of a totally new character. This attracted and was fueled by upwardly mobile entrepreneurial and intellectual groups as well as workers and peasants.

By the end of the period of colonial control, the overwhelmingly largest city in each country (again with the qualified exception of Japan) was a Western-founded or largely Western-developed port.[15] Japan is a qualified exception in the sense that Tokyo became a major port and strongly primate city whose multimillion growth after 1870, albeit in Japanese hands, resulted primarily from Japan's new involvement with the West. Tokyo became (with Yokohama as its adjunct, a city which like Kobe started life as a Western-founded treaty port on a previously unoccupied or nonurban site) a more uncompromisingly "Western" city than any in Asia, although as Edo it was a big city long before Perry. Even Japan was unable to exclude Western privilege after 1853; Shimoda, Hakodate, Nagasaki, and Niigata were "opened" as treaty ports in addition to Kobe and Yokohama. Extraterritoriality and the treaty port privileges remained in force until 1899 and Japan did not recover full tariff autonomy until 1911. Bangkok, it is true, became the Thai capital by historical coincidence on the eve of the major nineteenth-century Western drive in Asia. But its growth from small and inauspicious beginnings in 1782, as a refuge for the defeated court at the end of a disastrous war with Burma, on the deltaic fringe of the country amid the protection of tidal marshes, to its modern primacy as the center of Thailand took place under Western dominance and was fueled primarily by Western efforts to stimulate external trade. The same applies to Rangoon, although there the Western hand was stronger.[16] These new port cities became not only far larger than the traditional capitals or inland cities; they had taken over their functions as new national centers, institutionally and ideologically as well as economically.

In the larger countries such as India and Indonesia, port cities founded de novo by Westerners occupied the first several places in the size hierarchy. In India, Calcutta, Bombay, and Madras, in that order, remained the big three until after independence, as they had been since at least 1850 despite the shift of the colonial capital from Calcutta to Delhi in 1911 in an effort to legitimize the British imperium. The Indonesian hierarchy at independence was led by Batavia (now Djakarta), Surabaja, and Semarang. All of these Indian and Indonesian port cities had arisen on sites either vacant until the planting of the first Western fort, or occupied by small villages. In the smaller countries, the one major city which dominated the urban hierarchy in multiple primacy was the Western-colonial port: Colombo, Rangoon, Bangkok, Singapore, Cholon-Saigon, Hanoi-Haiphong, and Manila. As centers of external trade, all these cities were still more sharply dominant. More than 90 percent of India's foreign trade in the 1930s passed through Calcutta, Bombay, Karachi, and Madras, in that order.[17] None of them were in existence before the seventeenth century and all developed with the impetus provided by Western entrepreneurs. A similar proportion of China's foreign trade in the same period passed through the treaty ports of Shanghai, Tientsin, Dairen, Hankow, and Hong Kong—Canton.[18] In the smaller countries, foreign trade was to the same or to a greater degree concentrated in the one port which owed most of its development to Western initiative. Apart from simple size primacy, the new intellectual life of each Asian country came to center in the colonial ports. All lines of modern internal communication focused on them, and they dominated publishing, information, and education. They were the leading bases of the new Asian nationalism and cultural renaissance.[19]

They were also the seats of colonial or semicolonial bureaucracies, concerned both with political and financial administration and with the management of new commercial and industrial enterprises. The bureaucracies were staffed by Asians as well as by Westerners; they served as an important vehicle of Westernization and as a school of Asian nationalism. Although the number of Asians employed in the Indian Civil Service, the Chinese Maritime Customs, and their equivalents elsewhere was never very large, many were involved in lower-status posts associated with these and similar organizations and hence were offered an important model of integration and organization. By comparison, most of the surviving indigenous cities, inland centers and traditional capitals, tended to remain largely outside the new world of change being shaped in the colonial ports. The old channels of advancement, the avenues for ambition and for public service, shifted from their traditional lines spatially as well as institutionally, and increasingly centered in the ports. Factory-based and power-driven manufacturing, when it came, was almost exclusively confined to these same cities. This of course further augmented both their economic bases and their capacity to transform their hinterlands.

In all these respects there are parallels to the role played by Western-founded or Western-developed port cities in the modern growth of Africa and Latin America.[20] Calcutta, Batavia, and Shanghai had their semiequivalents in Accra, Lagos, Buenos Aires, and Sao Paulo, which acted as funnels for the export trade and entry ports for the transformation of each country along European lines. They too were "head-link" cities, bridges between each area and a world across the sea.[21] Similar roles, and of much longer standing, were played by many of the port cities of North Africa and the Middle East: Algiers, Tunis, Alexandria, Istanbul, Basra, and in a quite different context by ports which linked white overseas colonies with the homeland: Sydney, Wellington, Capetown, Durban, Montreal. But the differences from the Asian case seem at least as important as the parallels. In none of these non-Asian areas was there an indigenous system as highly developed, as large in its mass, as confident in and identified with its own tradition, and hence as difficult to move as in every Asian area. Accordingly, Ghana, Nigeria, Argentina, Brazil, Algeria, or Turkey were far more fundamentally transformed through the agency of their head-link cities. Although elements of original and pre-European culture remained (outside of Latin America, also the indigenous people as a whole), they were for the most part in full retreat, subsidiary in virtually every way to the dominantly Western new hybrid model generated in and spread from the ports. By comparison, a relatively confident but small force of Westerners in Asia at every period, including the high tide of Western power and prestige in the nineteenth and early twentieth centuries, were competing and attempting to manipulate an enormously larger, more stable, and resistant mass. At the beginning of the confrontation and for some time thereafter, even in relation to the West, Asia was far from underdeveloped, "backward," or unsophisticated. Technologically, economically, institutionally, as well as in more general cultural terms, Asia remained in most respects at least in the same league with the West (however such things may be measured) until late in their confrontation. Even as the traditional orders began to weaken and crumble they never wholly lost their self-sufficient cultural identity or their ability to function without succumbing completely to a Western-style model.

However effective and compelling the Western model and Western power became, and however much it was able to manipulate and to provoke responses from the Asian systems, it was never completely able to move or to prevail against the mass. The mass was immense, in area, in numbers of people, and in the weight of deep-rooted and highly developed traditional culture. The forces impinging on it were heavily concentrated in the port cities, on the fringe of each country; they stimulated new urban growth in some areas along newly built rail lines, but touched only lightly and selectively the rural areas where most Asians continued to live. Diffusion of the forces for change was centered in communication lines, literate groups, and areas of commercialization, fanning out from the highest concentrations in the ports but never encompassing more than a small part especially of the larger countries, except in the most tangential fashion. The story is told (unfortunately I no longer remember by whom) of interviewing in rural India in the 1950s where to the interviewer's question "Do you think things are better for you now, or were they better under the British?" a frequent (though not majority) reply was "Who are the British?" However typical or atypical this may have been, or how much precisely it may mean beyond simple communications friction, it is a useful reminder that even in India, where one would have supposed the Western impact to have been basic and all-pervasive if only because it began so early and lasted so long in the form of full colonial sovereignty over most of the country, the Western presence did not carry all before it.[22] There was certainly an enormous increase in the degree of impact during the nineteenth century, especially compared to the earlier period when it would seem Westerners in Asia counted for nothing. But this does not mean that at the high tide of their power in Asia they counted for everything.

Part of the reason for the tunnel vision of Westerners about their own accomplishments in Asia has been the gospel of modernization, in the terms used in the first chapter of this book, as it reflects ethnocentric self-satisfaction and confusion between *meum* and *verum*. "Westernization" and "modernization" have been confused by Western pride. The West happened to be the first to pursue and achieve a number of universally desirable goals: national integration, industrialization, mass literacy and political participation, scientifically based improvements in agriculture and medicine, a revolution in transport and communications and with it a widening of both economic and cultural horizons. All of these and other related goals came to be shared by most of the rest of the world as an answer to each culture's perception of its own needs, not as an effort to replicate the Western *value* system. Each culture has pursued at its own pace its own path toward these goals, and each is producing culturally specific results. The original stimulus or challenge of the modern West, especially as an actual or potential conqueror, was of course the basic dynamic which initiated all these changes. But to call the result Westernization or to equate what is labeled "modernization" with the Western model, as is commonly done, is to misunderstand what has happened, and to demonstrate that ethnocentric Western pride is still obscuring Western vision.

All societies are to some degree dualistic, combining tradition with change. Change is not and need not be uniform. Because Asian countries, in their pursuit of the universally desired goals listed above, chose in some respects to follow different development models from those offered them by the West, or altered and adapted those models, or reacted against them, does not mean that change was not happening or that it was somehow less "modern." Because other countries chose in other respects to follow more closely originally Western models does not mean that they were more "modern." Nor does striving for universally desired objectives such as industrialization or medical advances mean that their achievement must produce a society like those of the West. The wide diffusion of bicycles, sewing machines, radios, political parties, chemical fertilizers, and hospitals does not mean that all or even most of Western values or culture have been or should be similarly diffused. Nor are "traditional" and "modern" necessarily antithetical; not only do they often coexist happily, but tradition may prove in some cases to contain highly effective vehicles or instruments of change. Many traditional Asian institutions and forms proved surprisingly resilient or have been capable of adapting to meet new pressures without losing their essential character. This is neither bad nor "backward" nor in any way remarkable, except as it may help to illuminate differences between institutions, countries, or cultural contexts.

Change may indeed take place in many instances more effectively, sometimes more quickly and more stably if it can come about through the agency or under the auspices of traditional forms in some degree, sometimes even through traditional institutions. But there is no universal norm, which is the objection to the term and the connotations of "moderniza- tion" at least as it is commonly used. All societies grow out of their own traditions. Since traditions vary enormously, so will the nature, the pace, and the pattern or direction of change vary. Where tradition is strong, as in most of Asia, change must be related to it, either harmoniously and accommodatingly, or in terms of a revolutionary dialectic. China is the most talked of case, in the first respect before 1949, in the second after 1949, as revolution responded explicitly to tradition and was shaped by the dialectics of elitism, the urban-rural dichotomy, regional-central ten- sions, and other legacies of the Chinese past. But despite the greater Western impact on India and an earlier and greater receptivity there to certain kinds of change, India may be a still better case of a system where change has been accommodated within tradition as well as vice versa.[23] It is foolish to deny that the major impetus for change in Asia after about 1800 came originally through the Western presence. It is equally foolish to conclude from this that Western models did or should sweep all before them. Change continued to respond to and to be conditioned by persisting Asian tradition. Asian responses were also conditioned by the processes of change which went on being generated within their own cultures as well as by the introduction of new alien elements. It was ,the confrontation of these two different dynamics which has shaped modern Asia. There remains the importance, and the fascination, of examining how and why each Asian area responded differently to the Western impetus in working out its own distinctive resolution.[24]

One seminally important difference between traditional Asia and the nineteenth-century West is the notion of progress, and the aggressively confident attitude toward change and the future which accompanied this notion in the Western mind. None of the Asian traditions shared such a view. Especially in the Chinese mind, change and the disharmony it threatened were to be distrusted or even resisted, particularly where it appeared to confront rather than to accommodate or to serve existing institutions and values, as of course some change did. Western drive did represent, however, a disruptive confrontation. Flushed with the success and power of its own burgeoning industrialization, the nineteenth-century West saw itself as having a duty to spread its "higher civilization," to replace the backwardness of all other cultures.

Western writings about Asia in the nineteenth and early twentieth centuries are full of such sentiments. Here is Bayard Taylor, an American at Aden, the symbolic gate of Asia, beginning a tour in 1853:

> I have never felt more forcibly the power of that civilization which follows the Anglo-Saxon Race in all its conquests, and takes root in whatever corner of the earth that Race sets its foot. Here on the farthest Arabian shore, facing the most savage and inhospitable regions of Africa, were Law, Order, Security, Freedom of Conscience and of Speech, and all the material advantages which are inseparable from these. Herein consist the true power and grandeur of the Race, and the assurance of its final supremacy.[25]

Such a model of superior civilization, the railways and steam engines it had created, the power and wealth which flowed from industrialization, could confidently be expected to make its own conquests, to persuade by example. But where blind and stubborn people persisted in sticking to their own different ways, it was right for the West to force its own system on them for the general good. Such a task need not even be distasteful, but noble and ennobling, a self-sacrificing for the general benefit of mankind— the White Man's Burden.

To inculcate, if necessary by force, the Protestant work ethic, Victorian morality, nineteenth-century Christianity, public cleanliness, impatience with traditional ideas, competitive drive, and desire for innovation in the belief that progress was real and possible and deeply rewarding, especially in its Western form, if only people could be made to push for it, was an inspiring mission. A social and political system which could create such values must clearly be superior to one which did not. Since no Asian system did so (with the later qualified exception of Japan, which was accordingly much admired by Westerners), they were all clearly inferior and both needed and somehow deserved Western tutelage. If this process and its results could be profitable to Western merchants and industrialists, as of course they saw that it could be, so much the better. But there was also a sense of obligation based on the nineteenth-century belief in progress, a universalist conviction that the West, through its apparent mastery of a new technology, had produced a gospel which was good news for all mankind and which therefore the West had a duty to spread. Resistance to this gospel, even temporizing or desire to adapt aspects of it to fit their own cultural situations, tended to increase Western insistence and aggressiveness. One can see both such sentiments on the Western part rising, especially in China, as Chinese resistance to "modernization" or to Christianity continued even after successive decades of Western example and exhortation. Many Westerners became violently anti-Chinese, labeling them both stupid and evil because they would not make themselves over in the obviously superior Western image and despite the long record of patient Western evangelism.

The nineteenth-century belief in progress was central, as was its absence in the traditional Asian mind, until Indians first picked it up as part of their acceptance of the British model as an appropriate means to rebuild India. Faith in progress is not a cultural universal, and has not been a historically consistent part even of the Western outlook.[26] Asian respect for the past, view of historical evolution as essentially cyclical, and emphasis on preserving harmony and avoiding conflict or disruption are at least as common a norm.[27] The modern West was impelled toward its more futuristic and aggressive view in large part by its apparent success in winning "control over nature," bending natural forces to the service of man, freeing man from nature's "tyranny." Man's new creations, science and technology, had become the keys to the universe, and the world was being gloriously remade accordingly. Even poets caught it, as in Tennyson's famous lines in "Locksley Hall," based, as he acknowledges, on his trip in 1830 on the first train from Liverpool to Manchester:

> Forward, forward, let us range
> Let the great world spin for ever
> Down the ringing grooves of change.[28]

The contrast and the implicit conflict with the traditional Asian view are obvious.[29]

From the West's point of view, recently emerged from relative "underdevelopment" (in its own terms), change could more easily be seen as improvement, and the conflict which brought it about and which it engendered—conflict with nature, conflict among groups—accepted or even sought as necessary and desirable. From the Chinese point of view, with its real accomplishments in the past and its own positive attitude toward that past, change—and the present and future—were more easily regarded as degeneration, and the disharmony and conflict which change brought something to be feared. Especially was this so, of course, when the agents of change were alien intruders whose technological power and growing aggressiveness were intrinsically threatening.

This kind of Western role and the ideas which accompanied it were not apparent until the nineteenth century, for they were in large part a product of industrialization and the new strength as well as unbounded confidence which it imparted. Even trade was now seen as a vehicle of beneficent change in an almost millenarian, at least a missionary, sense although Westerners had been trading in and with Asia for some three centuries without troubling themselves with ideas about it beyond simple profit. As Richard Cobden, the apostle of free trade, put it in 1838:

> Commerce is the grand panacea which, like a beneficent medical discovery, will serve to innoculate with the healthy and saving taste for civilization all the nations of the world. Not a bale of merchandise leaves our shores but it bears the seeds of intelligence and fruitful thought to the members of some less enlightened community; not a merchant visits our seats of manufacturing industry but he returns to his own country the missionary of freedom, peace, and good government, while our steam boats, that now visit every port of Europe, and our miraculous railroads that are the talk of all nations, are the advertisements and vouchers for the value of our enlightened institutions.[30]

This is the kind of thinking which lay behind Western zeal to "open" Asia. They confidently expected that the colonial ports would, through the vehicle of trade, spread not merely a profitable but a healing and ennobling transformation of all of Asia where their influence could be made to reach. Particularly as such efforts ran into resistance Western arrogance increased, as did their dislike and growing contempt for those whose resistance to such an obviously superior model demonstrated their "backwardness," and the Westerners were convinced of the need and justification for more forceful methods. Rutherford Alcock, an archetypal representative of the forward British policy in China as minister and ambassador, echoed Cobden's views, and also misapplied Darwin four years before the publication of *The Origin of Species,* by expressing in 1855 sentiments which grew out of the delusions of the Victorian West rather than from Darwin's careful biological research:

[Commerce is] the true herald of civilization . . . the human agency appointed under a Divine dispensation to work out man's emancipation from the law which governs the life, and growth, and decay of nations as clearly as it does the life of man. . . . Man's efforts at civilization invariably—when the race to be benefitted is inferior and weaker, intellectually and physically, than the nation civilizing—have but one result: the weaker has gone down before the stronger. . . . There must be . . . an assertion . . . of the dignity and rights of other nations immeasurably their superiors in all that constitutes a nation's worth . . . truckling and temporizing will never have any other issue than to add insolence to arrogance, and impractibility to conceit.[31]

Many other Westerners were equally confident of the moral rightness of their civilizing mission, flowing from their sense of total superiority. Alcock quotes his American colleague Edward Cunningham, also consul at Shanghai (and simultaneously a partner in the trading firm of Russell and Co.):

. . . the exercise of self-restraint and the practice of justice are not consistent with the treatment of a nation of the 17th century in knowledge and policy as if it were one of the 19th, with the treatment of a child as if it were a grown man. The civilized world, moved by philanthropic feelings, is too apt to consider any attempt to procure further advantages of trade with Eastern nations, though equally advantageous to them as to us, except by simple request, as unmannerly and unchristian. The sentiment is founded on a noble principle, but overlooks the childish character of the people with whom we have to deal, and whom it may be considered our mission to guide and enlighten.[32]

Darwin's own work, when it appeared (*The Origin of Species* was published in 1859), did not in fact support such arguments and stressed instead the importance of a balance in nature rather than contemporary human attacks on it. His findings dealt not with modern man and his ambitions but with evolutionary processes of a totally different sort and on a far vaster time scale. But the post-1860 West was already bent on a "civilizing mission" to transform the rest of the world, and spokesmen were not lacking to misinterpret and misapply Darwin's ideas about "the survival of the fittest" to justify and even to ennoble what the West was doing overseas. Social and political Darwinism of this sort became the reigning philosophy in the world of the colonial ports in Asia.

Built on recent shifting ephemeral coastal alluvium, as nearly all of them were, the situation of the colonial ports symbolized their tangential position. So did their physical appearance, as hybridized versions of Western cities, unplanned growths for the most part lacking in monumental or cosmic character but surrounded by water and focused on the harbors and docks which linked them with a world overseas. The ocean tides which lapped against the wharves were appropriate tokens of the role these cities played, bringing goods and ideas in from the sea and carrying away from Asia what they could skim off. They were outward rather than inward facing, as Asian cities heretofore had been, and connected to a supranational and external world of Westernization far more than they were to the world of each country whose alluvial periphery they occupied. In each country to differing degrees, they did succeed in rearranging long-established patterns of settlement, movement, and resource use. This was accomplished from the outside through the use of new and imported techniques which could manipulate factors of time and cost—mechanized transport and production—and new techniques of management and organization. Through such means, and despite their isolated positions on the tidal foreshores, they produced a basic reorientation of each country, away from its traditional inland concerns and along new routes of movement leading to and from the new centers of ferment in the colonial ports. These cities were not particularisticly Asian, let alone national in the old sense, nor were they coherent symbols of a homogenous culture of traditional consensus. They were alien and physically chaotic growths which neatly symbolized the disruption which they introduced into each Asian order. As open windows on the rest of the world, they were small and marginal but enough to admit a draft which in the end frayed or shredded much of each Asian traditional system and reshuffled the pieces with others imported from outside to produce a new national structure in each country.

Such an analysis of course glosses over basic differences in the Western impact from one area to another, but the grand colonial design was essentially uniform in the Western mind, and one can see some of the same results in each country. Missionaries, traders, and consuls or colonial administrators played similar roles in India and China as elsewhere in Asia. The ports themselves were, as pointed out, strikingly similar, not merely in physical layout—the complex of bund, racecourse, club, trading firms, consulate or colonial government buildings, hotels—but in their ideological world. The empire builders, taipans, adventurers, and even to a degree many of the missionaries, were from the same stamp in each port. They lived, talked, and worked by the same values, referents, shibboleths, codes, tastes, and goals, amid the potted palms and the bars or smoking rooms of the Taj Mahal Hotel in Bombay, the Raffles in Singapore, the Hotel des Indes in Batavia, the Peninsular Hotel in Hong Kong, the Cathay Mansions in Shanghai, or the Imperial Hotel in Tokyo. Their ladies helped to put on endless amateur performances of Gilbert and Sullivan operettas at the British Club or the church hall, differing little from one end of colonial Asia to the other, like the men who strolled home after the performance humming "For he is an Englishman," or, "A British tar is a soaring soul . . . his fists are ever-ready for a knock-down blow . . . and this should be his customary attitude." Englishmen, Russians, Parsees, Frenchmen, Americans, Dutchmen, Armenians, and even Middle Eastern Jews like the Sassoons and Hardouns who made fortunes in Shanghai, were all part of this glittering but artificial cosmopolitan club-land world of the colonial ports. They jostled each other, but they were jointly trying to do the same kinds of things in each country, and to impress uniformly on the Asian landscape their vision of the grand colonial design. The essence of my argument in this book is that they failed to do so, that the separate Indian and Chinese contexts were sufficiently varied and sufficiently powerful to warp and deflect even so powerful a Western drive, and to produce as a result strikingly different outcomes.

Chapter 3

The Western Effort in India: From Petitioners to Rulers

The sea routes eastward from Europe led first to India, and although the Western drive was pan-Asian and efforts to penetrate China, Japan, and Southeast Asia followed only a few years after 1498, Western strength tended to remain greatest in India because of its relative proximity to the European home base. There was also ample reward for Western traders in India, intervening opportunity between Europe and East Asia. The spice trade was of course the first and most profitable venture, but Southeast Asian sources soon became more important than Indian, and spices were replaced by textiles as the leading commodity in the trade between India and the West.[1] A major objective especially of the English in their efforts overseas was to find a market for their woolens, persistently ignoring both the Asian climate and the better quality of Asian textile production. The same myopia was still shaping British dreams of the China market into the twentieth century. In India, as in China, the English found from the beginning that their woolens could not be sold in any significant amounts, and that the market would take in fact very few Western goods of any sort, at least until well into the nineteenth century after Western industrialization had gathered momentum and began to have something attractive to offer for export to Asia.[2] Indian cloth (primarily cottons, secondarily silks) of all grades was superior in quality and lower in cost. It was profitable to buy these goods for bullion, first trading them in Southeast Asia for spices which were sold in Europe, and then, after about 1650, transporting them directly to the West. The cheaper grades of cottons were sold in exchange for slaves in Africa or to West Indian slave plantations; the better grades and the silks found an eager market in Europe, where Indian cottons had a great vogue. English consumption became so great after about 1660 (especially with Restoration tastes for

36

luxuries) that parliament in 1701 prohibited their import, and in 1720 even their use or wear; re-export to the continent, however, continued, and even domestic consumption could not apparently be wholly prevented.

The major original Western base for this and all other Indian trade was Gujerat and its chief port of Surat, on the west coast and hence closest to Europe but also a long-established center of trade, especially in textiles, for many centuries before the European arrival. The spice trade, mainly in pepper, continued to center on the Malabar coast farther south—including Cochin, Calicut, Mangalore, and Goa—but it became relatively less important among Indian exports. Much of the cottons moving into export channels came from Gujerat itself, still a major cotton-growing and textile-manufacturing center, but some, especially of finer quality, was assembled overland by Gujerati merchants from other Indian areas, notably Bengal. A great drought-induced famine in Gujerat in 1630 resulted in the death of many weavers and grossly disrupted the export trade, providing the Europeans with an additional incentive to seek other sources of export goods rather than dealing only with Gujerati merchants. The two principal source areas were Coromandel (southeast coast north and south of the present city of Madras, which began as an English foundation later, in 1639) and Bengal. Heretofore the English had held off from direct efforts in eastern India, in part because of the intervening opportunity offered in Gujerat and by Gujerati merchants for goods from 'elsewhere; in part because eastern India was that much farther away, especially by sea, and lacked adequate harbors even for the ships of the day; and in part because of the prior and originally stronger position there of the Portuguese, who had established a virtual monopoly of India-Europe trade especially in Bengal.

The productivity, riches, and trade potential of Bengal were however legendary. In particular, the finest of all the cotton textiles (which the English and others had been buying in Gujerat) came from there, notably the incredibly light muslins produced mainly in the vicinity of Dacca and famous even in the West since Roman times. In the seventeenth century, the Emperor Aurangzeb (ruled from 1659 to 1707), in a widely repeated story, was said to have reproved his daughter for appearing naked in court when she was actually wearing seven thicknesses of Dacca muslin.[3] Bengal also produced and exported sugar, silk (which was cheaper than French or Italian silk even after transport to Europe), lac, and saltpeter, the last almost a contemporary Bengal and Bihar monopoly and very much wanted in Europe as an ingredient of gunpowder. It was considered superior to saltpeter from any other then known source.[4]

The Portuguese position in eastern India (they began trading at the port of Chittagong in eastern Bengal in 1518) and the trade profits to be won there did attract the envy of the Dutch and the English, as expressed for example in 1616 by Sir Thomas Roe, ambassador from Westminster to the court of the Mughal Emperor Jahangir:

> The number of Portugalls residing there is a good argument for us to seeke it; it is a signe that there is good doing. An Abby was ever a token of a rich soyle, and store of crows of plenty of carrion... We must fyre them out and maynteyne our trade at the Pike's end.[5]

Appropriate sentiments from an Elizabethan! The disruptions caused by the great Gujerat famine of 1630, and the waning of at least relative Portuguese power which coincided with rising English power and ambition combined to bring English ships and ultimately factories and bases into eastern India.

The chief Portuguese base since at least 1537 had been at the town of Hughli, some twenty-five miles upstream from the later site of Calcutta, reachable by the ocean shipping of the day and a good place from which to tap the trade of Bengal. Hughli was captured by Mughal forces in 1632; the Portuguese were expelled and their factory sacked. Their prominence in trade and their warehouses of goods had made them targets for a powerful and rapacious state. For a time at least, the Dutch, French, and English were able to win some favor from Mughal officials as counterweights, on both land and sea, to the Portuguese, and also against Portuguese piracy with which Indian forces were unable to cope. English trading factories were established first on the fringes of Bengal, at Harihapur (near Cuttack) on the Mahanadi delta in 1633, and at Pipli and Balasore in the 1640s, somewhat farther north but still within present day Orissa (see the front endpaper map), following the permission granted in 1634 by the Emperor Shah Jahan for English ships to trade to Bengal. In 1651 the Mughal governor of Bengal granted full trading privileges to the English East India Company in contrast to earlier Bengali attempts to exclude them, Bengal retaining a degree of autonomy even under Mughal rule. In the same year an English factory was established at Hughli; factories followed at Kazimbazar and Patna (central inland Bengal as it then was constituted) and at Dacca by 1668. Dutch factories were established at about the same time in many of the same places, but growing preoccupation with their trade and holdings in the Indies made them less and less serious rivals. The French role in Bengal, as in India, was always secondary if not marginal, although periodically it was threatening.[6]

Meanwhile English and Dutch attention was also given to establishing a position in Coromandel, where the Dutch had been trading since the first years of the seventeenth century, at the then major east coast market of Masulipatam at the mouth of the Kistna River (see the front endpaper map), which served in effect as the port of the kingdom of Golconda. The Dutch had also established a factory farther south at Pulicat, but refused the English request for permission to trade there in 1611. The English joined the competition at Masulipatam, and in 1623 founded their own factory at Armagon, between Pulicat and Masulipatam, where in the absence of an effective local state they build the first English fortifications in India by mounting twelve cannons around their factory. Complaints of interference from the local governor at Masulipatam led to the removal of all English Coromandel trade operations to Armagon in 1629, but it proved to be a poor source for the cotton textiles which were the most sought trade good. In 1639 the chief agent there, Francis Day, sailed south to find a better base which could also be free of both Indian and Dutch interference. The old Portuguese settlements at Mylapore and San Thomé dating from the 1530s (both now within metropolitan Madras) were apparently willing to welcome a nearby English base as a counterweight against the Dutch at Pulicat, and Day found promising local sources for "pintadoes" and calicoes.

At the mouth of Cooum Creek and around the shallow lagoon to which it led was the tiny village of Madraspatam (perhaps originally Madre de Dios? Christianity long antedated the Portuguese in south India) on what Day considered a good site for the new English base. Accordingly Fort St. George was founded there, defended from the beginning by walls and cannon as if it were a piece of English property. The fort had to repel Indian assults in the 1690s and 1710s, and repeated French attacks (succumbing to a French conquest from 1746 to 1748) during the long though interrupted Anglo-French struggles of the eighteenth century. It represented the first step in what was to become much later a British imperium in India. Cooum Creek could take ships of only some fifty tons, but there was no better harbor on the east coast[7] and the local rajah was not only willing to sell the land for an English settlement but appeared likely to leave the English traders alone.[8]

A position in Coromandel was additionally important as a forward base for the penetration of Bengal. Fort St. George acted as the general headquarters for this effort, which could not have been mounted from Surat, the original English factory (though never a territorial base) far on the other side of India on the Gujerat coast. In any case, the English were now attempting to break out of the traditional trading pattern by going to the sources of the goods rather than dealing, as they and other foreigners had been doing, through Gujerati middlemen at Surat, which had for centuries been the chief Indian port for overseas trade and where the Westerners never controlled or dominated the scene. Fort St. George provided for the first time a reasonably secure and independent base, especially necessary for the assault on Bengal where there was chronic trouble with arbitrary and powerful Mughal and local state actions, no secure English base but only factories in existing market centers, and continued threats from Portuguese, Dutch, and French rivals. Meanwhile Madras prospered as a trade center, helped in part by the final Mughal conquest and devastation of Golconda and of Hyderabad, the Golconda capital, in 1689. Many artisans and merchants from Hyderabad and from Masulipatam, its port, fled to Madras, which became from that time the chief commercial and port center of Coromandel, and in time of south India as a whole.

All of the British settlements in India, and to a degree the colonial ports elsewhere in Asia, were to grow to a major extent as a result of in-migration from a chronically disordered, violent, or economically declining hinterland from which the Western-dominated ports offered a relatively secure haven. The new port cities generated new labor demand and offered substantial new economic opportunity. In a sense, the rise of Madras was fortuitous; any other spot which the English might have picked in Coromandel would probably have done as well. Their ultimate victory over French and Dutch competition, and their rise to hegemony in India, ensured that their base, which was also the administrative seat of a Presidency, in south India would become the major city of that large region and would draw to it the bulk of the region's commercial activity as well as its external trade. From the beginning, the English Company made consistent efforts at each of its own settlements, including Madras and later Bombay and Calcutta, to attract weavers, dyers, spinners, and other artisans to live and work there under English protection and patronage. The conditions of late Mughal India helped to make such efforts successful.

Although Bombay island (then containing only a tiny fishing village) was ceded by Portugal to England in 1661 as part of the marriage contract between Charles II and the Infanta Catherine of Portugal and hence antedates the establishment of an English territorial base in Bengal, the growth of the Bombay settlement remained very slow and its acquisition was fortuitous rather than being part of a concerted English plan to extend their penetration of India. The Company did not even bother to occupy it permanently until 1668, and left their chief factory at Surat until 1687. Eastern India, and especially Bengal, remained the prime goal—and the major scene of English, Dutch, and French operations—for at least the subsequent century. The Portuguese, Dutch, and then the English traders in Bengal had for the most part not attempted to take their ships up country but dealt with local brokers (*dallals*) who bought for them on consignment at each inland mart goods which were then brought down the Ganges and its many distributaries (including the Hooghly) for transhipping into ocean vessels at Pipli, Balasore, and other places on the edge of the delta, none of which were satisfactory. The approaches to Balasore were too shallow even for the ships of the time, and cargoes had to be transhipped in an exposed roadstead, to be carried to and from Balasore, ten miles up a tidal creek, in small boats:

> Our ships in Ballasore road do generally ride in a hard and dangerous Roadstead and many of our men come to Sickness and Death by their constant labour of rowing so far in such a rough sea, which we would willingly prevent all that in us lyes.[9]

But although Balasore was also inconveniently far from the major trade centers of Bengal, navigation within the delta was hazardous. As an early English observer put it in 1620, "We are mere strangers, the coast is too dangerous, and our shipping too great [i.e., deep draft] to adventure there among so many shelves and sandes."[10]

Equally important was the well-founded European fear of Mughal and Bengali state power and its recurrent arbitrary confiscations, exactions, and even physical attacks on the merchants themselves as well as on their goods and factories, which the Europeans were powerless to prevent. The Dutch and English did begin after about 1650 to try their ocean-going ships on the Hooghly from time to time. They found that they could make use of a relative deep and somewhat protected anchorage and occasional lading place just above a bend in the river near the site of a small village called Sutanuti, the place which later became Calcutta. But despite their anxiety to take their ships and factories as far inland as possible to the chief markets, they were increasingly discouraged by their inability to cope with the local political and military pressures. In 1686, Job Charnock, the English Company's chief agent at Patna on the Ganges, then the principal commercial center of Bengal, was publicly whipped by the Mughal authorities for an alleged slight to the local Nawab, who also stopped all shipping. The English withdrew to their factory in the town of Hughli but were again attacked, retreated to their anchorage at Sutanuti, and finally returned to Madras in 1689.

These adventures, typical of much of the European experience in seventeenth century Bengal, helped Charnock to convince the Company Directors at Fort St. George that they must have an independent base in Bengal, one which could defend itself militarily, be free from arbitrary exactions, and be located as far as practicable from any existing urban or administrative center and from the attentions of rapacious officials. He had urged since 1689 that such a base be established at Sutanuti, and in 1690 he found his opportunity. The Company was encouraged by the accession of a new Nawab of Bengal who was apparently eager for trade revenues and fearful of English naval strength. He hoped to use this strength against the Portuguese and to control their piracy, so he promised the English compensation for the earlier confiscations and freedom of trade if they would return to Bengal. The Company decided to try again, moved also by the need for a safer anchorage and one closer to the source of goods than Balasore.

> Therefore if the Moors will allow us to fortify ourselves at Chutanutee [Sutanuti] where our ships may go up and ride within the command of our guns it would be much better for us though it should cost us a bribe of thirty or forty thousand Rupees to the Great Men to be paid when we are possessed of the Mogulls Phirmaund [*firman* or *farman*—a charter of trading privileges and exemption from transit dues] for that and for the twelve articles made with Mr. Charnock [i.e., the draft of an agreement from the then Nawab of Bengal in 1687], but the confirmation of these articles we insist upon in right and will not purchase them.[11]

Charnock reascended the Hooghly in August of 1690 with a small company and made the first permanent English settlement in Bengal at Sutanuti, soon to be called Fort William, and shortly after the turn of the eighteenth century, Calcutta. Its first few years were difficult and uncertain, marked by a very high death rate and recurrent trade interruptions; the imperial *farman* was widely ignored locally, and there was trouble with banditry. But in 1696 there was a change far more significant than was generally realized, at that time or since: the infant settlement was given official imperial permission to fortify itself against the threat posed by the local rebellion of Sobha Singh, and the walls and guns of the original Fort William rose beside the Hooghly. This was of course a tacit admission by a traditional-style state of its own inability to keep order, especially on the fringes of its supposed territory, a recognition of the military power of the English, and an acknowledgment that their presence in Bengal was also desirable as a stimulus to trade and the revenues and indirect profits which it yielded to the state. This was not an uncommon pattern in many traditional political systems, but fortification of Sutanuti marked a turning point, on the eve of the Mughal collapse, between Western impotence and insignificance earlier, and Western strength which grew as Indian power declined. The grant of *zamindari* rights (land revenue collection and administration) to the English in 1698 for the three preexisting villages and land in the immediate vicinity of Calcutta was a further acknowledgment of all the above, and, together with the formal recognition of English power and responsibility for defense and the preservation of order, began the process which led, through progressive extensions of both sorts of authority, to the British imperium in India.

In 1717, after many petitions, the Mughal court granted a new and wider-ranging *farman* giving trade privileges and freedom from transit dues and inspection to the English factors at Madras, Bombay, and Calcutta and adding thirty-eight villages to the Calcutta *zamindari*. This was the Magna Carta of the English in India. No such privileges were given to any other foreigners, nor to any Indians. The *zamindari* and freedom from search and restraint of trade clearly departed to some degree from the mode in which the Mughals attempted to deal with supposedly subordinate groups. Special privileges and even autonomy were traditionally granted in return for acquiescence to Mughal rule, but the concessions granted to the English in 1717 were made to a new order of petitioners, as later became clear. Although the agreements were periodically broken and Calcutta itself captured by the army of a new Nawab in 1756 in a last flourish of imperial fire, they helped to lay the basis for the retaliatory expedition of 1757, Clive's victory at Plassey, and the final securing of the English position in India.[12]

On the west coast, the chief English factory which had been functioning at Surat since 1609 was shifted to Bombay in 1687. Despite its silting harbor near the mouth of the Tapti River, Surat remained a larger trade center until about 1750, although trade and shipping there continued to be dominated by Indians. Bombay offered the same set of advantages as Calcutta: a defensible base independent of any Indian state. Its growth for the first several decades was stymied by Portuguese strength and flanking bases on the west coast, by the continued counterattractions of Surat plus the Portuguese establishments at Diu, Goa, and elsewhere, and by a crippling combination of piracy at sea and a virtual blockade by land on the part of the marauding Marathas who were then in the early stages of their bid for national power. Their widespread raiding campaigns effectively sealed Bombay off from its hinterland until the second half of the eighteenth century. Only then, with the disappearance of both Portuguese and Mughal power and the weakening of the Maratha threat, did Bombay begin to grow significantly and become able to take full advantage of its unique asset: the only adequate natural harbor anywhere on either Indian coast. The final outbreak of war against the Marathas brought the conquest of the other almost adjoining islands in the bay (since linked by landfill), the peninsula of Salsette, and a piece of the surrounding mainland by 1781, now open to the further expansion of English power and penetration, although the extinction of Maratha power was not completed until the surrender to the British of the last Peshwa in 1818. West coastal piracy was finally ended for good by a British naval expedition in 1819, and Bombay at last had free access by land and sea.

The stress from the beginning was to preserve Bombay as an independent base, like those at Madras and Calcutta, protected from the exactions and depredations of both state and brigand power, defended by its own fort and ships. From the earliest days there were efforts, as in the other two English settlements, to attract Indian traders and artisans so that Bombay could produce its own trade goods (especially cloth) and could tap trade elsewhere. A few, including Parsee merchants, followed the English there from Surat as early as 1671, in effect progenitors of Parsee leadership and collaboration in the boom economic growth of nineteenth-century and post-Suez Bombay. Artisans came too, although for some time only in small numbers. One of the earliest and ultimately most important of such groups were shipbuilders, from Surat and elsewhere, induced to move to Bombay by the East India Company. In 1736 this movement included the chief shipbuilder at Surat, Lowji Nassarwanji, a Parsee who became the superintendent of the Bombay Dockyards which from that time on dominated shipbuilding in India.

Bombay became not only the chief naval base for the British position in Asia but an important builder of both coastal and naval shipping of high quality, including British ships of the line.[13] Weavers also, and other artisans and traders, were enticed to Bombay, given the increasingly disordered state of the surrounding areas after about 1680 and the relative security and new opportunity offered by the English settlement. They came from Poona and from nearer inland and coastal centers where the combination of piracy, Mughal extortion, civil war and Maratha raids had created a grim environment. As early as 1676 the factors at Surat wrote to those at Bombay: "We desire you . . . to use all just means possible to invite and encourage weavers of all sorts to inhabit on the island." The message was apparently still necessary in 1784 in a letter dated March 15 from the Directors in London to the Company Council in Bombay:

> By the exercise of a mild good Government people from other parts may be induced to come and reside under our protection. Let there be entire justice exercised to all persons without distinction and open trade allowed to all, and, as often as necessary or as the force allotted will enable you, let convoys be provided to the ships. . . . An able honest man [an eighteenth century Robert Hart?] must ever direct the customhouse at Bombay . . . a constant pursuance of these rules will naturally draw people to leave the oppressions of other country Governments and come to you, while freedom and exact justice subsist in our settlements. . . . It is our earnest desire that as many people as possible, especially those of circumstance, be encouraged to settle at Bombay . . . they [must] have all the reasonable privileges that can possibly be given them.[14]

This was in some ways the motto and the sales pitch of all the colonial ports in Asia, increasingly self-satisfied as it became increasingly successful, but certainly most successful of all in India.[15]

Why should this have been so? The answer is surely to be found at least in part in the nature of the Indian context. Unfortunately we know very little especially about the economic detail of that context, much less than we know about either contemporary Europe or China. The bulk of the source material, at least that which has survived, is Western records and observations. This is in itself however symptomatic of a major character-istic of the Indian context about which we can be quite certain and which was enormously significant: the weakness of the central state and of any national system, the chronic prevalence and recrudescence of disorder, the persistence of regionalism, and the almost complete lack of political or administrative continuity except for what was ultimately provided by the British. Although Western records and first-hand accounts of sixteenth-, seventeenth-, and eighteenth-century India are varied and relatively plenti-ful, most pronouncements about the Indian context must be tentative, given the imperfect state of our knowledge, and must also guard against over-generalization, since major regional differences persisted and it may often be misleading to speak in all-India terms.[16]

Nevertheless, we can assume that there *was* a context and that it was the controlling factor in explaining why and how the Western effort produced the results it achieved in India, which contrast so sharply with what those same efforts produced in the very different context of China. This is the focus of the following chapter.

Chapter 4

The Mughal Context

India at the beginning of the Western presence was far from being eco-nomically or even politically underdeveloped, let alone culturally. It was at least productive enough to be self-sufficient, to generate some external as well as internal trade, to support large and often magnificent cities, temples, palaces, and imperial grandeur, and to maintain a population probably many times the size of contemporary Europe's, if not of China's. There was both absolute and individual wealth, but it was grossly maldistributed among groups within the population and spatially over the country. There was also a considerable trade, and a relatively sophisticated set of merchant groups and commercial techniques.[1] But most trade goods came from a multitude of small-scale and spatially scattered producers. Western traders complained chronically that they could never obtain adequate amounts of the goods they sought (especially textiles) and for which they had external markets. As Morris puts it, "commercial activity, international and domestic, must have constituted an infinitesimal portion of total economic activity on the sub-continent. . . ."[2] He goes on to demonstrate, by ingenious extrapolation of what limited data exist, the essential plausibility of his assertion.

Local marketing systems with a radius of a few miles, which exchanged primarily local agricultural products mainly through barter, appear to have dominated the commercial sector in India to a greater extent than in China or in Europe. Long-distance marketing was also hampered by the intricate Indian mosaic of separate languages and cultures; it was above all else a centrifugal rather than centripetal pattern, in trade, in culture, and in social and political systems.[3] The units of which it was composed were both relatively small for the most part and relatively unused to mutual interaction except on a minor and superficial plane, for example, the trade in a few high-value commodities. The Indian trade which was important to each European country engaged in it and which did have much impact on European economies was of relatively negligible importance or had little impact in the far larger mass of India as a whole or even of those areas where trade was proportionately more important, such as Gujerat or Bengal, themselves almost certainly more populous than any European country. The largest groups of skilled artisans were attached as virtual slaves to the Mughal court and its workshops, or to provincial governors, where they produced luxuries for the elite. Sophisticated hand craftsmanship even for more utilitarian goods, such as textiles, was no substitute for and was indeed inimical to high productivity.

There is little reason to assume that agricultural yields at this period were significantly higher, indeed they are more likely to have been lower, than when they began to be measured more systematically in the late nineteenth century after the beginnings of significant net increases in irrigation inter alia. Yields as of the 1890s were estimated, as yields must necessarily be, at probably less than one-half, perhaps as little as one-third, of best-guess average yields in China or Japan in about the same period.[4] Indian agriculture as a whole suffered most importantly from a chronic moisture shortage, made much worse by the pronounced seasonality and the yearly vagaries of monsoonal rainfall.[5] Compensatory efforts through irrigation were never as fully developed as in East Asia for a variety of reasons. The most important may well have been chronic disorder which discouraged most forms of capital investment by cultivators, groups of cultivators, or local or national administrations. The latter were relatively weak, discontinuous, and far more exploitative than constructive in their impact on the agricultural system. A further relative disability vis-à-vis East Asia in particular was the virtual absence in India of the use of night soil, because of cultural reasons related to Indian notions of ritual purity. There was also much more limited use even of animal manures, for which there were too many competing uses as fuel and plaster, a problem more successfully avoided both in East Asia and in Europe where animal manures were of great importance in maintaining and increasing yields. The Indian climate with its precarious water balance reflecting very high evaporation rates restricted vegetation cover and inhibited its recovery so that it could contribute relatively little, by European or even East Asian standards, to fuel needs. Metal and metal tools seem to have been scarce and expensive in comparison with Europe or East Asia, perhaps in part reflecting the fuel problem but also a shortage of known workable ores until later nineteenth-century discoveries. This too must have contributed to low agricultural and industrial productivity.

Areas of higher productivity in agriculture or handicrafts and those which had a surplus for export to other areas or abroad were widely scattered, separated by extensive tracts of marginal subsistence agriculture. Communication was difficult, expensive, and frequently dangerous. India was very poorly supplied with usable internal waterways in particular contrast to China. The best of the river systems, the Ganges, was indifferently navigable at best in its lower reaches by shallow-draft boats within the delta, but could not carry much more than barge traffic farther inland. The Indus and its tributaries were no better. The advent of steam did make somewhat more use possible of these two streams, but never on a significant scale relative to the area and population to be served. The other Indian rivers were even less navigable, their heavily braided deltas choked with silt brought down by the spates of the monsoon, and their upper courses drying up to near-trickles during the long dry period between monsoons; these problems were evident also in the two master streams of the north, the Ganges and the Indus. India was too large and physically and culturally diverse to be effectively integrated by preindustrial land transport alone, but roads were in any case relatively few (again in comparison with either China or Europe) and were apparently chronically bad for the most part. This was a reflection of the relative weakness of the politico-administrative system; the Mughals did make some effort at road building, albeit for primarily military reasons, but the network was inadequate in scope and was not well maintained. Here again the Indian climate was a factor; the violence of monsoonal rainfall imposed special needs for road construction and maintenance which in practice were rarely met; most roads were literally impassable for many months each year. Coastal shipping links between west and east, around the tip of the subcontinent, were too long and too exposed to piracy to offer an adequate alternative even for the littoral areas, let alone the vast inland bulk of the country. Finally, the acute shortage of adequate harbors along the whole of the east coast and large stretches of the west above Malabar further discouraged coastal shipping.

This was altogether a crippling handicap for an area of India's size. It greatly restricted the possibilities of regional specialization and hence of economic growth, even in so apparently coherent and potentially productive a region as the lower Ganges basin. If one may take the lower Ganges as the most promising area, it pointedly illustrates the deficiencies which inhibited Indian economic growth before the British period and the development of mineral, tea, jute, and other resources. Outside the immediate area of the delta, exchange by water was severely limited despite the existence of a master stream which however could carry very little traffic, and that only seasonally. The Ganges was chronically silted, alternately in spate and falling to expose sand bars. This was of course a reflection of the Indian climate, which also imposed severe restraints on agriculture, producing drought and crop failure in some part of the Ganges basin almost yearly. In the absence of continuous or even effective political integration or administration, nothing was done to improve navigation, nor to provide irrigation except for pitifully inadequate village-level efforts with small tanks and shallow wells. Incentives for making large permanent investments in irrigation or land improvement projects were seriously weakened when control over them or even the survival of the project could not be assumed in a context of recurrent disorder. The contrast with China is striking, with the Yangtze basin, or indeed with other size-and-circumstance analogues such as Atlantic France or lowland England, where, as in the Yangtze basin, there was a cumulative accretion of labor and capital investments over many centuries adding to the productivity of the landscape.

While there was certainly some Indian interregional trade (at what precise scale remains unclear), it was far less important proportionately than in Europe from at least the fourteenth century, or than in China at probably any period since the Chou (fifth century B.C.), where it was also on a much greater absolute scale. The deficiencies of transport not only helped to keep India far less highly developed commercially than China but also helped to explain why neither a national economy (even on a partial basis) nor a genuine national polity emerged until the weakness of internal communication was alleviated, beginning in the nineteenth century under British management in the form of roads, railways, and coastal and riverine steam shipping.

In part for this reason, each area tended toward political autonomy. Each regime which attempted to rule India or even north India from the center had to spend a disproportionate share of its resources and energies in putting down chronic regional efforts to break away, not just in the campaigns to establish a central order in the first place but as a continuing problem which was never effectively solved for more than a few years. This in turn imposed heavy expenses on the center and a permanently insatiable need for revenue. The Mughal system, being most recent and least imperfectly known, was the context of the period with which we are concerned. Throughout the Mughal period (1526–1759, although the latter date, while official as marking the death by assasination of the Emperor Alangir II, is somewhat arbitrary) there were large-scale military campaigns in progress, mainly against regional rebellion, in all but a few of the years. Regional states or would-be states were semichronically involved not only in rebellion against the center but in fighting with one another or in raiding to control revenue-producing territory along their own peripheries. Production and trade were thus caught in a double squeeze and suffered from the devastation occasioned by fighting as well as from the rapacity of revenue seekers. Economic distress and political ambiguity or chaos also furthered extensive banditry, and there were large areas where the writ of no state ran. Land, goods, and trade which escaped official grasp risked falling prey to local bandits, some of them highly organized and in effect controlling territory which lay across many of the important trade routes. One significant clue to the nature of the Indian context in this period is the apparent extent of cultivable land abandoned or left unused until the second half of the nineteenth century, primarily it would seem as a result of insecurity. The contrast with Ch'ing China and its record of extension and reclamation of cultivated land is striking.

The Mughal government is credited with taking as much as one-third of the gross production of the areas it controlled in taxation in various forms.[6] The tax-farming *zamindars* collected additional sums on their own account. Regional states, for example Bengal, which like other regional entities teetered back and forth across the line between Mughal control and autonomy, squeezed further amounts, as they were obliged to do to support their own military efforts and political apparatus. While the land tax was the chief source of revenue, trade did not escape and was milked at innumerable duty points, in every large town, at every provincial boundary, and often at arbitrary intermediate points. Wealth in private hands attracted state attention and risked expropriation. As the French traveler Francois Bernier put it in the 1660s: "Let the profit be ever so great, the man by whom it has been made must still wear the garb of indigence."[7] All of this of course increased the price of trade goods, and restricted their scope and market. Unfortunately, neither the Mughal nor regional states used or could use revenues to any significant degree to enhance productivity, or even to ensure the minimum conditions of security from plunder or to enhance safe, low-cost transport and exchange.

At the village and small town level, where most Indians lived and most production centered, social and political organization were provided on long-established lines by village councils (*panchayats*) and through the leadership of what have been labeled "dominant castes." Village efforts were directed at protection against the inroads of the state or of any extravillage forces, which had repeatedly proved destructive to village welfare through taxation, extortion, warfare, and banditry. In these terms, the Indian village was perennially closed, or as closed as it could be made, to all outsiders.[8] In the larger towns, Mughal or regional state officials managed an exploitative revenue system which preyed, in addition to the land tax, especially on merchants, but in an often uneasy alliance with local landowning elite. The political orders milked the economy but did not feed it, a disastrous pattern which helped to keep India in turmoil even at the height of Mughal power and which brought that power down in effective terms after less than two hundred years. Revenue was used primarily to finance warfare; in this sense, the economy was bled so that the state(s) could then further weaken it by diverting energies from production in order to produce instead devastation. The Mughals did do some road building, as already indicated, and the roads were used for commerce, but their chief purpose was military. Nonmilitary expenditures were largely limited to administration (much of it in turn devoted to revenue collection), and to monumental building and gorgeous display in an effort to legitimize imperial power.

But the chief need for and use of revenue was the economically self-defeating one of warfare. The Mughals were never able fully to control the revenue and administrative system of more than small areas; they had to keep fighting in an effort to extend their authority. Administrative weakness and preoccupation with warfare were mutually reinforcing. The state was never able to establish an effective centrally controlled bureaucracy; administration and hence political power were in effect subcontracted, with disastrous results. However inescapable this may have been, it was not the result of simple perversity on the part of the Mughals. The obstacles already pointed out as standing in the way of national or interregional integration were formidable and would probably have defeated the most determined centralizing effort, especially by an alien regime. In any case, the subcontracting of power to local and regional agents, a system in some ways reminiscent of feudalism and, like it, symptomatic of the inability of the center to control or administer on its own resources more than a small area around the royal capital, led in the case of Mughal India to a ruinously exploitative system. Administration and revenue-collecting rights (*jagirs*) were granted to those (*jagirdars*) who for various reasons the Emperor wanted or was obliged to favor and whose assistance (but rarely whose loyalty) was obtained in this way.[9] Lest *jagirdars* build up local power bases, an obvious and serious risk, assignments were kept temporary and were moved around. Given the weakness of the center, this was essential, but it had the predictable effect that most *jagirdars*, with no long-term interest in the areas assigned to them, stripped them and especially their cultivators to the bone.

This in turn fatally weakened both the incentive and the means for peasants or any others involved in agriculture to invest labor or capital to increase productivity. With the additional risk represented by chronic banditry in many areas, and periodic large-scale warfare, it is not to be expected that any producers would put out effort or resources to create improvements or greater production which was so heavily liable to expropriation or destruction. It is also hardly surprising under these circumstances to find both an extremely limited interregional trade (given the absence of significant disposable surplus plus the problems of transport) and large groups of landless rural laborers in acute economic distress—a further recruiting pool for banditry.[10]

One must not overstress the negative aspects of the Indian context; merchants and trade did survive, the Mughal power remained amply sufficient to overawe the Westerners, and the system as a whole functioned well enough to produce material conditions for most people most of the time which struck contemporary European observers as comparing not unfavorably with conditions at home. To most of them, the Indian rich seemed richer, but the (far more numerous) poor poorer than in Europe. It was perhaps mainly a loss in potential; India could have been so much better off—for example, under the kind of management, whatever its shortcomings, which was being provided for contemporary China under the first century or so of the Ch'ing. A critical aspect of the Indian context was the vulnerability of the merchant group, for all its sophistication. As Spear puts it, "In times of tumult, the men of commerce were the first to suffer."[11] Their chief defense was to appear "too humble to be worth the notice of the lords of the earth." In practice (as opposed to theory) merchant-state relations in China were far more sustaining of the merchant, and the state was also able to maintain a much larger degree of civil order. Lack of it in India, even at the height of Mughal power, was probably the greatest single disabling factor for the growth of production and trade. Nor did the strength or majesty of the Mughal state, as an alien dynasty of conquest and in the absence of national coherence on a cultural basis, sustain a sense of Indian unity. Little concerted opposition was offered to Westerners fishing in India's troubled waters, and even when their power became noticeable and began to eat away locally at indigenous sovereignty, they were more often joined by Indian collaborators than resisted by Indian patriots.

The attraction especially of the English was that they *could* maintain order in the areas they controlled. They had the strength and the organization otherwise lacking at least on the local scene, and they had an obvious interest in doing so in order to sustain production and the trade which was their sole objective, unlike the Mughal state's view of trade as a source of revenue only. The insignificance of the Westerners to begin with undoubtedly also helped them to insinuate themselves locally; they did not appear to be a threat until the Mughal power was collapsing, too late for concerted opposition. Even Aurangzeb, the last effective Mughal emperor (r. 1659–1707), was reported by François Bernier to have complained, after belatedly realizing the strength of the Europeans, that his tutor had told him "... the whole of Feringustan [Europe] was no more than some inconsiderable island, [that its kings] resembled petty rajahs, and that the potentates of Hindustan eclipsed the glory of all other kings."[12] Apart from its sycophant overtones (and its striking similarity to Chinese official attitudes), this reflects, for all that it may not in fact have been a grossly inaccurate description, an innate Indian sense of cultural superiority which, as in China, still persists and which helped to blind Indians to the danger which the Western presence posed. Thus Indians believed that the Europeans "have no polite manners, that they are ignorant, wanting in ordered life, and very dirty."[13]

The parallel with China, as both peoples buttressed their own sense of worth in the face of foreign counterclaims and blows by looking down on their challengers as crude, uncivilized barbarians, is illuminating especially given the clear contextual differences in other respects. By Indian or Chinese standards, Westerners were indeed crude, especially the aggressive, adventuring, swashbuckling representatives of the West in early modern Asia, and cultural relativism was not attractive to Asian minds. The more threatening the Westerners, the more Indians and Chinese were impelled to look down on them. "India in the minds of her inhabitants is the queen among nations, and other men are mere barbarians by comparison . . . all the courtesy, courage, and arts and sciences of Europeans cannot give us the position which birth bestows on Indians even in the poorest circumstances. . . . In the interior a white man hardly as yet escapes public ridicule."[14] That sense of worth the Westerners, for all their successes, never wholly took away from Asians, even in India.

The death of Aurangzeb in 1707 marked the effective end of Mughal power, at least on any national scale. The Maratha revolt, fed by Aurangzeb's repressive and intolerant policies, was in full spate, the Mughals were in retreat everywhere in the south and in many regions of the north, and their ability to maintain even a holding action was fast waning, especially as they increasingly lost revenue bases. The Westerners on the spot did not see this clearly at the time and continued their obsequious petitions to the Mughal court for trading privileges, as in the Surman Embassy of 1714–15, where the English representative described himself as "the smallest particle of sand," giving "the reverence due from a slave" or in the several petitions of John Russell, chief company agent in Bengal in the early eighteenth century, who regularly kissed the feet of the Nawab of Bengal, an Indian equivalent of the *k'e-t'ou.*[15] The English were of course attempting to insinuate themselves as subjects of the Great Mughal, or of regional Nawabs, not in any sense as rivals, and hence behaved as all other petitioners had to do. At the time of the Surman embassy they were seeking an extension of their *zamindari* in the Calcutta area as well as trade privileges, for they had already found that the defense of their settlement and their military actions against the Marathas and others in that troubled region overstrained their financial resources. They needed a larger revenue base, and were pursuing the standard Indian means for acquiring it by petitioning in effect for a *jagir,* albeit on a very modest scale. It was a further evidence of weakness that this was ultimately granted two years later in 1717, a tacit admission that foreigners could do what the Indian state was incapable of, and that foreign power was seen as sufficiently great that concessions must be made to it.

Western efforts of the preceding century, through successive embassies to the court, had failed to convince the still all-powerful Mughal that concessions of any kind were appropriate; the emperor refused to deal in treaties or in permanent grants of privileges. By 1715 the climate was changing. The English account of the Surman Embassy reads a little like

INDIA AT THE HEIGHT
OF MUGHAL POWER, 1707

accounts of the Macartney mission to Peking in 1793, but with a radically
different outcome.[16] There was a formal retinue and procession including
160 bullock wagons carrying presents for the emperor as well as supplies
for what was expected to be a protracted mission. From Patna to Delhi the
embassy had to travel by road, a journey which took three months, over
atrocious tracks and with continual harrassment from large armed bands of

robbers, even along the imperial highway from the recent capital at Agra, the royal way to Delhi. Here was surely an unmistakable sign that all was not well with the Mughal power, but despite a dramatic entry into Delhi with drums, trumpets, a cavalry escort, and a scattering of money in the streets, the English embassy was largely ignored and was in any case put off with endless pretexts. They might never have been heard if the emperor had not fallen ill and asked advice and treatment from Dr. William Hamilton, who had accompanied the embassy. Hamilton's success—perhaps also fortuitous—was followed after a protracted interval by an imperial reception, and ultimately, after the embassy had long gone, by an imperial *farman* of 1717 granting all the English requests, including the *zamindari* of five villages in the vicinity of Madras. The English were still humble petitioners, dependent on chance favor, or so it seemed.

Nevertheless, they had already fortified their three bases at Madras, Calcutta, and Bombay, already acquired de facto sovereignty over small surrounding areas at the first two, and were successful when no Indian group was in preserving order and security in their own territories even in the rapidly and grossly deteriorating conditions after 1707. Maratha raiding parties and larger armies were all over the north and parts of the south, but English forces kept them out of the expanding Calcutta *zamindari*. The invasion of Nadir Shah from Afghanistan in 1738–39, which tumbled the last appearances of Mughal power and sacked the capital at Delhi, was blocked in its thrust into Bengal by the English who had in effect taken over the defense of Bengal and in this case protected its chief city of Patna against the invaders. The final defeat of the Marathas, again at Panipat (guarding the approaches to Delhi), by an Afghan army in 1761 (which then withdrew) left the English in effect masters of an otherwise masterless house, fresh from their own victory over the forces of the Nawab of Bengal at Plassey in 1757. Plassey was the outcome of a retaliatory response to the Nawab's storming of Calcutta in 1756.[17] He attacked Calcutta primarily because the English refused to desist from further fortification, and his action seems a reasonable enough effort to check the erosion of Indian sovereignty. But the Nawab and his regime, like the Mughals, no longer represented an adequate rallying point for most Bengalis or Indians. Many must already have seen that the English offered a better promise of order, and in particular of conditions favorable to trade, since they were themselves traders.

The contrast with the both rapacious and ineffective indigenous politi-

cal orders was enough, apparently, to tip the outcome of Plassey. Clive
sailed up the Hooghly at the head of a small and nondescript force hastily
put together from garrison troops and European idlers in Madras to meet
the vastly superior army of the Nawab some seventy miles north of
Calcutta. His strategy and tactics were outstanding, he made clever use of
an early morning mist, and he was able to inspire and lead his rag-tag
forces with great effectiveness to operate as a single organized body. Even
though the Nawab's army was less well led or disciplined, its numbers and
fire power might have decided the outcome had it not been, apparently,
for a fifth column on the Indian side. Evidence is understandably inadequate, but the impression and the story persist that Indian merchants,
commercial agents, and money lenders who saw their bread as being more
heavily buttered on the English side bribed sections of the Nawab's army.
Marwaris and others had long been lending money to both sides, largely to
pay troops, and had learned that the English were better loan risks, and
better administrators, than the Nawab.[18] English military success in India
stemmed also from stronger, more coordinated leadership and organization, which multiplied the effectiveness of their much smaller numbers and
made for an army instead of a collection of individuals or groups.[19]
Regular pay, uniforms, and esprit de corps produced loyalty and coherence, all largely new on the Indian scene in these terms. In any case, the
critical reinforcements on the Indian side at Plassey, which might have
swept the field, never turned up. Many Indians doubtless did feel that they
had much to gain from the defeat of the old order and the installation of
the English with whom they became willing collaborators. Given the
Indian context, such an attitude is understandable, nor were Indian collaborators necessarily traitors; they had no responsible indigenous order to
which to offer their loyalty.

There had long been wealthy Indian merchants, guilds, letters of credit
and other means for the transfer of funds, bills of exchange, some
development of banking and credit, and some long-distance shipment of
goods. All of these things existed also in classical and medieval Europe.
India did not evolve commercially beyond such a level, and in part for this
reason could never mobilize resources on a large scale. The commercial
structure as a whole, like the individuals who manned it, was also at the
mercy of a rapacious state, with which it had no sustaining links, as did
Chinese merchants. "The guild power in India remained purely money
power, unsupported by any authority of a political or military nature. It

collapsed as soon as the king found it convenient to call in the aid of priestly or knightly elements."[20] Merchants and commerce were more important in some areas than in others. Gujerat in particular stood out, partially because of its marginal position on the west coast, long consequent tradition of overseas and coastal trade, and degree of independence from heavy Mughal control, which at least was never complete. The presence of the Parsees in Gujerat, as an entrepreneurial group which had fled from Hormuz in the eighth century to escape Islamic persecution, was perhaps a further factor, although the Parsees won major prominence only later, as collaborators of the British after about 1780.

But even in Gujerat, merchant status, though not tied to caste, tended to be hereditary (and normatively inferior) and there was no protection against the state when it chose to intervene or expropriate. As Pearson points out merchants and rulers were separate, and on occasion antagonistic orders; merchants were left to make their own arrangements, but the state could move in on them arbitrarily.[21] They lacked the sort of understood symbiotic connection with the state and with the status system through membership in the gentry group which most Chinese merchants enjoyed. There were no means by which wealth could be converted for those who acquired it into social status or political power. Most Indian merchants had no literary education and were often barely literate, although often able to keep accounts.[22] Finally, business partnership was rare, let alone limited liability; commerce was conducted largely by family units, and there were no adequate devices to pool resources for larger enterprises. All these factors helped to limit economic growth and trade, to leave at least potential gaps in the Indian system which Western entrepreneurs could fill, and to make the Western model an attractive one to many Indians. There was no Chinese-style gentry-dominated commercial structure with its stake in the status quo, its links with officialdom, and its own extensive scale of operation which left little room for outsiders and which actively opposed change. Many Indians, especially merchant groups, were eager for it and were ready to welcome even Westerners if they could offer, as they did, a more stable administration favorable to trade.

The most obvious need was peace and security; their absence was probably the greatest single factor working against economic development in terms of both production and exchange. Job Charnock had complained in his time, still in the relatively high period of Mughal power, while acting as the Company's agent in Patna in 1678, ". . . the whole kingdome lying in a very miserable feeble condition, the great ones plundering and Robbing the feebler, and no order or method of government among them. The King's *hookim* is of as small value as an ordinary Governour's."[23] In such a situation, determination and organization could accomplish much, especially when supported by sea power, even on the part of numerically small groups of Westerners. The English proved particularly adroit, as compared with the heavier-handed Portuguese and Dutch, in insinuating themselves into this troubled landscape without gratuitously antagonizing the Indian powers, and by offering themselves as agents and defenders against the older and seemingly more threatening activities (including piracy) of the Portuguese. They were in fact welcomed (barbarians to fight barbarians), and later provided further service against the Marathas and against the powerful Mugh (Magh)[24] pirates of the Arakan coast, whose depredations in Bengal could be countered only by English power at sea.

The English alternative to the Portuguese style is well illustrated in the correspondence about the original fortifications at Calcutta: from the Council at Fort St. George dated January 26, 1698, "We approve of your fortifying Chuttanutte [Sutanuti] . . . but you must carry it so evenly and calmly with the government there that they may connive at, if not approve your ffortifications [*sic*] . . . do not take any advantage thereby to quarrell with or oppose them . . . merchants desire no Enemyes, and would create none."[25] The last phrase surely fits the character and objectives of the English East India Company of the time and speaks the mercantile mind of early modern Europe. But continued success and rising strength led to growing confidence, spilling over into the arrogance which reached its peak in the imperialist mind of post–Suez Asia and especially in treaty port China. With the completion of the first Fort William, the beginnings of such a change can be traced even in the early eighteenth century:

It is plain even to a demonstration to all that know any thing of the Moors tempers that a show of power is the best way to keep the English in India free of the Natives Insults. . . . If they find you alwayes on your guard and in a good posture of defense and your Carriage to them Civill and obliging they will be very unwilling to assault you . . . let them see you will neither give them any affronts nor sitt down tamely under any where it is in your power to do your Selves justice.[26]

Power was to be held in reserve and diplomacy stressed, as they were later in China. But the Indian context increasingly tempted and rewarded the Westerners to use their rising power in a deteriorating situation significantly different from that in which gunboat diplomacy was employed (and with far less reward to the Westerners) in nineteenth- and twentieth-century China. Chronic disorder combined with predatory rulers to create a virtual jungle in which there was little concerted resistance to determined interlopers, and little reason for Indians to attempt to defend their own traditional system, at least not in terms of the political orders. Most of the evidence in the early period of the Western presence deals with Bengal since it became the first major area of Western efforts to penetrate inland instead of dealing with agents at coastal markets, as at Surat. But although Bengal had a tradition of rebelliousness (in some ways, including its geographical marginality on the coast far from the center of imperial power and its strong sense of separate regional identity, a parallel to Kwangtung), there is little reason to assume that disorder and predation were worse there than in most of the rest of India, especially not in the several other areas on the fringes of Mughal control and hence involved, like Bengal, in a devastating see-saw conflict between the center and regional powers, or left to the anarchy of banditry and piracy. There was instability and conflict between regions and the center and also interregional conflict; none of the regional nuclear areas which might have produced bases of stability in themselves (analogous, for example, to Szechuan or Kiangnan) were in fact able to do so. Seventeenth-century Western commentary on conditions in Bengal can be matched by nineteenth-century observations on conditions in areas not yet brought under British rule. Here are two seventeenth-century descriptions:

> Bengalla is at present in a very bad condition by means of the great exactions on the People. The Nabob (Nawab) being ancient and extremely covetous, and his officers long experienced in the business of these Countreyes, there are noe Wayes of extortion omitted whereby to gratifie their master's humour, and Hughly being in his Jaggeer [lands assigned to him as revenue collector] for his own pay, and that and Ballasore both under one man's Govt. makes Merchants business very troublesome.[27]

> The King's Governour hath little more than the name, and for the most part sits still whilst the Nabob's officers oppress the People and

> monopolize most Commodityes even as low as grass for Beasts, canes, fire wood, thatch, etc., nor do they want wayes to oppress the people of all sorts who trade, whether natives or Strangers.[28]

As a modern Bengali historian has put it, "The impact of a complex alien administration and a superior economic system naturally proved ruinous to this rotten edifice."[29]

Into the nineteenth century, areas which remained outside British administration continued to manifest similar problems, as for example, early nineteenth-century Saurashtra, in the Kathiawar peninsula of west coastal India (just southwest of Gujerat): "This country is divided in a very singular manner; and it would not, perhaps, be an easy matter to point out the paramount power."[30] "Conflicting jurisdictions, autocratic legal systems, weak governments, and ill-defined borders all discouraged peaceful settlement."[31] Banditry was pandemic and was described as "too great to allow of Guzerat [or Saurashtra] being considered a settled country; cattle-liftings and such like irregularities were looked on as daily occurrences; and a stranger could not stir to travel from one place to another without a guard of some twenty or thirty *kolis* [local farmers who doubled as part-time bandits and counterbandits] or horsemen."[32]

Piracy remained an equally great problem, as it had been for many centuries. "The Nawab of Junagadh, finding his forces too meager to protect sea trade, closed the most infested ports. Bhavnagar, facing a similar threat, entered into a cooperative alliance with the British to root out the pirates. Navanagar made an alliance with the pirates!"[33] As late as the 1840s the Political Agent of the British in Saurashtra during 1839–43, before the British took on active administrative responsibility for the area, wrote: "The traditional policy of the state was to maintain inaccessibility. Forests, difficult passes, vile roads, thick jungles, were the bulwarks not only of the capital but of most of its towns and villages."[34] Spodek acknowledges, and many other contemporary and later accounts make clear, that such conditions were in general typical of most of India outside the Company's territories, as they had been of most of the country as a whole when the English began their territorial intrusion. It is hardly surprising that they succeeded—or perhaps more accurately that they fell increasingly into the role of keepers of order over more and more Indian territory, to protect trade and to guard their own domains as well as interregional commerce against disorder spreading from adjacent areas.

Many modern Indian historians have recognized, as the bitterness engendered by British colonialism has receded, that the Mughals, themselves an alien and intolerant dynasty of conquest, imposed on India an exploitative rule which largely disregarded mass welfare. Their rule plunged the country into chaos and suffering through its military campaigns and its subsequent failure to maintain order, whatever its accomplishments for a time in imposing a more or less uniform administrative system over some areas. These are of course relative matters, and one should also attempt to see them in the context of the times. Contemporary China (late Ming) and Europe ("l'etat, c'est moi") were hardly free of exploitative and oppressive rule, and Mughal administrative achievements were surely significant. But any such comparison leads me at least to see the impact of Mughal rule, especially after Akbar, as increasingly destructive and with net negative consequences economically. The Emperor Akbar (r. 1556–1605), an inspiringly large-minded and dedicated ruler, was unfortunately not followed on the peacock throne by anyone who could be so described; warfare in the provinces came to be echoed microcosmically in court intrigues and power struggles in the capital, culminating in the cruelly intolerant and repressive reign of Aurangzeb. Even a Muslim historian, Khafi Khan, writing in the 1720s, described the state of the country as follows:

> It is clear to the wise and experienced that now, according to the ways of the time, thoughtfulness in managing the affairs of State [and the practice of] protecting the peasantry and encouraging the prosperity of the country and increase in produce, have all departed. Revenue collectors ... having spent considerable amounts at the Court [i.e., to obtain the office], proceed to the *mahals* and become a scourge for the revenue-paying peasantry. ... Since they have no confidence that they will be confirmed in their office the next year, nay even for the whole of the current year, they seize both parts of the produce [the State's share as well as the peasants'] and sell them away. It is a God-fearing man indeed who limits himself to this and does not sell away the bullocks and carts [of the peasants], on which tillage depends, or, not contenting himself with extorting the amount of his expenses at the Court, of his troopers and the deficit on his pledge, does not sell away whatever remains with the peasantry, down to the fruit-bearing trees and their proprietary and hereditary [rights in the] land. ... Many *parganas* and townships which used to yield full revenue have, owing to the oppression of the officials, been so far ruined and devastated that they have become forests infested by tigers and lions; and the villages are so utterly

ruined and desolate that there is no sign of habitation on the routes.[35]

Khafi Khan was of course writing during the nadir of political degeneration after the death of Aurangzeb, and the text does tend to imply that things had been better earlier. No doubt this was true—nor is it hard to conceive of things having been better than this description—but what we know of the earlier Mughal period, to which modern Indian historians are our best guide, suggests that then too the *jagirdar* system among other aspects of Mughal rule lent itself too easily to abusive expropriation. From the early eighteenth century the three tiny English territorial bases at Madras, Calcutta, and Bombay, which had seemed so insignificant and so pre- carious, began to grow and prosper as secure alternatives to the kind of environment described by Khafi Khan: first, mainly for merchants, artisans, and commercial agents, who were more mobile; then, increasingly for originally peasant in-migrants. The progressive collapse into disorder after about 1710 set in train the virtual ruin of most traditional Indian merchant groups over the ensuing century and their trade bases at places such as Surat, Calicut, Masulipatam, and Hughli; thus, in effect, the merchants were impelled to shift their activities to the new towns growing up around the English forts.

Perhaps the best evidence for the weakness of the indigenous Indian commercial sector (or sectors, given India's regional fragmentation) is the success of European and English traders and entrepreneurs in moving in on the Indian economy, at the expense of Indian merchants as well as in partnership with some of them. As detailed in later chapters, this was in total contrast with the foreign failure to find any but the smallest of entrants or niches into the Chinese economy. Commercial success in India was followed in the nineteenth century by the spread of British-built rail lines linking the foreign-founded port cities with their hinterlands, draining goods to them from all parts of the country, and diffusing in return not merely imported goods and the products of new India-based factories but new foreign-style ideas. Finally, British sovereignty made possible massive British investment in the production process: a plantation sector, mines, new and greatly increased production of commercial crops for export (jute, cotton, wheat, tobacco), and the dissemination of steam and electric power. Traditional inland cities were transformed into growing industrial centers, using power-driven machinery and Western methods in both production and organization: Kanpur (Cawnpore), Allahabad, Ahmadabad ("the Manchester of India"), and others.[36] More and more of India was being drawn into the pattern of development set by the Western-founded colonial ports.

For all of these reasons and in all of the ways detailed in this chapter, India was in a condition to accept not merely colonial rule but fundamental change along the lines offered by the British. Individual Indians were accordingly willing to become collaborators as fellow entrepreneurs and fellow administrators. China and individual Chinese resisted colonialism and collaboration, both economically and politically. China was culturally homogenous and confident, and therefore relatively impervious, while India was culturally fragmented and disillusioned, and therefore susceptible. China was also economically far more successful and left no such opportunities or attractions as Westerners found in India. In China, foreigners had no choice but to collaborate with the Chinese, as traders, or as resident but not sovereign bodies. Intellectually also, the Indian response to the Western effort was in striking contrast to the Chinese experience. The following chapter attempts to describe this response, to explain it, and to explore some consequences.

Chapter 5

Colonialism and Collaboration

The Battle of Plassey established the English as the paramount power on the subcontinent. Although this was not immediately apparent to anyone, including the English, their paramountcy was not effectively challenged until independence nearly two centuries later. This was not merely, not even primarily, the result of British military power. While that power was disproportionately effective and was also deployed against a wholly disunited opposition, it was never great enough to maintain the British position by force alone. In addition, the Indian Army was indeed Indian; the number of British officers never exceeded its twentieth-century peak of forty thousand. And why was there no united opposition, even on a regional basis? Even in the administrative system the British ruled but did not govern, leaving that primarily to Indians who willingly served the Raj. The number of British in the Indian Civil Service never exceeded nine hundred and reached that figure only quite late in the colonial period. Remembering the vast size of the territory defended and administered in British India alone (not counting the so-called Native States) and the total of its population, it is obvious that the British could never have done it alone, and indeed that they never even considered doing so. In other words, most Indians were willing collaborators; some were also competitors, but in an overall context which accepted British paramountcy as axiomatic, until well into the twentieth century.

To most Indians who had any degree of political consciousness (throughout the colonial period of course a small but powerful minority) the Western-British model, if not British colonial rule, was genuinely attractive. As an alternative to the Mughal and post-Mughal order or disorder there was simply no contest. Very few Indians troubled themselves until much later about the greater degree of foreignness of the British, including the racial distinction. For one thing, the British themselves were far less concerned or self-conscious about it until after about

1860, with the rise of racism as an element in the final flowering of Western imperialism in Asia. Western arrogance then acquired a new bite, but in the earlier period there was little reason to see the Europeans (with the possible exception of the Portuguese) as any more arrogant, certainly not more oppressive, than the Mughals or many of their Indian power rivals. But probably most important, the subcontinent had seen too many alien conquests, all of them by people whose foreignness had both racial and religious aspects, to regard the English as significantly different, at least for the first century or so. Nor was there an Indian *national* as opposed to regional cultural awareness which could stimulate resistance.

The important difference about the English was that they offered, as no other alien or indigenous system had done in Indian memory, a degree of civil order and a set of new attitudes and techniques focused on economic growth from which some Indians as well as Englishmen could gain. Obviously all Indians could not and did not gain, and very few gained as much as the English, but the opportunity was there and became real for many, especially by comparison with opportunity under Mughal rule. It was concentrated in certain groups, preeminently the chief collaborators in the commercial-industrial sector (including some who later became competitors, e.g., the Tata and Birla enterprises, the cotton textile industrialists of Bombay and Gujerat, etc.) and the emerging group of Western-style professionals and civil servants. Others did well from land-owning because of the changed opportunities offered by the *zamindari* system as institutionalized by the British under the Permanent Settlement of 1793 in northeastern India.

In the wholly new setting of the colonial ports, divorced from traditional channels of status, advancement, and economic success, many Indian groups rose to prominence from previous relative obscurity. The Setts (Seths) and Basaks of lower Bengal did so through their early relationship to the English Company as bankers,[1] the Marwaris, in a more independent response to new opportunities in an expanding urban-commercial world, especially in Calcutta. The groups which rose with the colonial ports, including newly rich landowners and *zamindars*, literary figures, civil servants under the British Raj, and new professional men as well as merchants and industrialists, formed the new regional elites who increasingly dominated Indian politics and thought, while the power of the traditional elites was eclipsed or destroyed in the wake of the Mughal decline.[2] Some groups, including some peasants who were drawn into the production of new or newly expanded cash crops (indigo most notoriously), suffered at least in the sense that they took little or a disproportionate part in the gains.[3] But probably most of those, including peasants, drawn into the money economy benefited thereby and were in any case able to pursue their own economic interest and to manipulate new sets of choices (e.g., cash crops versus subsistence) to advantage. The most obvious and probably most important change here was improved transport, especially railways, the effect of which was spatially uneven but which, together with increased security, speed, and lesser costs greatly widened the market and produced substantial new net benefits for nearly all who were able to take advantage.[4]

It is impossible to guess at the extent to which average, peasant, or most other group welfare rose or declined under British rule except for the cases mentioned above, which even in total were probably a minority of the population.[5] It does need to be stressed, however, that the appropriate datum is late Mughal India; it is against that datum that the ensuing period is to be compared and was compared by the Indians of the time. This is a point commonly overlooked or misrepresented by anticolonialist historians, many of whom assume or argue for a much more favorable assessment of the state of the country as of the early eighteenth century than the evidence permits. Peasants—probably nearly all of them—and the great bulk of the Indian population certainly suffered during the Mughal period; most people were probably less well off at the end of it than they had been at the beginning. That seems very much less likely to have been the case for the period 1757–1947, nor is there sufficient evidence to suggest any substantial worsening of income distribution.

However reasonable or unreasonable such generalizations may be, any attempt to assess the impact of British rule on mass welfare is not the issue at this point; that is important, but not fully relevant to my purposes here, which center on explaining how and why British rule was generally accepted rather than resisted. Why did so many Indians become enthusiastic collaborators long before there was any significant effect on mass welfare? Why as a result was the impact of the Western-founded port cities so much greater than it was in China, and what sorts of consequences did all this have for the evolution of modern India? The British impact on mass welfare cannot be measured satisfactorily. Not enough is known about welfare levels in late Mughal India or at almost any point during the British colonial period to say with any assurance let alone precision what was happening over the two centuries or more involved, nor what the specific causal factors may have been.

Although we are also largely in the dark about population totals and growth rates until late in the nineteenth century, it is nevertheless sugges- tive that population was clearly continuing to grow throughout the British period, and especially rapidly in its last decades. Whatever the causes (although increased irrigation, transport improvements, genuine if modest industrial growth, and the establishment of civil order are not likely to have been irrelevant), this is not easy to reconcile with assertions of net or mass economic decline. Population growth brought its own problems, as in China and elsewhere, and doubtless contributed to much distress, but it is not likely to have taken place or to have continued if India's circumstances after 1750 or 1800 were in fact worse, or not better, than they had been before. No one questions that some people and some groups suffered from cruel exploitation under British rule, nor that much individual British wealth was extorted thereby; this does not necessarily make British rule worse than what preceded it or what might have existed in its place if the British had never come along. British rule, like any other attempt by an alien power to manipulate the affairs of others elsewhere—i.e., im- perialism—came to be resented whether or not it was economically de- structive of Indian welfare. It is not necessary in order to justify indepen- dence or to castigate alien manipulation to prove that originally foreign rule was or is bad for people materially. And whatever its material results, it may often not be perceived or labeled as imperialism. The problem is one of definition, under what circumstances and by whom.[6]

Until well into the nineteenth century few Indians saw the British presence or even British rule as insupportable, as something to be resisted. Even then it was a tiny minority; the events of 1857, variously labeled the Indian Mutiny and the First War of Indian Independence, are not properly regarded as the birth of the movement for Indian independence however else they may be interpreted. Of course, there was resentment on the part of some against British rule, and especially against mounting British arrogance, but 1857 is best characterized as an effort on the part of a small group to use this resentment (such as exists at almost any time against nearly every ruling system, let alone an alien one) to reestablish their own special privilege by moving back quite consciously to something like the Mughal order. The lack of promise which such a course offered to most Indians is demonstrated by its failure to attract adequate support. And despite the ruthlessness of its suppression by the British, the half-century which followed saw the further rise to prominence in national life of Indian collaborators, including most signficantly those who are credited with founding modern Indian nationalism. They were people who saw the British model as a promising path to something which they themselves identified as "progress," and to the strengthening and rebuilding of India.

The man now accepted as the first important figure in the political evolution of modern India, M. G. Ranade, was preeminently such a person. A Maharashtrian Brahmin who became the first graduate (in 1862) of the British-style and partially British-founded University of Bombay, he strove all his life for reform of traditional India along avowedly British lines. As a lifelong civil servant in the British Indian system, and ultimately as a judge on the Bombay High Court, he epitomized the profoundly Westernized collaborator who believed in the virtues of the British system because he was himself a part of it. Far from opposing British rule, such men welcomed it, not because they profited by it (although most of them did) but as the best vehicle for the beneficial redevelopment of India. To them it represented no inconsistency to retain at the same time a degree of identification with Indian tradition; they were not iconoclasts like those in early Meiji Japan, rejecting their own tradition (however briefly) in favor of a Western model which they saw as superior. They argued instead for Western-style change as the best way to rejuvenate and extract the best from a national past, in order to improve a present which they saw as weak, degenerate, and even "backward" in terms of recent or current local models, including of course the Mughal legacy.[7] Traditional India was to be preserved but "modernized"; there was to be an Indian cultural renaissance, "democratic" reforms in education, and a grafting of liberal constitutionalism onto the framework of traditional Indian society.[8]

While Ranade was the first to become an active political reformist, there were others before him (and many after) who argued for the same ideas. The essayist Gopal Hari Deshmukh was already publishing in the periodical press of Maharashtra and Bombay in the late 1840s letters which stressed the need for and benefits of British rule and criticized what he saw as the backwardness of Hindu society.[9] He advised India to become more commercialized and industrialized and to discard what he saw as the useless and unproductive customs of Hinduism, to abandon the joint family in favor of the nuclear family, to eliminate early marriage and allow widow remarriage, to break the repressive aspects of caste, and to recognize the value of Western mores. Ranade, Deshmukh, and later figures such as G. K. Gokhale, G. G. Agarkar, and even B. G. Tilak[10] were to dominate the later nineteenth-century political scene with the same essential message in western India as Rammohun Roy and his followers were doing in Bengal. Even those who resented British rule saw the British model as the best one for India.

Hindu revivalists and traditionalists, called into existence by foreign rule and its arrogance, interacted with and further stimulated Indian critics of indigenous institutions. While the British challenge did impel some Indians to look into their own past in search of value, few of those who did so were uncritical, and even they rejected the preceding eight centuries of Islamic domination. What value they found in the supposed golden age of Hinduism, a hazy millennium and more ago, provided occasion for more attacks on indigenous tradition by the now-dominant group of contemporary Indians who saw the past as an obstacle and felt an urgent need to free India from its stultifying tradition as they saw it. What was needed was a complete break with what had gone before, to build a new India on consciously Western lines. The process went far beyond the kind of reexamination of tradition which Chinese intellectuals and nativists engaged in. For all the bitter denunciation of old China by Lu Hsün and his circle, they did not prescribe its remaking through adopting the Western model. The Indian ferment induced by foreign presence evolved into a far more sweeping synthesis which more and more explicitly sought to apply the Western formula to India's perceived problems.

Deshmukh's contemporary V. K. Chiplunkar, another Maharashtrian Brahmin, was a bitter critic of British and especially missionary arrogance, but even he acknowledged that "the English language is like a tigress, and one who is brought up on her milk should never be a weakling . . . the study of books in that language is likely to create such excellent virtues as energy, self-reliance, bravery, etc."[11] Chiplunkar and Deshmukh, like Ranade, were both civil servants in Bombay Presidency, collaborators and converts of the new British-run world in which they moved.

Even as such sentiments evolved toward a movement for independence at the end of the nineteenth century, the result suggests, at least in terms of the political or philosophic rhetoric, comparison with the American colonies a rough century earlier rather than with the types of response to imperialism elsewhere in Asia. It was converts to the British model who were asking for their freedom, not rejectors of an alien system. These highly educated subjects of the Raj were not yet in open opposition. They supported the government, but they were increasingly critical of it, and by its own standards. They faulted it for being untrue to the long-established values of the British political order which they had learned to admire at school and university. While they remained loyal, at least to such a set of ideals, and their activities stayed well within legal bounds, they were an ever louder and more embarrassing problem to successive Viceroys. As Anil Seal puts it:

> Theirs were not movements which could be dealt with by a whiff of grapeshot; lawyers from the high court could hardly be ridden down or Surendranath Banerjea be blown from a gun. These men spoke highly of British justice. They asked God to bless the British Queen. They had friends inside the British parliament. But they spoke of the "Un-Britishness" of British Rule in India.[12]

Whether parallel or not to the American colonies in the 1760s and 1770s, how utterly and totally different from the Chinese response to the Western model. The difference may well revolve primarily around the Indian perception that initially there was not a preferable domestic model to defend, and that the best way for India, as well as for themselves, to get ahead was to become a collaborator, even if one who ultimately demanded political independence. The British system represented and promised success; its foreignness was incidental, at least until late in the game, and was in any case far from a new experience for Indians. Individual Chinese later toyed with some of these ideas in their despair over China's weakness, but few were willing to go so far toward acknowledging that the best way for their own country was the Western way. The Indian nationalist reformers, like the economic entrepreneurs, came to believe in "progress" in a Western sense as an article of faith, and in the Western model as the best means to gain it. This implied at least a degree of rejection or a downgrading of the past, and hence (since the past was indigenous) of one's own tradition. Indians were far more ready, and had far more reason, to do this than did the Chinese. When at last the Chinese Communist Party rejected the past, it was a selective rejection, or even a resorting, and not one which substituted Western models for indigenous ones.

But it was not just a political contrast which British rule offered to recent and current alternatives in India. Nor was it, of course, an accident that political criticism of British rule and the collaborators who later began to voice it were almost exclusively centered in the capitals of the Presidencies—that is, in Calcutta, Bombay, and Madras, where the beginnings of modern Indian education along strictly British lines and the first modern Indian universities had also arisen. All the developments touched on above first took shape in the colonial ports, founded and dominated by the British. Such stirrings took place also in the other colonial ports throughout Asia, including the China treaty ports. The difference in India is that what began there spread, perhaps not to engulf the entire country but to create and shape virtually all change which took place in the country and to create virtually de novo the people, groups, institutions, and ideas which ruled India at independence. The treaty port Indian became, without need for apology, the dominant modern Indian, where the treaty port Chinese and all that he stood for, after a late and brief period of power and influence, has been rejected by a nationalist revolution.

In India, it began early, in the absence of an attractive or even viable indigenous alternative. In Bengal, Indian agents were serving the East India Company before the end of the seventeenth century, groups who found in collaboration a secure road to wealth and hence became allies. Many of those who became rich, especially after Plassey, came from humble beginnings; their new wealth was not only secure but was admired in the Western-dominated world of Calcutta. By 1835 two Indians were serving on committees and on the board of directors of the newly founded Calcutta Chamber of Commerce; the year before had already seen the establishment of Carr, Tagore and Co., a genuinely joint Anglo-Indian commercial venture. Eight years later, in 1843, the Bengal British India Society was founded, joining Western-minded Indian businessmen, intellectuals, and landowners with British residents in an association which discussed the "progressive improvement" of Bengal, Calcutta, and India. Identity of interest between the British and this new Westernized Indian bourgeoisie was epitomized in 1888 when David Yule, an Englishman then chairman of the Bengal Chamber of Commerce, presided over the first annual session of the Indian National Congress.

Dwarkanath Tagore (1794–1846) and Rammohun Roy (1772–1833) are perhaps the two best known and earliest models of the new kind of Indian who was emerging in the colonial ports, one a Western-style commercial entrepreneur, the other a political philosopher, reformer, and writer. Both were profoundly impressed not just by the material success of the modern West but by the Western self-image, and especially by the early nineteenth-century British vision of the good society. They sought to transform India in that image, preserving what they saw as the best of its own tradition, primarily what could be reconciled with, or at least was not antagonistic to, modern Western notions (for example, accepting the monotheism of the Upanishads and Hindu doctrines of tolerance and good works, but rejecting, like the British, *suttee,* religious-sanctioned violence, much of caste rules, and what they saw as the "extremes" of Hindu communalism) to produce a visionary blend, a "progressive," "rational," "liberal," order, free from "superstition," bigotry, and social injustice. Tagore (the grandfather of Rabindranath [1861–1941], the Nobel laureate poet and prophet of ecumenical cosmopolitanism) probably was the more appropriate to his times, and Roy a generation or two ahead of his; Western-oriented political philosophers and reformers generally followed after successful commercial entrepreneurs in finding the British model attractive and rewarding. Dwarkanath Tagore was far from being the first to do so, but he became a more wholehearted and articulate spokesman for the development of India on the model of British social and political institutions than anyone before him. He was also the first Indian to hold a status position in the East India Company, at the Board of Customs. But he owed that position to his previous success in the Western-style commercial world of Calcutta, as an entrepreneur.

Tagore founded and directed the first Western-style bank, pioneered India's first modern coal mining (and later railway) enterprise at Raniganj in West Bengal, organized the first Indian-owned steamship line, and was the moving spirit behind the founding and management of Carr, Tagore and Co.–clearly an enthusiastically committed recruit to what is referred to as modernization, i.e., Westernization–and, equally to the point, an outstandingly successful one. He made money, and he used it in part to help spread the gospel which had done so well by him as founder, promoter, or sponsor of public institutions striving for development along British lines: newspapers, associations, British-style schools and colleges, and especially joint Anglo-Indian enterprises of all sorts. He was an early supporter and, from 1833 to his death, principal of Hare's Hindu College, founded in Calcutta in 1817 as the first of many higher-level educational institutions designed to produce English-trained Indians who could be effective Westernizers. Tagore was also, like nearly all Bengalis who won commercial success, a landowner, a *zamindar.* There too he made continuous efforts to stimulate his fellow Bengali *zamindars* to work together in support of social reform, education, and Westernization.

Bengalis in fact became less and less prominent in the commercial life of Calcutta after Tagore's time. They were hampered by British competition and discrimination, especially in this city which was also the colonial capital and to a greater extent than in Bombay which remained a much more Indian city and one where Indians (largely Gujeratis) dominated the commercial and industrial scene. But landowning was a highly profitable and perfectly rational (as well as prestigious) outlet for Bengali capital earned in trade; it was not necessarily a bad bargain, or one to which most wealthy Bengalis were forced. Others found Western-style professions, especially law and the civil service, also more attractive and rewarding than trade, a pattern which helps to explain the disproportionate role played by Bengalis in the national life ever since as articulators of the literary and political values of Western society. But the majority of literate Bengalis (and literacy was and remains higher there than in most of the rest of India) were also intellectuals, amateur or professional, writers about the discussers of the events of their day as traditional Bengali and Indian culture hybridized with the Western model in this first and greatest Indian arena of their meeting.

Perhaps as a result of their strong identity with their own traditional literary heritage, Bengali intellectuals seemed somehow to be able to manipulate the new Western modes almost effortlessly, not really merging them with tradition but keeping the two separate while remaining at home with both. While in politics, economics, and social change Gujeratis, Madrasis, Punjabis, U. P. men, and others became more prominent, as well as more complete synthesizers, blenders of traditional and Western strands, Bengali articulateness, mastery of new Western modes, success in the law and the civil service, and distinctive *panache* kept them in the forefront of the national scene where traditional India and the West were evolving in interaction toward modern India.

Tagore was consciously following a British formula in promoting a paternalistic, gentry-like role for his fellow *zamindars,* urging their responsibility for the welfare of their tenants and for the improvement and commercialization of agriculture, and also their political duty as leaders and reformers to organize for cooperative action toward Western-style change. He saw the rising middle class in general as the chief agent of economic growth and of the building of a new and strengthened India. Like him, they lived increasingly in Western style, to match their Western ideas, and sought like him to promote joint Anglo-Indian ventures of every sort. Tagore and several of his Indian colleagues actually fought the Court of

Directors of the East India Company in a protest movement in 1829 against the restrictions then in force limiting European (including English) settlement in India, and published in this connection several articles stressing the good which Westerners had done for India. Tagore built a rural villa outside Calcutta where he entertained and cultivated his British and Westernized Indian friends in a garden house surrounded by clipped green lawns and equipped with a sumptuous ballroom and European paintings. His dream of equal partnership in the building of a modern and Westernized India was to fail, especially as later-day British imperialism and associated racism brought growing mutual hostility. Indians accordingly turned increasingly to the rediscovery of their own cultural identity. But Tagore nevertheless epitomizes the more or less happy blending of British and Indian elements which did take place, in Bengal and by degrees in much of the rest of India but especially in the colonial ports where the blending began and from which it spread. Literate, politically conscious Indians by the twentieth century, whatever their grievances against the Raj, were genuinely, as Jawarlahal Nehru described himself as being, half English and half Indian, children of the new bourgeois collaborators who found both British reality and British ideas at least as attractive, compelling, and rewarding as even the best of their own Indian tradition.[13]

Lacking the means and the will to govern India except in a supervisory role, the British actively attempted to create collaborators who could assist them by doing the work of administration, the preservation of order, and the commercial development of the country. In the words of Macaulay's famous "Minute on Education" of 1835, what was wanted was a new sort of Indian elite, "a class Indian in blood and colour, but English in tastes, in opinions, in morals, and intellect."[14] This was the original blueprint of the education system of British India, which went on producing more Tagores, and more Nehrus.[15] But that process depended of course on Indian willingness to follow such a course, something already established long before Macaulay wrote. The earliest evidence, from the beginning of the English presence in Bengal, was the appearance of Indian collaborators who easily merged their own patterns of behavior and values with those of their trade partners. By the nineteenth century there were the beginnings of group explorations of this rapidly expanding hybrid culture in the form of regional associations. These were first organized in the Presidency capitals where the activities of the East India Company had first produced an alternative to traditional patterns. The associations attracted Indians who had won new and higher status in this hybrid but English-dominated world and who were at home there not only linguistically but culturally and politically. Most of the associations arose specifically to meet the needs perceived by Indians to foster English-style education rather than remaining dependent on either missionary or traditional Hindu schools. Graduates of the first such Indian-founded schools and others who had passed through mission establishments founded new associations, where their group sense was heightened by the ostracism they suffered at the hands both of orthodox Hindus and of British colonialists, as well as by the shared excitment of their commitment to a newly emerging movement whose goal was a renascent India—along British lines.

> These students . . . debated subjects of the most general kind—free will, fate, truth, virtue, and the hollowness of idolatry; their heroes were the *philosophes,* and their handbook was Tom Paine's *Age of Reason* . . . they galvanized Calcutta in the late 1820's, flaunting their renunciation of orthodox Hindu society.[16]

Seal adds in a footnote: "It was rumoured that the college boys recited the Iliad instead of their matras. Others refused in court to swear by the holy waters of the Ganges and met at Derozio's house to eat beef and drink beer . . . (or) sherry and biscuits." The same intellectual scene was reproduced as first Bombay, then Madras, then in a flowing tide virtually all urban centers with a college or university joined the movement begun in Calcutta, Indian intellectuals and bourgeoisie choosing Westernization, for itself and as the best means they could think of for the redevelopment of India.

Independence has brought relatively few changes. The Westernized bourgeois elite who rose to status, wealth, and power under colonial rule, children of the colonial ports who fought and won political freedom on a platform of representative parliamentary government British style made little effort to dismantle the colonial legacy. Under Nehru's daughter, India is still dominated by the same group, a coalition of Western-trained and Western-oriented bourgeois intellectuals, civil servants and politicians, urban entrepreneurs and industrialists, and rural landowners. Despite vague endorsements of "a socialist pattern of society" (itself of course a Western notion) there has been no significant break with the hybrid but dominantly capitalist pattern of colonial institutions, still less a revolution. The rural masses are to be appealed to and guided toward material improvement, but not mobilized or made the central figures of power or policy despite their preponderant majority in this still overwhelming peasant society. India remains a basically Asian country, ruled and shaped by a small elite who in many respects are indistinguishable from their Western counterparts. The fundamental economic, social, and political structure inherited from colonialism remains largely unchanged. To India's Western-ized rulers, genuine mass egalitarianism and the revolution needed to establish it are not attractive.[17]

Independent India continues to pursue the Western urban-industrial model of economic growth, focused on concentration. The newly emerg-ing middle class elite became the effective managers of India under British tutelage, and rightly demanded independence on the grounds that they were at least as able as the colonialists to run the country on Western lines; they themselves had become equivalent to Westerners in education and training, in attitudes, in values, and in goals. For the most part, they supported the gospel of modernization as Westernization. After nearly thirty years of independence, there may now be some tendency for a more distinctive pattern of development to assert itself, a set of solutions more particularly South Asian. The Gandhian legacy has tended to remain largely lip service, at least in terms of its impact on actual policy, with few exceptions. But it and other indigenous approaches and values, including a move toward the rural and peasant end of the spectrum, may be strength-ened as both Westerners and Asians increasingly recognize that the Western model of over-concentrated urban-industrial growth, the legacy of the colonial ports, creates as many problems as it solves, may fail to serve real welfare, and may be destructive both of the environment and of the quality of human life.[18] In India, nativist groups are increasingly elbowing themselves into influence and power, via the regionally, culturally, and linguistically separate traditions and bases of which the subcontinent has long been composed. Indigenous and traditional emphases are thus, be-latedly, picking up new strength.

In any case, the Western model of consumerism and high per capita incomes is especially inappropriate for South Asia. It is unrealizable even if it were desirable; it establishes a false and needlessly frustrating perspec-tive; it warps planning priorities; and it does not and cannot serve mass welfare needs. South Asia's circumstances, needs, and wants are pro-foundly different from those of the West. Western-style "progress" is beginning to be questioned as the prescription for South Asia. To raise these questions, however, is to underline still further the gap between South Asia's middle class and thoroughly Westernized managers and the mass of its people, sharing a subcontinent but living otherwise in different worlds. Perhaps they can begin to close the gap and to move toward the South Asian end of the spectrum. So far the "modernists" and the newly rising nativists are competing for power and influence rather than attempting to work together; it is rivalry and mutual disapproval rather than synthesis. The institutional structure inherited from colonialism, the attitudes and values of the elite nurtured in the colonial ports, stand in the way.

The colonial ports did indeed transform India. The same effort and the same message carried over to China fell on different ground.

Chapter 6

Steps to China

Whatever the rewards for Western traders and colonialists in India, the prospects of the China market continued to draw Western ambition from before Columbus, as even under revolutionary new circumstances they still do. If India was seen as rich, China was richer, even more populous, and hence both a source of profitable trade goods and an immense potential market for Western products. India, and later Western positions in Southeast Asia, were seen as valuable in part as forward bases for the Western effort in China.

Southeast Asia, however, was also attractive in itself, as a source of valuable trade goods (pepper, tin, and spices most importantly) and as an area where large numbers of Chinese merchants had long been engaged in trade and had even established permanent settlements. Perhaps the Westerners might be able to deal directly with them in their Southeast Asian entrepôts, obtaining Chinese goods and marketing Western commodities with less effort, greater profit, and fewer restrictions than in China itself. At the same time, Southeast Asian trade could be tapped, and Western bases established there which could serve as way stations to Canton and, when conditions made it possible, as support for a larger-scale assault on China directly. It was a combination of such motives and ambitions which ultimately led to the foundation of Singapore in 1819. But the process was a long one, extending over nearly two centuries, and even the success of Singapore did not prove sufficient. As a British colony, Singapore did indeed become the predominant entrepôt for Southeast Asian trade, despite the Dutch retention of Indonesia. But it never was able to serve as an adequate alternative to a Western position in China for providing access to the China market which was still the prime goal. Chinese flocked there, continuing a long history of trading in the Malay archipelago, but as emigrés rather than as agents, representatives, or intermediaries of direct access to El Dorado.

Nevertheless, Southeast Asia lay athwart the routes from the West to

80

China, via India, and as the Western grasp extended eastward, powerfully drawn by dreams of the riches of China, it was natural that efforts would be made to use Southeast Asia as a lever in addition to tapping its trade for its own sake. Western frustration in China itself increased the motivation somehow to circumvent the restrictions imposed by the mandarinate and to attempt to create in Southeast Asia a base where Western merchants could deal directly with their Chinese counterparts, free of the crippling incubus of official interference and of the barriers which Westerners confronted in their efforts to operate as entrepreneurs in China as a whole. Ch'ing policy (1644–1911) toward foreigners and foreign trade continued trends already evident from mid-Ming (1368–1644) in regulating such contacts as much as possible in order to protect China's Great Harmony from their disturbing influences and to concentrate resources on internal development. China's experience with foreigners was that they were troublesome, and that neither they nor their trade offered anything which China needed or wanted. By 1759 the arrangement which had been followed in practice for many previous years was more formally institutionalized in what is referred to as the Canton system. Western merchants were to be limited to Canton, on the outer fringe of the empire, and denied permission to trade elsewhere. Only those foreigners who came as members of official tributary missions bringing gifts and performing obeisance to the Emperor were permitted to go beyond Canton, en route to Peking. Foreign trade was made a state monopoly, and in their dealings at Canton, Western merchants were obliged to work only with the official Co-hong, or consortium of Chinese firms, which set prices and determined the conditions of trade as in effect an arm of the government. No Westerners could deal with other Chinese merchants, nor trade at other ports. At Canton they were forbidden to enter the city and were virtually confined to their trading factories outside the city gates. They could not bring in women or arms and could not reside permanently but only during each year's trading season, from September to April.

By comparison, a Southeast Asian base for trade with China came to seem more and more attractive. But Southeast Asia was a complex welter of separate and often rather ambiguous units—sultanates large and petty, relict empires, trading groups and their bases, numerous and effective pirate groups such as the Bugis, city-states, and even larger relatively empty areas of upland and rainforest where economic or political organization were at best unclear. In addition, there were a number of outside contenders for commercial primacy, including the Chinese as well as the Portuguese, the Spanish, the Dutch, the English, and south Indian, "Arab," and Malay traders. Among the Westerners, the Portuguese had of course arrived first and had established a strong position in the area. By the time the English began to think seriously of extending their effort to Southeast Asia, the Dutch had already ousted the Portuguese and were in an even stronger position, as explained later in this chapter. The English were caught, in their mounting eagerness to get at the China market, between crippling restrictions at Canton and a confused and high-risk landscape in Southeast Asia. Although the idea of a Southeast Asian base remained alive, it was understandable that the first efforts were concentrated on trying to improve access in China itself.

In addition to the English and Dutch (and somewhat later French) direct trading ventures at Canton,[1] which had begun on an occasional basis earlier in the seventeenth century, the directors of the English Company at Fort St. George (Madras) tried in 1698 to extend their Indian operations to China by sending a shipload of English and Indian goods under Robert Douglas as supercargo. Douglas was detained at Canton by Chinese delaying tactics and negotiation (as so many were to be in later years) and was in the end forced to take back most of the goods previously sold after the Chinese found that they could be bought more cheaply at Amoy (how and why are not clear since Amoy was supplied with English goods via Canton). Douglas had originally contracted to buy silk at an agreed price, but this was raised and the amount reduced before delivery because of heavy silk purchases meanwhile by the yearly Manila galleon; the English were obliged to fill out their cargo with other goods not originally contracted for. Douglas then tried to sail to Ningpo to buy the silk wanted and also to sell off the English goods which had been returned in Canton, "But our Ship was not Sufficed to go nearer than Chusan . . . where I mett with many new troubles, ours being the first English ship that ever loaded from thence."[2]

Douglas was closely followed at Chusan by Allen Catchpoole, originally from Calcutta but operating now as president of the short-lived rival East India Company known as the "New" Company. Catchpoole tried to establish a factory and settlement on Chusan, but was forced to withdraw in 1702. Still seeking a forward base for trade with China, he and his company settled on the island of Poulo Condore, off the south coast of

Vietnam (see the front endpaper map), hoping to make it into a major entrepôt for the entire China coast, the role later played by Hong Kong. His account of the island praises its excellent harbor and healthfully cool climate (presumably by contrast with Calcutta—it could hardly have been very cool although it doubtless benefited from sea breezes) and dilates on its great commercial future.[3] However, Catchpoole and his entire company were massacred by their Macassar garrison in 1705. Influenced by this series of unpromising experiences, even on the part of a rival company, the directors at Fort St. George decided in 1706 to give up the China trade as impracticable.[4]

This was to be only for a time, however, for although there were no further schemes to use India as a forward base for selling English goods in China, Indian goods under British entrepreneurial management came to dominate China's imports by the mid-eighteenth century and almost to the end of the nineteenth. These were of course primarily opium and cotton, first raw cotton and later cloth and cotton yarn, demand for the latter in China rising as opium imports declined after about 1870. What was referred to as the "country trade," in which private European merchants not attached to the East India Company bought and shipped Indian goods for sale at different places within the Indian market, had been an element of some importance in the commercial landscape from the beginning of the Western presence. Sugar, textiles, and other Bengal and east coast commodities, for example, were carried by private traders to Surat and later to Bombay in exchange for raw cotton or for Company bills of exchange.

Many Company officials invested privately in this trade, and it began to expand beyond simple exchange between Indian east and west coasts. Raw cotton, textiles, and other Indian goods were in demand in Southeast Asia, and the booming West Indian plantation sector provided a vigorous market for Bengali sugar and for cheap cotton prints. Shipments of Indian goods in this "country trade" to Malacca and to ports in the East Indies were purchased, it was noticed, among others by Chinese merchants for reshipment to Canton, and it was natural for Western traders involved to attempt their own direct ventures to such an immense potential market. One of the commodities involved in the early India-Southeast Asia country trade was opium. It had long been grown in India (and in China) for use as a drug, but apparently not smoked until the diffusion of tobacco from the New

World via the Spanish Acapulco-Manila-Canton link. As with other Indian goods, private European merchants found that opium shipped to Southeast Asia was being purchased in part by Chinese for resale in China.

Chinese production of both cotton and opium was unable to keep pace with demand; both plants were introduced into the agricultural system relatively late, cotton from India (where it was probably cultivated by the third millennium B.C., earlier than anywhere else in the world) not until Sung times. Opium appears to have been known and used first in Asia Minor at least by classical Greek times, if not earlier, and to have spread to India via Persia some centuries later, but not to China before the T'ang. Its use on a large scale for other than medicinal purposes does not seem to have begun in China until the seventeenth century, but demand thereafter rose sharply and continually outran domestic supplies. India had a climatic advantage for the production of both crops, since both are susceptible to moisture damage, especially at harvest time, and do best in a semiarid situation. The Indian agricultural system was also more able than the Chinese system to expand rapidly in new or subsidiary crops, given the presence of much unused or abandoned arable land (see p. 51) which under the British order could now be cultivated without displacing food crops. In any case, under British rule cash cropping increased rapidly as new capital, markets, and transport became available. In addition to jute, the growth of Calcutta came to depend importantly on Bengal opium, as did the rise of Bombay on Gujerat, Maharahstra, and Deccan cotton, much of it exported in raw or more finished form to China. Raw cotton alone exported from Bombay and Surat increased in volume almost ten times between 1784 and 1788, and remained at the new high level into the nineteenth century.[5]

The best quality opium came from the Patna-Banaras area (including parts of what is now Bihar) produced and taxed under Company monopoly and sold at auction in Calcutta for export by private traders, first to Southeast Asia and then increasingly to Canton. The proceeds from its sale at Canton were made over to the Company in exchange for Company bills payable in London. This built up funds at Canton for the purchase of teas on the Company's account, by far the largest British import from China. Until the growth of this triangular "country trade" carrying Indian cotton and opium to Canton for exchange on London, British purchases at Canton had been financed in large part by bullion. By the time of the abolition of the Company's monopoly of trade in India in 1813, the import of Indian goods to China was in effect paying for nearly three-quarters of British purchases at Canton. In addition, of course, the trade provided a profitable outlet for a booming Indian production of cotton and opium which also swelled the Company's Indian revenues. After 1813, mushrooming Agency Houses succeeded the individual private traders in India. Many of them had representatives at Canton, the immediate predecessors of the British firms which blossomed there after the end of the Company's China monopoly in 1833 and after 1842 went on to dominate the treaty ports, whose Anglo-Indian flavor (see chapter 1) thus had clear and direct roots.

The China trade had at least as much impact on India as on China. As already suggested, the growth of a Chinese market for cotton contributed importantly to the growth of Bombay and to the rise of Indian entrepreneurial groups there, as well as helping to stimulate and to finance the beginnings of Indian industrialization in the form of the Bombay and Gujerat textile industry, which supplied a large share of Chinese textile imports; by the end of the nineteenth century India had the fourth largest cotton textile industry in the world. Opium was involved too in the modern commercial growth of western India, since the secondary production area of Malwa in Maharashtra, yielding a lesser grade and cheaper opium sometimes referred to as "country" opium, and outside the Company's control until the 1830s, provided large trade profits to Parsee entrepreneurs operating out of Bombay and selling Malwa opium at Canton. Marwaris were also involved in financing Malwa opium production, through advances, and probably owed some of their later success elsewhere to capital earned thus. Parsee profits, earned both at the Bombay and the Canton ends (where Parsee firms remained prominent especially in the opium trade into the 1850s) went increasingly into Bombay industrialization and specifically into cotton textiles, one of the great success stories of modern Indian entrepreneurship. By the 1860s the Parsees were ready to abandon opium even at the Indian end to more recent recruits (including Middle Eastern Jews like the Sassoons and the Hardouns, who moved into the opium business and treaty port real estate after 1870 in China) in preference for the greater profitability and security of investment in booming Bombay industry.[6]

Especially after about 1780, it was increasingly the profits earned from its double role in the triangular opium and cotton trade with China which kept the English East India Company afloat financially, and which also kept it competitive in the Canton market, since it could sell opium, cotton, and saltpeter at relatively low prices and still afford to offer relatively high prices for tea and silk. Operations in India and in China, as elsewhere in Asia, were combined in the Company's accounts, but it seems reasonably clear that by the last decades of the eighteenth century the Indian side was a substantial loser and that China profits saved the Company from bankruptcy.[7] In China the Company functioned only as a trader, while in India it was more and more functioning as a government, increasingly spending more than it earned and in particular having to finance out of its own revenues the cost of keeping order and of conducting the series of small-scale military campaigns along the edges of its expanding territories after Plassey and into the nineteenth century. Apart from its vital role in balancing the Company's books, however, the China trade was irresistibly attractive. The tangential Western involvement in it under the Canton system gave, for all its frustrations, a tantalizing glimpse of the vast size and wealth of the market. If only Western traders could get free access to it, their fortunes would be made. The English also dreamed, as they were to go on doing a century or more later in the face of all the evidence, that here at last was a country northern enough to buy British woolens[8] and perhaps also British metal goods, since the Indian market for both had been a disappointment.

There were several efforts to trade along the China coast north of Canton, including the ventures by Douglas and Catchpoole referred to previously and the more dramatic undertaking by James Flint in 1755, all of which ended in failure, as did the subsequent and larger-scale diplomatic campaigns in the missions of Viscount Macartney and Lord Amherst in 1793 and 1816.[9] An early and continuing counterstrategy, of which Catchpoole's settlement on Poulo Condore was an example, was to establish a base or bases in Southeast Asia in the hope of attracting Chinese merchants there and using this channel as a means of free or at least officially unregulated access to the China market. Indian and a few English goods were in fact sold to China in this way, as already indicated, and this degree of success prompted a series of greater hopes and plans.

Southeast Asia was however not free of problems from the British point of view. In a sense, they exchanged Chinese monopolistic control for Dutch, especially after the consolidation of the Dutch position on Java following the foundation of Batavia and the building of a fort there by 1619. Under the vigorous leadership of Jan Pieterzon Coen (Governor-

General of the Indies from 1618 to 1629) and his able successors, the Dutch East India Company became de facto sovereign over most of Java by the end of the seventeenth century. More important from the point of view of would-be Western competition, the Dutch were largely successful in maintaining a virtual monopoly of the trade of at least the central Indies. Batavia was well placed, as Coen saw, to control traffic through the Sunda Straits, the principal entrant to the Indonesian archipelago, and to serve as a central base for the policing of Indonesian waters as a whole and the enforcement of a Dutch monopoly. With the help of this strategically located base, the Dutch were able first to outflank the Portuguese positions at Goa and Malacca and then virtually to eliminate Portuguese trade competition throughout the Indies. They continued also to improve on ship design and naval gunnery to produce faster, more maneuverable, and militarily more effective craft which they used with vigor and organization to drive out the by now more cumbersome and less effective Portuguese ships.

The same set of advantages, stemming from the possession of a strategic base at Batavia and an aggressive and highly competent fleet pursuing a well-organized policy of monopolistic control of the trade of the Indies, proved a match also for the somewhat later-arriving English. The Dutch took Malacca by storm from the Portuguese in 1641, but in effect demonstrated the strength of their new position by allowing Malacca to decay, no longer fearing competition in their own waters from any base east of Bengal. The main preexisting trade centers of the Indies in indigenous hands were conquered, including Macassar; several of the spice-producing outer islands, such as Amboina and Ternate, occupied; and all trade concentrated in Batavia. By the end of the seventeenth century the Dutch position was supreme and apparently unassailable except perhaps along the margins of the Indies area. They had gradually scaled down their effort in India, and especially as the English built up their own bases at Madras, Calcutta, and Bombay tacitly acknowledged that their status there was at best marginal, while the strength and profitability of their position in the Indies suggested continued concentration of their efforts there.

Whatever the logic of such an arrangement from the Dutch point of view, many of the English continued to feel that it must be challenged. This was much less, if at all, based on any hope to dislodge the Dutch but rather on the recurrent strategy to use a base or bases somewhere on the fringes of the Dutch realm in Southeast Asia as a forward position for a commercial assault on China for which the English bases in India were too distant. It was also hoped, as in Catchpoole's vision, to attract significant numbers of Chinese merchants to such a base conveniently close to Kwangtung and Fukien and tempting as an alternative to the tightly controlled Canton system. It was known, of course, that Chinese merchants had been numerous and active in virtually all Southeast Asian trading centers for centuries. Why not create or take over such a center, on the northern edge of the Dutch sphere under English management, and make it into a free port through which both Indian and English goods could be sold for the first time in real volume to China, outflanking the arbitrarily and artificially limiting constraints imposed by the Canton system and in effect giving access to the entire country rather than merely to the Co-hong?

It was a genuinely exciting prospect, if only a way could somehow be found to circumvent the Dutch power. It was certain that the Chinese would continue to buy, and probably in increasing amounts, Southeast Asian tin, pepper, and other spices, so that whatever the real Chinese demand for English woolens or other goods (as opposed to the warping and stunting effects supposedly exerted on the market by the Canton system), a brisk trade could be counted on in a combination of Southeast Asian products plus Indian cotton and opium. An early English factory establishment at Pattani (near the extreme southern end of the east coast of Siam—see the front endpaper map) in 1612, intended not unreasonably as an appropriate base of this sort, had to be abandoned in 1623 in the face of overbearing Dutch pressure, despite its great distance from Batavia on the northern fringe. The same fate overtook slightly later English efforts at Bantam and Bandjarmasin (west Java and south Borneo, respectively—see the front endpaper map), although both of these were perilously close to the center of Dutch power at Batavia and were hence more easily countered.

The first man who tried to put all these strategies together in a concerted scheme on behalf of the English East India Company, aimed at the penetration of the China market via a Southeast Asian base, was Alexander Dalrymple. Earlier Company servants and private traders had pursued the same goal for over a century and a half and, as indicated, had founded abortive bases in a variety of places, but Dalrymple was the first at least to publish a wide-ranging blueprint for the expansion of British trade and influence along such lines and to attempt to execute a grandiose strategic plan as opposed to the planting of a single factory. He was originally posted to Madras as a writer (clerk) in the Company, arriving there in 1753, ultimately becoming a member of the governing council at Madras. His *A Plan For Extending the Commerce of this Kingdom and of the East India Company* was published in London in 1769, after his project had been begun on the ground and was already in serious trouble, but still urging with enthusiasm and conviction the great rewards to be expected of it. It is not easy even with the advantage of hindsight to fault Dalrymple's general argument, and his eloquent enthusiasm is contagious. He was in effect an earlier version of Raffles and displayed many of the same compelling qualities. His *Plan* was a persuasive statement of the multiple advantages to be won from an English-managed trade base on the northern fringe of the Indies, as summarized previously, and with the chief goal held up as successful penetration of the China market through an end run around the Canton Co-hong. He was well aware of the strength of the Dutch position and was also thoroughly familiar with the several earlier English attempts to break that monopoly and to found bases along the margins of Dutch control. He played the role of a gadfly in Madras and from his seat on the council urged the Company not to abandon such a promising strategy merely because earlier attempts had failed, but to support a better thought-out and more concerted plan such as his.

The English had been expelled from Java with the capture of their base at Bantam by the Dutch in 1682, and the factory which they had founded to take its place at Bencoolen on the southwest coast of Sumatra (see the front endpaper map) was poorly placed for anything but the local Sumatran trade, mainly in pepper. Bencoolen not only was far on the wrong side of the Sumatran barrier, and hence a long detour from the route to China, but also was exposed, like all Sumatran west coast harbors, to a chronic and dangerous offshore swell. Furthermore, the prevailing winds made the rocky coast dangerous as a lee shore for much of the year, and the mountains which rise directly behind the steaming equatorial littoral hampered access and constituted a largely barren commercial hinterland. Dalrymple urged instead the planting of a base on the northern edge of the Dutch sphere in the approaches to China. Borneo was at this period largely unclaimed and unused by the Dutch and acted in effect as an immense buffer zone. Just off its northeast coast, at the southwestern end of the Sulu Archipelago and hence beyond even Dutch pretensions territorially, lay the island of Balambangan, which became Dalrymple's candidate for the key to China. The Sultan of Sulu was eager for Western protection against Spanish pressures and claims from Manila and hence was willing to cede the island to the English Company in 1761. Dalrymple and his party took possession of it in 1763, although a supposedly permanent settlement was not made until ten years later in 1773.

A base in the Sulu archipelago might profit from another advantage, as Dalrymple argued. His extensive surveys of the area in the course of which he studied passages, routes, winds, and soundings, and his research into Company ship logs along various routes to China convinced him that passage through the Sunda Straits instead of via Malacca, thence between Borneo and Celebes, and (depending on the season and winds) either through the Sulu Archipelago or from it around to the east of the Philippines and into the open Pacific would make it possible for sailing ships to reach Canton, or other China coast ports, easily at every season instead of being limited to the six months, more or less, of the southwest monsoon on which ships using the Malacca route had to depend. Similarly, departures from Canton could be made by this route at any season, an equally great advantage especially in the race to get each new season's teas on the London market as early as possible so as to command the best prices. Dalrymple's extensive surveys and soundings and the charts which he produced from them were of great value to the Royal Navy, and also commanded respect from the Company. The harbor at Balambangan was deep and well protected. The only disadvantages of the scheme were the shortage of local or even regional trading goods and the distant, insecure, and exposed position of the island. In the end, these were to prove crucial, but the strategic design was appealing.

The settlement was never a success. The trade results remained unprom-ising, and the English at Balambangan were never able to develop ade-quate control over the production, marketing, and price of local goods or of spices. It was very far from Madras, the nearest English territorial base of any consequence, and the Company was fearful of making the addi-tional investment which would have been necessary to ensure adequate control. Part of Dalrymple's plan was to use this new base, as Raffles was later to urge for Singapore, to extend English trade into Southeast Asia in competition with the Dutch, from a secure settlement which could also serve as a naval base between Madras or Bengal and Canton where a fleet could be maintained, refitting and stores provided, and antipiracy cam-paigns mounted. This was indeed the same rationale as later prevailed for

Singapore, but Singapore was far better placed both for trade goods and for its function as a base. The Company remained nervous about its naval position in eastern India, especially while the French remained a threat, without a decent harbor anywhere on the Indian east coast and none at all which could be used safely during the monsoon. Bombay was too far, and in any case ships based there could not beat up into the Bay of Bengal for military or commercial purposes during the northeast monsoon. It was under such circumstances that the French had captured Madras in 1746, and that the French fleet under Admiral de Suffren had swept the Bay in 1782. A secure base to the east was wanted as much to protect the British position in eastern India as to support an assault on China, and Balambangan was hardly well placed to serve the former need, which cautious planners were likely to put first in any case.

Dalrymple had opponents in Madras who tried with some success to undermine his scheme, and there was apparently a conspiracy of sorts to discredit him. He appears to have been a determined, even obstinate man who easily made enemies. The successful implementation of his scheme would have required a large capital investment and the detachment of other resources, including military and naval forces, in an admittedly risky venture at a time when it could reasonably be argued that there were safer, more necessary, and more profitable alternative uses for scarce Company resources. In a way, Dalrymple's *Plan* was thus not given a fair trial; it also ran into bad luck with personnel, poor trading seasons, and large-scale peculation on the part of Company servants posted to Balambangan. The Company governors in Madras were fearful of antagonizing the Spanish, from an exposed and distant forward base eminently vulnerable from Manila, and seemingly approved Dalrymple's plan only if it could be carried out with minimal expense and risk. Since these were clearly impossible or at least unreasonable conditions, the scheme ended in failure. The settlement and factory at Balambangan were finally abandoned in 1775 after a series of misadventures and a successful attack by resentful Suluans.[10]

Dalrymple's vision, however, remained very much alive in the minds of many and was of course ultimately realized in the founding of Singapore. By that time overall British strength in Asia had greatly increased; the French threat in India waned and then disappeared, while Dutch power suffered an eclipse as a result of Holland's conquest by Napoleon and the consequent temporary loss of the Dutch possessions in the East to

British occupation under the guidance of Raffles. Although the Dutch East Indies were later returned (to Raffles's disappointment), Ceylon was retained and the British position in Malaya strengthened. The newly reestablished Dutch position in the East Indies was too strong to challenge, and with rising British power the old goal of China was now given primacy. By the 1780s, ironically soon after Dalrymple's failure, the Company was beginning to be willing to pursue more vigorously a forward policy east of Bengal and specifically to establish a secure base or bases, with the investment necessary to make them secure, along the route to China. These bases could serve not only as avenues into Southeast Asian trade but as places to which Chinese traders might be attracted as buyers of British-owned goods from Britain, India, and Southeast Asia and could at the same time provide support for the British effort to penetrate China itself. China remained the great El Dorado, continued to resist Western efforts at penetration, and therefore tempted especially the English, with their sense of rising commercial and military power, to mount more and more direct and strongly supported assaults.

Malaya was closer to the Company's Indian bases and yet near enough to China to serve this purpose while at the same time lying outside the sphere of effective Dutch or Spanish power. With the single exception of Malacca, Malaya itself had been almost entirely neglected by Western traders because it produced no significant amounts of spices or other trade goods. The Portuguese and later Dutch fort at Malacca was designed primarily to guard the straits entrance to the Indies and the South China Sea. This passage also served and still serves as the major route to China itself, but Malacca never generated more than a very small volume of trade. The English had been trading off and on since 1605 at Acheh, on the northernmost tip of Sumatra (see the front endpaper map), and for a brief period (1669–76) had maintained a supposed trading factory on the Malay side of the straits in Kedah, the latter with such poor results that it was quickly abandoned.[11]

But by the 1770s the pull of the China market and the English appetite for it, as well as their power and ambition, had become far more important than earlier interests in the Southeast Asian trade per se. Dalrymple had, despite his ill-fated adventure at Balambangan, helped to establish the case for a forward British base along the route to China, and Malaya now seemed the obvious candidate. Francis Light, agent at Acheh of an association of country or private traders, was also sensitive to the larger designs and needs of the British position and the Company's requirements. He called on the Sultan of Kedah in 1771 and received from him a proposal to admit a British settlement at Penang, on a small island enclosing a deep and protected harbor between it and the mainland of Kedah. The Sultan suggested that the British should share in the trade of Kedah (tin, wax, and pepper, all readily salable in China) and build a base there in return for protecting the Sultan against Siamese pressure and against chronic and devastating raiding by well-organized Bugis marauders from Selangor to the south. Light accepted and began to trade, but also passed word to the Company at Madras which sent out a mission to negotiate with the Sultan of Kedah on the Company's behalf. Mismanagement, high-handedness, and lack of appreciation both of Malay customs and of the potential advantages of a base at Penang led to the failure and withdrawal of the mission in 1772,[12] but the logic of an eastern base which could support an assault on China persisted, especially one which could at the same time help to guard the British position in the Bay of Bengal at all seasons and could also collect Southeast Asian trade goods for sale at Canton in exchange for tea.

British purchases of Chinese tea continued to increase and to outpace the supply of silver dollars, interrupted while Britain was at war with Spain from 1779 to 1785. Imports of Chinese tea into the United Kingdom rose from just under 700,000 piculs in the years 1776–80 to over 1,145,000 piculs between 1786 and 1790.[13] It was the expanding country trade from India, in private hands, which continued to provide the funds for these purchases. But the Company became understandably more and more anxious to acquire a more direct or controlling role in so vital an enterprise, through the establishment of a base of its own in Southeast Asia where its own ships could pick up cargoes for sale in Canton and where it could also have a secure position along this vital route. Warren Hastings had returned to India as governor-general in 1774. He was keenly aware of both the needs and the enormous attractions of the China trade, and supported a number of schemes designed to strengthen the British approach. He was well acquainted not only with Dalrymple's *Plan* but with the arguments and the experience of the Balambangan adventure. Dalrymple's chief accomplishment was that his general strategy continued to exercise imaginations and stimulate solutions, until the final successful founding of Penang and Singapore.

Perhaps the most melodramatic of Hastings's several schemes in this connection was his dispatching of a mission to Tibet in 1774 under George

Bogle. It was designed not only to increase the flow of Tibetan gold in exchange for the British woolens which had proved superfluous in both India and China, thus providing the Company with specie for tea purchases at Canton, but also to attempt to use Tibet as a backdoor to China. British woolens might thus be introduced into the markets of northern China, and there was also some hope that the Dalai Lama might be used as a client advocate for British trade interests directly with the Court at Peking. Not surprisingly, the scheme came to nothing, and Tibet was in effect closed off in any case by the Ghurka invasion of 1778.[14]

In 1778 Hastings then attempted to found a Company factory at Tourane in Annam (southern Vietnam), where large fleets of Chinese junks had traded regularly for centuries. This too failed, largely as a result of the civil war then going on and the absence of any stable authority to deal with. Still in pursuit of Dalrymple's original vision, three more ventures in the Indonesian archipelago followed: an expedition to Celebes in 1782, one to Acheh in 1784, and one to the island of Rhio (south of Singapore) in the same year. All failed to win a foothold. The Company was finally persuaded to try again at Penang, while the local Sultan of Kedah still welcomed a British presence. Penang lay conveniently on the margins of Dutch power and also within the shadowy fringes of both Siamese and Burmese claims or pressures.

Prompted by further urgings from Francis Light, an expedition was sent out, this time directly from the Company's headquarters at Fort William (Calcutta) in 1786, under Light's command, to found a settlement, a trading factory, and a fortified base on Penang island, in treaty with the Sultan of Kedah. There for the first time a British base east of India survived and succeeded. Within a few weeks of its founding, on a previously almost uninhabited island, Chinese traders had joined the British and Indian personnel there and Malays from the mainland increasingly settled at Penang, all attracted by the relative security created by the British presence and by the prospect of unhampered trade. Tamil merchants from south India followed. Penang became an early microcosm of the pluralistic society of Malaya, drawing to it in particular a growing share of the Chinese traders and entrepreneurs who had been part of the Malaya scene for centuries but who now began to find, under a British-managed order, expanding commercial opportunity. This was of course an important part of the original design, to attract Chinese merchants and to use them in effect as an avenue to the immense market from which they came.

The other principal part of the plan, to generate Southeast Asian trade goods for sale at Canton (and incidentally also to sell Indian opium, cotton, textiles, and some British goods to Southeast Asia) also succeeded, and on those grounds as well Penang was seen as a success. Company ships and private country traders on their way to and from China called there in rising numbers, and although Penang never became a significant naval base, it was extremely useful as a way station and also served as a growing nucleus for Straits trade by local or regional merchants in their own ships, both Chinese and Malay. By 1811, the total population was estimated at about twenty-five thousand, of whom ten thousand were Malays, seven thousand Chinese, six thousand Indians, and two thousand others, mainly English.[15]

One of the reasons for its success was that Penang, like Singapore and Hong Kong after it, was run as a free port unlike the Dutch bases; it (and later Singapore) thus cut increasingly into the previous Dutch monopoly. But however successful it became regionally, Penang did not achieve its principal goal, the widening of the door to China—nor did Singapore. That problem remained to be fought out in China itself. There was no mass flocking of China-based merchants to use the British bases in Malaya as an alternative to Canton, nor could the Straits Chinese be used as agents or avenues to crack the China market. Some help was derived for the Company's payment balance problems for a few years through a combination of sales of Indian and British goods in Southeast Asia and trading of Southeast Asian tin, pepper, and birds' nests (all available at Penang and Singapore) at Canton in exchange for tea and silk, but this was neither the chief original purpose of the settlements nor did it ever make a really significant impact. As the volume of the trade at Canton continued to rise, the relative importance of contributions made by the British bases in Malaya declined, and the Company indeed began to worry about the expense of maintaining and administering them, which they did not see as being offset in direct financial terms by their help toward improving the British position at Canton. The earlier shortage of silver, however, had disappeared by about the end of the century and was increasingly replaced by a reverse flow, out of China to the Company (via the private traders) to pay for booming imports of opium brought directly from India in the country trade with no help needed from Penang. Chinese merchants continued to supply the China coast, as they always had, with the bulk of its demand for Straits and Southeast Asian goods, including Malayan tin and pepper, carried directly to China in their own ships. With the additional efforts from Penang to increase this trade and to send private British cargoes as well, the market for Straits produce at Canton began to be oversupplied and prices dropped disastrously.[16]

Singapore was ultimately founded with some of Dalrymple's original strategy in mind. But by that time one of its important purposes was as a counter to possible Dutch threats and as a base from which to move in on the trade of Southeast Asia (in which of course it succeeded) rather than only to serve as a forward staging area for an assault on China. Such a possibility did apparently remain in Raffles's and the Company's overall planning, and Raffles in particular saw from the beginning the immense strategic advantages of Singapore's location. It did indeed command the route to China; but it also could command the trade of Southeast Asia and, once securely fortified and fitted out as a base at a time when British military and naval power, fresh from the Napoleonic wars, was in the ascendancy, could push a deep salient into the Dutch sphere, end the Dutch threat, and reap a large share of the trade profits on which the Dutch had previously grown rich. Raffles could not have foreseen the much later booms in tin and rubber which virtually created the modern economy of Malaya and became in consequence even more important factors in the growth of Singapore. But even by 1819 the dreams of forging the means in Southeast Asia for the penetration of China were dimming, and the British effort in Malaya was already beginning to aim increasingly at other, more local or regional goals.

Nevertheless Singapore, like Penang, was founded with the primary intention of expediting and safeguarding the route to China, through the Straits of Malacca, and of serving as a sustaining base for Company, private, and later naval vessels along that route, some two-thirds of the way from Calcutta to Canton. The Dutch return to Java after the Napoleonic Wars (in keeping with Castlereagh's conviction that a strong Dutch state must be preserved as a counter to the French at home and abroad) meant that the Sunda Strait was no longer an attractive route, and it was in any case a longer one. The Straits of Malacca must be securely in British control, and this required a base at its southern end, the tip of the Malay Peninsula, as well as Penang at its northern end. Raffles sailed from Calcutta, via Penang, late in 1818, with the objective of founding a fort and settlement on an island or on the tip of the Johore mainland near the southern end of the Malacca Straits. At the end of January of 1819, after surveying other possibilities, the expedition landed at Singapore, then practically uninhabited but still encompassing the jungle-covered ruins of the defensive wall around the ancient Indianized city of Sinhapura ("the lion city"), which Raffles as a keen amateur historian knew well. A treaty was signed with the Sultan of Johore giving the British title to the island. Within the first year Malays and Chinese from Malacca and elsewhere began to flock to the new settlement for the security it offered as well as for its rapidly growing commercial opportunity. Like Penang, it was maintained perpetually as a free port, and very soon began to attract a fast rising share of the trade of peninsular and insular Southeast Asia, lying close to the geographic center of the region and projecting into the Java Sea.

Singapore's possible role in the China trade was also seen from the beginning. As the London *Times* reported on July 31, 1820, "Our occupation of Sincapoor . . . is on the part of England a purely defensive position to cover her direct trade with China." Canton was only a few days away even by Chinese junk, and this also suggested the possibility that if the tenuous British position at Canton should crumble or become even more seriously disadvantageous, Singapore could become the main opium base for China and could receive tea, silver, and silk in exchange.[17] It did not, of course, ever play that role, but it did to some extent prefigure the role of Hong Kong as a free island entrepôt close to a major Asian coastal trade flow. It was also an economic phenomenon whose brilliantly successful growth rested extensively on the entrepreneurial efforts and hard work of the Chinese who from its early years dominated its population. Singapore flourished in these terms far more as a Chinese than as a British colony, as of course it still does.

But it was the lure of China itself which led the British to found Singapore as well as Penang, and it was China which remained the chief prize of Asia in the Western mind. The harbor and base at Singapore were used and were useful for the British forces engaged in the First Anglo-Chinese War of 1840–42. Without such a base and staging area the campaign would certainly have been longer and more costly to the British, and knowledge of the advantage which Singapore could give them in fighting a war in China probably helped to stiffen their resolve and to move them from negotiation to military action. But the China world proved far too resistant and too self-contained to permit access to it through a *nan-yang* entrepôt. Chinese might go there in great numbers, as they did to the Straits Settlements, but the mountain itself would not come to Mahomet. A paramount British position was established along the track to China through Southeast Asia, but while other benefits flowed from this establishment, the chief prize and chief objective remained elusive. The battle for it would have to be joined in China itself.

Chapter 7

The Western Effort in China: Confrontation and Competition

By the time of the first Anglo-Chinese war of 1840–42, the industrial revolution had been well launched in Europe, and Westerners were enormously more effective contenders on the Asian scene than they had been in da Gama's time or in Clive's or Wellesley's or Raffles's—or so it would seem they must have been. British forces had little trouble in destroying Chinese military resistance. There was the further difference from the Indian scene in that China was genuinely a national unit; defeat of the imperial army and navy and the occupation of Nanking, where the treaty was signed, meant the defeat of all political entities or forces. But it was not just military effectiveness, critical though that was, which enhanced the West's momentum. It was, and was easily seen by both Westerners and Asians as being, a notably successful society which had produced industrialization. The material strength and welfare which flowed from industrialization and the new technology made the whole system attractive, including the newly vigorous, confident, and mass-based nationalism which was part of the nineteenth-century West and which appeared to be causally interrelated with material success. The attractiveness of this package spilled over to include, especially in the minds of Indians, aspects of other Western institutions—dress, language, political and philosophical ideas, economic or commercial techniques, science and technology, and intellectual values and vogues—which also were seen as associated parts of an overall model which had proved itself more effective than any other.

Sections of text of chapters 7 through 12 have appeared in different forms in Rhoads Murphey, *The Treaty Ports and China's Modernization: What Went Wrong?*, Michigan Papers in Chinese Studies, no. 7 (Ann Arbor: Center for Chinese Studies, University of Michigan, 1970), and in "The Treaty Ports and China's Modernization" in G. W. Skinner and Mark Elvin, eds., *The Chinese City Between Two Worlds* (Stanford University Press, 1974), pp. 17–71.

The weight of this system was now aimed also at China, for the first time (after three centuries of effort) under conditions as of 1842 which would seem to guarantee its prevailing, at least to the extent that it had already done in India. The long dream of a vast Chinese market and the many earlier efforts to grasp it could now be realized. There was surely still the same pot of gold at the end of the rainbow stretching from its solid western end in Bombay or Karachi, arching over Penang and Singapore, to the China coast. British and Parsee fingers had already begun to touch it at Canton well before 1842; expectations were buoyed of what might be possible once Chinese political restrictions and stonewalling had been swept aside by rising Western power. The China trade had become the major money-earner on the East India Company's books, as pointed out in chapter 6, and private traders were also making profits—pressing both for the expansion of trade in general and for the elimination of the Company's monopoly which was finally accomplished in 1833. By 1796 China's imports had already become larger by value than her exports, and specie hence had to be remitted to finance the supplies, especially of Indian raw cotton, which was by then the chief import.[1] The link with India was generically close. Opium, grown and sold in India as a Company monopoly (see chapter 6) and marketed in China like Indian cotton and Southeast Asian tin and pepper by private traders who banked their proceeds with the Company in exchange for bills on London, passed cotton as China's chief import by value in 1823.[2] Foreign pressures for the expansion of so profitable and potentially large a trade and tensions between private traders and the Company and between both and the Co-hong led directly to the war of 1840–42. In this pattern the Indian base and its role in the China trade were clearly of major importance.

British possession of Hong Kong, by the terms of the Treaty of Nanking, soon came to represent what Hastings, Dalrymple, and others had wanted for so long, a secure and well-located entrepôt and base under British control from which a frontal assault could be mounted on the China market. The special privileges granted to foreigners for residence and trade at the five ports opened by the Treaty of Nanking (Canton, Amoy, Foochow, Ningpo, and Shanghai) were further points of attack and entry. The assault rested also on the already well-developed British staging areas in India and Malaya, the pattern of colonial penetration and manipulation which had been so successfully worked out there, and the confident sense of mission and achievement which this experience had generated. The

Western effort, buttressed now by steam and steel, saw itself, after three centuries of slowly and then more rapidly rising effectiveness, as approaching its high tide. Having prevailed in India it confronted a defeated China with confidence.

Operative links with the Indian base continued to sustain the expanding front of the Western drive on the China coast. About three-quarters of the trading firms in China as of the early 1850s were British (most of them related directly or indirectly to firms in India), Parsee, and Indian. Clipper and other sailing ship networks, and later steamship and telegraph or cable lines, linked firms and commercial, military, and diplomatic operations among British Asian bases, with China as the forward wave. It was not surprising that the China treaty ports soon came to look in many respects like the Anglo-Indian models from which they were derived: anchorage, docks, go-downs, bunds, the club, the racecourse, consulates, churches and burying grounds, Sikh policemen, and the offices and residences of the foreign merchants with square, columned buildings of Anglo-Indian style fringed with wide verandas or arcades, a genre soon christened on the China coast as "Compradoric." Commercial, diplomatic, and military personnel moved or were shifted from port to port and between India, Malaya, and China, with the Indian pool providing for several early years the bulk of the British China contingent, including Sir John Davis, interpreter, trade superintendent, and then governor of Hong Kong, and George Balfour, first British consul at Shanghai. Davis came from an old Anglo-Indian family, his father having been a Company director in Calcutta, and Balfour had been a captain in the Madras Artillery.

They and their commercial brethren of similar antecedents brought with them to China a faith in the superiority of the British way and its Empire, a determination to make these matters clear to the Chinese, and a conviction that they both should and would prevail through a combination of firmness, rectitude, and the innate virtues and hence self-promoting attractiveness of the system which they represented and advocated. Like most Englishmen of the time, they fully endorsed Richard Cobden's sentiments (quoted in chapter 2) about commerce as "a grand panacea" and as a powerful and self-generating instrument of civilization, which they had no difficulty in equating with Westernization. The "opening" of China, primarily through the agency of an expanded trade, would thus be beneficial to both parties, benevolent and uplifting as well as profitable. Why did this Western effort, despite its apparent strength, confidence, and favorable circumstances, fail to achieve its goals in China, and fail to transform let alone "civilize," the country, even to the same extent that it had succeeded in India? Answers to this question will be pursued along several different lines in the remaining chapters of this book.

China was both enabled and stimulated to resist the Western model because it had long been sustained by its own productivity and its indigenous system of management.[3] Western techniques were not seen as offering an essential or desirable alternative, especially not when the price was an erosion either of Chinese cultural identity or of Chinese sovereignty. Western technology, methods, and ideas were resisted because they were not seen (with a few exceptions) as advantageous, not merely because they were foreign. Nor was this simply cultural narcissism. China could cope, as India could not, and well enough even in hard material terms that Western-style modernization was examined critically, selected from sparingly (e.g., steamships, arsenals), but as a general or prescriptive package dispensed with. In China "progress" did not carry the gloss that many Indians attached to it.

In India, it may be said that the English fell into the role of rulers in the absence of a viable indigenous alternative. In addition to China's more highly developed economy, system of management, cultural pride, and sense of self-sufficency, the Chinese proved adept at both diplomatic negotiation and at resisting the implementation of concessions once granted because of their conviction that foreign incursion was something to be resisted. In the face of such obstacles, the several Western states involved were as often rivals as allies. Encroachment by one was feared by all the others, especially in the imperialist atmosphere of the later nineteenth century, and there was rarely concerted action. But the home governments were never willing, even separately, to press the issue with China, either militarily or diplomatically, as vigorously as their representatives or nationals in the treaty ports continually urged. China was too big a problem to attempt to take on, especially against the combined resistance of the Chinese and of rival Western states, and given the Chinese skill at diplomacy. But why could not the attractive power of the Western model, established in the treaty ports,[4] transform China by example, as it had transformed India? What kept it from penetrating more of the country, its economic system, its values and institutions, the allegiance of its intellectuals?

Let us begin with the compradores, the first and the most effective of the treaty port Chinese. The word is Portuguese, from *compra*, "to buy," applied to the Chinese agents of foreign traders who had been essential from the beginning of Western contact. But even after the destruction of the Canton system and the theoretical freedom of foreigners to move around the country, they remained dependent on local knowledge. Chinese currency, weights, and measures represented a tangle of confusion which the foreigners could not sort out on their own while they confined their activities so largely to treaty port land and persisted in regarding the Chinese language as something beyond their powers. The language barrier was never significantly dented, and hence the services of the compradore remained essential. The China market was huge and regionally varied, a profusion of goods, consumer patterns, buyers or sellers and their credit ratings, prices, measures, standards of quality, and regulations or exactions. Local officials and guilds had their own systems of control, taxation, squeeze, production, and management to which all commercial dealings had to adjust. Trade was competently managed by sophisticated merchant guilds within a network where long-standing personal and kin connections were paramount and where direct and indirect official ties were also often important; there was no place for outsiders. To most foreign merchants this was an unknown world in which they could not attempt to function, except for a very few (mainly Russian merchants in the tea trade) who learned Chinese, acquired some knowledge of the market and its varied characteristics, and were able to dispense with Chinese agents to their own profit. These few and some hundreds of millions of Chinese (plus the missionaries) seemed to manage to learn the language, but most treaty port merchants declared, virtually as a point of pride, that it was impossible and somehow not even fitting for a "civilized" person to learn Chinese.

Their compradores did all that for them, charging both retainers and commissions and in most cases becoming wealthy. They often loaned funds to their employers, served as guarantors, and most also engaged in trade on their own account. After about 1870, many of them began to invest in shipping lines, mining, textile manufacturing, and other nontraditional enterprises. With their close and usually admiring association with Western merchants and their acquired familiarity with Western commercial techniques, they were cast by many as the logical spearheads of modernization, the operative links between the West and China, who moved easily between both worlds. In time however they became more at home in treaty port land than in their own country, and their brief taste of political power as one of the wings of the Kuomintang (KMT) was a symbol of the degree to which the KMT government did not represent the real China. While the foreign position lasted, however, and up to the end of the treaty port system, they remained indispensable to most foreign firms, even the Japanese. The British Chamber of Commerce at Tientsin published in 1930 a report on "The Present State of British Trade in North China" which stressed the continued importance of the compradore, a figure

> on whose recommendation business is accepted and declined. . . . The Japanese merchants in Tientsin also use compradores and their terms of contract do not materially differ from those used by British companies. . . . Efforts on the part of foreign merchants to deal direct would result in loss of trade in the treaty ports, where the risk is already sufficiently great.[5]

Like the British, the Japanese firms imported only on order from Chinese buyers, obtained and screened by their compradores. Foreign firms remained in effect commission agents, as they had been since their first trading contacts with China.[6]

The persistence of the compradores was, however, also a symbol of the continued self-sufficient viability of the traditional Chinese economic system. New Western commercial institutions planted in the treaty ports— modern banking and finance, insurance, joint stock companies—and the new technology of steam and steel seemed full of promise for China as a whole, but in fact they made little impact. Most Chinese did not see a need for them while they were able to continue satisfactorily on traditional indigenous terms. The treaty ports grew very rapidly, but not primarily because of any close integration with the rest of the Chinese economy. Their commercial innovations and their rapid growth as overseas trade centers were new phenomena, but in those terms remained an artificial graft which never grew into an organic union with the late-traditional economy of China. It was the new and different kind of economic opportunity they had created which was mainly responsible for their growth. This is perhaps most clearly shown in the case of Shanghai, a relatively small center of regional trade in 1842, which became by far the largest city in China—and yet not of China, as the attitudes and behavior of both its Chinese and its foreign inhabitants demonstrated. The Shanghai model did not spread—except to other treaty ports. The trade which it handled linked it primarily with other treaty ports and with Europe and America rather than with China. And in the most innovative or revolutionary aspect of the Western model, its foreignness was unmistakable. Over one-half of the factory-based power-driven manufacturing in China was in Shanghai; most of the remainder was distributed among the other treaty ports or in Manchuria.

The Japanese invasion of 1937 marked the end of the treaty port era. By this time, with the single exception of Peking, all of the largest cities—Shanghai, Tientsin, Canton-Hong Kong,[7] Wuhan, Nanking, Chungking, Mukden, and Dairen, in that order—were coastal or riverine treaty ports dominated by their commercial functions as opposed to the administrative character of the largest traditional cities. Their populations were, of course, overwhelmingly Chinese, but a new kind of Chinese, most of whom promised to be the indigenous agents for the remaking of China along Western lines as in India, following the path of the compradores and discarding the less appropriate selective self-strengthening models of Chang Chih-tung or Li Hung-chang and the crippling disabilities of the *kuan-tu shang-pan* system.[8] The treaty ports also provided a political sanctuary and a challenge which bred a series of increasingly revolutionary thinkers as well as the founding of the Chinese Communist Party. But while the treaty port system lasted, they remained a relatively powerless minority, outnumbered and outgunned by treaty port Chinese who were more compliant followers of the Western model and who accepted many of its values and institutions. The impact of the treaty port radicals was to be long delayed.

Anil Seal has convincingly argued that any successful colonial system requires indigenous collaborators, that external pressures for change can be effective only if they can find internal support in the persons of those who come forward to stand between the outsiders and the domestic masses and who can transmit change.[9] In colonial India, the context from which Seal primarily writes, and in Southeast Asia and Japan in very different ways such a pattern is clear. In effect, Calcutta, Colombo, Batavia, and Tokyo conquered Banaras, Kandy, Djogjakarta, and Kyoto, through the agency of at least partly Westernized Asians operating in and from the environment of the port cities. The problem for the external forces may be to find enough collaborators and of the right sorts—the wrong ones may be discredited, or alternatively may subvert the colonial power. Briefly put, it was the latter which finally happened in South and Southeast Asia. In China since 1949, it has been the former.

It was tempting to assume, as many wishful foreigners did, that the treaty ports, although never in any sense dominating the country at large, had attracted and then transformed into a new kind of Western-style entrepreneur and innovator enough Chinese collaborators to then transform China. Many of these recruits, it may be argued, were drawn from traditional merchant groups who contrasted their position under the traditional order where "the rapacity of the civil officers discourages the accumulation of wealth" (in the words of the British consul at Tientsin in his Report for 1862) with the new freedom offered in the treaty ports—security of property and accumulation, the protection of nonparticularistic law, a stable civil order, the ready availability of capital at low rates of interest, expanding opportunities for constructive as opposed to parasitic uses for capital—and, in traditional parlance, hastened to be transformed. The first Chinese efforts at industrialization were in every case in the treaty port urban areas—the arsenals, iron works, and other enterprises of the self-strengtheners at Shanghai and Wuhan, and the first privately owned Chinese factories, financed mainly by ex-compradores.[10]

The treaty ports were also, as already mentioned, havens for political and ideological dissidents and in time havens for open revolutionaries and their political parties. The Tung Meng Hui and the Kuomintang could not have come into effective existence without having been able to depend on the treaty ports as secure retreats, nor could the many earlier revolutionary thinkers have survived and published, as for example Wang T'ao, most of whose active life was necessarily lived in Hong Kong and Shanghai.[11] The same is true of the succession of dissidents who followed him, including K'ang Yu-wei,[12] Liang Ch'i-ch'ao, Yen Fu, Ts'ai Yuan-p'ei, and their influential journals published in Shanghai and under foreign legal protection. Three-quarters of all the publishing in the entire country took place in Shanghai, including a number of reformist Chinese-language journals such as *Shen Pao, Shih Pao, Shih-wu Pao, Min-li Pao, Su Pao, Ta-lu Yüeh-k'an,* and others flourishing around the turn of the century and after, followed by increasingly radical journals with titles like *New Dawn, New China,* and *New Youth* in the aftermath of the May Fourth Movement. Such activities in the sanctuary of the treaty ports, and openly inspired by their example (both negatively and positively) as all Chinese nationalists acknowledged and Sun Yat-sen made clear from his havens in Hong Kong and Canton, helped to throw China into a turmoil of radical change such as it had never before seen in its long history.

Change was also in the air in the treaty ports and in the hinterland through Chinese students returning from abroad, especially from Japan (where most of them went) which after 1870 was busily reorganizing itself on Western lines. They brought new ideas and perspectives as well as pressures for radical reorganization in China. Overseas Chinese in Southeast Asia, America, and Europe contributed ideas, support, and money to revolutionary causes in China. Some of the country's own elite were exploring radical new departures. Western books were being translated into Chinese and widely read. Radical newspapers and journals published in the treaty ports circulated widely outside them and were probably read by many more than the subscribers. The growing body of students in newly founded Western-style universities, especially in Peking, as well as in the treaty ports, formed an increasingly vocal and active radical group pressing for change. Most of all these forms of activity centered and were generated or reinforced in the treaty ports themselves. The ports offered an example of strength, integration, success, and wealth, as well as oppression and exploitation, all flowing from Western technology and Western institutions. Wang T'ao and those who followed him saw China's problem as basically institutional rather than technological; it was this which made them revolutionaries.[13] Their earlier prototypes in India, also on the rimland in the colonial ports, in time spread their activities, agents, allies, and converts inland, and set the stage for the emergence of contemporary India. Karl Marx saw what was happening:

> From the Indian natives, reluctantly and sparingly educated at Calcutta under English superintendence, a fresh class is springing up, endowed with the requirements for government and imbued with European science. . . . The time is not far distant . . . when that once fabulous country will thus be actually annexed to the Western world.[14]

Jawarhalal Nehru, writing nearly a century later on the same theme, felt that India's

> peculiar quality is absorption, synthesis [and that] the old culture managed to live through many a fierce storm and tempest, but

though it kept its outer form, it lost its real content. Today it is fighting silently and desperately against a new and all-powerful opponent, . . . the capitalist West. It will succomb to this newcomer.[15]

Why did the treaty port Chinese, both collaborators and radical reactors, who seemed to be following the Indian path, not achieve a similar conquest? The retention of Chinese sovereignty was an important reason, as examined in the next chapter. Apart from simple and stultifying resistance to change, the chief negative result of the persistence of Chinese sovereignty was the progressive collapse of civil order, which no Chinese government after 1850 and until 1949 was able to reverse significantly. Chronic disorder helped to blunt the treaty port impact even while it also weakened the indigenous economy. The experience with railways in India and in China provides a convenient means of comparison, partly because some comparable data are available and partly because, together with steamshipping, railways were both the chief material monument of the Western impact (as well as the prime means of increasing commercialization and industrialization) and the most obvious measure of that impact. Admittedly China's unparalleled network of navigable waterways, especially from the Yangtze southward, opened much of the most productive part of the country to steam shipping, an advantage which India largely lacked as described in chapter 4. Traditional-style Chinese shipping also used this water network on a very large scale and made railways far less necessary. For this reason what railway building occurred in China was concentrated in the north, where the first major coal and iron deposits were found and worked on a large and mechanized basis, dependent on railways for their modern-style exploitation. But in its transforming or enabling consequences substitution of steam for traditional shipping (only very partial substitution at that, as detailed later in this chapter) in central, south, and coastal China did not compare with the construction of a national rail network.

The beginnings of a rail skeleton were built in China, largely at foreign urging, with foreign capital, and for the most part against the resistance of the traditional official-gentry incubus. But for most of the brief existence of what can be called a rail system, from about 1902 to 1936, many of the lines were blocked, cut, or critically hampered by civil war, troop movements, and commandeering of rolling stock.[16] The contrast with India is clear, where a huge rail network operating in a context of internal stability and administrative efficiency acted as a powerful agent of economic and

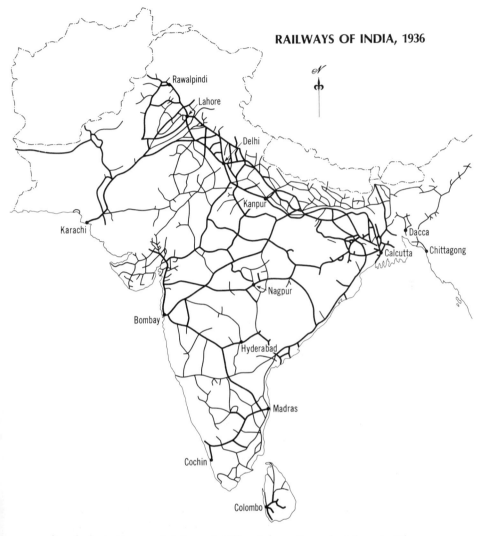

RAILWAYS OF INDIA, 1936

cultural change, generated in and diffused from the colonial ports. They were the hubs of the railway system, and development elsewhere in the country followed their pattern.

Most direct India-China comparisons of a quantitative sort are difficult, given the much greater completeness, variety, detail, and accuracy of the Indian economic data, at least from about 1870. There are, however, sufficiently comparable railway figures for both countries from about 1912, including the peak period of the Western presence and effort.[17]

These figures are shown in the following compilation:

	Undivided India (excluding Burma)	China (excluding Taiwan, Tibet, and Manchukuo)
Million square miles of territory	1.57	3.5
Population, 1931 (millions)	339	ca. 470 (?)
Miles of railway track, 1936	44,832	6,032
Billion ton/miles of goods carried, 1912	15.3	0.14
Billion ton/miles of goods carried, 1925	19.2	0.25
Billion ton/miles of goods carried, 1936 (last prewar year in China)	20.8	0.40
Billion passenger/miles, 1912	14.7	0.1
Billion passenger/miles, 1925	19.5	0.23
Billion passenger/miles, 1936	17.7	0.27

Several recent studies bear out the truth of Vera Anstey's statement that the Indian railways created "not only a national but a world price for most articles of general consumption, whereas previously prices fluctuated enormously [as they continued to do in China] from district to district."[18] John Hurd's work shows that railways produced an India-wide market for food grains, prices for which continually converged toward a single all-India price as the market expanded.[19] M. B. McAlpin has demonstrated the influence of railways on increasing cultivation of both food grains and nonfood crops for commercial sale, and has assessed the dimensions and implications of this change.[20]

But even before the building of railways, the spread of commercial cropping under British management or in response to more general commercialization of the economy had begun to transform large sectors of rural Hindustan, especially in the Ganges valley. Before the end of the eighteenth century, cotton and indigo had become major commercial crops in Oudh and were moving through a series of rapidly growing urban markets tied directly into the Calcutta network. Overseas markets available through Calcutta were absorbing most of this increased production.[21] Further evidence of the effects of the widening of the market achieved through the principal agency of Calcutta and Bombay can be seen in the vigorous growth of both new and old urban centers in north India, commercially tied in one direction to the major ports and in the other to their rural hinterlands which were being drawn into a newly commercial world and hence creating a need for urban services. Rapid town growth on such a basis is apparent from about 1790, and is traceable to the expansion of the new port-based commercial economy into the interior, especially as it stimulated the spread of cash cropping.[22]

Some more general economic comparisons may be possible on the basis of two detailed national income studies, that by Liu and Yeh for China and by Moni Mukherjee for India.[23] Both studies use some of the same categories, and it was therefore possible to construct the following composite tabulation using their data.[24]

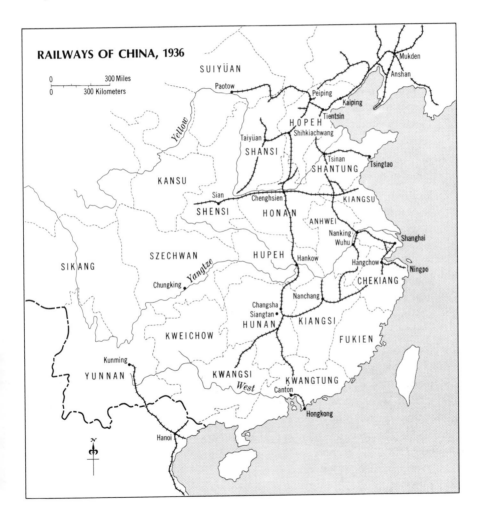

RAILWAYS OF CHINA, 1936

CONTRIBUTIONS TO NET DOMESTIC PRODUCT,
NET VALUE ADDED, PERCENTAGE OF TOTAL

	India 1946	China 1933
Agriculture	45.2	65
Manufacturing and mining	17.3*	10†
Commerce and transport	19.5	14.6‡

*Of which small enterprises were 10.8 percent.
†Of which handicrafts were 7.1 percent.
‡Of which peddlers were 3.1 percent, old-fashioned transport,
4.4 percent, modern transport and communications, 1.4
percent.

These may be taken as at least sample measures of the extent to which
the Indian economy was altered by the Western impact, and to which the
traditional Chinese economy remained much less affected. This was not
however merely the result of internal disorder after 1911. Nineteenth- and
twentieth-century China, despite its political problems, was not an economic wilderness, as has sometimes been too easily assumed from the
supposed "backwardness" of traditional commercial methods and production technology or the heavy hand of the bureaucratic state. The absolute
levels of Ming and Ch'ing production and trade were immense, compared
to India and probably to any other contemporary national system. They
cannot be measured precisely, but what evidence we have from gazetteers
suggests even in per capita terms a level of interprovincial trade equal to or
greater than northwest European levels as late as the first decade or
quarter of the nineteenth century.[25] The absolute total was far greater. A
large sector of the economy was monetized and a number of commodities
were produced for and distributed over a multiprovince, national, or
external market: raw cotton and woven cloth from several centers in
Chihli and Kiangsu, silk from Hangchow and Soochow, rice from
Hukuang, sugar from Szechuan and Kwangtung, porcelain from Ching-te
Chen, tea from Fukien, and a long list of lesser goods such as iron tools,
paper, dried or preserved foods, and the several commodities marketed as
official monopolies, most of which were also traded and smuggled privately. A large proportion of total trade was probably local only; perhaps
in some respects this was merely, in Sol Tax's phrase, "penny capitalism,"
but the total number of pennies was vast. And there clearly was a
transprovincial and national market for a number of goods, of which
cotton cloth, rice, and salt were probably the most important.[26]

The Japanese consul at Amoy in 1898, Ueno Sen'icho, reported that in the whole of the Foochow district there had been traditionally no local production of cotton cloth, and that until very recently all cloth consumed had been imported from Kiangsu and Chekiang; his report indicated a similar situation in most of Kiangsi and eastern Kwangtung. Only within the preceding few years had local cloth production begun, almost entirely as a female occupation carried on in households and making use of imported Indian yarn.[27] Much of the cloth supply for these southern areas probably came from Kiangsu. Hatano Yoshihiro in his study of the cotton cloth industry cites data from Ch'ang-shu in Kiangsu in 1901 to the effect that cloth made there had long been sold in large quantities to Fukien, Kwangtung, Kwangsi, and Kiangsi, and as far as Szechuan as well as northward to Shantung, Chihli, and Shansi. These data include estimates of total cloth sales from Ch'ang-shu alone of three million rolls a year, of which only one million were marketed in Kiangsu, the balance being shipped to other provinces.[28] These are indications of a high degree of commercialization and a well-developed exchange economy before the onset of any significant foreign influences on production or transport.

Tribute grain shipments, involving a complex and demanding transport linkage, provide further indication of regional specialization and exchange. Grain actually transported to the capital averaged over three million *tan* yearly during the Ch'ing, carried in between seven thousand and eight thousand ships from the eight provinces concerned.[29] To this should be added about an equal amount to cover "wastage" in a variety of forms along the route, plus similar varieties of "squeeze" and peculation at the sources.[30] However, the tribute grain shipments became by the nineteenth century a predominantly commercial operation, managed by merchants.[31] The grain ships were officially exempted from customs and transit duties and were authorized to carry a fixed quota of trade goods tax-free, but commonly they exceeded this quota and nevertheless paid no tax partly because customs officials en route feared being accused of delaying the tribute rice.[32] The grain shipment itself was increasingly commercialized by commuting payments into "easy delivery silver," a practice begun as early as Sung but increasingly common in Ch'ing.[33] By 1834, according to the *Veritable Records* for that year, half of the tribute grain was being collected as silver, and in the most densely populated areas of Kiangnan tribute rice money amounted to 20,000 or 30,000 taels yearly.[34]

This was a reflection of a highly monetized economy. Commission fees for commutation, tax farming, sale of tribute grain en route and privately in the capital, and various forms of squeeze associated with each enterprise all helped to nourish a cloud of merchants. It was far from being an official undertaking any longer. Trade goods other than rice appear to have become by far the dominant cargo of the grain ships, especially if illegal and smuggled as well as legal goods were included. By 1799 one scholar asserted that each ship carried one to two thousand *tan* of private merchants' goods which successfully escaped inspection and taxation.[35] Grain ships carried a similar supply of commercial goods on the return trip southward, including some of the tribute rice being shipped back on private account.[36] Merchants usually traveled with the boats, buying and selling a wide variety of goods in great volume along the way and acting as virtually the sole managers of the entire affair. The other personnel on the boats, and even the officials, were in effect the employees of the merchants.[37] One rough measure both of the magnitude of the shipments and of the nature of the late traditional economy is provided in the grain-equivalents used for commutation: one ounce of silver for four piculs of rice, government scrip (*ch'ao*) worth five hundred cash for one picul, one piece of cotton cloth for one picul, one *chin* of cleaned raw cotton for 0.2 picul, one ounce of gold for twenty piculs, or one piece of silk for 1.2 piculs.[38] Large numbers of private as well as official merchants were involved in this trade, legal and illegal.[39]

Nor did traditional style junk traffic apparently suffer substantially, if at all, from the later introduction of steamships. "The traditional structure was stimulated rather than depressed by competition from more modern forms."[40] The treaty port impact in this, as in so many respects, was not what the foreigners intended. Into the 1930s and 1940s, junks and their traditional commercial networks continued to hold their own and even expanded their activities, helped presumably by overall increases in commercialization but also by their traditional reliance on personal credit and old-style brokers who knew the market rather than on capitalized or modern-style entrepreneurs. They were far less disrupted by civil disorder than were the railways, as well as charging very much lower rates, the lowest rates of any carriers. The dense network of waterways, especially in the Yangtze watershed (which still contains half of China's population and more than half of its urbanization and commercial activity) made junks better able to serve all parts of the market, through capillaries as well as arteries; this and their relatively smaller capacities also meant that their service was flexible, they could more quickly be dispatched as needed, loaded and unloaded, and hence often could deliver goods more promptly. Watson's collection referred to previously includes a number of articles detailing the persistence of junk transport and citing figures to show that both their gross tonnage and their haulage were increasing rather than decreasing into the 1940s and that in both respects they remained more important than steamships by an overwhelming margin.[41]

One of the important cargoes, in addition to grain, was salt, although it was widely acknowledged that the quantity of smuggled salt was at most periods at least as great as the total legally traded, despite the severe penalties for smuggling.[42] Wide variations in salt prices, both temporal and spatial (primarily as a result of fluctuating tax or levy demands, irregular enforcement of regulations, and transport problems, as well as normal economic cycles) encouraged speculation on a massive scale and increased smuggling incentives.[43] As with the grain tribute, there was extensive leakage, but apparently to an even greater extent. In early nineteenth-century Lianghuai, for example, the salt tax collection turned over to the government was a little over two million taels, while the actual tax collected was about eight million, and the Lianghuai transport merchant's outlay for that area's share of the salt trade was between twenty and thirty million taels.[44] Merchants and officials invested both in the legal and illegal salt trade as well as in the rice trade, in pawnshops, etc., using capital derived from speculation and/or smuggling of salt. The wealth of many of them and the size of the trade which they manipulated are indicated by the dimensions of the special levies exacted from them at periodic intervals, to meet unusual military expenses or other financial crises: the Lianghuai salt merchants alone "contributed" four million taels toward the costs of financing the expedition against the Gurkhas in 1792, and two million for the Miao campaign in 1795.[45] But our attention should not perhaps be focused too much on the abuses of the system. A study by Professor Thomas Metzger deals with a highly successful and rational reform in the system of salt deliveries, quotas, transport, and taxes carried out by T'ao Chu in 1832–34 and designed to reduce smuggling by eliminating the incentives. It worked very well, at least for a few decades. Metzger concludes: "little could have been accomplished without expert and dedicated officials. . . . The effectiveness of T'ao and his subordinates does not easily tally with the theory that the Ch'ing bureaucracy, except for anomalies, was a mass of corruption, paralyzed by suspicion, and operating on sheer inertia."[46]

Especially as the nineteenth century wore on and population increased faster than production, while at the same time political disorder mounted, the economy was no longer keeping pace with the rise in numbers; merchants or those with capital also increasingly sought speculative or predatory activities as the best means of survival. But whatever relative decline there may have been seems likely to have been fairly slow, at least until perhaps the 1930s. In any case it did not destroy the ability of the traditional commercial sector to continue to control the bulk of the market and largely to exclude foreign entrepreneurs and their technology. Nineteenth-century China was perhaps caught in a "high-level equilibrium trap," as Mark Elvin, Albert Feuerwerker, and others have suggested,[47] in the sense that while the economy was highly productive and reasonably commercialized, it had lost the power to increase production or exchange even proportionately with population increases. It lacked in particular the ability to evolve the massive new technological infusion which was the only escape from what had become a closed and shrinking circle. Political decay and final collapse made such a solution doubly beyond reach, and at the same time imposed new burdens on the economy and on the civil order. In the end, and after the foreigners had been expelled, a revolutionary new political order provided the means for technological transformation. But however much consumption levels may have fallen up to the 1930s (and there is no hard evidence that they did so significantly), China remained productive and competent enough to serve its own market adequately and to support a merchant group and a commercial system which was able largely to exclude foreign merchants, their goods, and their methods.

Ch'ing official and actual policy toward merchants and commerce, often characterized as ruinously oppressive, is probably better seen as reflecting the close mutuality of merchant and bureaucratic interests. The state depended in part on the commercial sector and hence attempted to ensure that it would thrive; in general, trade was not heavily taxed, but to a considerable extent, the bureaucracy lived off the merchants. Merchants, for their part, benefited far more from contact with officials (including a role in the management of government monopolies) than they suffered from taxation or extortion. Commercial success depended on official connections, but the embrace was more nourishing than stifling.[48]

More directly relevant to the treaty port model, the level of indigenous urbanization in China was also relatively high. Perhaps as much as one-tenth of an immense population (more in some areas such as Kiangnan) lived in cities before the planting of the treaty ports, and perhaps more than half of this mass of city dwellers were supported by or in some way engaged in trade, transport, manufacturing, or their management. Given the size of the total population, this meant that something over one-third of the world's urban population was in China. Urbanization had been gradually rising and maturing for centuries, even millennia; change of this sort was not rapid or suddenly innovative, as in Japan, but more slowly cumulative.[49] Urbanization and attendant commercialization were by the nineteenth century in no sense new or even recent experiences. Even Adam Smith was impressed enough, at second or third hand, to write:

> The great extent of the empire of China, the vast multitude of its inhabitants, the variety of climate, and consequently of productions in its different provinces, and the easy communication by means of water carriage between the greater part of them, render the home market of that country of so great extent as to be alone sufficient to support very great manufactures, and to admit of very considerable subdivisions of labour. The home market of China is perhaps in extent not much inferior to the market of all the different countries of Europe put together.[50]

Smith also remarks elsewhere on China's strong commercial advantage in possessing such a vast network of natural and artificial internal waterways, and on the enormous traffic they carried, matters commented on subsequently by nearly all foreign observers at first hand.[51]

The most important difference between China and India in this connection is that in China the traditional indigenous economic system remained very much more effective, right through the nineteenth and into the twentieth century. There was little vacuum which the foreigners could fill. The great economic drive of European export to China, in textiles, met with strong competition from traditional textile production, and, especially after about 1917, Chinese machine manufacturing. Although imported yarn (and later yarn from treaty port factories) captured a growing

share of the market, it did not become predominant; cloth imports at their
peak reached only about one-quarter of total consumption. The strong
position of Chinese handicraft textiles was apparent quite early, but most
foreigners continued to dream despite the accurate assessments of a few.
One of the earliest of these was the report prepared in 1852 for the
Foreign Office by W. H. Mitchell, assistant magistrate at Hong Kong,
addressed to Sir George Bonham (governor of Hong Kong, 1848–63) and
published with minor changes and updatings as "Report on British Trade
with China" in the Blue Book of 1857–59. It reads in part as follows:

> Since the British plenipotentiary who signed the Treaty of Nan-
> king in 1842 informed his countryman that he had opened up to
> their trade a country so vast 'that all the mills of Lancashire could
> not make stocking stuff enough for one of its provinces' the en-
> deavour to supply China with manufactured cotton has been the
> most interesting and generally the most perplexing of the enterprises
> which merchants in this country have been engaged in. The
> Lancashire and other manufacturers soon found that however cor-
> rect the plenipotentiary's statement might have been as far as it
> related to the consuming capacity of China, it was wrong either in
> ignoring the producing power which the country possessed, or the
> difficulties in the way of introducing cotton goods into the interior.
> Amongst the disappointed merchants in China were several who
> took the latter view, and who thought—even at a time when, as now,
> the labouring classes of Chinese at Hong Kong, where no duty at all
> is charged on cotton goods, preferred wearing the more durable
> fabrics of their own country—that English manufactured cottons
> were prevented from circulating freely in the interior by the heavy
> inland duties levied on them, an opinion which led to the emphatic
> assertion of the transit dues regulation in the treaties of 1858. There
> were some however, who saw that it was the producing power in the
> people which made them independent of foreign supply, and the
> larger experience of the last few years has made the view of this
> faction clear enough.[52]

A few years later, the commissioner of Customs at Tientsin in his
Report on Trade for 1866 pointed out that

> Cotton is grown extensively in China, and the people weave it
> into a coarse, strong cloth which is much better suited to the wants
> of the peasants and working men than the more showy but less
> substantial product of Foreign machinery. The customers of the

British manufacturer in China are not the bulk of the people but only those who can afford to buy a better looking but less useful article.[53]

The commissioner listed the relative weights and prices of Tientsin- and British-made cloth, indicating that the British article was significantly more expensive per unit of weight and adding that

the Chinese say that the superiority in strength of the Native article over the Foreign is greater than the difference in weight between them. . . . No transit passes are applied for by Foreigners to protect imported cotton piece goods from undue charges on their way into the interior, and it is to be inferred from this fact that if the inland charges in this part of China exceed the Treaty transit dues [i.e., half of the import duty] the excess is so small that the native merchant does not think it worth his while to try to get his goods passed into the interior under foreign protection.[54]

Note that it was the "native merchant" who remained responsible for the marketing even of imported foreign goods.

As in the case of India, there has long been a too-easy assumption that imports of machine-made cloth ruined a large share of traditional production. Even for India, this is in serious question,[55] but for China virtually all the evidence (except, as in India, for yarn) points the other way, including the chronically disappointing trade figures and the tiny scale of cloth (as opposed to yarn) imports even at their peak by comparison with the size of the market. As late as the 1930s in Hopei, Fang Hsien-ting estimates that small-scale handloom weavers still accounted for four-fifths of the total cloth production.[56] By that time, machine-spun yarn was in use even by hand weavers (originally imported from India and Japan, later obtained in greater quantity from Chinese factory production), and foot-treadle and Jacquard looms were common.[57] Nearly all of the cloth was sold commercially, much of it in interprovincial trade, and profitable use was made of mechanized transport, especially the railway lines and motor roads with which eastern Hopei was relatively well supplied.[58]

Hatano's study of the cotton industry cites a Japanese report of 1898 on the areas around Shanghai (of all places!) which suggests among other things that hand-spun yarn continued to be important:

The general characteristics of the producing area are like those of Nara, Ibaraki, or Saitama before the importation of foreign yarn. The people are very primitive, and stress only frugality, diligence, and honesty. . . . The investigators were surprised to find no hired labour from outside either in rich or poor households, all of which were individually operated. They use hand-twisted yarn made by themselves from home-grown cotton for both the warp and the weft. Although some progress has been made in recent years with the importation of foreign yarn, they still stubbornly adhere to their old ways. . . . We have heard that the reason is that they dislike receiving a small price as the result of having to buy the raw materials and not using their home-grown cotton.[59]

In the vicinity of Sha-shih in Hupei, the raw materials were either hand-spun yarn alone or a combination of machine-spun warp and hand-spun weft. The cloth was sold in Szechuan, Yunnan, Kweichow, Kwangsi, Hunan, and elsewhere, either by local shops directly or through merchant-travelers (*hao-k'o*) sent out from these areas to lay in stock. The system was clearly economically rational and commercially successful. As late as 1913, according to Hatano, hand-spun yarn continued to be used on a large scale. He refers to the gap between recorded yarn imports in that year (358 million pounds by weight), Chinese-made machine-spun yarn (estimated at between 220 and 250 million pounds), and total yarn consumption in China, where power looms used only about 15 million pounds of yarn. Hand-spun yarn used in combination with this machine-spun yarn clearly must have amounted still to a vast quantity.[60]

The persistence of indigenous production so late, and its ability to adjust to changing conditions by taking advantage of technological innovations, tell us something about the reasons for the foreign failure either to penetrate the market with their own goods or to see the complete form of their technology triumph even in Chinese hands. Ch'en Shih-chi has provided a broad survey of this and similar areas in Shantung and Hunan where hand weaving preserved a strong position into the 1930s.[61] Hand-woven Chinese cloth remained more durable and cheaper by weight than foreign machine-made cloth, and continued to enjoy an enormously greater sale. The traditional cottage-based silk industry saw similar changes after about 1880, when mechanical silk-reeling equipment was introduced, although here weaving as well as reeling (the equivalent of cotton spinning) was quickly taken over almost entirely by concentrated factory units,

leaving the traditional producer only the function of supplying cocoons. [62]
The silk industry, especially in Kiangnan, also illustrates responsiveness to
technological change, as well as vigor in its earlier ability to recover with
almost miraculous speed from the devastations of the Taiping Rebellion,
whose full destructive force fell on the Kiangnan silk districts. The traditional system clearly retained considerable regenerative powers, and in the
typical case of silk production remained almost entirely in Chinese hands.
Given the newly widened export markets provided through the treaty
ports, silk production expanded rapidly in a rational economic response.
Silk exports more than doubled between 1868 and 1900, and rose again
by 50 percent between 1900 and 1930. Mechanical innovation proved
relatively easy to introduce in textile production from eighteenth-century
Britain on, but the Chinese experience does not suggest a deteriorating or
stagnated economic system. [63]

Imported cotton cloth (and later cloth manufactured in the treaty
ports) was sold mainly in the cities, predominantly the treaty ports
themselves, to the wealthier and more Westernized minority who used it
because it was fashionable; it made very limited inroads in rural or inland
areas, where over 90 percent of the people continued to live. Imported
cloth never accounted for more than one-quarter of total Chinese cloth
consumption, and in the mid-1930s 60 to 70 percent of total cloth
production was still handwoven. [64] As for domestic factory-produced
cloth, Chinese-owned factories accounted for over half of that total in the
mid-1930s, and China became a net exporter of both cloth and yarn in the
1920s. [65]

What was true of cloth was, in differing ways, true of almost every
other would-be import. Part of the foreign problem was Chinese resistance
to new commodities, well summarized by S. G. Checkland:

> Selling in China of course means discovering within the Chinese
> consumption pattern hitherto unexplored desires capable of re-
> sponding to the manufactured novelties and factory processed
> fabrics of the West. This meant altering the traditional culture of the
> Empire—the very thing that had rendered the Chinese so hostile to
> the newcomers. Little was to be hoped for from the attempt to
> interest the Chinese in a variety of new and untried things. [66]

Checkland's study is based on the private papers of the Rathbone family
and on records of the firm of Rathbone, Worthington and Co. at the

University of Liverpool. These records graphically illustrate the difficulties all foreign firms experienced in their effort to penetrate the China market. Given the volatile prices, the fluctuating exchange rates, the problems of selling almost anything on commission-consignment, and the need for multiple Chinese agents, business "expenses in China were heavy beyond all Indian experience." The firm ultimately made most of its profits in speculation on the great variety of money exchanges, currency, and credit. As early as 1851, one of the partners accurately foresaw this: "Profits will be made as much in the management of the funds and the exchanges as in any other way."[67]

But a great deal of the Chinese reluctance to buy foreign goods or to adopt foreign business methods or technology was entirely rational and not culture bound: traditional Chinese goods and methods were equal or superior, and prices as low or lower. The only significant exceptions were cotton yarn (though its success was far from complete, as shown previously), kerosene, and cigarettes, the last two being items not present at all in the traditional economy and, at least in the case of kerosene, demonstrably superior to domestic alternatives without being substantially more expensive. However, cigarettes, like machine-made yarn, matches, and a number of other lesser goods of originally foreign manufacture, came increasingly after about 1915 from Chinese producers using Chinese raw materials.

As the Chinese producer successfully moved into the production of goods which had been earlier foreign monopolies (and as the consumer accepted clearly preferable new alternatives like kerosene), so the Chinese entrepreneur took advantage of changing conditions to invade new fields of trade and investment. He had never been replaced as the commercial manager of the domestic market for either imports or exports, despite foreign efforts. After about 1860, and especially after 1920, he took advantage as an investor of the new opportunities for profit offered by foreign innovation in steamships, mining, banking, and factory production in the treaty ports. One estimate gives a total of 400 million taels of Chinese capital invested in *foreign* enterprise in the late 1890s, by which time Chinese owned about 40 percent of the stock of Western firms in shipping, cotton spinning, and banking, and held shares in roughly 60 percent of all foreign firms in China.[68]

Steamship enterprises attracted the earliest major Chinese investment outside of trade itself. Chinese merchants subscribed about one-third of the original capital of the first three foreign steamship companies founded at Shanghai between 1862 and 1868, and nearly 80 percent of the initial capital of the China Merchants Steam Navigation Co., the first such enterprise owned and operated by Chinese, in 1873–74.[69] Large amounts of Chinese capital were also later invested in new mining and manufacturing enterprises, especially cotton textiles and tobacco.[70] By 1894 Chinese investors, and some managers, were represented in about three-fifths of the foreign firms in China.[71] Profits obtainable from landholding (especially as land prices rose in response primarily to continued population increase) and from the traditional government monopolies such as salt were becoming at best static or declining, and Chinese investors were fully able to perceive and to act on changed circumstances.[72] Foreign undertakings were more attractive to Chinese investors than the officially sponsored *kuan-tu shang-pan* efforts, which were chronically plagued by capital shortages.[73] But it was not just in foreign enterprises that Chinese investors played a prominent role. They came, especially after World War I, to dominate even factory-based manufacturing with their own enterprises in almost every field, leaving foreign firms by the 1930s with less than one-third of China's total modern manufacturing output.[74] In steam shipping, perhaps the most important Western-introduced innovation, Chinese owned well over half of the total capacity by 1931.[75]

Chinese success in competing in machine manufacturing, steam shipping, and as investors in other Western or Western-style enterprises should not however be taken to mean that foreign technology or methods were making major inroads into the traditional system. Feuerwerker's careful summary of the available data, based primarily on the Liu-Yeh study, shows handicraft production in 1933 accounting for 67.8 percent of total industrial output and factories for only 20.9 percent.[76] A large proportion—perhaps one-third—of this 20.9 percent was in Manchuria, which had become a separate political entity and a separate and very different, far more industrialized, economic system under Japanese management (see chapter 11 for a discussion of Manchuria's separateness). Modern machine manufacturing which had developed in China Proper by the 1930s was almost wholly confined to the major treaty ports and a few nearby satellite towns; well over half of it was in Shanghai alone. And the entire modern nonagricultural sector of the Chinese economy, very broadly defined as encompassing factories, mines, utilities, construction, "modern" trade and transport, trading stores, restaurants, and "modern" financial institutions, is credited by Feuerwerker (following Liu and Yeh) with only 12.6 percent of net domestic product, while he gives the share of agriculture and the traditional-style nonagricultural sector (handicrafts, "old-fashioned" transport, peddlers, traditional financial institutions, personal services, rents, and government administration) as 87.4 percent. As for steam shipping, although it did grow, it did not do so at the expense of traditional shipping, which through the 1930s probably accounted for over 80 percent of haulage by water.[77]

It may require effort to see nineteenth-century China as anything but disintegrating. Our perceptions have been warped by our tendency to attribute to that period the conditions prevailing in the 1920s, 1930s, and 1940s, the decades which are now best known and on which most of the existing detailed studies are based. The Chinese economy and its per capita consumption levels may have been suffering a slow decline throughout most of the nineteenth century, but it approached the levels observable and recorded in the 1920s or 1930s only gradually. The economy, and individual sectors and entrepreneurs, also showed considerable resilience, in recovering from the devastation attendant on rebellions, floods, and famines and in adjusting to changed conditions, as for example the ability of handloom weavers to enhance their competitive position by changing to machine-spun yarn and foot-treadle looms. Chinese merchants were very quick to make use of steamships when they entered the scene, recognizing especially the value of the insurance which could be obtained on the cargoes thus carried. Resistance to innovation was in many respects rationally selective, not blind; it rested on calculated self-interest rather than on unthinking reaction or xenophobia.

This was a situation quantitatively and qualitatively of a wholly different order from that in India. Although there was a substantial pre-British commercial sector in India, it was both much smaller and less highly developed than in China. It impressed the early Europeans, and is looked back on by some contemporary Indian historians with nostalgic pride.[78] But the economy of Ming and Ch'ing China was on a very much larger and more sophisticated scale, and the Indian economy after the seventeenth century was overtaken by an avalanche of chaos from which it never recovered except under British management. Habib also acknowledges that much, perhaps most, of India's seventeenth-century economy was dependent on "the Mughal ruling class, and after its collapse . . . merchant capital had no choice but to atrophy."[79] The contemporary estimates which Habib cites to suggest the order of magnitude of the commercial sector, including city populations, before the collapse do not bear comparison with similar estimates for China. Indian cities and merchants may well have struck contemporary observers as larger and richer than any in Europe, but this is more impressive to an Indianist, or a historian of Europe, than to a student of China.

In China there was no place, and no need, for outsiders. Foreign energy and missionary zeal in the treaty ports, their vision of "progress," were met mainly with indifference or with antagonism. Ch'ing and successor governments followed the long-established techniques of compromise with these latest barbarians on the empire's frontiers. They could not be ejected, and so they must be pacified, contained, given small concessions, but the body of China must be kept inviolate. The government might even employ some of them, or use their help in suppressing rebellions, but they remained barbarians. Although China might have to accommodate itself to certain barbarian ways and even make use of some barbarian techniques, this was only to keep itself free from their depredations. But apart from official policy, China was proof against even the technically competent, economically "developed," and superconfident West. It was not, as the foreigners perennially complained, the resistance of officials, the foot dragging of the gentry, the "backwardness" or xenophobia of the Chinese consumer, the inadequacy of railways, the continuation of the *likin* (internal transit tax), the transit pass system, or the lack of support from their home governments which aborted their dreams of trade profits. They were attempting to invade an economy and a set of producers and entrepreneurs who were able to beat them at their own game, especially on home grounds, enough so at least to remain in charge. The mass of Chinese consumers were low-income and frugal people, unable and perhaps even unwilling to expand their purchasing, at least not to accommodate foreign goods. The market had little elasticity, and it was already adequately served.

The foreign effort probably strengthened China economically more than it weakened it. Much of the capital generated in the treaty ports was drained off as profits or for reinvestment in the metropolitan countries, but there was significant new net investment in China—significant, that is, within treaty port land and within the relatively small and isolated "modern" sector. Foreign efforts to widen external markets were accompanied by increased production of foreign trade goods, and the level of domestic commercialization also rose in partial response to new and expanded transport facilities introduced by foreigners. The availability of new commodities which did represent a net advantage over traditional alternatives: machine-spun yarn, kerosene, and matches, benefited indigenous production and welfare and enhanced the competitiveness of domestic producers. New employment was created in the treaty ports, especially after the beginnings of large-scale manufacturing following 1895, and in this new environment a trained labor force and a small group of technicians and managers of industrialization began to grow.[80]

Admittedly all these tendencies toward greater commercialization, specialization, and interdependency made the economic system more vulnerable to disruption, and more dependent on foreign capital and markets. There was certainly a foreign stranglehold on key sectors of the "modern" economy, and it was used ruthlessly to block or destroy Chinese efforts to compete. Modern mining and railways (the latter through loans rather than directly) were predominantly foreign owned, as were most of the largest insurance and financial institutions and large-scale manufacturing enterprises. They used their special legal status under extraterritoriality, lesser burden of Chinese taxation, diplomatic pressure, and the sharp practice which attaches like a corollary to power to maintain their position at Chinese expense. Indemnities extracted from the Chinese government further increased the drag effect which the foreign presence created on the Chinese economy. In a larger and more important sense its chief effect was a weakening of the state, which contributed to the state's inability to provide the kind of leadership which played such a crucial role in Japan's economic success after 1870. But as late as 1931, over three-quarters of all foreign capital invested in China was in Shanghai or Manchuria.[81] The role played by foreign investment was marginal.

A symptom as well as a cause of this marginality was the pronounced weakness of the forward and backward linkages of foreign-owned industries. Ninety percent of foreign-owned industrial output in the 1930s was concentrated in enterprises directly serving foreign trade: processing egg products (dried, powdered, and frozen eggs for export), providing import substitutes (cigarettes and cotton yarn), and maintaining public utilities (electric power, gas, water, communications) in the treaty ports.[82] Components for these enterprises were either produced directly *in situ*, imported (e.g., machinery), or acquired directly from the agricultural producer as raw material. Output also went directly to the consumer, the exports abroad, and the goods or services consumed domestically primarily to residents of treaty ports and immediately surrounding areas. Other export goods which received little or no industrial processing, e.g., tung oil, silk, hides, handicraft products such as straw braid, also moved directly from rural producers to treaty port godowns and out to overseas markets. Imports were mainly consumer goods, which like domestic output went mainly to the market in the treaty ports themselves. The treaty ports remained largely separate from most of the rest of the Chinese economy. New economic activity in them did proportionately little to stimulate new economic activity elsewhere in the country, and its net impact was thus very much less than the total of investment or output might otherwise suggest.

It is impossible to discover in any quantitative terms either what was happening during these years to average or mass economic welfare, or the net effect of the foreign presence on it. I am not impressed by any of the several attempts to measure statistically the levels and changes in overall production, per capita income, or consumption in China as a whole up to or even beyond 1949. Such attempts, in my opinion, may mislead as much as they help in the effort to understand what was happening to the Chinese economy. There are in fact almost no statistical knowns of any precision (outside the relatively tiny spheres of foreign trade and "modern" industry) about population, production, or rates of growth and change therein at a national or even regional level throughout the period being discussed here. When the basic statistical data are so poor, the results of attempting to manipulate them may be worse than guess work, not only because they may well be farther from rather than closer to the still unestablished "truth" but because the use or extrapolation of flawed statistical data may give the seductively deceptive impression that something definite has been established. At best, manipulation of such data, or surrogate data, does not advance our knowledge or tell us with confidence anything not already known or knowable from other evidence. At worst (and most commonly) the deductive or analytical structures built on such unsound foundations lead away from, not toward, what reality may have been while at the same time giving the illusion that they are achieving the opposite.

Many of the existing studies which, especially in recent years, have attempted to address what was happening to the Chinese economy during the century of foreign domination deal with particular cases or small areas, any of which are likely to be unrepresentative.[83] What I myself was able to observe (and can report only impressionistically) in the western provinces and elsewhere in the China of the 1940s should not be considered a reliable guide to the economy as a whole. We simply do not know with any precision what average national living standards were or what was happening to them, quite apart from the fact that national averages even if known may become relatively meaningless in a country the size and variety of China where the regional realities of specific time and place are so easily obscured. By the twentieth century the traditional economic system had probably lost the capacity to maintain stability, let alone growth, but the specific picture was far from uniform or clear. There was certainly disintegration and suffering at many times and places, and there was also at least modest prosperity and order at others. Especially outside the clan-dominated society of the south, there was also considerable erosion of the traditional collectivity, aggravated after about 1900, into a situation of relative and progressive chaos where dog-eat-dog behavior became more common and the few predators lived on the misery of the many. North China was probably worse off economically than most of the rest of the country, beginning with the disastrous famine-and-flood decade of the 1920s. The warlords, with their campaigns also concentrated in the north, were an additional and highly visible element of this era; the result was, and looked, that much worse. But for China as a whole it is exaggerating to picture even the 1920s, 1930s, and 1940s as a period of unrelieved, universal, and limitless mass misery, just as it is exaggerating to blame whatever *was* happening to the economy on the foreign presence.

The economy and its welfare levels, the society, the polity were probably in worse shape by the 1920s and 1930s than they had been a century earlier. This has been overlooked or misinterpreted in the tendency to assume that all of the post-1850 years belong in the same indistinguishable bundle of deterioration. But as suggested, China even at its nadir was able to cope with its basic economic and organizational or management needs until quite late, despite the degeneration of the center. The political landscape was disintegrating, which is what the foreigners saw. The rest of the landscape, which they saw far less clearly and knew little about, went on functioning with little impairment. The economy retained a surprising degree of resilience, demonstrated in the ability of groups and entrepreneurs to adjust to changing conditions, to turn them to advantage, and to remain largely in control despite foreign efforts to dislodge them.

The foreigners and their aggressively ambitious activities were only marginal factors in what deterioration took place in China. The dust which they raised, their arrogance and exploitation, their confident drive and self-image, the kinds of responses all this engendered in the treaty ports where its weight was almost entirely concentrated, the agony and remorse of the Chinese intellectuals exposed to or living in the treaty port world, the emulative behavior of the compradores and the new "modern-style" Chinese entrepreneurs—all this obscured what was happening in the real China, the countryside, villages, and towns outside treaty port land; namely, very little relating significantly to the foreign presence. China continued to respond to its own far older problems and paradigms: population outrunning production, the high-level equilibrium trap, the progressive rot at the center as a dynasty grew old in office, the period of relative chaos which, as so often before, followed dynastic collapse.

It was when the Chinese began to put things together again that the legacy of the foreign impact became important. While the treaty ports lasted, their influence was slight in material terms. But the intellectual and psychological impact was profound, in a way which became fully apparent only after 1949. Things were reassembled in a new way, new because of the Chinese experience with the West, but with the West as challenge, as threat, and also as the original but decultured source of a new and potentially liberating technology. It was not Western civilization which triumphed, but a new and newly self-conscious Chinese answer, stimulated to revolutionary restructuring by the Western challenge even while it made prominent use of industrialization and Marxist-Leninist doctrine and organization. The ultimately revolutionary treaty port impact on the Chinese mind now overshadows the limited impact on the economy, and is dealt with at greater length in chapter 12. But the chief focus of this book is on the Western experience while colonialism lasted. Its legacies now seem more important and should not be ignored, but we need first to distinguish what happened while the foreign effort was in progress, and why the experience in China was so different from that in India.

Differences in indigenous economic effectiveness were critical, but so were the differences in self-image. There was a far longer and greater *Chinese* legacy of a notably and self-consciously successful society. A century in the wilderness, relatively speaking, was only a brief interval in Chinese history, one whose brevity and atypical nature become clearer as it recedes into the past. The cumulative capabilities and achievements of the longer Chinese experience were still retrievable, still viable resources to be drawn on, in 1950 or 1970, for the pursuit of national integration and modern economic growth. This is an important reason why that effort since 1949 has been so successful, even though it followed on what seemed to be a set of circumstances which had reduced China to chaos and its people to helplessness in their ability to cope with their own basic problems, let alone with modernization. We can now see more clearly that such a picture was at best misleading, that China's seeming disorganization was temporary, and that it could not have been complete. This was also true in 1850, in 1900, and even in 1930. The following chapters will examine, in somewhat greater detail, this Chinese base on which the foreigners of the nineteenth and early twentieth centuries attempted to make their mark.

Chapter 8

The Chinese Base:
Politics, Values, and Livelihood

A communication [to Queen Victoria, from Imperial Commissioner Lin Tse-hsu]: magnificently our great Emperor soothes and pacifies China and the foreign countries. . . . This is because he takes the mind of heaven and earth as his mind. . . . We are delighted with the way in which the honorable rulers of your country deeply understand the grand principles and are grateful for the Celestial grace. . . . But . . . there appear among the crowd of barbarians both good persons and bad, unevenly. . . . We find that your country is some sixty or seventy thousand *li* from China. Yet there are barbarian ships that strive to come here for trade for the purpose of making a great profit . . . taken from the rightful share of China. By what right do they then in return use the poisonous drug [opium] to injure the Chinese people? . . . Of all that China exports to foreign countries there is not a single thing which is not beneficial . . . the things that must be had by foreign countries are innumerable. . . . foreign countries cannot get along for a single day without them. If China cuts off these benefits . . . then what can the barbarians rely upon to keep themselves alive? . . . On the other hand, articles coming from the outside to China can only be used as toys. We can take them or get along without them. They are not needed by China. . . . Nevertheless our Celestial Court lets tea, silk, and other goods be shipped without limit. . . . This is for no other reason but to share the benefit with the people of the whole world.[1]

The assumptions reflected here, including the image of China as wholly self-sufficient, supremely civilized, and magnanimous to outside barbarians (who are lumped together as not worth distinctions), and of Britian as a distant island barbarian lair (of somewhat uncertain and unimportant location) resonate with the Ch'ien Lung Emperor's even more famous letter of 1793 to George III. Although the relative circumstances in 1793 were more in keeping with these images, Lin's words represent a Chinese mind set which altered very slowly and very little almost to the end of the dynasty. Foreign-induced changes, of any sort, were to be resisted not only because they were foreign, not to say contemptibly barbarian, but because the chief aim of both government and morality in the Chinese view was the avoidance of disruption and the preservation of harmony, the social order which any outside stimuli threatened. Ethnocentricity, cultural pride and sublime self-assurance, knowledge of China's achievements in the arts of government, management of society, production, national power, and more cultivated pursuits further strengthened an overall cultural impermeability which was more than proof against repeated military defeats or eagerly aggressive merchants and missionaries. The simple size of the country was a further major bulwark. Well over twice the size of India, and with its provinces the size, population, and productivity of separate European states, China was simply too vast to be moved, let alone transformed by marginal seacoast contact with a relative handful of foreigners, however vigorous or effective they were. The contrasting impact of the West on Japan may help to underscore this point when one remembers that over 90 percent of the Japanese population lived and still lives within fifty miles of the sea and within the same distance of Japan's six major cities, all of them seaports—the whole within a small, compact island country with easy internal communication by both land and coastal routes.

China was not unused to the presence or the occasionally importunate demands of foreigners (barbarians), a few of whom had indeed on a few occasions threatened or defeated Chinese sovereignty. There were consequently long-established techniques and forms for dealing with resident or visiting foreigners, designed both to guard against possible threat and, for the most part more important, to minimize their potentially disruptive effect on the sociocultural order, the Great Harmony. Foreigners were to be kept at the margins of the Empire (Canton in the case of Western sea traders, following an ancient pattern) and their behavior and activities closely watched and controlled. The Westerners were merely one more in a long series of barbarians to be fitted into this system, which on the whole had worked well enough for long enough that the Chinese saw no reason to consider an alternative method of coping with this latest set of outsiders. The best way to accede to their demands (at least enough to satisfy them) and at the same time to limit the disruption and trouble they might cause was to fit them into long-established roles for such people who sought the magnanimous favor of the Celestial Empire.

These roles were defined within the traditional tribute system. As John Fairbank has explained, the treaties which the Westerners obtained and which they saw as giving them a privileged position from which they could manipulate and transform the country were from the Chinese point of view merely a set of devices to fit these particular barbarians into the pattern of tributary relations which had successfully channeled into relative harmlessness the activities of so many barbarian groups in the past.[2] They too had been granted small areas within or beside a few cities for residence and trade, where they had been expected to maintain order among their own people according to their own laws (extraterritoriality). Consuls were the equivalent of headmen who were collectively responsible for the behavior of their countrymen. Tariffs had never been designed as protection but only as a source of revenue, nor was foreign trade large enough for tariffs at any level to be a major financial matter. The most-favored-nation clauses in the treaties were easily related to the magnanimous and benevolent Imperial wish to show impartiality, as from one far above their level, to all barbarians.

The Westerners saw the treaties as a license for the rapid expansion of their effort, the long-awaited "opening" of China. The Chinese saw them as an agreed set of limitations which were designed to restrict this new set of barbarians. These noncoverging views, productive of endless mutual misunderstanding and friction, persisted through successive treaty signings and minor wars not only to the end of the dynasty, but to a measurable degree to 1949 and beyond. Certainly the two views never coincided—and why should they have done so? The Kuomintang government, whatever its weaknesses, was still Chinese, still a conscious heir to a long tradition, still unable and unwilling to acknowledge that China was beholden to or in some sense inferior to the West or that Westernization—especially as the treaty port Westerners proposed it—was the best or only course for China to follow. Basic Chinese sovereignty was never seriously questioned. To that important degree, the Chinese view prevailed; it stuck to its premises and faced down a determined and seemingly all-powerful Western challenge. Circumstances of course played a part in such an outcome, primarily inter-Western rivalries, and the prospect of full colonial responsibility for the Chinese empire was in any case dismaying. But the staying power of the Chinese self-image despite all the blows heaped on it by the modern West is impressive testimony to its strength.

The Chinese self-image more than anything else was what blunted the Western effort, what kept it from achieving the degree of success, in its own terms, which it won in India. Shanghai never became a Calcutta, in the sense that it exerted little influence which could be seen, while foreign-dominated Shanghai lasted, toward reshaping the rest of the country. It and the other treaty ports remained for the most part isolated and tiny islands of Western dominance and Western-style change, in a much vaster and wholly Chinese sea which resisted Western efforts both to exploit and to transform it, and in the end rejected them, even though China ultimately adopted leading but decultured Western techniques.

In India the Westerners eventually constructed their own colonial environments in which the port centers and their commercial and administrative nets could set in train a process of more widespread transformation. In China, such a set of conditions conducive to Western-style change was never accomplished, and foreign trade alone, even through the many-sided agency of the treaty port, proved not to be an effective vehicle of transformation. Almost as if it were in traditional Chinese terms, the treaty port merchant, foreign or remolded Chinese, was reduced to manipulating the fringes of the economy which he found rather than attempting to transform it, as the colonial administrators in India succeeded in doing. Such a difference is neatly symbolized in the contrasting situational patterns. With the single and very late exception of Tsingtao,[3] all of the Chinese treaty ports arose beside the walls of preexisting major Chinese trade centers. Indeed, the Westerners specifically sought such locations, anxious to place their own efforts (as they put it themselves) to "tap" the China market as close as possible to where the action already was, places which had been major commercial nuclei for centuries. Having destroyed the fabric of the Co-hong and the restrictions of the Canton system, the foreigners nevertheless did not accomplish the creation of a new system, but only a graft onto a massive trunk already there, a graft whose shoots never bore the fruit the foreigners hoped for.

It did produce some centrifugal growths, but the dominant pattern of Chinese urbanization, of economic and cultural life, remained, as it has always been, centripetal. The treaty ports were not new cities but only new adjuncts to existing urban trade bases, selected by the foreigners precisely because they were already important commercially. The foreign stimulus which was the primary cause of the rapid growth of Shanghai, Tientsin, and Hankow especially was accompanied by some deflection of traditional trade flows (helped by the extension of steamship lines) and certainly by a significant increase in foreign trade (even though its absolute total remained very small). But the urban hierarchy was only partially altered and the Chinese economy as a whole only marginally affected.[4] Foreign efforts, successively frustrated in their aim to transform China, came to be almost entirely directed not toward changing the Chinese economy or "developing" it but toward garnering a share of existing trade and diverting as much of it as possible into external channels—an effort which, as discussed in a later chapter, was not notably successful. Where Manchesterian principles served in South and Southeast Asia to "open" each country and to fuel its transformation through the operations of an expanded marketplace (albeit with some help from colonial administrations), the Chinese proved resistant to these supposedly vitalizing currents, as the Chinese state was able to resist the imposition of colonial control.

The two were certainly interrelated; China could resist a colonial takeover in part because its indigenous system was able to continue functioning effectively in its own way, and it was enabled to do so because China was never politically or militarily taken over by the West. Territorial sovereignty was critically important. Even within the Chinese sphere, the Manchurian case demonstrates the crucial difference which territorial sovereignty (de facto from 1905, by conquest from 1931) made in the degree to which genuine transformation could be achieved. On a much smaller, indeed a critically smaller, scale, the same may be said of the treaty ports themselves. Although nominal Chinese sovereignty was preserved there, foreigners in effect ran the treaty ports, including the areas within them of wholly Chinese settlement (after about 1870 in most cases). In the ports, Westernization and modernization, physical, technological, institutional, and ideological, bulked large. In most of the rest of China, 99 percent of both area and population, where Chinese sovereignty reigned, most elements of the indigenous Chinese system perdured. Beyond the ports, foreigners were not in general free to own land,[5] develop mines, build railways (outside Manchuria), or involve themselves directly in the production of goods, preservation of order, or manipulation of institutions. There were few significant new cities and no substantial skewing of the rank order of existing cities, except for the major treaty ports, no proportional inland parallels to the growth of Kanpur, Bangalore, or Bandoeng, and no basic remaking of the internal economy such as urban change of this sort might have reflected. The few towns which became cities as a result of their new function as railway junctions or mining centers—Chengchow, Shihchiachuang, Tsinan, T'angshan—remained relatively small until after 1949 and did not disrupt the existing urban hierarchy.

In South and Southeast Asia the essence of the Western impact could be seen in the growth of the colonial port cities, and in the total reordering of the internal urban hierarchy. Nearly all of the colonial ports were founded by Westerners, in the context of a crumbling domestic political order and on sites previously empty, with the explicit purpose of escaping from existing trade centers and urban bases of the indigenous system. Territorial sovereignty began with the ports themselves—something never achieved in China even within the foreign concessions—and spread from there. Western management of trade, preservation of order, administration of local affairs, and military power became demonstrably more effective than indigenous alternatives, as came to be seen by the Asians themselves, and there was accordingly less resistance to the spread of Western sovereignty than in China.

There was no parallel to the enduring Chinese sense of national-cultural identity, its unquestioned assumption that the Chinese tradition was in fact superior to any barbarian model, however effective, and that it would be defended against any efforts to compromise it politically. As suggested, this sense of confidence and coherence was strengthened specifically in the contest with the Westerners by the concrete achievements of the traditional Chinese system. Deteriorating it may have been in a relative sense, but it never, even after 1911, sank to the level of chaos which characterized eighteenth-century India. China held together, its Great Tradition sadly tarnished but still intact, and its Little Tradition, in the management of production and trade, still functioning well enough to keep even ambitious and determined Western entrepreneurs from making serious inroads. In the main part of China outside the limited arena of the treaty ports, livelihood, society, and management went on much as they had always done, substantially unaffected by what from the treaty port vantage point seemed such momentous strides toward transformation. China's continued sovereignty helps to explain why, but it is equally important to understand how and why the Chinese were able to preserve it where other Asians had failed. A single-minded determination to do so by any available means (including some Western-style "self-strengthening"), an adroit diplomacy, a deeply based confidence that sovereignty was worth preserving, plus the support of an ongoing system of production and organization which owed nothing to foreigners and was capable of continuing without them at an acceptable level of success, all contributed to this outcome.

One can hear the Westerners cumulatively losing patience as successive decades of effort failed to produce access to the pot of gold, and failed to transform this "backward" civilization, despite the example of the treaty ports. The Chinese did not seem to know when they had been beaten, or that they were hopelessly outclassed, but insisted on remaining Chinese—outmoded, heathenish, cumbersome, and blind to the promise and rewards of "progress."[6] Here is Archibald Little, a classic representative of the imperialist mind at the turn of the century:

> The open ports are oases of light in a waste of darkness and stagnation. . . . All our modern ideas of progress and the possibility of improving their lot seem non-existent in the official as well as in the popular mind. . . . Doubtless there is a leaven at work in our presence in China which will in time leaven the mass, and the more points of contact in the shape of treaty ports are created the quicker will be the advance, but to the outward eye only a small radius around each port has been so far affected. . . . A treaty port established means a new centre of activity, higher wages, and a vastly increased employment for the laboring classes; to the surrounding country it means an increased outlet for their productions and a steady rise in values. To the officials and the gentry it means a concrete example of the gains to be derived from Western methods of progress as opposed to the stagnation involved in fixing their ideas in the past. . . . To the people generally our settlements yield a specimen of order and cleanliness in a wilderness of dirt and discomfort, which they do nothing to alleviate until stimulated by our contact. . . . The time must come when Western modes of thought will have taken hold.[7]

Little goes on to urge "a show of force" as the only way to get the Chinese to see the point. His views are typical of the treaty port mind, evolving from early expectations through frustration and becoming in later decades more and more bitter. It was infuriating that the official Chinese accounts of their dealings with foreigners still preserved the language and imagery of the tribute system, that the Allied expedition in 1860 was described as having ended in the foreigners being driven back to their ships and their representatives for thirty years thereafter kept pleading for the favor of a celestial glance, as Little states. "In no other spot on the globe have I felt myself such an object of contempt as in Peking."[8] – this only two years before the Boxers took over the city.

Treaty after treaty had reconfirmed and extended Western "rights" to invade the Chinese economy, to manage concession areas, to control and administer foreign trade, to move goods within the country without paying local transit taxes, to operate steamship lines on internal waterways, to finance rail lines, to open more and more treaty ports (many of them far inland), and to extract more and more privileges, guarantees, and indemnities from the weakening Ch'ing government – until finally it fell (more perhaps of it own weight than as a result of foreign pressures on it). But still the stubborn Chinese would not accept the Western gospel; still the treaty ports remained isolated bastions of a "progress" which China went on rejecting. It was indeed maddening, especially given the Western vision of potential riches and their self-image as working for the *good* of the Chinese in offering them so clearly superior a model for their own development. A very few Westerners reminded their colleagues from time to time that the Chinese were after all Chinese and chose to remain so as well as to remain in control of their own affairs. These few, however, made little impression except to attract spiteful comment and allegations of treason or of "going native." The dominant Western view was that the Chinese were dishonest, lying, disgusting, pig-headed, cruel, densely ignorant, morally rotten, their music a din of confusion, and their language totally impossible for any civilized person to learn, lacking as it was in any logic or reason – all these things must be so if the Chinese have persisted for so long in ignoring or resisting what the Westerners have tried so hard to do for them. Other foreign sentiments, bracketing Little's in time, repeat the same message. Here is G. W. Cooke of the *Times* in 1858:

> It is impossible that our merchants and missionaries can course up and down the inland waters of this great region and traffic in their cities and preach in their villages without wearing away at the crust of a Chinaman's stoical and sceptical conceit. The whole present system in China is a hollow thing, with a hard brittle surface; we try in vain to scratch it, but some day a happy blow will shiver it. It will all go together.[9]

Part of the reason for Cooke's belligerence was doubtless the recent and still current context of the second Anglo-Chinese war, but later commentators echoed his views. A nation which saw itself as militarily powerful as well as outstandingly successful (and saw a close relationship between the two) was continually frustrated in what it also saw as its reasonable and even magnanimous aims in China, and despite its repeated ability to defeat the Chinese militarily. It was understandably frustrating. On the whole, the Chinese, with their own totally different view of reality, seem to have managed the hundred-year interaction with the Western imperialists with much greater aplomb, and with much greater skill and success. There were indeed a great many "happy" blows, and in the end the political structure crumbled, but China did not "all go together." Nor did it respond to what the Westerners saw as their own shining example. Here is J. W. Wilson, a major general in the United States Army interested in railway development in China, on "progress":

> The Chinese city [at Shanghai] is all inconceivably squalid and offensive to foreign eyes and nostrils, and fills the foreign soul with a sentiment of unutterable disgust. In the foreign settlement all is bustle, enterprise, and progress. In the native city all is sloth, squalor, and arrested development. . . . Progress has planted her foot firmly on the banks of the Wusung [*sic*] and from her safe abiding place in the foreign city is sure, slowly but inevitably, to invade and overcome the whole vast empire.[10]

But the Chinese were, it turned out, not like other people.

> As a human entity, the Celestial stands alone. . . . His aims are undirected by any train of thought to which we are accustomed. The Chinaman unites in his attributes a marked ability with an utter lack of honesty, truth, or affection. . . . Conceit and vanity are a national inheritance. . . . There is no limit to the supreme ignorance inherent in the Celestial. . . . The truth is that the normal Celestial is built on a different design to the Western man, and it is for this reason a matter of extreme difficulty to appreciate either his reason or his conclusions. . . . The whole social system of China is one systematic fraud.[11]

The Chinese returned the favor in an ironic symmetry. It was a monumental case of mutual noncomprehension, willful and stubborn on both sides, but with the Chinese owning the ground they stood on.

> It is monstrous in barbarians to attempt to improve the inhabitants of the Celestial Empire when they are so miserably deficient them-

selves. Thus, introducing [*sic*] a poisonous drug for their own benefit, to the injury of others, they are deficient in benevolence. Sending their fleets and armies to rob other nations of their posses- sions, they can make no pretense to rectitude. Allowing men and women to mix in society and walk arm in arm through the streets, they show that they have not the least sense of propriety. And in rejecting the doctrines of ancient kings they are far from displaying wisdom. . . . How can they expect to renovate others? They allow the rich and noble to enter office without passing through any literary examinations and do not open the road to advancement to the poorest and meanest in the land. From all this it appears that foreigners are inferior to the Chinese and therefore must be unfit to instruct them.[12]

The charges were of course accurate, and were in balance not nearly as culture bound as the common Western charges against the Chinese. The Chinese compared Western assertions and doctrine (including Christianity) with Western actions; Westerners compared Confucian doctrine with Chi- nese behavior; both saw humbug—but it was China's country.

Western arrogance was probably clearest and most resented in mission- ary attitudes and behavior. It was also the missionaries who attempted to penetrate and directly reform the country as a whole outside the treaty ports, as the merchants for the most part did not. Missionary arrogance became tempered somewhat toward the end of the century as the empha- sis shifted from evangelism to good works and education, in recognition of the essential failure to convert any significant numbers of Chinese. But although the effort became for many less direct, arrogant overtones and assumptions remained. Christianity could still serve as a superior model even to non-Christians as benighted as the Chinese, and through the vehicle of Western medicine or Western learning China's soul might yet be saved and China itself converted to the new gospel of progress. But however softened by newer views, the missionary effort came on strong and never really lost the bite of its first assumptions. Here is an early posttreaty account from the 1840s, describing a preaching journey made in Kwang- tung by George Smith and the famous Charles Gutzlaff, visiting villages and entering buildings without invitation:

We met in some native dwelling where the tenants of adjoining huts were congregated, Mr. Gutzlaff stationing himself at the door to allow free ingress but to prevent the egress of any refractory individual. . . . We told them they were pirates and robbers, wicked men, living without God, and exhorted them to repentance.[13]

The Chinese are a patient people, and these particular missionaries were not lynched. But Chinese bitterness and anger are understandable, as in the following proclamation posted on the city wall of Ichang and noticed there by Lieutenant J. E. Stokes, commander of the Royal Navy escort *Opposum,* who had accompanied the Special Mission of the Shanghai Chamber of Commerce up the Yangtze to Szechuan in 1869:

> We the scholars and people of seven districts of Ichang, on a subject on which we have conferred and consulted together: We know how, for the food we eat and the land we move on, we, our fathers and ancestors, have been for more than two hundred years indebted to and imbued by the deep benevolence and great virtue of the present dynasty. . . . Now there is a country, by name England, in a corner of the ocean, insignificant yet offensive, and with a people obstinate in their lawlessness, sudden as pigs in their appearance, and as destructive as wolves in their ravages, with a rooted desire to injure the people for their own glorification. . . . They think to add to their territory, and proclaim themselves a great nation. . . . What they rely on is an inaccessible port [Shanghai? London? Hong Kong?] and wickedly do they deceive men. Their fire wheels [steamboats] go up and down like the wind; and no matter whether a place is prosperous or otherwise, nowhere do they not do their best to entice away men to ravage. . . . They have encroached upon Hankou, and now desire to disturb Ichang . . . and have designs on our land and property, with various other evils innumerable as the hairs on the head.
>
> How in these enlightened days are we to grant permission to such born-wicked demons as these to come? On account of this we must all be bound over to be unanimous, and with care found a secret society, and in order to make a clearance of these imps, establish certain rules, as below:
> 1. if a native slays a foreigner, the society will give him 40,000 cash
> 2. if a native burns or destroys the steamer, a present of 100,000 cash will be given him
> 3. if any Chinese merchants privately selling land to foreigners for the erection of hongs [trading firms] or shops are slain, no notice must be taken of it
> 4. if a Chinese merchant lets a house or rooms to foreign merchants . . . no notice will be taken if they are all destroyed. . . .
> All must get in accord with this, and to give peace to the country. A special notice. T'ung-chih, eighth year, third month, 15th. day [April 26, 1869].[14]

China was hardly free from arrogance—vide its longstanding attitudes toward those it labeled "barbarians," i.e., all non-Chinese. This remained the chief problem faced but never cracked by the Western effort. If the Victorian West was confident of its own superiority, China was equally confident, as for two thousand years past, that *it* had a monopoly on superiority in all that mattered under the heading of civilization. The confrontation between two arrogant cultural narcissists led inevitably to conflict, but the Chinese were on home ground. China went on seeing the Westerners as unnecessary, undesirable, and potentially dangerous Outsiders. Successive military and diplomatic humiliations did not alter this view. Westerners remained "foreign devils," and the imperturbable Chinese assumptions about the nature of reality were never wholly destroyed. Robert Fortune provides in an account of his third visit to China, from 1853 to 1856, the story of an amusing incident which foreigners resident or visiting in China at any period will recognize as familiar: "A small boy who had been looking at me with great reverence for some time, and on whom I flattered myself I had made a favorable impression, undeceived me by putting the following simple question to his father: 'If I go near him, will he bite me?' . . . When I objected to my Chinese friends to being called 'white devil,' they expressed surprise and regret, but asked if we were not white devils, and if not, what were we?"[15] *Toujours la politesse,* but a very Chinese politeness.

By the 1930s, many of the treaty port foreigners were convinced that China had gone to hell. Chinese nationalism was showing new vigor, kindly Western instruction was being rejected together with the special provisions for the instructors, Chinese merchants were making inroads on even the small economic sphere which Westerners had won, and even extraterritoriality was threatened. The editor of *The China Yearbook,* published annually in Shanghai, H. G. Woodhead, was as typical of his time as Little had been of his. Woodhead was a self-appointed but accepted spokesman for the Old China Hands, having lived and worked in treaty port land since 1902 in Peking, Tientsin, and Shanghai as a newspaper man. In 1931 he made a trip up the Yangtze, and his account of it, titled *The Yangtze and Its Problems,* might well have been titled instead "The Foreigner and His Problems with China."[16] It is a series of wailings about the foreign failure to dent the Chinese mind or the Chinese system, and about the dire consequences which will surely result, punctuated with nostalgic vignettes of how good things used to be when the foreign governments had some backbone and stood up to the Chinese. He despairs over the lack of commercial (i.e., foreign-controlled) development in Szechuan, "a naturally wealthy province which has been in direct communication with world markets for more than forty years,"[17] and at Hankow: "When Hankow went Red in 1927, labour got completely out of hand."[18] "It is our compradores today; it will be ourselves who will be intimidated by armed police when the gunboats leave."[19] There follows with no apparent sense of irony on Woodhead's part a long section admiring the foreign racecourse and club at Hankow:

> It is not unusual for the day's turnover at the Race Club's meetings to exceed $150,000 ... approximately ten million dollars per annum. ... Hankow possesses what must, for a foreign community of its size, be the finest Race and Recreation Club in the world. ... An orchestra of Russian musicians plays every evening and on Sunday before lunch. The Club is the rendezvous for men, women, and children every evening, and for most of the day during week-ends and bank holidays. Chinese are only admitted during the race meetings.[20]

Woodhead is bitter about the rendition of the British concession at Hankow to Chinese control in the Chen-O'Malley Agreement of 1927 (this is what he meant by Hankow "going Red"), which he felt had turned over a superb example of Western progress to be ruined by Chinese inefficiency, graft, barbarism, chaos, and extortion. On the fighting at Nanking in 1927, the damage to foreign interests and residents was "so wanton that it might have been the work of wild beasts rather than men. The fact that these outrages remained unpunished [he seems to have forgotten the foreign naval shelling of the city] appears to have resulted in a feeling of permanent hostility toward foreigners. Several inexcusable outrages have occurred since."[21]

Especially seen forty years later, Woodhead's view, the treaty port view, of reality seems more distorted than the Chinese, whom he castigates as if they were somehow the intruders: "the various labour unions are constantly putting forth the most preposterous demands."[22] Outside the treaty ports in the real China

> the foreigner passes into a world in which medieval conditions prevail. ... Protests to the local Chinese authorities against treaty violations and lawless interference with foreign property are for the

most part cynically ignored. . . . I did not meet a single foreigner
who considered it possible to obtain elementary justice in a Chinese
tribunal. . . . The Chinese authorities, who lop off heads right and
left, who tax the people to the breaking point, and who force them
to accept a worthless paper currency could easily put a curb on the
lawless actions of the unions. But they almost invariably pretend
when appealed to that they cannot interfere with the will of the
people, as if the latter influenced them in the slightest degree in any
other connection. The lawlessness of the unions is tolerated, if not
fomented, because foreigners are the chief sufferers therefrom.[23]

Whatever the truth of this last remark, the Chinese were still adept at
keeping the foreigners at bay. Politically weak they might be, but long
experience in manipulating barbarians served them well. Their sovereignty
had been chipped away at on the edges, they had had to give ground, but
as in 1842 they did not consider, despite successive defeats and unrelieved
pressures from those supposedly all-powerful and all-virtuous "guests,"
accepting the foreign claim to be the arbiter of China's destiny nor
abandoning their efforts to keep China essentially inviolate.

Dreaming of El Dorado to the last, Woodhead closes his account with
bitter reflections on what might still be: "The possibilities of trade in West
China cannot be exaggerated. When, if ever, haphazard taxation is abandoned and the present obstacles to the free movement of commodities are
removed, a huge new market and an enormous supply of raw materials will
be opened to the world."[24] How maddening to have the greatest power on
earth denied this prize after nearly a century of effort, and how hateful of
the Chinese to be so stubbornly and stupidly unwilling to recognize their
own best interest in following the Western path! The Westerners could
span the globe with telegraph and steamship lines, but they could not
penetrate China—nor learn the Chinese language. They remained dependent on their compradores to the end, and were obliged, in part as a result,
to content themselves with the tiniest share of the China market. Even at
Canton, which was exposed to Western pressures far longer than any other
part of the country, foreigners remained largely confined to their island
base on Shameen with the gates on the two bridges locked every night.
Obstructions placed in the river in 1841 and again in 1884 and 1891 to
impede the passage of foreign naval vessels were not finally removed until
1905;[25] the city walls were not taken down until 1923.

What sustained the Chinese resistance to a Western takeover, not just politically or economically but ideologically and institutionally, was also their unshakeable sense of national-cultural identity. It was in turn strengthened by their pride in their own past, and by their ability to keep their traditional system of social and economic organization and management functioning at an acceptable level even while the imperial political structure was crumbling and during the political chaos which followed 1911. China was far more than a state, far more than a government. Colonial rule may be said to have created nationalism and national consciousness almost de novo in most of South and Southeast Asia, whereas in China a vigorously self-conscious and unitary culturalism had existed for some two thousand years before the Westerners arrived.

Chinese tradition did come to be questioned by some although it was wholly rejected by very few. But neither criticism nor rejection of tradition involved a loss of identity for most even of the severest critics. Was Lu Hsün, perhaps the bitterest of them, alienated from Chineseness? Was Sun Yat-sen? Perhaps the cosmopolites of treaty port land were alienated, those figures and their tiny world of unreality analyzed by Joseph Levenson.[26] Their translations of Pirandello and their apeing of Western manners symbolized their deracination. But they were truly marginal men, speaking to or for almost no one but themselves. They were creatures of the fringe like the treaty ports which had spawned, inspired, and sheltered them, and like the treaty ports were almost totally divorced from China. For virtually everyone else at every level and class, Chineseness, the pride and conviction of being Chinese, was not in question however seriously some intellectuals might question the appropriateness, rightness, or viability of this or that aspect of the Chinese tradition, even *The Tradition* as a whole. Somehow that was separable, a different thing from being Chinese.

What identity crisis there was (and I would argue that the phrase does not really apply to China, certainly not in the same way as to the rest of Asia), was limited to a few, and almost wholly in the non-Chinese world of the treaty ports. Some intellectuals wanted what they labeled as modernization, were enthusiastic for "science" and "democracy," and recognized the need for sometimes drastic and basic change. But there was, except for a few in the treaty ports, no surrender to the West, no thought of renouncing instinctive commitment to an unambiguous Chinese identity. China was in need of reform, of strengthening, even of purging and rebirth, but still a country and culture to be proud of belonging to. There was no significant deculturation, such as took place in other parts of Asia, and even more in Africa or elsewhere where indigenous cultures lacked the ascriptive stature, strength, long history of achievement, and self-satisfaction or pride of the Chinese. The Chinese sense of identity was sharpened by the confrontation with the West, where in other cultures and societies identity was eroded. Nationalism in the Western sense had not been previously part of the Chinese experience, since the Empire had no rivals. Now that a rival had appeared, Chinese culturalism evolved for the first time into Chinese nationalism. In any case, it was in interaction with the challenge of the Western model that the Chinese sense of identity became newly conscious and newly important. There was no surrender, and only the most limited ground given—given in order to strengthen China by adopting some aspects of the Western model, *not* in acknowledgment of the superior worth of Western civilization.

But as stated, even these attitudes, agonizing though they were for some, were limited to a very few in the treaty ports. The enormous majority of Chinese, not just peasants, were little if at all troubled by such dilemmas, as they and their circumstances had been so little affected by the impact of the West through the supposedly transforming agency of the treaty ports. Their world, the real Chinese world, remained separate and largely unruffled except by its own indigenous or self-generated problems and turbulences. Whatever the marginal men in the treaty ports did or thought made little difference, whether they were Chinese or foreign, to most of their contemporaries. The importance now attached to the would-be modernizers, reformers or radicals, the compradores, the cosmopolites, the Yung Wings and Wang T'aos and Yen Fus, the Lu Hsüns and Pa Chins is derived in part from hindsight. We know what followed, and how their influence in the end contributed to it. But in their own time their impact on events was slight and their audience, which they did influence deeply, was largely limited to fellow out-of-favor intellectuals as powerless as themselves, a tiny group on the fringes of action. They found little response in the China of their day, which was not receptive, as colonial India was, to gospels of radical change, especially not in alien garb. The Chinese context had first to alter—and to be altered—for their message to become relevant and central after the treaty ports as foreign bastions had been swept away. While they lived and struggled and wrote, while they looked into the Chinese past to find meaning for the present, the seeds of change these intellectuals in the treaty ports were creating through their writings lay largely dormant in the soil of the rest of China. It took time for them to germinate. In May of 1919, in the Hunan peasant movement, in Yenan, finally in 1949, long after most of these writers were dead, the seeds they had planted sprouted as a new generation schooled in their writings became the shapers of events. But even while they lived, while they agonized over China's weakness and degradation, while they sought new and radical patterns of restructuring, they were never alienated from a sense of their own *national* identity. China perdured.

An American Baptist missionary writing in the 1890s, for all his own cultural bondage and his remarks about the "inevitable" working of the "leaven of progress," caught this sense of China forever which remained in the minds of nearly all Chinese whatever the West might appear superficially to be doing to humiliate, overshadow, or outclass them and however compelling the Western model might thus appear to be:

> The people are very proud and nationalistic. They are as firmly persuaded that the Emperor of China is the rightful Universal Sovereign as Roman Catholics are that the Pope is the rightful head of the universal church. I have heard Chinese, in other respects intelligent, speak of the war of the English against China as "rebellion" and foreigners who oppose the will of the Emperor as "rebels." Whatever may be their acknowledgement of the fact that there are de facto governments in the world, they feel that there can be only one de jure Emperor, the Viceregent of Heaven upon earth, and that the Emperor of China is the man. . . . The Chinese are the model race, to whom all others must look up with deference.[27]

Not so in the rest of Asia. Most politically conscious Indians, lacking their own national tradition and seeing crippling deficiencies even in indigenous regional traditions, recognized the value of Western models and indeed welcomed British rule as the obvious path to progress, a Western concept which they enthusiastically adopted. India, like Ceylon, like most of Southeast Asia, and like even Japan, experienced an identity crisis so different in kind and degree from China's that the same phrase cannot meaningfully be applied to China. To differing degrees in each of these countries, indigenous attitudes, cultural styles, techniques, patterns of thought, notions of social and political organization—the whole stuff of traditional society—were found wanting and to varying degrees rejected, directly or indirectly, in favor either of outright and avowedly Western models or of what one may call the colonial hybrid which in the end prevailed, under the leadership of the new Westernized national elites in Bombay, Calcutta, Colombo, Rangoon, Bangkok, Singapore, Saigon, Batavia, Manila, and Tokyo. They questioned their indigenous cultural identity to the point of denial, or to the point where they chose instead to make themselves into, or to see themselves as, "liberated" from their own cultural heritage in favor of a new, hybrid, and heavily Western set of values and behavior patterns which they explicitly regarded as "superior." This did in the end bring its own agony, and in most cases a painful process of later readjustment associated with political independence. With the final destruction of old-style colonialism in the ashes of World War II, a resorting of values and modes which has been referred to as "second-wave nationalism" can be seen from Baluchistan to Lombok to Hokkaido.[28]

Although in the end she may have accepted a partly alien (and carefully decultured) modernization as the price of survival and self-respect, China never had a comparable identity problem. The Western challenge merely reinforced existing Sinocentric pride. All foreigners had always been barbarians to whom China had been magnanimously willing to condescend. After 1840, the new barbarians revealed themselves also as bandits, clever, effective in certain ways, but savage and frequently evil. Nor was this Chinese perception warped, let along paranoid. Their strong sense of cultural continuity, however, prevented any surrender. And the limited impact of the treaty port era, cultural-ideological as well as economic, continued to underline their foreignness and their marginality. The circulation of radical Chinese journals became increasingly widespread from the treaty ports after 1911 in a China where stability was disintegrating. But the influence of these journals strengthened the *Chinese* sense of crisis, not the cosmopolitanization of China, as did tend to be the effect of the circulation of "modernizing" publications from Calcutta, Manila, and the other colonial ports. The Japanese situation was different, but here the vastly greater size of China and its sharply contrasting experience over two millennia with cultural borrowing were crucial. To China, *foreign* had come to mean *inferior;* to Japan it could mean *possibly better* in a country which in any case was too small and too accessible throughout to ignore foreign pressures. A German physician who visited Japan in the middle 1870s, a few years after the Meiji Restoration, received a startling but revealing reply from a Japanese friend whom he questioned about Japanese history: "We have no history. Our history begins today."[29] Such an attitude at any period including the present is utterly inconceivable in China. Early Meiji rejection of the past was of course very brief and the Japanese sense of identity survived vigorously, but the Chinese experience and the Chinese adjustment were basically different.

In India, Western values and Western "civilization" were embraced enthusiastically along with Western technology.[30] Most politically conscious Indians were caught up by the Western notion of progress, and pursued it with few backward glances at the indigenous tradition which would be abandoned. Here is Bholanath Chandra, a Bengali reporting in English on his travels in northern India in the 1840s and 1860s:

> Day by day is the dominion of mind extending over matter, and the secrets of nature are brought to light to evolve the powers of the soil and make nations depend upon their own resources. . . . The rail turns the courses of men, merchandise, and mind, all into new channels.[31]

Contrast this with Chinese attitudes toward railways. Chandra's fellow Bengalis Rajendralal Mitra and Kisoricad Mitra echoed his sentiments:

> There is nothing in *status quo* in the universe. Change is the law of existence.[32]

> Progress is the law of God, and cannot be arrested by the puny efforts of man. As knowledge is acquired, facts accumulate and generalization is practiced, skepticism arises and engenders a spirit of inquiry, resulting in the triumph of truth.[33]

As did Girischandra Ghose:

> The final cause of the advent of the English in India is to forward the progress of mankind toward perfection. They are the destined instrument in the hand of Providence for this great work. . . . The march of civilization throughout the world is forward. . . . Progress is a necessary condition of creation. . . . The course of nature is perpetual development.[34]

So vigorous an espousal of Western-style progress was understandable only as the reciprocal of attitudes toward the Indian tradition and its past. India was recognized in effect as bankrupt, with nowhere to go but up, and no way to get there except the Western way:

The peninsula presented one unbroken surface of ignorance, dense, appalling ignorance.[35]

The Hindu social fabric at the beginning of this century was in a miserable state . . . based on a debasing cruel superstition and supported by the power of a handful of Brahmans. . . . In the course of half a century, the strongholds of superstitution . . . have been stormed and rendered untenable.[36]

Disorder and anarchy were the results of this sectarian bondage, aggravated by the "tyranny" of "feudal" landlords. The Mughal conquest made matters still worse; in a nineteenth-century Indian view:

The Mahometans introduced into this country all the vices of an ignorant, intolerant, and licentious soldiery. The utter destruction of learning and science was an invariable part of their system, and the conquered, no longer able to protect their lives by arms and independence, fell into the opposite extremes of abject submission, deceit, and fraud. . . . The English are to be thanked for having delivered India from the tyranny and villainy of the Mahometans.[37]

This was the view in differing degrees of most nineteenth-century Indian intellectuals, of which one more example may be given:

When India lay sunk in the mire of idolatry and superstition, when Mahometan oppression and misrule had almost extinguished the last spark of hope in the Indian mind, when Hinduism . . . had degenerated into the most horrible and abominable system of idolatry . . . the Lord in his mercy sent us the British nation to rescue India.[38]

As the English model almost uncritically was seen as superior and desirable, so its language and educational system were enthusiastically praised and adopted.[39]

Good learning means Western learning.[40]

. . . We must know English as thoroughly as Englishmen. . . . It is the language of Milton and Shakespeare, of Newton and Bacon, of Locke and Hume. . . . Can you afford to give up such a language for the poems of Kritibas and the doggrels of Kavi-kankan?[41]

Such attitudes did give way over time to others more critical of actual British rule and more supportive of indigenous values. It was supportive at least in the sense that reformist-minded Indians sought less to reject everything in their own tradition and more to revive the best of it, cleansed of what were now recognized as defects such as the rigidity of caste, the ban on widow remarriage, the "superstitious" aspects of Hinduism, and so forth. But this did not involve any abandonment of the earlier enthusiasm for Western-style progress or for a largely British model of development as the best course for an India which must fundamentally reorder its own tradition and produce a new, consciously hybrid civilization. Indeed Indian receptivity to and even eagerness for change in this context was unquestionably greater than on the part of their British rulers. The British were by comparison traditionalists who resisted change, as Gunderson ably argues in the paper from which I have drawn so extensively above. In part the reasons no doubt were the weakness of the indigenous political system or systems, the loss of sovereignty, the virtual absence of an Indian aristocracy after the seventeenth or eighteenth centuries with a stake in preserving tradition—the absence, in other words, of any group resembling in the slightest the Chinese gentry or its official or literati components—and the long history of successive invasion, conquest, and cultural mixture which was so prominent a part of the Indian experience. Whatever the reasons, the indigenous Indian system as a whole, such as it was including its economic aspects, was not and could not be seen by most Indians as a source of value and identity sufficient to stand against the power and the counterattraction of the British model. This model was exemplified and administered by exponents who were also the political rulers of India, merely the last (though apparently most effective) in a long series of foreign conquerors. The contrast with China was total. Indians could have few illusions about the superiority, let alone universalism, of their unaltered tradition, and had little reason not to respond positively to a new foreign alternative whose foreignness was far less important in their minds than its promise of change, development, and improvement.

As Joseph Levenson has stressed, there is an important difference between culturalism and nationalism, although both may sustain identity.[42] In the Chinese case, as some traditional values came to be questioned by the relatively few who were affected, Chinese identity was supported by the beginning of new nationalist feelings and loyalties. As Levenson describes it, this involved a shift from universalism-cosmopolitanism to provincialism, but it left identity intact. Nor did criticism of certain traditional values mean abandonment of cultural membership. No one in China wondered in all this turmoil who he or she was, as nearly all other Asian intellectuals caught up by Westernization did wonder while they groped for solutions. China was in danger, but not Chineseness. Which China to embrace or to try to build, how much and what kind of selection was appropriate from Western techniques, may have been a problem, but "a sense of where you are," what team, what part of the playing field, was never lost.[43]

The Japanese agony may have been briefer, concentrated in the first decade or so of Meiji, but Western pressure there involved a real threat to national identity. Unlike the Indians, the Japanese, having if only for a time questioned their identity, returned to it strengthened by their own success in managing an incredibly smooth balancing act. Modern Japan's fruitful and comparatively serene cohabitation with the Western world is an affair which has left Japanese identity inviolate. This has been easier for the Japanese, like their wholesale adoption of Chinese civilization in the eighth century and their volte-face after 1945, because their national sense of identity has been almost genetic rather than cultural. By comparison with Chineseness, Japaneseness has been far more value free. The right to rule or to wield authority in Japan has not been revocable as in China, nor dependent on morality, but far more unquestioned. The Japanese system of both government and society was hierarchical and authoritarian but not in itself associated with particular values: it could and did accommodate and vigorously pursue radically different or even contradictory goals at different times without disrupting the Japanese sense of national group identity derived from common genetic linkage, a supposed common but divine ancestor, and common group experience as residents of an ethnically homogenous and isolated island kingdom.[44]

China suffered infinitely more in a prolonged struggle, at least in part because she never even briefly considered the idea of changing the basis of Chineseness. This may have been a losing game after about 1870, but to play any other was nevertheless unthinkable.[45] Whatever the pain, it was still better to be Chinese. Where choices could or had to be made, as they often did, between "development" and sovereignty, China both before and after 1911 chose the latter. Up to 1949, China was more successful in resisting colonialism than in achieving modernization. Sovereignty and viability could be preserved, even on poor-man's terms, without surrendering to the Western gospel.

Observers have been misled by the noisy action in the treaty ports, by their much-trumpeted role as harbingers of national transformation, by the questionings and responses of the relatively few Chinese intellectuals there, and by the deterioration of the national political order into assuming that China was falling apart in the face of Western blows and moving toward Westernization. Something was happening all right, but the noise did not mean what the foreigners thought it meant. China was beginning to tune up for the overture to a revolution which would sweep the treaty ports away. But while it lasted, treaty port land and the real China touched one another very little. Their interaction was further minimized by the spatial concentration of the modernizing sector in the few scattered dots of the ports, or the political struggles centered in Peking or Nanking. The traditional imperial order also touched the village world lightly and infrequently, but it was at least an order of which the village was aware and to which it felt a relationship, at times a partnership, however distant. The foreignness of the treaty port order and its lack of traditional imperial channels of articulation with the village world made it far more separate.

Outside the few big cities and those served by railways, steamships, or motor roads—most of the country even in population terms—changes related to the modernizing sector were minimal even up to 1948. Skinner's study of rural marketing estimates that by that year only about 10 percent of the traditional standard markets in the country as a whole had yielded to "modern" trading systems.[46] In Szechuan, where most of his primary data were gathered, he found none that had so altered, despite the treaty port status and steamship services since 1899 of its largest city, Chungking, on China's major internal trade highway, the Yangtze. Over most of China the long-established nested pattern of marketing systems survived basically unchanged until the advent of the People's Republic, covering the economic and social landscape with its efficiently operating honeycomb of interaction and remaining the principal channel of internal trade and the sociocultural nexus. It was vigorous and flexible enough to adjust as necessary to changes in population, regional political conditions, and new commodities, but was rarely and briefly disrupted. It was a much less fragile and uncertain sector than the many times smaller one where modernization was being attempted. Its relative success in riding out essentially undamaged the mounting storm of disaster which, from a Western point of view, seemed to overtake China after 1850 or after 1900 is ample testimony to its effectiveness. It suggests that our attention has been focused to a misleading extent on the modern sector in jumping to the erroneous conclusion that China was hopelessly degenerating or no longer viable.

Change of course there was, and not for the better. The traditional system began to lose its continuing viability at an accelerating rate after 1900. But although its future was bleak, the indigenous economy in its local and regional bases was far from being in ruins, as our current perspectives and our knowledge of political disaster in the first half of the twentieth century have tended to suggest. Skinner's study is a useful corrective to this view, and in effect shows us the far larger China where the old currents of economic and social integration continued largely unruffled by the winds which were tearing at the more obvious official edifices of the traditional system. As the political center weakened and finally rotted, regional and local continuity in management kept much of the functionally beneficial aspects of the system going, despite mounting instability in other terms. To see the rise of regionalism after 1850 as either symptom or cause of general deterioration may well be missing the point. Exclusive attention to recorded political events at earlier periods in Chinese history may be similarly misleading. The Japanese monk Ennin, who made detailed observations in late T'ang within a few years of the dynasty's final collapse, records no political chaos but describes relative order and prosperity.[47] Presumably there were ample indications of decay at the center; the implication is that they did not importantly affect the basic fabric of Chinese civilization with which he was concerned. One may reach similar conclusions from accounts of late Sung, as for example Jacques Gernet's, focused on Hangchow.[48] Even in the Sung capital within a few years of its downfall one is shown an effective system in operation in which people seem to have been little touched by the weakening of the central bureaucracy. In late Ming too, as recorded by Ricci, the undeniable ossification overtaking the national administration does not seem to have been reflected in what was happening at the local level.[49] Ricci shows us a prosperous, well-ordered, vigorous, and highly civilized China which, like Skinner's picture of the 1940s, may be a useful antidote to generalizations based on the knowledge of imperial political decline.

Because we know a good deal more about the last few decades of the Ch'ing we may be reluctant to find a similar pattern there. And yet we may still be mesmerized by keeping our eye on the wrong ball, the modern sector and the political center. The rest of China, its traditional and regional sector, did in fact manage to go on functioning, at least well enough to enable it to hold the field against foreign encroachments and to buttress its own sense of self-sufficiency. One informant's recollections of village life in Kwangtung extending from about 1880 to 1950 offer some support.[50] His village and its area, some hundred miles southwest of Canton, was described as orderly, modestly prosperous, largely free of banditry, and surrounded on all hillsides by forest. After 1911 it was increasingly plagued by troop movements, banditry, interruptions in its normal communications, and wholesale removal of the trees by both troops and villagers. Emigration of young adult males became common after 1900, and by the 1920s the area fit the stereotypes of twentieth-century Kwangtung. But this condition was reached quite recently and should not be attributed to the nineteenth century. In Szechuan, more remote from the forces operating on Kwangtung and more typical of most of China, Skinner's data and my own observations from the early and middle 1940s suggest that even then the quality and conditions of rural life had not yet greatly changed for most people. They were suffering the kind of slow decline one might expect from growing overpopulation, and were beginning to be more seriously troubled by civil disorder, but they had certainly not fallen into chaos in the way that many Western generalizations about China, based on their reading of major political events and lumping the whole of the period since 1850 into one, would have us believe.

The fabric of traditional Chinese culture and society was richly and tightly woven. The fraying or breaking of one or a few threads—even the thread of central political power—did not destroy the fabric. Modernization ultimately came to China, but hardly in the form the treaty ports had striven for. Their efforts to transform China failed, but their example helped to push China into revolution. As both example and counterexample, the treaty port legacy also shaped the Maoist version of modernization. And one may argue, with Marion Levy, that the imitative behavior of the treaty port Chinese, as well as the activities of the Western-influenced radicals harbored there, was in effect a poison helping to corrode the traditional system.[51] The treaty ports were both irritants and goads, and they provoked in the end a massive reaction. But the reaction was *Chinese,* and in Chinese terms, not hybrid, not Western style, a new national answer to the Western challenge.

Chapter 9

The Chinese Base:
Economic Sophistication

The period 1850–1949 was an out-of-character interval in the wider context of Chinese history, something which developments since that time have helped to make clearer. If we had been better historians, we could have appreciated this sooner by paying more careful attention to the centuries which preceded 1850 instead of waiting for the People's Republic to correct our vision. Being overtaken by events does have its compensations however; hindsight is usually clearer than foresight, and in this case the lesson has been a sharp one. It should also help us to understand that the characteristics now once again so visible were not, could not have been, totally in eclipse during the brief century following the Opium War. They were masked by Western confidence, derogation, and assertion, by the erosion of Chinese confidence, and certainly by the culture-bound Western picture of the China of that era which has shaped all our judgments, Chinese and foreigners. Reiteration of "backward," "incompetent," "weak," "deteriorating," "chaotic" could not, whatever the truth of the matter, fail to affect what both speakers and hearers believed. This makes it harder to find out what the reality may have been, but one now has the advantage of greater freedom from the context of the times and from the particular culture bondage associated with it. We have our own different bondage, no doubt at least equally blind but different enough that we can at least reexamine the past with a new perspective.

With the help of this new perspective, conditioned in large part by what has happened in China since 1949, one can see more clearly in the eighteenth and into the nineteenth and twentieth centuries a smoothly functioning, proud, successful China manned and directed by people whose stereotypic Chineseness is now easier to accept as industrious, highly organized on a local level, competent producers, managers, and entrepreneurs, running a productive economy and continuing to do so

156

even as the upper-level political order degenerated. The collapse of the polity, though far from unprecedented in Chinese history, was certainly a major matter, and it did in time seriously weaken the economic and social base. The relation between polity and society in China has always been generic, but it was also possible for the system of livelihood and local organization to continue on its own momentum for some time after the central polity began to decay.

Those who managed that system were the inheritors of a uniquely productive agrarian base without equal in the world either in scale or in per acre yields, of a tradition of hard work and group effort, of a highly developed system of water transport, and of a level of technology which in many respects and until the eighteenth century was more advanced (and made more contribution to economic welfare) than in any other culture elsewhere. Although by the nineteenth century this technological and organizational base was no longer able to produce sustained growth and needed a radical new infusion—which was ultimately provided after 1949—it was still functioning effectively enough to resist during the period of Western effort to infiltrate it. The industriousness did get through even to contemporary Western observers because they saw it as threatening. Some of them from time to time showed awareness of other positive characteristics which they recognized not merely as pragmatic but as part of a high level of Chinese effectiveness. The organized quality of Chinese life, the collective nature of the economy and society, also made an impression on some, as did the long cumulative experience on which this rested. The Chinese economy had been "sophisticated" even in Western (i.e., commercial) terms since at least early Sung; there was no shortage of skilled managers and entrepreneurs, nor of competent labor.

All of these things help to account for the speed and success of economic growth and national development after 1949, when strength at the center was restored. A vigorous new government could draw on an immense reservoir of individual and institutional potential, quite apart from its equally important revolutionary nature and goals. China stands out as *qualitatively* different from the rest of the so-called developing world (and from much of the "developed" world as well) in its long-acquired experience with creating and managing a complex, sophisticated, productive system; the reservoir is deep, and has been so for a long time. There were periods in which it was being drawn on more than added to, but it was never substantially drained as the much smaller Indian reservoir was, by repeated and devastating breaches in the entire system and in the civil order on which any accumulation must rest. Nor even during the century following 1850, even though disorder did have a major negative effect, was the reservoir drawn down enough that the viability of the extrapolitical system was seriously impaired—as witness in particular the resilience shown in willingness and ability to adapt to changed economic or technological conditions and to remain competitive in the face of foreign pressures or infiltration.

Undergirding it all was the immense productivity of the agricultural system, nourished by a uniquely intensive system of cultivation orchestrated on a group basis and distinguished by such practices as transplanting, double cropping, intercultivation, soil renewal, and fertilization with nightsoil provided through an intricate and yet beautifully simple supply system. Some of the foreigners saw this too and recognized Chinese agriculture as a model of effectiveness whose superiority had ensured its spread throughout East Asia.[1] The complex system of irrigation which so enhanced agricultural productivity and which was an essential part of the model also attracted their admiration. Rice is a physically demanding crop but if it can be provided with a controlled water supply in a warm climate and grown in heavily manured and puddled fields where the water level can be altered or drained at will, its productivity can be increased manyfold. All these techniques had evolved since the Han, with a particular spurt in Ming and early Ch'ing, to a peak of effectiveness. The agricultural system too by the nineteenth century had exhausted its ability, with the technology available to it, to sustain the continued increases which had become necessary, and had ultimately to be transformed by new technology. But it was nevertheless a remarkable achievement, a model of productivity for two millennia, and it did not lose its effectiveness overnight.

As in all preindustrial economies, agriculture was the chief source of wealth, but the difference in China was the margin of surplus which agriculture produced. It was ultimately the engine of trade, of urbanization, of the imperial system, of Chinese civilization as a whole; and more than anything else it accounts for the sheen of imperial China. Even in terms of per capita consumption levels, it appears that the productivity of Chinese agriculture kept mass welfare at most times and places until perhaps the latter half of the nineteenth century above what it was in most other economies.[2] Agricultural surpluses were used for investment in other enterprises and also provided a cushion against periodic natural and human disasters. Nor did the operation of this productive system depend significantly on the state except for the maintenance of order. There were some large-scale works of irrigation, flood prevention, and canal building. But for the most part the operation was locally conceived and managed through smaller-scale group effort which was relatively little involved with the bureaucracy except at tax time and was hence to a degree self-perpetuating.

To review the earlier discussion in chapter 7, whatever the difficulties of establishing statistical knowns, especially for the agricultural sector, there is a variety of less precise (but possibly also less misleading) evidence to suggest that at least rural productivity and living standards did not grossly deteriorate until, or even in, the 1920s and 1930s in many, perhaps most, areas, and that the basic standard was well above minimum subsistence levels. This is the principal argument of Ramon Myers.[3] It may be urged, as some critics have done, that his evidence is overly selective, that he jumps to conclusions from inadequate evidence, and that the areas he describes were not typical despite his claims. But his conclusions agree with my own far more impressionistically based observations of Szechuan and of most of west China in the 1940s, insofar as they suggest that whatever the precise levels of material welfare and whether or not these declined in the first half of the twentieth century, they did not everywhere and perhaps not in most areas except for brief periods sink to, let alone below, the margin of subsistence. Acute economic distress certainly occurred in many places and at many times. The picture differed in each region and there was no single, national uniformity. But distress resulted more from drought, flood, or civil war, compounded by overpopulation, than directly from economic forces or from major deterioration of the economic system as a whole. Distress was usually temporary, and recovery rapid, again suggesting a surprising degree of resilience and a potential margin in the economy which we have been conditioned to overlook or deny.[4] Peasant economic behavior was rational and adjusted readily to changing circumstances. If all this was true or even partly true for the twentieth century, it must surely have been at least as true for earlier decades.

Although small-scale peasant agriculture dominated the economy, there were other components which were equally impressive and important in sustaining China's self-sufficiency, well-being, pride, and reluctance to

acknowledge that the modern West offered a better alternative model. It
has been Joseph Needham's contribution to show us this other China:

> China to Europeans has been like the moon, always showing the
> same face—a myriad peasant-farmers, a scattering of artists and
> recluses, an urban minority of scholars, mandarins, and shopkeepers.
> Thus do civilizations acquire "stereotypes" of one another. Now . . .
> we intend to see what is on the other side of the disc, and to meet
> the artisans and engineers, the shipwrights and metallurgists of
> China's three-thousand-year-old culture.[5]

Volume 4 of Needham's magistral work deals with many aspects of
technology directly relevant to the economy, beginning with road building
and its generally high quality, and including bridges, waterworks and
canals, and nautical technology. These traditions too survived the blows of
the nineteenth and twentieth centuries, as did the tradition of organized
mass labor for the construction of both large and small public works. One
could see it still alive in the building of the Burma Road or of airfields for
United States planes needing bases from which to bomb Japan. The
American command wanted them in a hurry but thought in terms of flying
in bulldozers in sections. While the Americans were still worrying about
logistics, the Chinese built the airfields in a few weeks, using mass organized labor and no mechanical equipment but the simple traditional tools
which had also built the Grand Canal. A Russian emigré who worked in
the late 1920s for the Liao River Conservancy Board in Manchuria as an
engineer describes in his memoirs the building of a canal by similar means,
"following traditions established in the dim past, with accuracy, precision,
and orderliness unsurpassed anywhere in the world."[6]

China's relative success economically did help, in the Chinese mind, to
mask the facts that it became *technologically* outdistanced by developments in the modern West and that its own development was stymied by
technological stagnation. Since it was mainly foreigners and their collaborators who were pushing for change through the adoption of Western
technology, Chinese resistance was the more understandable. Foreigners
complained about obstructionism, but their accounts of the economic
condition of the country, especially before about 1900, do not suggest a
decaying system of livelihood and commerce, or one where they could
expect easily to make a place for themselves as "developers" with something attractive to offer. A British Consular account of the Tientsin district

in 1862, within a year of the first effective foreign contact in that area, reads in part as follows: "The agricultural and industrial productions of this district are numerous and important. The population is large, but the means of living are abundant and cheap, and there is much less destitution in this than in many other far richer districts in Europe."[7] This may be read as typical of many foreign accounts from other parts of China throughout the period after 1842, and to some extent into the twentieth century. It suggests the extent to which even the Taiping Rebellion fell short of reducing China to the miserable level which accounts from the 1930s and 1940s describe. Although the Tientsin area was not directly affected by the Taipings, it had been heavily damaged by the Allied Expedition in 1860, and contemporary foreign accounts stressed the demonstrably lower level of prosperity in Chihli than in most of central and south China.[8]

Western descriptions of nineteenth-century China outside the treaty ports counter later stereotypes and give a reasonably consistent picture of general prosperity, great productivity, thriving commerce, and a well-ordered system of management and transport.[9] Positive and admiring Western assessments of China and its economy to some degree did yield over time to Western complaints of "backwardness" and poverty. China may have changed relatively little in any absolute sense, but the West changed dramatically and perspectives altered accordingly. After about 1870, Westerners began, as self-styled apostles of "progress," to see China in a new light. Like other non-Western cultures, it was more often viewed with condescension, or even with disdain and disgust. This is the image of China which the present Western generation inherited. It is not surprising that it misleads us in our efforts to reconstruct the past—or that those twentieth-century Western observations which continued to see the Chinese economy as a functionally effective system were discounted.

Let us look again at some representative Western accounts of China before arrogance and frustration began to blind their vision. Probably the best informed and most experienced first-hand Western observer was Robert Fortune, an English botanist sent to China in 1843 by the East India Company to obtain seeds and cuttings of the tea plant for smuggling out of the country in order to establish a plantation industry in India and Ceylon which could break the Chinese monopoly.[10] Fortune learned the language, disguised himself as a Chinese complete with false queue, and traveled very widely over most of the eastern half of the country. In all of these respects he was unlike most of the later foreign residents. He saw and wrote as a private individual, representing no government or religious cause but aiming to inform Western readers about this huge country whose civilization he clearly admired, though in no sense uncritically. He made four lengthy visits to China (the last in the early 1860s) and produced six books which inspire confidence in him as a careful observer of wide curiosity, and one who was well informed about economic and social conditions at home as well as in China. As a one-sentence summary of what he found, he includes a startling remark: "In no country in the world is there less real misery and want than in China."[11] Conditioned by later perspectives, many people will find themselves reading this sentence twice to make sure they have it right. But neither Fortune nor his printer was being careless. In a subsequent book about his third visit, from 1853 to 1856, he writes

> It is hoped that those who have been inclined to form their estimate of the Chinese character from what has been written about the low rabble of Canton will, after perusal of these pages, look with a more favorable eye upon the inhabitants of China when seen from other points of view. China is far more ancient as a nation, and as industrious if not as civilized, as ourselves. . . . The lower orders in China contrast favorably with the same classes in Europe, or even in India. . . . there is no apparent want, and certainly no oppression. The labourer is strong, healthy, and willing to work, but independent. . . . The poorest cottager had always a cup of tea for me which he insisted on my drinking before I left his house. . . . The farmers in China live well, dress plainly, and are industrious without being in any way oppressed. I doubt if there is a happier race anywhere than the Chinese farmer and peasantry.[12]

Fortune's views are echoed by many contemporary Western observers. F. E. Forbes, a retired British naval officer who traveled in China as a coin collector for five years immediately following the end of the first Anglo-Chinese War in 1842, agreed with Fortune in finding the atmosphere in Canton atypical of the rest of the country, where he was kindly received and deeply impressed. According to his account even the jails were comfortable, and the people "enjoy a fair portion of liberty and more happiness than falls to the lot of most nations. My own property suffered more from actual robbery in landing and passing the English frontier than during my whole sojourn in China."[13] The countryside is tranquil and prosperous, and "the economy of their agriculture is beautiful."[14] He describes a great variety of nonagricultural production and marketing, points out that "roads are ubiquitous and in good order" while reserving his greatest admiration for the "endless" network of water transport, and concludes that the Chinese are "the most contented, good humored, well fed, industrious, happy population that in the course of sixteen years of service in the navy and rambles in most parts of the globe I have ever met with."[15]

J. R. Ross, a British sea captain shipwrecked on Hainan in 1819, traveled overland with his crew to Canton and had thus an unusual and early opportunity to observe south China at first hand. His account was "confident in asserting that scarcely any people can be supposed to enjoy a more happy or contented life.... People of the poorest sort here are better clothed than the same class of persons even in England. ... We have seen nothing in the shape of a beggar."[16]

Other more widely read contemporary Western accounts make the same points, remarking on the absence of poverty, the high productivity, and the extensive and vigorous commercial sector. Many comment on what they identify as the innate Chinese love of commerce, common to all classes, ages, and sexes, and their skill as traders and entrepreneurs, not only the Cantonese but (in later accounts when foreigners were free to travel elsewhere) all Chinese wherever there was a commercial opportunity. The sour notes in the large number of Western works on China are in a small minority before about 1870 and can usually be directly traced to anger and frustration related either to Chinese adroitness in salvaging diplomatically and through subsequent foot-dragging or simple noncompliance what the foreigners thought they had won for themselves by arms and treaties, or to missionary failure to make converts and their consequent moral condemnation of the Chinese.

But even the few critics were impressed by all they saw of the hive of commercial activity and by its dimensions. H. H. Lindsay, on a visit to Shanghai in 1832, made one of the few attempts to guess at the actual volume of trade on the eve of the treaty port system.[17] He counted 400 junks, averaging between 100 and 400 tons, entering the port of Shanghai weekly during July. If this was typical of the year as a whole (there is no reason to think it was not since tribute rice shipments would not normally reach their peak until late summer), Shanghai was already one of the leading ports of the world with a volume of shipping equal to or greater than London's.[18] Most of the trade passing through Shanghai was domestic, but there was also substantial traffic with Java, Siam, Indo-China, and the Philippines. Although the volume of trade at Shanghai was clearly very large, it was almost certainly smaller than at Canton, and probably also at Foochow, Wuhan, and Tientsin, at least—unfortunately we have no estimates for those comparable with Lindsay's for Shanghai. That Shanghai despite its commercial prominence was only a small regional center in population terms tells one something about the bases of urban growth and functions in traditional China. By the 1920s, at the high tide of foreign power and commercial success, Shanghai again ranked among the first four or five ports of the world.

The Elgin expedition up the Yangtze reached Hankow in December of 1858, barely two years after the restoration of local order in the wake of the Taipings.

> The river was alive with boats [and the landing] so crowded with human beings that it seemed a problem how we should ever succeed in forcing our way through them. ... The streets themselves were superior to any I have seen in any other city of the empire. They were well paved and roofed over with mats. ... the shops were upon a much grander and handsomer scale than those at Canton or any of the open ports. ... We could scarcely credit that only two years and four months ago this bustling city had been levelled to the ground. Many of the townspeople assured us that not a stone had been left standing on another, so completely had the rebels demolished the shops and houses. ... No stronger proof could be afforded of the vitality of trade at this point, and of its importance as a commercial centre, than the marvelous resuscitation of Hankow.[19]

This was all a description of Hankow, which Oliphant recognized was inferior in size and grandeur to Wuchang if not to Hanyang, its two companion cities on facing banks of the confluence of the Han and Yangtze rivers. It was Wuchang which Oliphant felt was "worthy of being called the Queen of the Yangtze," though he also notes that he had to walk two miles through Hankow to reach open country.[20] He was impressed by the large number of coal junks from Hunan, other junks carrying oil, hemp, rice, and cotton from Hupeh, and the quantities of tin, lead, and copper arriving from Hunan; of sugar, tobacco, and opium from Szechuan; porcelain from Kiangsi; and tea from Hupeh, Hunan,

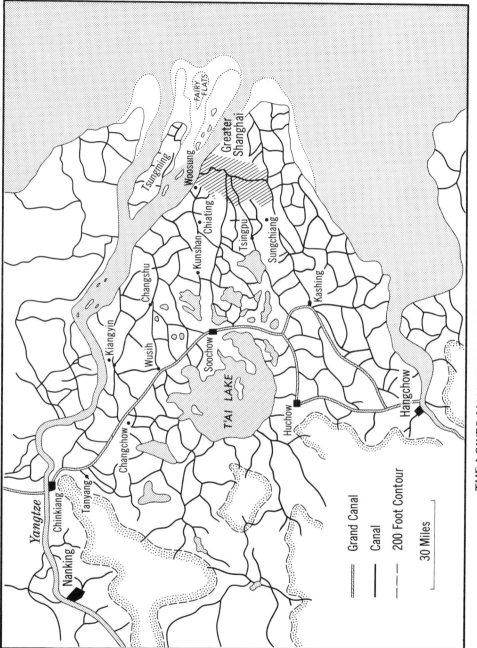

THE LOWER YANGTZE VALLEY, SHOWING WATERWAYS

Yangtze

Nanking
Chinkiang
Tanyang

Changchow

Kiangyin

Wusih

Soochow

TAI LAKE

Changshu

Kunshan
Chiating
Tsingpu
Sungchiang

Woosung

Greater
Shanghai

Tsungming

FAIRY
FLATS

Kashing

Huchow

Hangchow

Grand Canal

Canal

200 Foot Contour

30 Miles

Chekiang, and Anhwei. At the end of his account, he quotes Lord Elgin himself, in a prescient passage:

> My general impression is that British manufacturers will have to exert themselves if they intend to supplant to any considerable extent in the native market the fabrics produced in their leisure hours and at intervals of rest from agricultural labor by this industrious, frugal, and sober population. It is a pleasing but pernicious fallacy to imagine that the influence of an intriguing mandarin is to be presumed whenever a buyer shows a preference for native over foreign calico. [21]

Eight years later, A. S. Bickmore made a trip from Canton up the West River to Wuchow and thence, via Kweilin, with only one portage to the Hsiang River leading to Tungting Lake and on to Wuhan. He comments on the "immense" trade of Hsiangtan and the Hsiang River as a whole as well as what he could observe moving even along overland routes. On Tungting Lake he says:

> I enjoyed a view only to be seen in this land that numbers its population by the hundred million. As far as the eye could see and for several miles on either side, the whole surface of the water was perfectly feathered with white sails. . . . Twice I counted nearly 450 in sight at one time, and with the aid of my field glass fully a hundred more could be distinguished. Many were loaded with tea, many with coals, and many were just swimming along under huge deck loads of round timber. . . . The completeness of [China's] internal water communications [is] as much a wonder as the immense numbers of her population.[22]

Fortune's several accounts are full of surprises, and yet his manner compels trust in his honesty, accuracy, and detailed personal knowledge of what he writes about. His spoken Chinese and his dress, queue, and tinted skin were apparently good enough to deceive nearly everyone he met on his extensive travels (except of course for his own Chinese servants) into believing his explanation that he came from a distant province. His presence more than half a day's journey from one of the five "open ports" was of course illegal at this period, but he seems to have lost few opportunities to quiz people wherever he went. His account of a trip in 1848 through the silk districts south and west of Shanghai includes the following:

The merchant and silk manufacturer will form a good idea of the quantity of silk consumed in China when told that, after the war [i.e., 1840–42], on the port of Shanghae being opened, the exports of raw silk increased in two or three years from 3000 to 20,000 bales. This fact shows, I think, the enormous quantity which must have been in the Chinese market before the extra demand could have been so easily supplied. But as it is with tea, so it is with silk—the quantity exported bears but a small proportion to that consumed by the Chinese themselves. The 17,000 extra bales sent yearly out of the country have not in the least degree affected the price of raw silk or of silk manufacture. This fact speaks for itself.[23]

In a later book, he gives a detailed description of silk production and marketing, and uses a vivid analogy:

However large in the aggregate the production of silk may be in the country, this quantity is produced not by large farmers or extensive manufactures but by millions of cottagers, each of whom owns and cultivates a few roods or acres of land only. Like bees in a hive each contributes his portion to swell the general store. And so it is with almost every production in the celestial empire.[24]

The very size of this vast economy, and its composition of a myriad small producers and handlers, was of course an important reason why it was so difficult for the foreign impact to have any substantial effect. The stimulus necessary to move such a mass would have had to be immense. The increase in foreign trade which looked impressive to the Westerners remained proportionately tiny when compared to the bulk of the Chinese economy as a whole. Nor was it very effective in acting, as the foreigners kept hoping, as a "leaven" on the mass; it was not only too small, but too marginal, and at the same time represented too little that was new. China was well used to trade; somewhat more of it was deflected into external channels than in the traditional pattern, but there were very few new commodities, little change in production or consumption patterns or spatial concentrations, and little change in the management of trade, which remained predominantly in Chinese hands and by traditional methods. The foreign firms served largely as commission and insurance agents on behalf of Chinese buyers and sellers; their success as well as their standing within the community continued to depend on their Chinese compradores.

Fortune several times warns his readers not to judge China by the foreign experience in the five ports, especially not Canton and nearby Kwangtung which he says is full of petty thieves, surly and xenophobic peasantry, and scheming townspeople. He found Shanghai, Ningpo, Amoy, and Foochow only a little better and bearing scant comparison with the towns, countryside, and people he observed inland. He describes Hangchow however as a thriving, bustling place, full of prosperity and, like other cities and towns in the China he saw, with its walls, streets, and temples in excellent repair. Hangchow was "a place of wealth and luxury," where "all except the lowest labourers and coolies strutted about in dresses composed of silk, satin, and crepe." His Chinese servants, who came from elsewhere, said that there were many rich men in their country, but they all dressed modestly and plainly, while the natives of Hangchow, both rich and poor, were never contented unless gaily dressed in silks and satins.[25] Apparently neither sumptuary laws nor fear of public display of wealth had any force here.

Fortune's attention was also drawn to the prosperous appearance of the agricultural countryside with its well-tended fields and heavy crops. Like other later and earlier observers, he was impressed by the immense traffic on the waterways as well as by the frequent water mills using the current to power their machinery, and by the system of transferring even the largest boats from one water level to another in both streams and canals by the use of a windlass and an inclined plane. Most of his journeys he made by water, which also carried the great bulk of the trade of central and south China, but in the few places where he did use the roads he comments on the excellent state of their stone paving (presumably by comparison with contemporary English roads) and the dense traffic which they carried.

The account of Sir John Davis a decade earlier gives a similar picture.[26] His positive assessments are the more convincing when one remembers the nature of his experience: the frustrations of Company operations under the Canton system, the humiliation and provocation of the Amherst Mission, the chronic tension and irritation of his dealings as interpreter with the Cohong and the Kwangtung administrations, and his maddening and long drawn out controversy with Ch'i Ying and others over the infamous Canton "city question" from 1844 to 1848, which last he took back with him to England as his most recent memory of China. Yet Davis was profoundly impressed by the smoothness and effectiveness of China's self-regulating society (the phrase is mine, not his), based on the central virtue of filiality and its ramifications in the five relationships. He saw the system's tranquility as an important basis of the prosperity which he also recognized: "the machine works well."[27] He makes the by now familiar comments on "the cheerful industry" of the Chinese, and adds "It is certain that the bulk of the native population enjoys the results of its industry with a very fair degree of security, or it would not be so industrious."[28]

Despite his own experiences, Davis clearly cannot help liking the Chinese, whom he regards as immensely good-humored and competent (an impression most foreigners in China were still receiving in the 1940s), as well as admiring their civilization and economic success. Indeed he pays them the supreme compliment of comparing them with the English: "There is in short a business-like character about the Chinese which assimilates them in a striking manner to the most intelligent nations of the west. . . . It does not seem too much to say that in everything which enters into the composition of actively industrious and well-organized communities, there is vastly less difference between them and the English, French, and Americans than between these and the inhabitants of Spain and Portugal."[29] In fact, "The Chinese are very much our superiors in *true* civilization—in that which frees the majority of men from the brutality and ignorance which, among many European nations, place the lowest classes of society on a level with the most savage beasts."[30] Economically also, he anticipates in a more general sense Robert Fortune's remark about misery and want quoted above. In addition to Davis's statements already cited dealing with the level of prosperity, he mentions that as of the 1840s potatoes were still not widely grown even in Kwangtung, though they are "common" in Macao,[31] and had of course been introduced to China, via the Spanish base in the Philippines, in the sixteenth century. Like the delayed spread of kaoliang in the north after its original introduction from central Asia in the late sixteenth century, this may suggest that overpopulation or economic distress were still not pinching hard enough in these areas to make "inferior" or culturally devalued food crops acceptable. Another straw in the wind is Davis's observation that "the middling and poorer classes are amply accommodated with taverns and eating houses, where for a very small sum a hot breakfast or dinner can be obtained in a moment."[32] He joins the chorus of wonder over China's multitudinous inland water routes, traffic, and stone-lined Grand Canal, and points out that in many of the lesser towns "by far the most considerable buildings were the commercial halls belonging to the associated merchants and dealers."[33] Finally, mirabile dictu, "Europeans resident in China have generally found that their property has been as secure from violent invasion as it would be in any other country of the world.... The efficiency of the police has proved ... that the government was not only willing but able to do ... summary justice."[34] Did Davis have access to a time machine and arrange to transport himself into the era of the People's Republic?

The Abbé Huc included in his widely read travel account, *The Chinese Empire,* covering a journey from Tibet down the Yangtze and over the Meiling Pass to Canton in 1850–51, the first important foreign description of Wuhan, some ten years before Hankow became a treaty port.

> We took more than an hour to traverse the long streets of Han-yang ... [Wuchang is also] an immense town, a vast city, with multitides of enormous junks and a prodigious mass of shipping in the anchorage, one of the chief commercial places in the Empire.... [There is finally] another immense town called Han-keou ... at a confluence of a river that throws itself into the Yang-tse-kiang almost under the walls of the capital. These three towns, standing in a triangle in sight of one another, and only separated by the river, form a kind of heart from which the prodigious commercial activity of China circulates to all parts of the Empire. They are calculated together to contain nearly eight millions of inhabitants, and they are so closely connected by the perpetual coming and going of a multitude of vessels that they may almost be said to form one.[35]

This is not a picture which suggests an obvious place for the kind of innovation which the foreigners attempted to produce. Huc writes of Chinese trade with the West as follows:

> This commerce is doubtless of considerable importance to England and the United States, but its influence is very little felt in this vast Chinese Empire and this immense population of traders. The trade with foreigners might cease suddenly and completely without caus-ing any sensation in the interior provinces. The great Chinese mer-chants in the ports open to Europeans would doubtless feel it; but it is probable that the Chinese nation would not experience the least inconvenience.[36]

He goes on to say:

European productions will never have a very extensive market in China. . . . As foreign commerce cannot offer them any article of primary necessity [i.e., which they do not already produce themselves] nor even of any real utility, they will interest themselves very little in its extension, and they would see it stopped altogether not only without uneasiness but with a certain feeling of satisfaction. . . . China is a country so vast, so rich, so varied that its internal trade alone would suffice abundantly to occupy that part of the nation which can be devoted to mercantile operations. There are in all the great towns important commercial establishments into which, as reservoirs, the merchandise of all the provinces discharges. There is a constant bustle going on about them, a feverish activity that would scarcely be seen in the most important cities of Europe.

The immense population of China, the richness of its soil, the variety of its product, the vast extent of its territory, and the facility of communication by land and water, the activity of its inhabitants, all unite to render this nation the most commercial in the world. . . . The stranger is struck by the prodigious bustle and movement going on everywhere under the stimulus of the thirst of gain. . . . From north to south, from east to west, the whole country is like a perfect fair. . . . And yet when one has not penetrated to the centre of the Empire and seen the great towns Han-yang, Ou-tchang-fou, and Han-keou, facing one another, it is impossible to form an adequate idea of the amount of internal trade.[37]

What did the introduction of the treaty port system add to this? Huc's concluding remarks, about Hankow, make one wonder:

Han-keou especially, the Mouth of Commercial Marts, must be visited, for it is one great shop. . . . In all parts of the city you meet with a concourse of passengers, often pressed so compactly together that you have the greatest difficulty to make your way through them. . . . The shops are crowded with buyers and sellers. The factories also contain a considerable number of workmen and artisans. . . . The great port of Han-keou is literally a forest of masts, and it is quite astonishing to see vessels of such a size and in such numbers in the very middle of China. . . . Han-keou is in some measure the general mart for the eighteen provinces. . . . Perhaps the world could not show a town more favorably situated and possessing a greater number of natural advantages.[38]

The perspective of these observers was of course not ours. Theirs was the Europe of Charles Dickens and his Coketown, the Chartists, the Great

Hunger in Ireland, David Ricardo, and the early Marx. But many of their statements are simple factual observations, and the China which they show us, unrecognizable though it may be, was real enough. China in the first half of the nineteenth century did indeed compare favorably with Europe, in total agricultural output and per acre yields, in mass welfare levels, and perhaps even in commercial development. Certainly it did not occur to European observers that China was in any way "backward" commercially. Into this immense, prosperous, well-ordered, and commercially thriving country a small group of Westerners attempted to introduce an alien trade under their own management, to invade the domestic market with foreign goods, and to introduce Western commercial and (later) industrial techniques. It is not surprising that their accomplishments fell so far short of their goals. In spatial terms, the Canton delta, the Yangtze delta, the Wuhan area, the string of natural harbors along the southeast coast, the seaward face of the north China plain—all of the sites of the major treaty ports—were, long before 1842, the chief foci of traditional Chinese commerce and would have remained so even if the treaty ports had never existed. The treaty port system fell far short of making the kind of impact on the Chinese economy which the Westerners felt that it should, and therefore must, have done.

It is possible that the Westerners may have been misled to some extent, especially in later periods, by the probably or at least perceivably more even distribution of incomes in China than in Europe and concluded that economic opportunity was constrained in such a way that the different Western model would be attractive. But although there seem likely to have been relatively fewer very rich and the security of wealth was probably less than in Europe, there may also have been until quite late proportionately fewer wretchedly poor. Chinese society was composed overwhelmingly of small peasant proprietors, tenants, landless laborers, and small artisans, a number of petty but only a few large merchants, and a very small and fluid body of officials. There was little basis or opportunity for the kind of enrichment or the skewed income distribution characteristic of the modern West. Miserable poverty there doubtless was in China at every period, as in all societies, but the proportion of the Chinese population living on the brink of survival was probably low by comparison with Europe until the later part of the nineteenth century. Although there remains controversy among economic historians about the European experience, median economic welfare in Europe probably declined as a concomitant of the early stages of the industrial revolution and through most of the first half or more of the nineteenth century while at the same time the number of the newly rich was rapidly rising. Robert Fortune's analogy of the hive of bees fits the Chinese case admirably, as a description not only of a tightly organized system of production but of an essentially uniform, cooperatively based society which was fully self-sufficient and left few gaps which outsiders might fill.

For the period before 1842, there are also a number of foreign accounts, but most of them are based on hearsay or on second- and third-hand materials derived from the much earlier Jesuit observations.[39] They refer, despite the dates of publication of some of them, mainly to conditions well before 1800 or even 1750, so that they can be used only with cautious reserve in reaching conclusions about the condition of China in the nineteenth century. The large number of foreign accounts of conditions at Canton before 1842 and at the treaty ports after that date must also be discounted as giving a picture of a small and unrepresentative part of the economy and country as a whole, quite apart from other aspects of foreign myopia.

But there were of course two major foreign penetrations of the eastern sector of the country in the decades immediately preceding the establishment of the treaty system; detailed first-hand accounts are available from each: the missions of Macartney in 1796 and of Amherst in 1816. Both went northward by sea to Taku and Tientsin en route to Peking, but returned to Canton by inland routes and made detailed observations of what they saw along the way. Both followed the Grand Canal south to Yangchow, but the Amherst party was sent via the Yangtze to Poyang Lake and thence up the Kan River to the Meiling Pass, while Macartney was routed via Hangchow. Between them they covered a large swath through the most populous parts of the empire and were able to compare north and central China with what they knew from Canton. George Staunton, who as a boy of twelve had traveled with the Macartney mission, was also a member of the Amherst party as an interpreter and Old China Hand; his is the most complete first-hand account of both expeditions. The descriptions of Tientsin, as the chief urban and commercial center of the north, are essentially the same in both journals, and they agree also in the general picture which they convey of conditions along their routes as a whole: one of prosperity, order, agricultural productivity, very extensive internal trade flows, numerous large cities, and an immense population.

After noting the dense traffic on the Hai Ho and the great mounds of salt lining its banks which he had remarked twenty years earlier and which subsequent observers were also to comment on, Staunton describes the Amherst mission's approach and entry into Tientsin as follows: "The immense crowds of people which filled the space immediately behind the soldiers [drawn up along the banks of the Hai Ho] and formed an unbroken mass of population for a space of at least two or three miles was a sight which could hardly be equalled in any other part of the world. . . . The most perfect silence and tranquility seemed to prevail; nothing but contentment and good humour."[40] This suggests not only a large urban population, but a degree of order, discipline, and dignity totally at variance with our picture of what China was like in these respects by the twentieth century. As the Amherst party proceeded "through several streets of suburbs" and into the city itself "for about a mile" to the place of audience, "our route was kept perfectly clear and there was not the least tumult or molestation whatever."[41] The breakdown of administration and demoralization of the society which we tend automatically to associate with early twentieth-century China seem not yet to have become apparent. Here too one suspects that we have overprojected.

Both embassies were struck by the huge fleets of grain junks from Kiangnan which they repeatedly encountered on the Grand Canal and on the Pei Ho (between Tientsin and Peking). On many days they passed several such fleets, and they noted with admiration the stone facing, quays, and sluices at close intervals all along the Grand Canal, to regulate the level of the water and to adjust to changes in elevation. One stone-faced spillway was in particular remarked on between Tientsin and Peking "through which we were told there was a direct communication with the sea, then about a hundred lee distant, which admitted of the waters being let off when the river overflows."[42] It would seem that the problems of the Pei Ho, later so devastating, were under better control in 1816 than the foreigners were ever able to accomplish with all their efforts up to 1936.[43]

Four days' travel by boat south of Tientsin on September 11, 1816, as the Amherst party nursed their rage over the "insolent" rebuff they had received at Peking, Staunton is impelled nevertheless to write:

It is certainly remarkable that in so populous a country there should be so little appearance of mendicity; and whatever may be said of the character and system of the government in other respects this must be allowed to be a favorable symptom of the actual state of the country. It must also I think be admitted that in a country so generally cultivated, and in which the population is so considerable and wears the appearance of contentment, and of the enjoyment of a sufficiency of the necessaries of life, the government cannot be, practically, a very bad one; either the force of the laws, or of custom and public opinion, must be in effect adequate to secure to the people the fruits of their industry.[44]

And yet Staunton confesses that his experience in Peking had disposed him to see everything in the worst possible light, and that the treatment received had been "sufficient to make everyone in this party look on the surrounding objects with a jaundiced eye."[45] What he still records about the absence of beggars, the level of prosperity and order, and the virtues of the official-social system makes strange reading, as do Robert Fortune's observations a quarter of a century later, to almost any student of modern China; again one has to read it twice to make sure one has it right.

As the abortive embassy made its way southward, Staunton noted that the general level of prosperity seemed to increase in the towns and in the countryside. He comments particularly on the "vast inland commerce," confirms the Chinese estimates he has heard of a total of twenty thousand grain junks plying the Grand Canal, and remarks on the "endless series of thriving and populous towns."[46] "The lower orders of Chinese seem to me more neat and cleanly than any Europeans of the same class. They are not only not usually seen in rags, but even torn, soiled, or threadbare clothing is uncommon among them."[47] Pearl Buck's China was never like this! Once across the Yellow River, "everything improved [still more] in appearance . . . all the military stations are neatly whitewashed and painted and kept in perfect repair and instead of mud cabins we see the houses of peasants mostly built in a neat manner with blue brick. The joss houses are also handsome and numerous."[48]

It is altogether a picture of China which we in the West, with our short historical memories, have forgotten, even though it was confirmed as indicated by almost all foreign accounts into the second half of the nineteenth century, apart from those blinded by religious prejudice, angered by commercial or political setbacks, or based only on what could be seen in the treaty ports. Nor was this merely a little remote corner of the world which the West could easily overwhelm. The whole of Europe (including European Russia) numbered some 266 millions in 1850,[49] while China's population in that year has been variously estimated between 400 and 450 millions.[50] Even by 1950, the European total remained smaller than for China despite the increases resulting from industrialization. The West had certainly become technologically superior, but this was far from being enough to make a substantial impact on a Chinese economy whose mass was so large and whose existing techniques of production, management, and trade were self-sufficiently adequate to maintain welfare to at least bearable levels while at the same time feeding the conviction that China need not turn to Western models in order to survive.

It is necessary to correct recently inherited perspectives in order to see more clearly the China which Westerners attempted to transform, and also to look more closely at the Western effort, to sort out claims from reality, ambitions from accomplishments. That is attempted in the following chapter.

BOMBAY ABOUT 1790. Western sea power and one of its early beachheads; note fortifications and the eighteenth-century European buildings. *(From an engraving published in London in 1794)*

CALCUTTA ABOUT 1790. View over the Hooghly from near Fort William; note the mass of shipping in left background, and the original versions of the colonial treaty port architectural style. (*From an engraving published in London in 1794*)

BOMBAY STREET SCENE, 1964. A typically hybrid colonial port city with English still as its common language. (*Photograph by author*)

a

b

SINGAPORE (*a*) ABOUT 1850 AND (*b*) FROM THE AIR IN 1968. A Western-style city from the outset. (*From D. and J. Moore,* The First 150 Years of Singapore, *Singapore, 1969. Painting courtesy of the Singapore National Museum and 1968 photograph courtesy of the Singapore Ministry of Culture*)

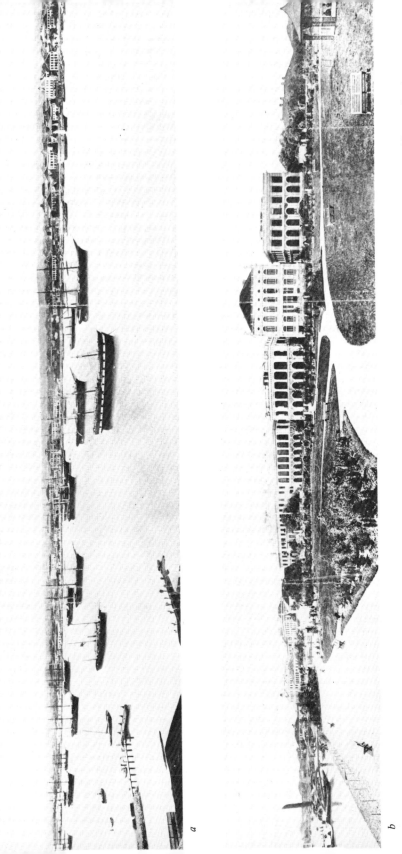

SHANGHAI IN 1876. (a) Toward the last days of sail as seen from P'u T'ung across the Huangp'u (Whangpoo); the treaty port architectural style, on an originally Anglo-Indian model, dominates the cityscape. (b) Foreground, the famous park on the Bund in its early days, from which later on Chinese and dogs were excluded. (From Ch. B. Maybon and Jean Fredet, Histoire de la Concession Francaise de Changhai, Paris, 1929, foldout)

a

b

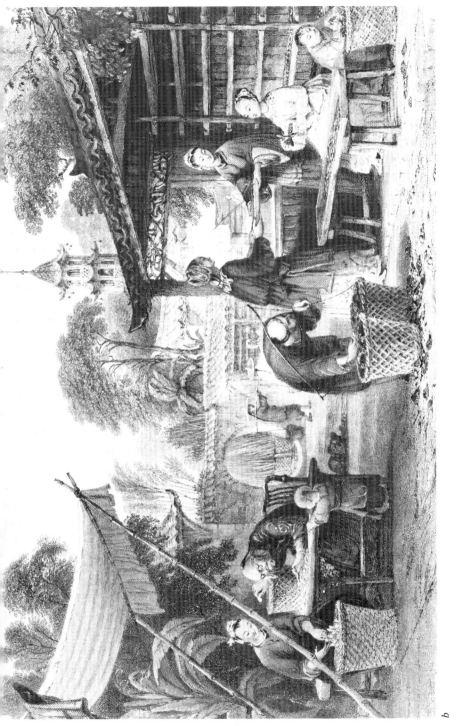

(a) House of Consequa, a Co-Hong Merchant and (b) Feeding Silkworms and Sorting the Cocoons. Engravings of T. Allom, a Western artist, between 1820 and 1835, wrongly showing Chinese women wearing Western dress but otherwise giving a reasonable picture of opulence and productivity in Canton. (*From original engravings courtesy of author*)

b

THE TREATY PORT STYLE AT ITS ZENITH, 1905. (*a*) Offices of a foreign firm in Canton, originally Russell and Co. (American) and (*b*) the Hankow Club. Anglo-Indian origins are still strongly apparent. (*From A. Wright,* Twentieth Century Impressions, *London, 1908, pp. 792, 696*)

Chapter 10

Chinese Merchants Versus the Foreigners

That magnificent market anxiously awaits the electric stimulus of foreign enterprise. . . . The calling of the Pioneer of Commerce is a calling higher than that of most men. For is it not a high aim and a noble ambition, the endeavour to inaugurate the advent of civilization by means of commerce, conferring . . . a benefit alike upon producers and consumers, British and Chinese? . . . it is not only their duty but their high privilege to see that the attempt to open up China shall not fail. The British merchant must be the conquering and irresistible vanguard of the great Army of Progress.[1]

[The opening of China] means the opening of the eyes of the Chinese people, and the younger generation will emerge from the chrysallis of superstition, ignorance, and oppression to bask in the sun of Western enlightenment.[2]

Foreign ambitions and expectations in China were indeed sweeping. To what extent were they realized? Certainly there was change taking place during the century after 1842. How much of it represented new departures, and how much of that can be ascribed to the impact of the treaty ports? Finally, how much of a role were foreigners able to play, either as agents of change or as participants in the evolving Chinese scene? To what degree did they remain outsiders?

One can be certain that the treaty port system produced a substantial net increase in foreign trade, both relatively and absolutely, and consequently some increased stimulus of commercial production for export. This was true even in long-established industries such as silk and tea, which the foreigners merely tapped but for which they created expanded overseas markets. There was a proportionately greater increase in later years in the production and export of commodities such as tung oil, eggs, bristles, wool, hides, peanuts, and straw braid. Given the scale of the Chinese economy, it must however be acknowledged that none of these increases, even if taken together, represented a large share of the whole and could not be said to be either new departures or sectors whose growth significantly changed the nature or operation of the economy. Foreign trade and production to serve it were minor and marginal adjuncts, in effect diverting into external channels slightly increased supplies of goods which had previously been circulated more domestically.

The major treaty ports did grow rapidly, especially after the beginnings of industrialization following 1895, and they did generate substantial new economic opportunity even though it was primarily confined to their own immediate urban areas. The spread of steamship lines, the beginnings of a railway system in some areas, and the growth of telecommunications were also accompanied by a more concentrated national commercial structure centered on the major treaty ports as the chief termini of these networks. A few dominant urban commercial nuclei began to emerge as transport improved and long-distance marketing became more important. This was the same process which took place under similar conditions in Europe and America with the growing dominance of one or a few metropolitan commercial centers in each country, especially for external trade, and the progressive relative decline of lesser centers (Bristol, Hull, Charleston, Bordeaux).

In China three levels of the concentration of urban functions began to appear. Shanghai and Hong Kong were central places and strongly dominant ports for foreign trade for the country as a whole, analogous to London, New York, Buenos Aires, Calcutta, or Bombay. At the second level, Tientsin, Hankow, and Canton played the same kind of role for north, central, and south China respectively. Dairen's position in Manchuria was similar, but Manchuria and its economy after 1905 were in effect separate from China.[3] The third level, smaller regional or provincial service centers, was represented by places such as Changsha, Chungking, or Foochow, all of them also part of the treaty port system. It was of course an overlapping hierarchy in which Shanghai and Hong Kong, like New York and London, included aspects of the whole country in their commercial hinterlands as Hankow, for example, included much of central China. The growth of commercial nodes at these three levels was a symptom of increasing commercialization and exchange beyond traditional levels, and one which in some respects by-passed or superseded traditional centers and lower-order systems.

Study of the yearly Customs *Returns of Trade* through the period 1864–1936 shows something of the nature of this hierarchy, at least for the trade which was recorded. Shanghai, Hong Kong, Tientsin, Canton, and Hankow increasingly exchanged predominantly with one another in the goods destined for export and in the distribution of foreign imports. Canton dealt in both respects overwhelmingly with Hong Kong to such an extent that, as suggested above, they were functionally almost a single city. For each of the four mainland ports, the other three were consistently the major trade partners by a large margin; Shanghai supplied Tientsin and Hankow with the great bulk of their imports of foreign origin, as Hong Kong supplied Canton. However, recorded reexports from each port accounted in every year for only a very small fraction of the value of the whole trade of the port. This suggests that much, perhaps most, of the actual reexports were not recorded, principally because they moved by Chinese carriers from the original port of entry, where they ceased on arrival to be foreign property and were fed into the domestic distribution system, most of which was beyond the purview or measurement of the Customs service. The figures also suggest, however, that the total amount of reexports was probably not very great and that each port was the dominant consumer of its own imports. The treaty port system was to a large extent an enclave economy, even though agricultural goods were drawn from parts of the rural hinterland for processing, consumption, and export. The trade in which they dealt, the beginnings of a new pattern of concentration, involved only the smallest fraction of or adjunct to the Chinese economy as a whole.

The four chief ports plus Hong Kong dominated the urban hierarchy in other respects as well, each serving as the cultural as well as industrial and foreign trade node for its quarter of the country—for the so-called modern sector, which remained a very small part of the whole. Such a role is apparent however in the concentration in the four major ports of both Chinese- and English-language newspapers, and in the function of each of these cities as an intellectual and (periodically after 1900) as a revolutionary center. Canton spoke for "modern" south China (aided in this case no doubt by the remoteness of Peking), Shanghai for the Yangtze valley, and so on. The even more marked concentration in these four ports of traditional and modern schools, technical colleges, and universities makes the same point. Outside of Manchuria, these four were also the first to develop a structure of both light and heavy industry, beginning with arsenals and shipyards, but going on into textiles, milling, and other consumer goods. Skinner's study referred to previously shows the early effects of rising commercialization and concentration on those rural marketing systems for which he has data and which were near enough to major centers to be acted on by the growing centripetal developments.

Expanded credit facilities for external trade, lower interest rates in the treaty ports where capital was relatively secure, the development of collection networks for export goods over much of the country by foreigners and their Chinese agents, and the emergence for the first time of a system of shipment of goods under single ownership from interior provinces through the hierarchy of treaty ports to Shanghai or Hong Kong for export, all encouraged economic growth and helped to account for the process of concentration. Although it involved only those few goods destined for export and hence only the smallest sector of the Chinese economy, this contrasted especially with the traditional series of middlemen and other agents who had earlier passed goods along from one part of the country to another.

By the end of the nineteenth century a few foreign banks dominated trade credit for the internal movement of most goods destined for export, or at least for those which are readily discernible through the files of the Customs Service and the records of foreign companies, possibly not a majority. Notes issued by foreign banks in the treaty ports circulated widely as an important element in the currency system. The Shansi banks had largely lost their trading role by the end of the nineteenth century and had been replaced in the financing of even internal trade by the rise of both foreign and Chinese banks. Other Chinese "native" or traditional banks, engaged to a greater extent in local commercial financing, survived and remained vigorous. Foreign banks appear to have shared the financing of trade with them in an increasingly nation-wide and interlocking system of credit which extended from Hong Kong and Shanghai through native banks in the interior to local dealers and collectors. Periodic financial crises in the treaty ports were related to failures of native banks in the provinces; defaulting by native banks or their calling in of loans weakened or contributed to the bankruptcy of foreign banks or firms; foreign financial failures reverberated similarly among Chinese firms and native banks involved in the trade in export goods.[4] Foreign and Chinese groups were partners in this trade, but the evidence from Customs records and other foreign sources suggesting a dominant foreign role may be misleading.

In fact, the period of supposed foreign dominance saw a vigorous expansion of the native banks which exceeded the growth of the new modern Chinese banks, as the native banks became more and more involved in the financing of internal commodity flows, either as part of the general increase in commercialization, or as the feeder system for exports and the distribution of imports. The Shansi banks shifted their earlier concentration on trade and interrregional remittances to a new near-client role as financers of the central and provincial governments. Their place was taken by a great expansion of *ch'ien-chuang* (literally, money shops), the institutions primarily referred to under the heading of "native banks." Their network extended to encompass the entire trading system, including foreign trade, and they often served as brokers between Western and Chinese financial circles, paralleling the role of the compradores but also frequently in direct association with them. They served as agents for funds deposited with them, paying relatively high interest and loaning out their funds at even higher rates. Foreign merchants in Shanghai, perennially seeking opportunities for profit which they largely failed to find directly in trade, speculated in the Chinese money market through the *ch'ien-chuang* and in their notes (*chuang-p'iao*), which were as widely used in trade as the notes issued by foreign banks and were accepted by them as legal tender. Foreign banks had to keep an account with at least one *ch'ien-chuang* which belonged to a guild in order to have access to the clearing house process and to have a means of cashing drafts, since the native bankers' guild controlled all these things, including currency exchange.[5]

The *ch'ien-chuang* dominated foreign commerce even in the treaty ports, where foreigners merely stood on the fringes and bought or sold on behalf of Chinese dealers. They provided a safe and relatively stable source of credit and facilitated the flow of capital between urban and rural areas by regulating exchange rates, supplying capital to urban buyers of rural goods, lending money to rural money shops who provided credit for villagers, and issuing letters of credit for funds in transit. The continued fluctuation of exchange rates, regional variations in currency and measures, and the confusions of bimetallism complicated the commercial scene and gave the *ch'ien-chuang* an indispensable role which the foreigners could not attempt to displace, as well as multiple opportunities for speculative profit. The article by S. M. Jones previously cited, which presents and summarizes much of this material, concludes that "The power of compradores and of native banking guilds over the relations between native and foreign banks belies the popular notion that foreign banks manipulated and controlled native money markets."[6]

The *ch'ien-chuang* were perhaps typical of many traditional institutions and groups which were strengthened by contact with new foreign enterprise rather than being destroyed by it. They recognized new opportunities for profit, and expanded on that basis. But the foreigners needed them as much as they depended for their growth on the foreign traders. The *ch'ien-chuang* provided essential avenues into the Chinese trading world, as did the compradores, and served as links between two basically different and separate systems. The personal and kin networks through which the *ch'ien-chuang* operated and which characterized the Chinese commercial system as a whole were impenetrable to Westerners.

Other evidence too suggests that in fact the great bulk of commerce, including much if not most of the increase attributable to foreign enterprise in widening the market, remained in the hands of Chinese merchants. Customs *Reports on Trade* at the treaty ports, the series of British, American, and French consular trade reports, and comments by a great variety of individual foreign observers all voice this complaint repeatedly from the beginnings of the treaty port system in the 1840s, again after the Treaties of Tientsin when the new terms failed to produce the hoped-for results, through the aftermath of the Treaty of Shiminoseki in 1895, and into the 1920s and 1930s.

To cite only a few convenient examples, the compradores and Cantonese and Ningpo agents of foreign traders at Hankow "speedily managed to monopolize the major portions of the business dealings of the port . . . and tend more and more to reduce the European mercantile community to the position of a mere agency for carrying on the transactions conducted on native account."[7] At Tientsin, "The returns made by the Consuls and Customs officers point out that it [the trade in foreign goods] is fast merging into the hands of the native merchants, who, having learnt to avail themselves of every facility (such as steamers, etc.) at the disposal of the foreigners, are fast ousting them from a participation in the profits to be made in China."[8] "That there is an immense trade at Canton there can be no question, but it is in the hands of the Chinese."[9] "It appears that the more the country is opened up, the more trade will fall into the hands of Native dealers coming from the old treaty ports."[10] "The superior economy of the natives is fast ousting foreigners."[11] "The import trade was becoming more and more the monopoly of the native dealer, while the Chinese are nothing if not conservative in the matter of foreign innovations. . . . The economic self-sufficiency of the Chinese was perhaps the most formidable barrier which we had as yet encountered in our career of industrial and commercial expansion . . . It was one thing to cease to import cotton goods from them; it was quite another to reverse the process as we were doing with considerable success in India."[12]

Traditional trade guilds not only persisted but expanded in numbers, even in the treaty ports themselves, alongside new Chinese commercial organizations. Mark Elvin has graphed the growth in the number of known and registered guilds in Shanghai in a pattern which quadrupled from 1842 to 1911.[13] New guilds continued to be formed after 1911, although the same sources are no longer available to indicate their numbers. To some extent the numerous Chinese chambers of commerce, which mushroomed especially after that time, paralleled as well as replaced the guilds and may therefore have been responsible for a slowing in the rate of new guild formation, but they were in turn based on the guilds and were often composed of specific guild representatives. Partly this expansion reflected the general increase in commercialization of the economy and concentration of trade in the treaty ports, but guilds and chambers of commerce arose also in a specific effort to counter Western efforts to infiltrate the market and to keep Chinese merchants in control. Traditional-style guilds did not of course have it all their own way,[14] but it was still primarily Chinese jostling Chinese for control of the growing commercial sector.

How in detail this control was exercised is hard to observe, secrecy and discretion being part of the guild system, but the results are clear. One is here in the position of the astronomer who guesses at the existence of a planet from observing its effects on the behavior of other bodies—in this case, the continued foreign complaints about the Chinese "stranglehold" on trade and their periodic unsuccessful confrontations with the guilds. One case in particular was widely reported in the *North China Herald* in 1879–80, having to do with the activities of the Swatow opium guild in closing out foreign competitors who then attempted to sue, formally charging a "conspiracy against foreign trade."[15] The evidence presented (despite the great difficulty of getting Chinese witnesses to testify; the few who did were apparently badly frightened and would give only evasive replies to questions) included actual letters produced by T. W. Duff (the principal plaintiff) and his partner clearly demonstrating the existence of a detailed and efficient network of collusion on the Chinese side, probably including even the Shanghai *tao-tai,* as suggested by the latter's delaying tactics in the hearing of the case as well as by his final judgment dismissing the charges, which had the effect of keeping the domestic sale and distribution of imported opium entirely in Chinese hands. Duff's assertions that this violated the treaties and the Chefoo Convention, and the *North China Herald*'s lead editorial of September 23, 1879, comparing the situation with the conditions of foreign trade under the Co-hong, were perfectly valid. But the continued operational weakness of the foreigners' position despite their apparent strength diplomatically, militarily, or legally is clear. It was a curious example of foreign blindness that the same issue of the *North China Herald* carried an article on the trial trip of the Ewo steamer *Kung-wo* on the Yangtze, which read in part as follows:

> The removal of restrictions upon trade from the banks of the mighty river inland, along its innumerable feeding creeks, united by a network of similar waterways, of which no man knoweth the limit, if trade were as it should be, untrammelled and open, there would be room enough for all who could launch ships on its mighty bosom without fear of even the most indirect interference of competition.[16]

What the foreigners objected to as "secrecy" and "conspiracy" was part of the tightly knit web of group relationships and decentralized, guild-based organization which was a distinctive aspect of the Chinese commercial system, in keeping with the traditional sociocultural system as a whole. It was very different from the modern Western experience, but this did not mean that it was not functionally effective. In the case of the Swatow Opium Guild, it was apparently simple enough for the variety of Chinese firms involved, at several levels, to agree in refusing dealings with foreign firms for the disposal of foreign-owned opium. The Swatow Guild was also able to get control of the likin collection in a large area of the lower Yangtze valley and in effect to refuse to accept likin payments from any but their own members.[17] Duff maintained in the court case that Chinese guilds controlled the sale of all goods imported by foreigners and that "there is something working, a system, a kind of underground current, beneath each foreign hong that is astonishing. Not a single one of us can trade independently and the treaty is no good at all so long as this underground system exists."[18]

Judging from continued foreign cries into the 1930s, the same underground system was never dislodged, although it would be more accurate to call it the foundation, in comparison to which the foreign efforts were a superficial and evanescent bit of marginalia. The British consul at Shanghai, Arthur Davenport, the principal foreign member of the special session of the Mixed Court which heard the Swatow Opium Guild case, neatly summarized what may have been an important reason for the foreign failure in China: "Our worst enemies in China are not the officials, nor are they that shadowy body that goes by the name of the literati. They are our own compradores and ex-compradores."[19] Some of them no doubt were compradores who used their connections and experience with foreign firms to good advantage in squeezing the foreigners out. But probably even larger numbers were traditional Chinese merchants who continued to manage their own highly developed system and kept it largely impervious to Western invasion, except as they chose, while remaining in control, to trade with foreign firms, making use of steam shipment for their goods, or buy and sell kerosene or machine-made yarn. Unfortunately for the latter-day investigator, it seems largely impervious also to any search for specific data, at least of the sort which Duff sought, except on an inadequate and haphazard basis. Conspiracy, or at least secrecy, was important to success, and we must still largely guess at the "conspiratorial" outlines of what the foreigners referred to as the vast, shadowy world of the Chinese merchant.

The two systems, Western and Chinese, though competing in the same market at least within the treaty ports and their immediate environs, remained largely separate. Chinese merchants in the treaty ports were also in many cases divided into separate groups: those who traded in the domestic market, and those who traded overseas, especially to Southeast Asia, where they were often dependent on overseas kin connections as well as on commercial organizations focused exclusively on foreign trade. There was little or no overlap in functions between the two groups; the overseas traders appear to have had few connections with the domestic market except through their immediate agents in the ports—a position close to that of the foreigners. To some extent this was also an urban-rural split. The treaty ports represented a new and exclusively urban phenomenon following a Western model, while the rest of China remained not only predominantly rural but characterized by cities, where they had developed, which were of a fundamentally different sort and which also had a far closer symbiotic relationship with their rural hinterlands.

In addition, none of the treaty ports ever had any administrative role (as opposed to political influence or gunboat diplomacy) outside their own concession areas, even in the legally separate but functionally integrated conurbation at each port outside the concession lines. The jurisdiction of extraterritoriality extended to foreigners all over the country, but this was hardly responsibility for the administration of territory. This further distinguished them from the colonial ports in the rest of Asia as well as from traditional Chinese cities, helps to explain their separateness from the Chinese system as a whole, and accounts in part for the failure of their model to spread. This is not to say that there was no spillover at all. In addition to the spread of steamship lines and the treaty port-centered trade they carried (with its wider economic implications), at shorter range the commercial sale of agricultural goods was greater within a twenty- or thirty-mile radius of each treaty port than elsewhere in the country, and in some cases such as the Yangtze delta hinterland of Shanghai there was a degree of satellite urban development with an increased commercial and light-industrial base (Wusih, Soochow, Huchow) related to Shanghai's proximity. But such developments were a result more of simple urbanization than of the particular model of urban growth which the treaty ports represented, and indeed were direct continuations of trends already apparent in traditional urban and demographic growth long before the founding of the treaty ports.

Industrial development in the immediate hinterlands of some of the treaty ports, such as silk reeling and silk and cotton spinning in Wusih or Soochow, and coal mining and associated metal industries in T'angshan, were perhaps more specifically connected with the new kinds of economic growth centered in Shanghai and Tientsin, respectively; but extensions of this sort were largely lacking in the hinterlands of Canton, Wuhan, and the lesser treaty ports. Part of the explanation is presumably that most of the capital earned in treaty port trade, both foreign and Chinese, sought investment outlets in the treaty ports themselves, in commercial speculation or landowning, rather than in industrial development elsewhere. In any case, capital for industrial investment selected locations which offered maximum advantage. These were predominantly in the treaty ports. Only in special cases, such as the Kaip'ing mines or the silk and cotton areas around T'ai Lake, did they happen to coincide with the vicinity of the treaty ports.

The separateness of the two systems, traditional Chinese and modernizing, was also reflected in the development of banking, as already suggested. Here most of the data refer to the treaty ports, where one might perhaps expect the modern sector to be dominant. In fact it seems reasonably clear that even in the treaty ports native Chinese banks of the traditional type did at least as much or more financing of domestic trade than was done by both foreign and modern Chinese banks.[20] Chinese merchants preferred to do business with the native banks, which were more liberal with unsecured loans and in general terms part of the same traditional system to which the bulk of the Chinese merchants belonged. There the interlocking network of personal and group associations was more important than Western notions of contract and liability. The native banks were also active, however, in speculative buying and selling of exchange on Hong Kong. Like the traditional merchant firms, they were quick to take advantage of new commercial opportunities created by foreigners, giving little ground to the intrusion of the modern system generated by Westerners. The native and the modern-style banks did, it is true, draw capital from some of the same sources, and there was some interlocking financing between them which involved the foreign banks as well. But such connections provided a necessary link between the treaty port sector of largely foreign trade and the far larger and mainly separate system of domestic production and exchange.

On the other hand, the modern Chinese banks which grew up especially after 1911 and were overwhelmingly concentrated in the treaty ports—an apparently promising Chinese response to Western pressures and models for modernization—were not importantly involved with the financing of either trade or manufacturing, apart from their late and brief involvement after 1928 with the textile industry. Private individuals and public institutions, not commercial or industrial firms, were their leading depositors, and they concentrated on government financing through loans and bond issues. These carried a high rate of interest and had the further attraction of greater security than commercial loans. The relatively high interest rate paid to depositors also contributed to rates charged to borrowers which were higher than most commercial enterprises found attractive.[21] This emphasis on government financing even on the part of the modern Chinese banks may suggest the persistence of merchant-bureaucracy ties. The foreign banks continued to dominate the financing of foreign trade, while Chinese native banks, with their wide geographical dispersal and network of connections throughout the traditional system, remained dominant in domestic commerce.[22] In brief, modernization and innovation in the treaty ports were mainly confined there, in banking as in other respects, as part of an alien system which remained in its essence apart from the country as a whole, where the traditional system, largely inviolate, continued its vigorous survival and indeed invaded even the treaty ports with success.

The backwash and multiplier effects of simple economic growth, let alone innovation, in the treaty ports were also limited by the degree of separateness of the two systems. The ports were economically, as they were legally, extraneous and tiny outposts of a system which remained foreign to China and made only limited material impact on it. The foreign impact was concentrated in external trade: in financing the movement (but not the production) of goods for export and in the sale to Chinese entrepreneurs of a few originally foreign goods—yarn, kerosene, and later, limited amounts of machinery. None of this grand total ever involved more than a small fraction of the Chinese economy, whose nature was not significantly altered, let alone transformed in keeping with the treaty port model. Even the beginnings of Western-style industrialization in the treaty ports did not spread significantly beyond them. Only the Western initiatives in steam shipping and railway building did spread, but despite the promise of this genuine innovation its impact remained limited both spatially and institutionally.

This was not merely because a large part of foreign profits were drawn off to the metropolitan countries or reinvested in the treaty ports themselves rather than in the rest of China, but resulted from the success of the traditional Chinese system in remaining master in its own house. The spatial pattern of innovation waves elsewhere in the world suggests that even in relatively small and highly developed countries such as Sweden the chain of innovation which runs between urban areas may have little or no connection with the temporally, spatially, and substantively different diffusion of separate innovation between rural areas. This appears to be the case whether the source of innovation is internal or external.[23] In semicolonial China[24] there was similarly only limited connection between the urban centers and the channels of Western-directed innovation and the far larger rural mass of the Middle Kingdom; the two might almost have been on different continents.

The "particularism" and "functional diffusiveness" of the traditional merchant, in Parsonian terms,[25] obstacles to modern business, were strong assets in his successful effort to exclude foreign competition. In this society where long-established family and personal connections took the place of legal contracts, no outsider (a status which carried greater handicaps even in a semicolonial China than anywhere else in the world) could hope to win a viable place beyond the artificial realm of the treaty ports. The role of law was traditionally minimized, in favor of moral virtue and of group norms and sanctions as controls on behavior; group (kin, occupational) networks largely replaced law for settlement of disputes, enforcement of obligations, and regulation of activities. Such a system left foreigners at an obvious disadvantage, nor was there a place for the protection offered by a law which was "no respecter of persons." In India, where antilegal attitudes were not as strong but where in any case traditional values and mechanisms were seen as decaying in disorder, Western ideas about the importance of law were picked up enthusiastically. Indeed many Indians, notably Bengalis, found the uses of British-style law more attractive, even fascinating, and more rewarding than most Westerners. This certainly eased and stimulated the adoption of Western commercial techniques, and of other Western values and institutions, as well as the invasion of Western entrepreneurs. In China, Westerners could not, almost by definition, become participants, even or especially as traders. And from the Chinese point of view, which in this matter was what counted, Western partners or techniques offered them no improvement on an indigenous commercial system which worked well and which, like other traditional institutions, persisted largely unaltered by Western efforts to infiltrate or "modernize."

Many observers have seen the absence in China of those qualities which they associate with commercial and industrial success in the West— "universalism" and "functional specificity" (the labels and circumlocutions vary)—as crippling disadvantages for economic development. Perhaps this was so, although it is arguable even beyond definitions of economic development. But there can be little argument that the traditional system was ideally designed to resist outside manipulation and to protect the Chinese merchant. The familial web enhanced rather than stultified his enterprises, and at the same time ensured that he would not be seriously challenged in his commercial control of this largely self-contained economy, although it may also have limited or even aborted his capacity for large-scale modern economic development.[26]

The Chinese merchant was also slow to make "modern" use of capital or to contribute to the building of an economic infrastructure. Without doubt this was a major roadblock to economic development however defined. But it rested on an individual rationality which was economically sound in the conditions prevailing in China, especially after 1850. Speculation, moneylending, and other parasitic or predatory (as opposed to constructive) uses of capital were both safer and more profitable, as well as faster. Where innovation offered reliable and immediate rewards, the Chinese merchant was quick to adopt it. The best illustration here is probably the almost instant response to the introduction of steamships. Merchants began by traveling on and shipping their goods by these safer and faster ships and not long thereafter ended by owning and managing the largest single shipping fleet in East Asia, the China Merchants' Steam Navigation Company.[27] But most industrial or long-term commercial investment could not begin to match the rate of return, security, and anonymity of traditional speculative and usurious ventures, especially without established and regulated institutions such as modern corporate enterprises or stock markets on a Western scale. The sharply varying prices of many commodities, temporally and spatially, offered strong attractions for speculation to those who possessed even small amounts of capital, and had the further important advantage of permitting the quick and not easily detected movement of funds from one venture to another. This minimized the risks of attracting unwelcome attention to the possession of money. To be a registered shareholder or involved in any "modern" enterprise, including those launched by officials after 1860, gave dangerously exposed identity to one's wealth and was to be avoided.[28]

It would appear that after 1911 this reluctance began to break down, and perhaps for other reasons as well (especially the weakening of Western competition and the rise in demand and profit margins during the first World War, although these abnormal circumstances did not last) industrial investment became more popular among Chinese merchants. Yen Chung-p'ing's study of the cotton industry lists nineteen cotton mills established in Shanghai, Tientsin, and Hankow between 1897 and 1910, of which twelve were founded by officials, three by compradores, and only two by traditional merchants or gentry (the remaining two involved families or individuals whose status is unclear).[29] However, of thirty-two cotton mills established in the same cities between 1916 and 1922, eighteen were founded by merchants (the term is not defined), only six by officials, three by "industrialists," two by gentry, two were owned publicly, and one was owned jointly by an official and two warlords.[30] The principal difficulty about these data is that none of the different status groups are defined. In both periods concerned, there was in fact often a good deal of blurring of distinctions between "merchant," "gentry," "compradore," and "official." If we take the data entirely at face value, they would suggest that the Chinese merchant-capitalist-investor was becoming more willing to risk his money in modern enterprises because many of the earlier objections to such investment were losing their force: profitability and security were attaching proportionately less to traditional uses for capital (land, usury, speculation) and proportionately more to industrial investment.

But again it was Chinese investors moving in on a previously foreign-dominated field, in pursuit of their own economic interest at least as much as because industrial investment was patriotic or "modern," let alone Western-inspired. Indeed it may be argued not only that this might have happened without the presence of the treaty ports at all, but that the semicolonial position of the foreigners and the aggressive role they attempted to play from their urban bases of special privilege may in fact have retarded rather than hastened the Chinese shift toward modernization. Modernization was clearly and exclusively of foreign origin; the special position and imperialist behavior of the foreigners made them resented rather than admired and the innovations which the foreigners attempted to push onto China were accordingly resisted.

When the Chinese entrepreneurs (as opposed to officials) did make up their minds to enter factory-based industry, they seem to have made a very creditable job of it. It was to an important extent their success, not merely Japanese- and Western-owned factories in China, which was by the 1930s impinging on the previously dominant position of the hand weavers in the cotton textile industry, and this in the face of Western and Japanese competition already in the field and with larger and cheaper sources of capital.[31] At first Chinese mills concentrated on the production of coarse cloth, but by 1930 "it is only a question of time until they crowd their competitors of today out of the market in most of the finer counts also."[32] This trend continued up to the outbreak of the war in 1937.[33] By 1934 imports of cotton yarn had also been largely displaced by domestic factory production.[34] The Chinese business man may have been, for a variety of reasons, slower than his Japanese counterpart to join the industrial revolution, but despite the obstacles he still faced in the 1920s and 1930s—domestic disorder, high interest rates, strong foreign competition, and many surviving traditional business practices—he apparently proved able to adjust successfully and to begin squeezing out the foreign devils even in this, their own field, though after 1927 with some help from a new but in many respects traditionalistic Chinese bureaucratic state.

The business parsimony of the traditional Chinese merchant and his reluctance to tie up capital in nonproductive overhead (which also had a dangerously high visibility) gave him an additional advantage over the foreign merchant with his far more expensive establishments and his taste for luxurious display and consumption.[35]   And throughout the semi-colonial period the integrative power of the guilds added to the protection which the web of relationships in traditional China gave to the Chinese merchant. Here the power of combination could be fearsome, especially when it was contested. Boycotts were the common guild weapon, and were of course used long before they became nationalist vehicles. H. B. Morse's little book on the guilds cites several boycotts which quickly brought the foreigners to terms, such as the dispute over the tea trade at Hankow in 1883,[36] and a later incident at Ningpo where the Ningpo *hui-kuan* effectively stopped all trade.[37]   The Customs Decennial Report for 1882—91 remarked of the Hankow tea dispute, in which the guild had stopped all selling of the tea: "The ever-united Chinese had advantage over the ever-disunited Europeans, and carried off the victory."[38]

The same sentiments are echoed at other treaty ports and at different periods:

> The Chinese have found out that they can better do their own business themselves. . . . The foreign community have underrated the capabilities of the Chinese and overlooked their perseverance and industry. . . . Chinese merchants purchase goods and take them to other ports or the interior, and re-sell them at prices with which the foreign merchant cannot compete . . . the same remark is applicable to exports.[39]

> . . . The foreign merchant and shipowner are being metamorphosed into the agent and carrier of the Chinese trader.[40]

> . . . Nine-tenths of the whole of the foreign trade are under the sole control, ownership, and combination of the Chinese. . . . The facilities afforded by the steamers travelling on the Yangtze (including

amongst primary inducements quickness and safety) being fully appreciated by the native traders, it follows that the bulk of the cargoes imported to Chinkiang in foreign bottoms is Chinese owned and on Chinese account. . . . The foreign merchant must rest satisfied with such profits as he may derive from his being simply the carrier of all this Chinese property.[41]

. . . This power of combining on the part of the Chinese is one of the most formidable obstacles the foreign merchant has to contend with. The markets are regulated by guilds and no single individual Chinese dare act in opposition to their decrees.[42]

. . . The foreign merchants have in great measure sunk to the position of mere commission agents.[43]

. . . The import and export trade are so monopolized by the Chinese that the share in foreign hands scarcely covers their expenses . . . the local trade is almost entirely in the hands of the Chinese [i.e., re-exports] or the compradores of foreign hongs . . . native buyers find it cheaper to go to the large market at Shanghae and with greater financial advantage supply their needs at auction there, for there is a larger assortment to choose from. The up-country buyers, [i.e., above Ichang] who have faced the dangerous passage of the Gorges and travelled down in discomfort so far as this by native boat are rather pleased to take the three days further journey in luxury and ease [by steamer] and have the opportunity of combining business and pleasure . . . the goods are brought here by foreign steamers or by vessels of the native company, and after re-packing are sent on to Szechuan, Shensi, and the far West under transit pass as foreign-owned goods, but 99/100, nay 999/1000 are entirely native-owned from the hour they left Shanghai.[44]

The established hongs are united in powerful guilds, exceedingly tenacious of their privileges. Something analogous to the old co-hong system seems to prevail. . . . Merchants from all parts of China do business in Chungking. . . . The bankers say they have relations with every important place in China and are prepared to grant and pay drafts to a practically unlimited amount on and at any of these places. . . . The foreign trade, or the trade in which foreigners are ever likely to be interested except as carriers, is utterly insignificant as compared with that in native products for native consumption. . . . The people in Szechuan as a whole are rich, and they recognize it themselves . . . the members of families who live on such a fruitful soil are able to remain at home and enjoy comfort in comparative idleness . . . this in turn leads to a great amount of home spinning and weaving of cotton, for their own use and for sale. . . . It is a matter of complaint in Szechuan that the money value of labor is rising . . . rice is about double its old price. These however we take to be some of the inevitable concomitants of growing wealth [*sic!*] [45]

The people are "rich," they enjoy "growing wealth!" Can this be the same country to which later foreign stereotypes were applied? But it is the same country, a part on which the foreigners made little material impact, although Szechuan was only one such part. It was however a different country from treaty port land, as the foreigners themselves recognized. They saw it as "mysterious" and separate even if they did not continue to see it, because of its profound differences from their own self-confident system, as the economic success which it was. Even where the two touched in a single city or treaty port, there were

Deux agglomerations distinctes: la ville Chinoise de 4000 habitants environ; la quartier de la gare avec la poste, le télégraphe, les magazins, et les hôtels. La première, là-bas, mysterieuse derriere ses murailles, à l'air de se tenir à l'écart, de regarder d'un oeil mauvais les habitats europennes, les repaires de ces diables étrangers, qui amènent avec eux toutes sortes d'engins redoubtes. [46]

A few foreigners did continue to recognize that "different" did not necessarily mean "backward," "degenerate," or "deteriorating." The Blackburn (Lancashire) Chamber of Commerce sent a commercial mission to China in 1896. Their report, in addition to commenting on commercial prospects and problems, includes a number of amusing and intriguing remarks reflecting their perception of China's separateness and yet effectiveness. In Szechuan, for example, they found

A perfect picture of rustic peace and happiness; nowhere is the idea of the old saw 'Man made the town but God made the country' better shown forth. . . . The people are prosperous but very rustic and plain in their habits. . . . One of the largest traders told us that he did not mind hanging up a watch as an ornament but saw no good in making it go, he thought it wasteful to wind it up. . . . We had a talk with the rustics . . . they had never heard of either England or Japan and called us foreign devils to our faces without the least intention of being impolite, but having no other term in their vocabulary. [47]

The Blackburn delegation, fresh from England, could undoubtedly see China with a far more open mind, as practical commercial men, than seemed to be possible for the Old China Hands in treaty port land, where they in effect walled themselves off. They were interested in making money, but not for the most part in understanding China. The "get-rich-quick-and-get-out" mentality was common to most foreigners in all parts of Asia from the days of da Gama, but it seems to have been less relieved by other perspectives on the part of most of those in China. Lacking any administrative responsibility beyond the concession areas, most Old China Hands saw little occasion to involve or even inform themselves about the rest of the country. Adam Smith's remark about the East India Company's servants in late eighteenth-century Bengal, "It is a very singular government in which every member of the administration wishes to get out of the country . . . as soon as he can, and to whose interest, the day after he has left it and carried his whole fortune with him, it is perfectly indifferent, though the whole country was swallowed up by an earthquake,"[48] became less and less appropriate a picture of the Englishman in India as the nineteenth century progressed. For the foreigners in China, the early search for a quick killing to the exclusion of everything else continued to be characteristic of attitudes and behavior into the 1930s, to an extent which was periodically recognized as shocking.

> "In two or three years at the farthest I hope to realize a fortune and get away," confessed a Shanghai merchant to his consul, "and what can it matter to me if all Shanghai disappeared afterwards in fire or flood? You must not expect men in my position to condemn themselves to prolonged exile in an unhealthy climate for the benefit of posterity. We are money-making, practical men. Our business is to make money, as much and as fast as we can.[49]

Such sentiments remained dominant among the foreigners in Shanghai and the other treaty ports until the whole structure was destroyed in 1949. Talk at the bars and clubs dealt with the price of gold bars and shadier opportunities for quick speculation. While they remained as exiles on the fringes of an elusive fortune, they tried to construct living conditions as much as possible like those of "home." Foreigners' houses sat within walled compounds, excluded Chinese except as servants, and boasted living quarters, complete with copies of *Punch,* the *Illustrated London Weekly,* or the *National Geographic* which might just as well have been in contemporary Birmingham or Philadelphia. Cooks were laboriously "trained" to approximate Western-style dishes, but there were complaints that "no Chinese could ever make good puddings." The unequaled Chinese cuisine was considered fit only for "the natives." There were exceptions of course, but they were exceptions. Probably the most famous symbol of imperialist Shanghai was the little park which was laid out in the 1870s at the end of the Bund, where Soochow Creek joined the Huangp'u (Whangpoo). A Scottish landscape gardener was employed to reproduce as well as possible in this exotic setting a Western-style area of lawn, shrubs, and trees where the foreigners could feel at home. Since this was such a consciously Western preserve, no one (until much later) thought it odd that one of the signs at the entrance of the park read "Chinese Not Allowed," while another read "Dogs Not Allowed."

Even if one acknowledges the emergence of a more clearly national market for capital as well as for goods, the relative security of capital in the treaty ports, the lower interest rates, and the substitution for the earlier more decentralized commercial system of a more concentrated one in the treaty port hierarchy, how much did any of this touch let alone transform the bulk of the Chinese economy? The changes were in some sense innovative, but they can also be seen as the logical continuation of processes already at work for some centuries as the Chinese economy had evolved since Sung times, and especially in Ming and Ch'ing, toward greater commercialization, urbanization, regional specialization, and long-distance trade, with the financial, production, and transport techniques appropriate to these developments keeping pace. Western industrial technology and its immediate fruits: steamships, railways, mechanized mining and textile production most importantly, were genuinely new and at least in the long run genuinely transforming. But they were taken up by Chinese and, at least until the end of the period of foreign dominance, fitted into a primarily traditional Chinese system which in larger terms remained but little altered, except that it was the better able to resist foreign efforts to invade it.[50]

It is useful however to make some effort at examining what statistical measures we have, direct and indirect, of the foreign economic impact rather than depending entirely on descriptive or impressionistic accounts. Trade figures, their meaning and implications, are considered therefore in chapter 11.

Chapter 11

What Do the Trade Figures Mean?

For all the well-deserved praise of the efforts of the Maritime Customs to measure China's foreign trade from 1864 to 1942, the Customs figures are grossly misleading. While there was certainly some real increase in trade, most of the growth recorded was statistical growth only. The monetary inflation during this period is relatively easily measured and adjusted for. But quite apart from that, the trade figures were swollen in their rises year by year and decade by decade as the Customs network extended its coverage, and as more and more trade goods shifted in their carriage from junks, sampans, carts, animals, and porters, whose freight was not recorded, to steamship and rail, where cargoes were recorded. There was also extensive double or triple counting, in ways which are detailed below. I conclude that the real growth of China's trade was modest, and that in this crucial respect the treaty port impact on the Chinese economy was very much less than the trade figures—and many people who have used them—would suggest.

Quantitative measures are particularly scarce and unreliable for most aspects of China before the 1950s, and the nature of what statistical data exist does not for the most part inspire confidence, in keeping with data from most so-called premodern systems. For most economies, however, foreign trade is relatively easily measurable and the statistics generated are therefore reasonably reliable even when no other data may be. Foreign trade usually moves in large carriers and in large lots, by definition crosses international frontiers with their apparatus of registration and control, and before leaving a country foreign trade goods are commonly assembled and often packed or reloaded in large warehouses in a port. Collection of tariffs and other dues provide further occasion for official involvement and record-keeping. These circumstances applied even in premodern states, and although smuggling has always existed, most international movement of goods was too obvious to avoid notice. There are ship counts and estimates of cargo capacities moving in and out of most ports in most countries, including China, long before regular, consistent, and comprehensive statistical series were established.

Originally through happenstance, the foreigners in the China treaty ports arrogated to themselves the collection of customs dues on foreign trade. During 1853 and 1854 the Chinese city at Shanghai was held by rebel forces of the Triad Society, a group which later merged into the Taiping Rebellion. The official Customs House operated by officials of the Ch'ing government was thus put out of action, and in this supposedly temporary emergency the British and American consuls at Shanghai agreed to collect the official customs dues owed by their own nationals.[1] From this on-the-spot expedient grew the Imperial Maritime Customs (after 1911, the Chinese Maritime Customs), an official organ of the Chinese government but by agreement headed by a national of the foreign country which had the greatest share of China's foreign trade. This of course was Britain, until first Japan and then the United States both exceeded the British share after 1910. The British nevertheless retained the Customs headship, partly by inertia and tradition, partly on the strength of their continued predominance among foreign investors in China, partly also as a legacy of the almost one-man creation of the efficiency and esprit de corps of the Customs Service through the long leadership of Robert (later Sir Robert) Hart.[2]

The Service was however staffed at lower levels by Chinese and the higher posts by a variety of foreign nationals in supposed proportion to varying national shares in China's foreign trade. Hart and successive inspectors general stressed that all members of the Customs Service were employees of the Chinese government rather than representatives of their respective countries. All foreign staff were required to learn Chinese, and in other respects as well the Customs stood out among foreign groups in China as freer of special interest, exploitative behavior, or blind arrogance toward things Chinese. In addition to recording trade and collecting the official dues, the Customs published annual and decennial statistics and prose reports on commercial and general conditions in the area of each treaty port which constitute one of the most important sources on the period. Periodic special publications dealt with particular industries or commodities (silk, opium, tea) and selected commercial problems. The Service also took on responsibility for establishing and maintaining a system of lights and navigational aids along the coast and major rivers, created and administered the first national public postal and telegraph service, and lent its support to road building. Nevertheless, it acted also as the manager of a system which imposed an arbitrarily low tariff on imports, agreed to in the treaties extracted from China by foreign governments eager to expedite the invasion of the China market by their own merchants.

However one chooses to assess the contribution of the Customs Service to China during the semicolonial period, its records are one of the few oases in the statistical desert of the Chinese economy. The *Annual Returns of Trade and Trade Reports,* published every year from 1864 to 1941 for each of the treaty ports open at the time, itemize the imports and exports of each port and give figures for original exports, reexports, coasting trade, and the origin and destination of imports and exports at each port.[3] The Customs was however concerned only with goods derived from or destined for foreign countries, including their domestic coastal and riverine movement, and domestic goods carried in foreign-built, foreign-style, or foreign-owned vessels. It was not concerned with the far larger domestic trade carried by junks, sampans, and rafts, nor with the domestic overland trade. This was supposedly left to the responsibility of the Chinese Customs ("Native Customs"), whose records were at best spotty and misleading reflections of actual movements, legal and illegal, and whose functioning was in any case severely hampered by general political instability.

How reliable a quantitative picture of China's foreign trade do the apparently orderly, conscientious, and business-like figures of the Maritime Customs give? They show a steady and substantial, if not breathtaking, increase in trade through the treaty ports from 1864 (when the series begins on a basis comparable with later years) until the 1930s. It is not merely that the dimensions involved look a good deal less impressive when compared with the mass of the Chinese economy, or with European trade with a great number of far smaller and less productive countries. A closer look at the figures, in the light of some study of the Customs *Reports on Trade* and other contemporary accounts, shows that to an unmeasurable but major extent the foreigners merely absorbed into their system and their statistics existing Chinese trade, and deflected some of it into export channels. Trade carried by junks which had originally gone unrecorded increasingly found its way into the Customs records as the network of collection and control expanded and became more efficient. Although considerable overseas as well as domestic traffic continued to move by junk, much of it shifted over time to carriage by steamship, which was recorded in the Customs figures. Some, perhaps a majority, of the increase in recorded trade represents only a change from junk transport, both domestic and overseas, to first foreign and then Chinese steamships as well. Much of the remaining recorded increase can be accounted for by the great expansion over time in the completeness of the Customs coverage. This last point is commonly overlooked. What happened in effect was a spread of the Customs statistical net from the original five ports to cover by the 1920s most of the country, through a total of sixty-nine treaty ports, forty-seven of them with Customs offices (see the back endpaper map). Their returns continued to swell the total of recorded trade, but the extent to which actual trade grew is not easy to establish.

> On a coastline of nearly 700 miles, studded with bays, harbours, cities, and towns and with rivers such as that called the West River penetrating far into the interior, there is one treaty port, Canton, and an open and free mart, the colony of Hong Kong. It is but reasonable therefore that if Chinese traders can purchase goods at Hong Kong and land them on the coast, they will not pass them through the foreign Custom-house at Canton but will ship them direct to their destination. The same may be said with regard to exports from these places. Hence it follows that no estimate can be formed of the foreign trade in this part of China from the published Canton Custom-house Returns.[4]

This was a true picture of the situation at the beginning of the statistical series, and although the special case of Hong Kong and the nature of the southeast coast made it particularly applicable to Canton, it was true to varying degrees of all of the other treaty ports then in existence as such. Covert smuggling was also acknowledged to be on a very large scale. As the treaty port system grew to include nearly every major port and inland market center in China, to a total of fifteen by 1870, forty by 1900, and sixty-nine by 1924,[5] its trade figures of course multiplied. At the same time, although smuggling was never wholly suppressed, it was considerably reduced in the sense that more of what had been smuggled goods now passed through Customs stations and helped to swell the figures. The Customs *Reports on Trade* periodically acknowledge that new Customs stations were established in particular areas to try to plug holes in the system, especially for the taxation and recording of foreign trade, as in

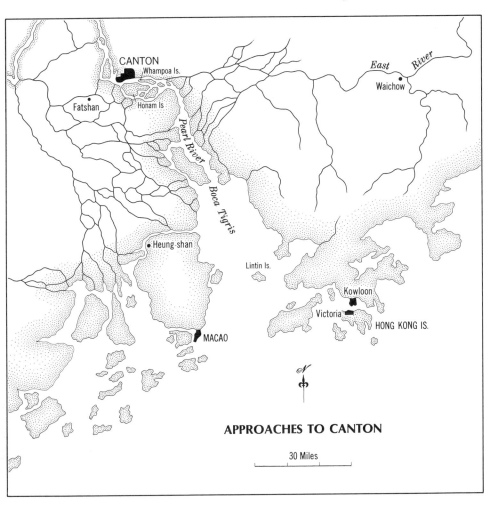

CANTON
Whampoa Is.

East *River*

Waichow

Fatshan

Honam Is.

Pearl River

Boca Tigris

Heung-shan

Lintin Is.

Kowloon

Victoria

HONG KONG IS.

MACAO

N

APPROACHES TO CANTON

30 Miles

the ring of such stations in the Canton delta area and environs at Pakhoi, Lappa-Kowloon, Kiaochow, Samshui, Kongmoon, and Swatow.

But the Chinese merchant, long experienced in the maneuvering necessary to survival in a bureaucratic state, was adept at anticipating and avoiding new instruments of exaction. His response to the opening of new Customs stations often had the effect of artificially inflating the trade figures not only by using steamships instead of junks but by shipping domestic goods from one mainland port to another, via Hong Kong, acquiring for them the favored status of foreign imports (which carried a very much lighter burden of duties) and at the same time tripping the counter at each Customs station. The same lot of goods might thus be recorded several times, in addition to being added to the total of both foreign exports and imports, in the course of its movement from domestic origin to domestic destination perhaps only a few score miles away.

> It frequently pays the Chinese merchant to ship native produce to Hong Kong in order to acquire a foreign status and become entitled to the privileges of a transit pass to cover its passage up the very river whence it came. . . . Hence it is that goods having the same provenance or place of origin in China may appear in two different import tables, of foreign and native goods, of the Imperial Maritime Customs. . . . The merchant or manufacturer in Europe or even in Asia, ignorant of this fact, may be led to think from these returns that there is really a market for his goods in China when that country is well able to and does supply its own needs.[6]

> The multiplication of Customs stations no more implies an increase of trade than frequent stoppages of a railway train at wayside stations imply an increase in the amount of goods carried.[7]

What real, as opposed to statistical, increases took place were heavily concentrated in foreign trade, but their amount cannot reliably be measured by the Customs series. Even so, the peak of the growth shown remained unimpressive on any international or per capita scale.

The total recorded value of the "whole" trade (i.e. domestic as well as foreign) of all the treaty ports (including Chinese goods imported from one treaty port to another, most of which went unrecorded in earlier years) rose relatively slowly until about 1890, and then more steeply to a peak in 1929–30, which it never subsequently regained in the face of Chinese boycotts, the world depression, civil war, and the Japanese invasion. The total recorded in 1870 was just over 100 million Haikuan taels. In 1890 it was 241 million, by 1910 just over 1 billion, and by 1930 just over 3 billion, an increase since 1870 of some thirty times. During the same period recorded foreign trade alone increased approximately twenty times in Haikuan tael values.[8] It should be noted that these totals included Manchuria, which by the 1920s represented nearly one-third of the total of Chinese foreign trade but which was in effect a separate economic system under Japanese management after 1905.

The separateness of the Manchurian economy is an important part of the argument here. It seems to me clear and substantial enough to warrant deducting Manchurian trade figures from any attempt to show trade volume, foreign or domestic, as a measure of the treaty port impact on the Chinese economy after 1905. By 1920, total Manchurian trade, in round numbers, reached 270 million Haikuan taels, while that of China Proper in 1920 totaled just over 1 billion. By 1925, these figures were respectively 365 million and 1.3 billion; by 1929, 559 million and 1.7 billion. Manchuria became a piece of outright colonial property, as China Proper never was. Japan was free to build railways, open mines, invest in agricultural innovation, and in general reconstruct the entire economy under its own control. The Japanese made these investments, like other colonial regimes, primarily in order to generate a flow of exports. They left the Manchurian economy highly commercialized, industrialized, provided with a dense net of railways, and concentrated on the production of trade goods. Exports rose dramatically, as the Japanese intended, but imports also flowed in, to feed industrialization and other new commercial enterprises. During the period of their de facto control, from 1905 to the outbreak of the Pacific war, Manchuria's population also increased by over thirty times. In all of these respects, Manchuria was a wholly noncomparable and separate sector of the former Chinese empire. What was happening there bore little or no relation to what was happening in China Proper, and especially not to the far more limited interaction between foreign investments and the Chinese economy or with foreign efforts to stimulate trade. Manchurian trade figures reflected a totally different and separate scene and therefore should not be lumped with the Chinese figures in any effort to measure what was happening to China.[9]

For China Proper, how much of the increase in the Customs figures represented a real rise in trade and how much a shift from traditional to steam carriage and from unrecorded to recorded is impossible to say. But the amount which should be deducted from the figures on such grounds seems most unlikely to be less than one-half and should perhaps be closer to two-thirds.[10] To give one specific example whose scale can at least roughly be measured, the tribute grain shipments, which had traditionally moved by junk from central to north China via the Grand Canal and by sea, began after 1872 to move by steamer (both Chinese- and foreign-owned) whose cargoes were recorded. This was a very large flow but clearly an artificial inflation of trade figures. What was true for tribute grain was true to varying degrees for nearly all other goods. During the same period, the exchange value of the Haikuan tael fell more or less continuously, dropping altogether by about two-thirds (from the equivalent of $1.60 [U.S.] in 1870 to $0.46 [U.S.] in 1930), as recorded in the yearly sterling and dollar equivalents published in the Maritime Customs *Annual Returns of Trade and Trade Reports*. Here at least is a precisely quantifiable measure of the extent to which trade figures departed from reality, and to a very large order of magnitude. Taking all of these matters into account, we may be left with a real increase of the trade of China Proper less Manchuria (mainly in foreign trade, although some of this may in turn only have been deflected from previously domestic channels) of at most three or four times; that it was in fact less than that is more likely.

But even if one takes the Customs trade figures as if they gave a picture of reality, the total dollar-equivalent value of the foreign trade of China (less Manchuria) which they recorded by the end of the 1920s put it in the same approximate foreign trade class as Mexico, Chile, New Zealand, and Brazil, and far behind Argentina, Australia, Canada, Denmark, India, Indonesia, or, of course, any of the industrialized countries of the West or Japan. In all of these countries one suspects that the trade figures were more in accord with real flows than in China. It is generally true that the proportional importance of foreign trade varies inversely with the overall size of the country, and directly with the degree of industrialization or commercialization; it is not particularly surprising that in any international comparison China ranked low. This is simply another aspect of the difficulty which foreigners encountered in making an impact on the Chinese mass. But China accounted for approximately one-fifth of world population, and yet its recorded foreign trade never exceeded 1.5 percent of the total value of world trade, and exceeded 1 percent only briefly.[11]

Especially on any areal or per capita basis, but even disregarding this basic measure, it was not a very impressive result of over four centuries of foreign effort to "open" the China market, for nearly the last century of which the foreigners operated with the powerful advantages of the treaty port system, extraterritoriality, and a variety of other special privileges and threats of force designed to enhance their commercial success. This is also an attempt to measure the growth of the sector on which the bulk of the foreign effort was concentrated. In per capita terms, China's foreign trade remained negligible and at its peak was probably smaller than that of any country in the world. It is questionable whether its total value ever reached 10 percent of China's gross national product, or perhaps ever passed 5 percent.[12]

It is perhaps not surprising that when even in trade the foreign impact was unremarkable, it was less effective still in the broader sphere of modernization. Almost as if it were in traditional Chinese terms, the treaty port men—foreign, traditional Chinese, or remolded Chinese—took their opportunity to manipulate the system they found rather than transforming it as the colonialists and their Asian partners did elsewhere. Trade alone was not, and should not really be expected to be, a sufficient agent of transformation. It did not produce innovation or the equivalent of modernization in the great premodern centers of trade in the West, including Portugal, despite Portuguese domination of overseas trade, especially with the East, for over a century after da Gama. The foreign and treaty port role in China may with some appropriateness be compared to the Portuguese century in Asia and their extremely limited impact on the areas whose trade they appeared, like the foreigners in China, so completely to control. Like the China treaty port merchants, the Portuguese never eliminated the Asian merchant groups, and perhaps more important, did not significantly alter the nature of existing trade, let alone affect the conditions or commodities of production. They were merely one more in a long succession of briefly successful entrepreneurs who left the Asian economy little changed from what it was when they found it and as it had been manipulated by others before them, including the Chinese. As George Masselman puts it:

> Nor did the Portuguese succeed in eradicating the Moslem traders. On the contrary, the old established trade flourished as never before. . . . We may conclude that the volume of Portuguese trade was exceeded many times over by the trade carried on by the peoples of Asia. . . . Thus the Portuguese, notwithstanding their strongholds, never succeeded in establishing even a rudimentary type of colonial administration in the sense of a European power gaining significant control over large areas. The long established pattern of Asiatic trade remained the same.[13]

As the only significant change brought about by the Portuguese was the introduction of Christianity (although often through forced conversions), so one may reasonably argue that, despite the discouraging total of converts, the post-1842 missionary effort in China was a more effective direct and indirect vehicle of change, and of ultimate modernization (primarily through the mission-founded schools), than the seemingly more impressive but evanescent commercial activities in the isolated islands of the treaty ports. Like the Portuguese, the treaty port foreigners and their Chinese imitators had a dominantly speculative attitude. They were neither free nor for the most part interested through investment and management to improve the means of production, or to "develop" the Chinese economy. Like traditional Chinese merchants, they were more often content to compete for slices of the cake rather than trying to make the cake bigger. Sir Frederick Bruce, the British Minister, writing from Peking in January of 1864, put it more pretentiously in arguing against Western efforts to force modernization on China: "Our office is that of the schoolmaster who educates, not of the tyrant who imposes."[14] But an alien schoolmaster was in a poor position to make a significant dent on a country as vast, effective, and self-satisfied as China, in the absence of the climate which full colonialism, its sanctions and its organizational structures, could create. The Indian and Southeast Asian experiences underline this point and help to explain why Western schoolmasters in China failed.

The great exception to these generalizations, and one that may be taken to support their validity, is Manchuria. After 1905, Manchuria was a piece of colonial property, probably even more effectively so than India or Java, especially in the sense that Manchuria was thinly occupied before about 1900, had no inherited economic, social, or political system whose vigor or inertia could resist change, and was therefore the more easily shaped by planned Japanese investment and by Japanese development policy in general. Without any of the built-in drags against change which characterized China Proper—its immense size and population, its existing level of economic and commercial development, the sanctity and relative effectiveness of the entire existing system, and simple national or xenophobic resistance to foreign-inspired change—Manchuria was the kind of tabula rasa where a developmental blueprint could most easily and quickly be translated into reality by a determined manager with technology, organization, and capital to invest. Manchuria was also distinct from China, and had never been ruled (except in small part and long ago, in the Han dynasty occupation of the Liao valley) by a Chinese government. The degree both of development and of transformation which the Japanese accomplished in less than forty years in Manchuria is extremely impressive. It tends to suggest not merely that trade alone changes little, but that for effective impact on any established Asian system, complete colonial control or territorial sovereignty was necessary. The cases of Java, Luzon,

Ceylon, Malaya, lower Burma, Vietnam, and India confirm this. Manchuria's course, though brief, and the level of foreign impact there were much closer to the experience of the areas listed above than to that of China.

Once again, size was also critical. Manchuria was manageable in these terms where China was not. One is struck by the contrast in the foreign impact between China and all of the above areas as well, none of them except for India larger than a Chinese province, and all the more easily taken over as colonial property. Something of the indigenous structures survived in each area, but there is no question of the basic remaking by Western agency of major aspects of their economies, cultures, institutions, and even their landscapes. Such sweeping change did not take place to the same degree in India as in much of Southeast Asia, except in the intellectual sphere, but China is over twice the geographical size even of undivided India (before 1947), a dimension which clearly helps to account for the major discrepancies between them in the results of the Western effort. India is also a peninsula, with no part of it more than 700 miles from the sea, where the strength and penetrating power of the West was concentrated. But perhaps the sharpest contrast is with the smaller cultural entities, among which Ceylon stands out as the smallest and is also open to sea-borne influences as a tear-drop-shaped island. The Portuguese and later other Westerners were seeking a lodgment at Canton only a few years after their arrival at Ceylon. They were in effect still seeking a position in China when the treaty port system ended, by which time not only the Ceylonese landscape but almost the whole of its culture and economy had been remade by the succession of colonial managers, to such an extent that even most of the Ceylonese elite no longer knew their own language as well as they knew English, and English ways. Artists worked in Western modes, writers wrote in English, Ceylonese judges sat in black robes and white wigs in an equatorial climate, while in the mission churches congregations sang the hymn about Ceylon by a former missionary: "Where every prospect pleases, and only man is vile." Ceylon's economy was overwhelmingly dominated by the Western-owned plantation sector, and its foreign trade (especially exports) was almost as large as that recorded for China.

The Maritime Customs figures do need to be seen, like the Western experience in China as a whole, in context within the rest of the Western effort in Asia. But they should also be examined in the context of the

Chinese scene, from part of which they were extracted. It was an anomalous part, and it is therefore misleading to take them, as commonly they are taken, as indicators of what was going on in the Chinese economy at large or of the extent of the Western impact. When one sets the Customs figures against general knowledge, or detailed accounts, of what was happening in the area theoretically being influenced or served by each treaty port, one is immediately struck by anomalies. There is a more or less consistent pattern of correlation between flourishing trade through the treaty ports (at least in recorded statistics) and catastrophic economic disaster in their supposed commercial hinterlands.

Customs returns at Tientsin, for example, show unbroken increases in the trade of the port throughout the dreadful famine years in Hopeh in the 1870s, and again in the 1890s and 1920s. In fact, boom years for trade both coincide with and immediately follow the years of worst famine, flood, and (in several cases) rampant civil disorder. While this sort of pattern is clearest in the case of Tientsin, it is apparent for all of the other major and minor treaty ports, enough so even to prompt remarks about it in many of the Customs *Reports on Trade*. But the point seems more generally to have been lost, or at least no adequate conclusions were drawn from it; the treaty ports seem clearly to have been serving, influencing, dealing with themselves primarily, as enclave systems, rather than with the far larger Chinese system which they were supposedly transforming. From the early years of the Customs series this dichotomy is apparent from a comparison of trade figures with what the Customs *Reports* themselves tell about events and conditions in the area of each treaty port, echoed by the closely similar consular reports. Both comment, near the beginning of the period, on the prolonged "anarchy" in Hopeh during 1866, 1867, and 1868, mentioning food riots, numerous "robber bands," and the plundering activities of an estimated thirty thousand troops of the Nien Fei rebels, who "ravaged the whole province to the south of Tientsin. . . . [But] the trade of 1866 was not at all and that of 1867 only partially affected." [15] The city itself had to be defended against the Nien Fei in both 1867 and 1868. Its transport and trade connections with the rest of the province were cut, and there was "terrible devastation" virtually throughout Hopeh. Yet the trade of the port increased to a new high in 1868.

Things recovered by the end of 1868, but the 1870s were a grim decade for most of the inhabitants of north China. 1871 saw a major and devastating flood in the lower plain of the Yellow River, yet Tientsin trade figures set successive new records in both 1871 and 1872. From 1875 to 1879, with successive crop failures beginning in 1876, there were severe famine conditions "of unparalleled extent and destructiveness over the greater part of North China commercially connected with Tientsin. . . . [But this] has only exercized a comparatively small influence on the figures representing the trade of Tientsin."[16] The influence is hard to find, since the trade figures continued their unbroken increase, although the Customs Report estimates that by 1879, 60 percent of the population of Shansi alone had died or fled and that conditions were only moderately better in Hopeh and Shantung.[17] The British consul's commercial report for the same year reads in part:

> It was naturally expected that the full effects of the disastrous famine which had prevailed during three years and had caused the deaths during that period of nine million of the inhabitants of those provinces which are supplied with foreign manufactures principally through Tientsin would be apparent in a falling off of the trade of the port in 1879. Countrary to expectations, however, the foreign imports showed an increase of 5,584,819 taels.[18]

The floods of 1890 were judged to be the worst in the thirty-year history of the foreign settlement at Tientsin, and also laid waste extensive parts of north China. Chinese officials estimated that twenty thousand people had been drowned in Hopeh alone, but as so often has happened in north China the excessive rainfall came too late to do more than wash away what few crops had survived the preceding drought of spring and early summer so that 1890 and 1891 were famine years also. The trade of the port however continued to flourish, and indeed both 1890 and 1891 were record years of outstanding magnitude.[19] In 1899, "the dry summer and consequent meagre crops have caused much distress; nevertheless, trade has flourished."[20] The beginnings of the great north China famine of the 1920s were apparent in 1919–20, when it was already being described as "the worst that has ever visited China" and as covering all of Hopeh and large parts of Shantung, Honan, Shansi, and Shensi.[21] But the trade of Tientsin for 1920 was the second best on record and the slight drop from 1919 was attributed entirely to "exchange prohlems." In fact, the import of foreign goods at Tientsin reached a new record in 1920, and the Inland Transit trade "was normal"–this also in the face of extensive civil war in the area through most of 1919 and 1920, including heavy fighting between the Anfu and Chihli cliques which cut the main rail lines several times and disrupted rail shipments for much of the rest of the time by commandeering and troop movements.

In 1921, with the famine in its worst year thus far and with over fifty thousand refugees in camps in Tientsin alone,[22] trade through the port broke all records to reach in both imports and exports the highest totals ever recorded. Some of this increase was in prices, but 1922 again broke the record, and with no increases in prices. Yet 1922 saw the famine continue unbroken, and was further marked by hard fighting on a large scale during spring and early summer between the Chihli and Fengtien cliques, including actions along the Tientsin-Pukou (Nanking) and Tientsin-Hankow railway lines. Chihli-Fengtien clashes punctuated much of 1924 as well, but in that year new record trade totals at Tientsin were again reached, only to fall before the still larger totals of 1925. Toward the end of this tragic decade and its "atmosphere of civil war which has hung over North China with very little intermission . . . civil war, bad harvest, depletion of the rural population, and constant interruptions of the means of communication have all combined to hamper trade [i.e., in 1928], and yet the total volume of imports and exports constitutes a fresh record in the history of the port."[23]

In 1928, famine conditions in north China had become even worse than in the earlier part of the decade, with the cumulative effect of successive years of crop failure; Shensi is estimated by that year to have lost 40 percent of its population by combined death and migration.[24] The Customs *Decennial Reports on Trade* for 1922–31 repeats the paradoxical juxtaposition of unprecedented catastrophe in the hinterland and unprecedented prosperity in the treaty port:

> Internecine wars with attendant dislocation of transport facilities, successive years of dearth caused by droughts and floods, brigandage waxing rife in the interior, the silting of the Hai-Ho [the river at Tientsin] above Tangku . . . [yet] disturbed as it was by drought, flood, and civil war, trade continued to show advances in value . . . despite continual military interferences with railway transport.[25]

"Disorder and banditry were rampant everywhere"[26] and secret societies mushroomed; the report estimates that the Red Spear Society had 100,000 followers in Hopei and 600,000 in Honan by the end of the decade.[27] This was of course in addition to the chronic fighting on a large scale between the Fengtien, Chihli, and other cliques in the immediate hinterland of Tientsin until 1927, which repeatedly cut the major rail lines for long periods, the attacks on the Kuominchun by Chang Tso-lin, Wu P'ei-fu, and Chang Tsung-chang during 1926, and the fighting which accompanied the final push of the Northern Expedition. All of this meant not merely dislocation of the economy and widespread destruction but an almost complete break in rail and other long-distance overland shipments. The *Decennial Report* states that "most of the rolling stock was carried away by the retreating forces; that available for trade fell off to only 5 per cent of normal."[28] It goes on to say that

> the deplorable state of the Hai-Ho continued to cause anxiety [i.e., internal trade movements by this channel were also sharply curtailed] and that there were successive poor harvests in which "crops suffered partly from being laid waste by military operations and partly from drought, followed by excessive rains." [A cruelly familiar pattern in north China.] It is a pleasant surprise to note however that notwithstanding the obstacles described above, the total value of trade exceeded the record of any previous year.[29]

The British Chamber of Commerce in Tientsin issued a pamphlet in 1930 titled *The Present State of British Trade in North China* which devotes most of its brief compass to viewing with alarm but which tells essentially the same story as the Customs *Reports*. The persistent dreams of trade with the immense China market are restated, but as so often, the wrong explanations are given for the fact that those golden dreams have been aborted: "the illegal taxation under which trade has groaned. . . . It is of first importance that trade be allowed to flow in its accustomed channels." But what were these accustomed channels?—not, one suspects, what the Chamber had in mind.

> The trade returns, full of suggestions of prosperity, are most fallacious [i.e., as a guide to prosperity for foreign merchants]. They reflect the courage and tenacity of the merchant rather than supplying any true index of the condition of affairs . . . profit is so reduced that the primary aim is to meet overhead charges and retain connections in the hope of less lawless times. . . . Given reasonable safeguards for trade and credit, and the restoration and maintenance of existing communications, the possibilities of Tientsin are incalculable. It is the business heart of North China and Mongolia. . . .

> The key to North China is Tientsin, the political and commercial
> importance of which appears to be so strangely overlooked.[30]

Given the foreign perspective at the time, it is perhaps understandable
that they should have been puzzled, but it seems clear that they were
profoundly wrong about Tientsin's or any other treaty port's role as the
"business heart" of any part of China outside the treaty ports themselves.
"The history of British trade in China is one long story of official
interference in various forms. The British merchant cannot in any way be
blamed for not having extended his activities into the interior by opening
branches at smaller inland towns."[31] It was convenient, and understandable, to blame "official interference" for the foreign failure, under Ch'ing,
warlord, and Kuomintang rule alike, but this was never the real reason.

The pamphlet concludes in language reminiscent of the Customs *Reports* on the same years:

> When one looks at the appalling conditions that have prevailed in
> China for the past several years one can only wonder there has been
> any trade whatever—civil wars, brigands, thieves, fire, murder, rape,
> earthquakes, drought, flood, famine, and disease have decimated
> millions. And as if these tribulations were not enough, the State and
> Governors have extorted taxation beyond belief and levied excess
> transport and other charges to the point where the harried merchant
> prefers any means of carriage rather than use the railway, even if it
> is available.[32]

It is indeed amazing that there was any trade, and hard to understand that
throughout the decade so described new records continued to be set.

The paradox is completed by what happened after 1929 (1927, 1928,
and 1929 were each in turn new trade-value highs): there was "an exceptionally good harvest in this province"[33] in 1930, an absence of flooding,
and a temporary end to significant civil disorder in the Tientsin hinterland;
rail lines and waterways functioned more or less normally and traffic
moved well on the Hai-Ho. There was a marked *decline* in the total value
of the trade of Tientsin for 1930. The same pattern continued in 1931: an
excellent harvest, relatively peaceful conditions, and a decline in the trade
of the port. The drop in world trade as a whole beginning in 1930 was of
course a contributing factor, and one can readily surmise, in addition to
the fragmentary evidence in the Customs figures and *Reports,* that a part of

the paradox is also accounted for by heavy imports of grain in famine years. But food imports, mainly grain and flour, remained a small proportion of total imports during those years and were in any case totally inadequate to make any impression on the gross food shortages. The continued increases in Tientsin's trade 1919–29 (with the single exception of 1926) also cannot be explained by postponed consumption in the city's hinterland in the early years of the decade. Grain and flour imports largely disappeared in 1930 and 1931, but the Customs reports do not apparently regard this as an important factor in the overall trade decline. With the recovery to something like normal conditions in north China,

> cheaper foreign cotton piece goods were largely supplanted by native ones, which not only compared favorably with foreign products but were sold at such low prices as to defeat most competitors . . . the match trade has been totally killed by the local article, and native cotton socks, candles, and common window glass outnumber the foreign articles.[34]

The success of Tientsin's trade during the 1920s rested also on exports, and here "Trade developed most satisfactorily during the decade . . . almost every item of the staple export showed an increase."[35] It is hard to avoid the conclusion that whatever Tientsin was doing as a Western-dominated commercial center, it was not significantly integrated with the economy of its supposed hinterland, and that at least its recorded trade reflected no more than a miniscule part of that economy.

Tientsin in fact prided itself on its position ahead even of Shanghai in many years as the chief distributing center for foreign imports, at least according to the Customs figures. Those figures do not however give an accurate picture, since a large part of Shanghai's port business was transit trade involving the reexport of foreign goods to other treaty ports, Tientsin among them, whereas Tientsin was the end of the treaty port line and distributed its imports (mainly from Shanghai) directly to the Chinese market. "Tientsin distributed in this way a volume of imports equal to the total of imports thus distributed by all the other treaty ports in China, including Shanghai."[36] Here incidentally was one more important source of statistical illusion, since the same goods would be counted as imports to Shanghai, exports from Shanghai, imports to Tientsin (and the other ports, which also received the bulk of their goods from Shanghai), and exports from Tientsin. By such quadruple counting, which was characteristic of the great majority of the goods moving through the Customs network, the recorded figures probably inflated the real import and export of goods by close to 100 percent.

But these unreal calculations were in any case making only relative distinctions among the treaty ports; they revealed little or nothing about the proportional importance of this trade in China as a whole. The disabling of the railway system which was such a feature of the 1920s in north China does in fact provide some indirect evidence on how small that importance was. The Customs *Decennial Reports on Trade,* 1922–31, include in the section on Tientsin a table estimating the percentages of inland trade to and from the city in the period 1922–31 carried by rail, boat, and cart. The percentage estimated as carried by rail does, understandably, drop during the period, but averages over two-thirds until 1926, and thereafter about one-half. Yet writing as of 1931, the *Decennial Report* concludes its discussion of the vicissitudes of the railway system as follows:

> The continued civil war has all but completely denuded the railways of their rolling stock for commercial transport; locomotives and cars once commandeered have found their way back to their normal stations only too slowly . . . All the lines are in a state of deterioration. . . . Whenever civil war broke out, the railway was always the first to suffer. The fighting might be terminated in a few months or even weeks, but the railway communications would be paralyzed for a much longer period. . . . Damage was always done to bridge works and other equipment.[37]

This may be compared with the 1930 account of the Tientsin British Chamber of Commerce cited above:

> The civil wars which have been carried out in China incessantly for the last few years when the railways have been seized by one warlord or Military Party after another for their own use, have practically crippled the majority of the railways. They have no funds to spend even on repairs and renewals to existing equipment, much less to consider any possible extensions.[38]

When even a railway system in such condition could carry one-half to two-thirds of the inland trade of Tientsin, and when the total trade of the port (which included exports derived from the hinterland as well as a large proportion of imports which were then distributed to places outside the city) could continue to rise throughout this period (in fact, it more than doubled between 1920 and 1939), two conclusions seem inescapable: (1) Tientsin's trade, for all its importance among other treaty ports, was a drop in the bucket of the economy of north China; and (2) Tientsin was not serving to any significant extent as the commercial center even of Hopeh, for the collection of goods for export or especially for the distribution of imported goods.[39]

Although Tientsin is an especially clear case, the same paradoxical pattern is discernible at Hankow,[40] and to some extent at Canton, as well as in a more general sense at Shanghai and for the treaty port system as a whole, which continued to show vigorously rising levels of trade while the Chinese economy continued to deteriorate, and declining levels whenever there was a brief recovery. In the Wuhan area, the 1920s were also a troubled period, chronically disturbed by war lord fighting which was periodically on a large scale in both Hunan and Hupei and involved troops belonging to Wu P'ei-fu, Wu Kuang-hsin, Chang-Ching-yao, Wang Chan-yuan, and others, in addition to the violence and disruption related to the fate of the Hankow government and to the Northern Expedition. The Pei-Han and Wuchang-Changsha rail lines were frequently cut, and operated at anything like normal levels for perhaps no more than one-third of the decade. There were also frequent and serious interruptions, attacks, and commandeering of river and lake craft. Yet the Customs-recorded trade of Hankow also showed a steady and substantial increase, nearly doubling between 1920 and 1929. With the restoration of comparative order after 1929, Hankow's recorded trade declined and the Customs *Reports* note the virtual disappearance of foreign imports of goods, which the Chinese produced more cheaply and at comparable or superior quality: cotton yarn, cotton cloth, candles, soap, and so forth.[41] And while the revolution of 1911 went largely unrecognized and uncelebrated by most foreigners, it was noted in reports from Hankow as a period of local disturbance, followed by comments on the continued rise in the trade of the port:

> In spite of riot and civil commotion in surrounding districts [including the] ceaseless and ubiquitous activity of the White Wolf Brigands whose bands infest Hunan, Kiangsi, and parts of Hupeh, the trade of Hankow for 1913 shows a larger total than that for 1912, itself a record.[42]

At Canton, too, total recorded trade values rose during the chaotic conditions in Kwangtung after 1911 and into the 1920s: fighting between Kwangsi, Kwangtung, and Yunnan forces, Cantonese efforts under Ch'en Ch'iung-ming and Sun Yat-sen to expel the Kwangsi clique from Kwangtung, and chronic stoppage of trade on the West River. Nevertheless, "The heavy cloud of political chaos which has for several years now hung over the trade of Kwangtung never ceases to show a silver lining in the form of a commercial buoyancy which augurs well for China's commerce."[43] Recorded trade totals did sag midway through the 1920s as a result primarily of Chinese boycotts—a largely urban movement—but recovered and by 1929 were over 20 percent higher than in 1920. Imports during this period included large amounts of rice coinciding with poor harvest years in southern Kwangtung or with years when disorder blocked the normal internal supply channels. As at other ports, including Shanghai, grain imports disappeared and total trade fell off with the return of more nearly normal conditions after 1929. Falling Haikuan tael values, the silver problem, and the early signs of the spreading world depression all help to explain what happened to treaty port trade statistics in 1930 and 1931, but they do not by any means explain away the paradox suggested here, nor can they account for the obvious discrepancies in the 1920s between rising trade levels in the treaty ports and rising distress in the rest of the country.

One possibly important explanation for the rise in treaty port trade during the 1920s and at similar earlier periods of distress in their hinterlands is the temporary migration, perhaps especially of wealthy Chinese (who had most to lose and were also better able to migrate) from their normal homes to the physical safety of the foreign concessions. We know from a great variety of contemporary accounts, official, Customs, and private, that this was a prominent and indeed predictable pattern whenever there was civil unrest after 1842, and that it was also periodically swollen by large numbers of destitute refugees from famine or flood as well as from soldiers and bandits. The demographic and real estate history of Shanghai is especially marked by this pattern, and in the political chaos into which China descended after 1911 and the additional blows of the 1920s all of the treaty ports became increasingly attractive havens for possessors of capital, and for the harassed *lao pai hsing* who lived near enough to survive the journey.[44] By their very nature as instant cities, so to speak, the treaty ports grew predominantly through in-migration rather than natural increase, and nearly all of them, or at least their concession areas, saw especially rapid population growth between 1911 and 1930. During this period Shanghai, for example, rose from approximately one million to nearly three and one-half million, the bulk of it after 1920.[45]

Figures of comparable reliability are not available for the population growth of any of the other treaty ports, but what fragmentary evidence exists suggests a closely similar pattern. Customs *Reports* estimate the population of Hankow (excluding Wuchang and Hanyang) at 289,000 in 1922 and at 804,000 in 1931, pointing out at the same time that immigration (specifically attributed to the flight from banditry and civil war) into Hankow in 1930 alone was estimated at 277,000, a figure which the *Report* assumes as broadly typical of at least the last half of the 1920s.[46] Estimates in the same *Decennial Report* suggest a substantial decline in the total population of Hopeh between 1922 and 1931, but an increase in Tientsin's population over the same period from roughly 800,000 to 1.9 million, attributed likewise to the in-migration of refugees and wealthy Chinese families.[47]

There is obviously no question that treaty port population totals swelled and shrank in close relation to the fluctuating level of civil order and economic well-being in their hinterlands, although it is difficult even to guess at the proportions of wealthy and destitute among those who sought refuge in the concessions. But whatever their economic status, these temporary migrants at each period represented a large net increase in local consumption, perhaps enough to account for a substantial share of the increased imports shown as entering the treaty ports during these periods. It is also a reasonable assumption that both the normal and the temporary "emergency" population of the treaty ports included a larger proportion of relatively wealthy individuals and families than was characteristic of the dominantly rural hinterlands, and that both these and the less prosperous elements of the population developed consumption patterns which included growing amounts of Western-style or imported goods.

In Canton, for example, an account of 1910 includes the observation that "fully 75 per cent of the male population of Canton wear the foreign cloth cap during the winter months."[48] This sounds like considerable prosperity as well as Westernization (at least in tastes), since the account makes clear that the caps were imported rather than domestically made. The well-to-do merchants and gentry who were doubtless less numerous in the treaty ports than the wearers of cloth caps but who, judging from contemporary accounts, were nevertheless a substantial part of the population, lived well and often ostentatiously so. Their normal consumption, increasingly oriented toward Western models, may well have absorbed a large part of the goods imported to each treaty port, apart from the imports (especially after 1895) destined for the support of the growing treaty port industrial sector, the spreading railway system, and the beginnings of large-scale mining enterprise. The foreign residents of the treaty ports, although never more than a tiny fraction of the total population in any of the cities, were also notoriously big spenders who were heavily (it may seem to an irrational degree) dependent on imported goods.

Some, perhaps most, of the remaining inflow of consumer goods may have been destined for higher income and/or semi-Westernized groups in the satellite towns within easy radius of several of the major treaty ports, as mentioned above—Soochow, Fatshan, Hanyang-Wuch'ang, T'angshan—and such nearby centers may also have absorbed most of the treaty port trade in producer goods, raw materials, and commercial services beyond the treaty port itself. It is of course true that nearly all of the industrial development which took place in China after about 1850, private and official Chinese as well as foreign, was physically located either in a few of the major treaty ports, in urban areas adjoining them which remained under Chinese jurisdiction (e.g. the Kiangnan and Hanyang arsenals), or in a few satellite towns of the sort just referred to. Industrial growth after 1895, and especially after 1915, became responsible for increasingly major shares of treaty port imports. Even for raw materials which were available domestically, such as wheat for flour milling (a leading industry in Tientsin and other north China centers), external sources were usually preferred. Given the almost exclusively coastal or riverine location of the treaty ports, bulky goods imported by sea could be laid down there in most cases at lower cost than for domestic equivalents, and usually at more reliable and consistent levels of quality. External sources became additionally important whenever the domestic hinterland was disturbed by disorder or by other interruptions in production. In this way as well, distress in the hinterland might semiautomatically produce an increase in treaty port trade.

Internally, domestic producers were doubtless hurt by famine, flood, and disorder, and their output presumably fell during such periods. Their access to market, as well as the actual cost of transport, was also affected adversely, and the combined effect created an enhanced opportunity for foreign imports in the treaty ports at the expense of what were normally domestic suppliers. Consumers in the hinterland may also have turned to foreign sources of supply in troubled periods for the same reasons. Even in normal times foreign cloth was often cheaper, and economic distress had the effect of reducing consumption of the slightly higher-priced but more durable and desirable Chinese cloth. But all of such changes were temporary, as the Customs trade figures suggest, and it seems unlikely that they were on a very great scale, especially since the foreign accounts do not mention any significant enhancement of the market for foreign goods outside the treaty ports which could be attributed to such causes.

The detailed trade figures show, as one might expect, a highly mixed pattern, as different commodities succeeded one another (for widely varying reasons) in both the import and export trade. Careful analysis and plotting of the mass of figures at Tientsin for the three periods mentioned above shows no gross and few significant exceptions to the general statement that the trade of the port increased when its supposed hinterland was in economic distress and decreased when the distress was relieved. Among foreign imports this was as true for opium (1876–81 and 1890–93) as it was for cotton and woolen cloth and piece goods in aggregate, and for "sundries." The major exception, in the period 1919–31, was metals and machinery (a combined category), which showed a more or less continuous increase through 1931—not an item likely to reflect economic developments outside the city itself, except for railway expansion and the growth of the Kailan Mines. The overall picture is not altered, and is indeed mirrored for the most part, by an analysis of so-called native imports. The figures for exports make a more confused pattern. Although in perhaps half of the dominant commodities there were unbroken or only slightly interrupted increases, usually relatively modest in any one of the three periods, most of the remaining export items showed substantial (though often erratic) rises during the supposed bad years, followed by declines closely parallel to the import figures once economic distress in north China was eased. Disaggregation of the trade confirms the general pattern and provides few clues, at least to me, which could challenge or extend the conclusions stated above. The only suggestion is the obvious one—that in bad times producers in the hinterland became proportionately more dependent on selling whatever goods they could, to consumers in Tientsin, other treaty ports, or abroad, who in such times were the only ones able to buy. Normal trading patterns were between inland, indigenous areas. In troubled times their interconnections were broken, or buyers were impoverished, and producers had thus to sell in Tientsin, which remained unaffected although possibly offering slightly higher prices as a reflection of scarcity. As for imports, with normal sources of indigenous goods closed or reduced, import substitutes were used instead both in Tientsin and in the hinterland.

But none of this constitutes a substantial interrelation between what was happening in the treaty ports and the mass of the Chinese economy. It may be possible to explain why treaty port trade figures rose and fell at certain periods, but not (except negatively) by reference to what was going on in the country beyond their limits—the area they were supposedly transforming. It seems unlikely that the presumed commercial hinterlands of the treaty ports were generating the trade increases shown in the Customs figures during and following periods of political and economic disaster. It is hard to avoid the conclusion that most of the market which the treaty ports served was encompassed in themselves and their local satellites. Their sharp political and cultural isolation from the rest of China was mirrored economically. Something must be wrong with our assumptions about the key role which it has been supposed the treaty ports were playing in the redevelopment of China. Most of the trade increases shown by the Customs figures were statistical rather than real. And most of the real increases were related not to China but to treaty port land. The foreigners remained outsiders.

Chapter 12

China Unconquered?

> The Empire of China is an old crazy first-rate man of war, which a succession of vigilant officers has continued to keep afloat for these 150 years past and to overawe their neighbors merely by her bulk and appearance; but whenever an insufficient man happens to have the command upon deck, adieu to the discipline and safety of the ship. She may perhaps not sink outright; she may drift for a time as a wreck, and then be dashed to pieces on the shore; but she can never be rebuilt on the old bottom.[1]

Macartney was to say the least premature in his judgment, colored as it was both by ignorance of the real state of the country and its relatively slight dependence on the imperial bureaucracy, and by his cultural prejudice. But he was remarkably prescient in forseeing that the Great Confrontation would in the end produce, though not in the way he and the later treaty port figures envisaged, a fundamental reordering of China. The critical element in the Western model was industrial technology, and the strength, wealth, and national power which flowed from it. This was of far greater significance, and with infinitely more potential for transformation, than was trade. Technologically, China became and saw itself as genuinely backward by comparison with the modern West. The traditional system had great staying power, as even Macartney saw; it remained remarkably effective, outside the national political sphere, right to the end. But China's relative decline technologically was simultaneously accelerating. This was not something which could be remedied either by tinkering or by attempting in effect to plaster a thin veneer in a few spots along the coast. The foreigners, the collaborators, and the self-strengtheners all tried to do essentially both of these, and it is not surprising that they failed to make any substantial headway.

Steamships, railways, power-driven manufacturing and mining, all entered China as a result of foreign pressures and with the help of a few Westernized Chinese. Unlike trade or commercial techniques, these were real innovations of genuinely revolutionary potential. Even though their scale remained small in terms of impact on the economy as a whole, they were an essential beginning, and they took place through the agency of the treaty ports in their role as beachheads of an alien system. Machine coal mining was typically begun by the former compradore Tong King-sing, anxious to obtain an adequate and reliable supply of fuel for his new steamship company.[2] Coal mining was later spurred by the development of railways as well as providing their chief cargo. There were thus the beginnings of a basic change in resource use and production, something which trade alone never did and never could accomplish, especially given the extent to which foreigners, their commercial techniques, their goods, and their agency were excluded by Chinese self-sufficiency and capability.

Technological change was a different matter, but it acquired even a modest momentum relatively late, predominantly after 1895 and mainly after 1919. Its spread was also hampered if not hamstrung by events outside the treaty ports after about 1900 and largely unrelated to them, including the progressive collapse of order. The problems which this posed for the railways have already been mentioned, but the so-called modern industrial sector as a whole, although it grew rapidly, never really emerged from an infant stage. To summarize the earlier discussion in chapter 7, the total output in 1933 of all of the modern industrial sector (i.e., eliminating handicrafts) is estimated by the Liu-Yeh study as 3.4 percent of net domestic product. By including estimates for the output of construction, "modern" trade and finance, and mechanized transport and communications, the same source shows the modern sector accounting for 13 percent of net product in the same year, while it estimates total employment in factory industry, mining, and utilities at about two million, or not more than 4 percent of the then current nonagricultural labor force.[3] What one may call a railway system, as opposed to a few separate lines, did not begin to emerge until after 1900, only a few years before the civil order began to collapse. Traditional carriers, especially junks, sampans, and rafts, continued to carry the overwhelming bulk of the traffic, as pointed out in chapter 7.

In all of these respects the impact of new Western technology was blunted by the retention of Chinese sovereignty, the continued capabilities of the indigenous economic system, general resistance to and suspicion of foreign-induced change, and the inability of the Westerners to own land, make investments, build railways—or restore order—outside the treaty ports. The foreign governments wisely chose to eschew either conquests or protectorates, however much their nationals in the treaty ports urged such a course, preferring to keep the Ch'ing in office as an almost client caretaker, to use bluster, threat, and gun-boat diplomacy, and to calculate the costs of attempting to take over China as far beyond reason. The Old China Hands never convinced their home governments that their interests in China were national rather than private concerns, nor that if only Chinese could be replaced by Western control, in some form or other, the potential of the China market would at last be realized. As the London *Times* put it in an 1875 editorial, "We are not in the mood to undertake the responsibility of another India."[4] The threat of conquest was nevertheless very real in the minds of many Chinese, but the galvanizing effects of the Western threat were delayed by comparison with the much smaller, more integrated, and more responsive setting of Japan, let alone the effects produced by actual conquest in South and Southeast Asia.

No substantial numbers of new-style innovators, gentry or others, appeared outside the treaty ports. Most owners of capital avoided industrial ventures, preferring speculative or predatory ventures in the *sauve-qui-peut* climate after 1900, or traditionally hallowed local philanthropy. The continued prominence of landholding as well as local charities as uses for capital does not suggest that the character of the gentry role was changing or that as a group they were a positive factor in the process of economic growth. Landholding became less and less profitable in the course of the nineteenth and twentieth centuries, especially by comparison with other forms of investment,[5] but together with philanthropy it remained the predominant means for enhancing prestige and legitimacy, another sign that the traditional system and its values had changed very little. The gentry also played a relatively minor role in the national as opposed to local political fumblings of the warlord period, although they did increasingly take over from a moribund central government most of its erstwhile local functions through the extension of traditional gentry management of local affairs. But relatively little gentry leadership developed to point the way to national regeneration or integration. The revolution of 1911 was to a large extent a gentry-led movement, in provincial urban centers and in some sense as a newly emerging group, though hardly a Western-style bourgeoisie. While they aimed at constitutional reform rather than at genuine revolution, their response was far more to internal problems, and at local and provincial levels, than to the treaty port model except in some superficial forms. The new group of reformers were anti-imperialist, as were their allies who organized boycotts in Canton and Shanghai, but the West was far more a target for them than a cause or shaper of their vision. The foreign threat united them, created in effect a new nationalism, but did not evoke a response which, as elsewhere in Asia, sought Westernization as the appropriate path to national development and strength.

What was true of the gentry was, at least in many respects, apparently true also of most of the new group of compradores and ex-compradores. Except for their association with the post-1927 Kuomintang, by that time no longer a revolutionary organization, they too pursued quick or speculative profit rather than socially or economically productive innovation. After all, they too had grown up in the absence of reliable civil order or of a sociopolitical structure which protected or rewarded innovation or even constructive investment. Nearly all of the compradores before 1911 purchased or attempted to purchase official rank or gentry titles,[6] and as much as possible also assumed traditional gentry roles in their native places, as landowners, founders and supervisors of local public works, compilers and publishers of local histories, and supporters of local charitable undertakings.[7] Many of the new schools in the treaty ports also, especially in Shanghai, were financed and organized in whole or part by compradores who were also active in organizing chapters of the Red Cross and similar organizations.[8]

The old governmental order did of course fall in 1911; the official side of the dyarchy was removed and the Chinese merchant and nationalist was now on his own. In the treaty ports there was, especially after 1900 and increasingly after 1911, what appeared in the perspective of the time to be a promising growth of new-style and openly Western-influenced Chinese entrepreneurs, some outright collaborators, some on the sidelines or functioning in both groups, for example in the Chinese Chambers of Commerce.[9] But most of whatever promise this sort of growth may have held was choked off in the context of what was happening in China outside the protection of the foreign concessions. No effective government emerged, stability was not restored, and no innovating leadership made itself felt. There was not a sufficiently favorable climate in which the new-style Chinese entrepreneur could flourish outside the little foreign islands.

In political or ideological terms, while they lasted the treaty ports did not help to integrate China, as the port cities helped to integrate South and Southeast Asia, in many cases for the first time. Instead, the treaty ports created a deep dualism. The early Communist vision was formed in these cities, but as a reaction *against* them, and its translation into successful action took place in the countryside in open warfare against the treaty ports. There was no blending of China and the West, but only a sharpening of the confrontation. No *national* group emerged from the treaty port context to speak or to act for China. The treaty ports instead multiplied the divisions among the traditional or reactionary gentry and official elite, the treaty port Chinese, and the new revolutionaries: the Chinese Communist Party and their student allies. The perspective of contemporary China has revealed the treaty ports as tiny and isolated islands in an alien Chinese sea which all along resisted, and then rejected them. The colonial port cities in India and Southeast Asia could not effectively be rejected; they had become too important a part of the essence of each cultural and political unit. They became also the dominant, almost the sole, nuclei of what each country was trying to achieve: both new and old cultural identity, economic growth, national integration, and the movement for independence.

The China treaty ports, in contrast, remained foreign in everyone's eyes, distinct from the country as a whole. When even the foreigners distinguished China from treaty port land, it is hardly surprising that the Chinese did the same. They could the more easily reject the treaty ports as alien and threatening. Traditional resistance to foreign-style innovation as unneeded, unwanted, and productive of disharmony was succeeded by the bitter Communist denunciation of the treaty port model.

Many Asian nationalists, including the Chinese (Ch'ing, KMT, and Chinese Communist Party alike) blamed colonialism for Asia's unsatisfactory economic and political progress, even for its moral and social problems. In South and Southeast Asia the evidence seems in balance to argue the opposite. In China the semicolonial system was never as effective as the nationalist, or Marxist, argument implied. China was a different case from that conceived in Marxist analysis. The imperialist effort did not destroy its ability to compete, or its ability to manage in its own terms and within its own largely unaffected world its own successful system of livelihood, values, and organization. The treaty port Chinese remained a resented and feeble minority, divorced from both the traditional order and from the emerging revolutionary solution. The KMT was controlled at least as much by unregenerate gentry as by treaty port men, as exemplified

by Chiang Kai-shek, who was both. And the Nanking government represented the apogee of power for the treaty port Chinese—not a very
impressive achievement. Treaty port intellectuals and political dissidents
had little influence in their own time on the course of events from outside
positions of political power. The reformers of 1898 were certainly treaty
port tainted, but hardly treaty port men.

It was students, in league with workers, the few intellectuals, and
nationalist-minded merchants, who in May of 1919 created the movement
which first exercised a direct influence on events. Their effort, which
succeeded in building the first truly national front, centered on protests
and boycotts *against* the treaty ports and all they represented: national
humiliation. Students and other earlier and later protesters and potential revolutionaries were of course both sheltered in and stimulated by
the treaty port world. It was the principal arena of national humiliation
and the point of maximum contact with the foreigners who were attempting to rape China, and at the same time it offered an example of
strength through nationalism. But the students and other patriots, especially the leaders of boycotts, used the treaty ports as their *targets,* never
as their even indirect model. It was, as it had to be, a new group, divorced
from both the traditional order and from the treaty ports, which inherited
the leadership of modern China.

But the vigor with which the treaty ports were rejected demonstrates their
profound impact on the Chinese mind. Materially, the treaty port system
and its drive for commercialization and modernization of the economy
must be seen for the most part as a failure, especially in the perspective of
the colonial experience in India. The supremely self-confident foreign view
of their role in China from 1842 to 1941 can now be corrected, as one
looks at the place through those years of the treaty port system, the
railways and colleges, the mines, factories, and banks, in the greater
Chinese context which overshadows them, or in the context of colonial
South and Southeast Asia. For all its vigor and self-confidence, the foreign
presence and its efforts at innovation made only the smallest of dents in
the material fabric of traditional China. The great majority of Chinese
were unaffected, directly or indirectly, in their way of life. Over most of
the landscape, as in the production process or in the urban centers outside
the foreign concessions themselves, there was almost no sign that external
forces were attempting to reshape the country. The foreigners saw them-

selves as the wave of the future, offering a model of "progress" which the Chinese could not and would not want to resist. But in fact, all but a handful of Chinese ignored or were little touched by it, continuing to respond instead to long-established internal forces and values.

Materially, China went on behaving for the most part as it had always done. Chinese merchants, most of them in the traditional mode, continued completely to dominate the marketing system and its financing, including the assembly and distribution of foreign trade goods. The overwhelming majority of consumer goods continued to come from Chinese producers, mainly of the traditional sort but including also most of the small total of machine-made goods. Railways and river or coastal steamers carried a very small proportion of total haulage, most of which continued to move by junk, sampan, raft, cart, pack animal, wheelbarrow, and human porter. A few commodities of foreign origin: kerosene, cotton yarn, cigarettes, found niches in the domestic market, as did originally exotic (New World) crops such as peanuts and maize, but all of these were in a relative sense inconsequentials. Foreign dreams of "tapping the vast China market" were never even faintly realized. The same applies to the growth of new exports. The total new production, let alone that part newly devoted to commercial sale for export, of commodities like pig bristles, eggs, sausage casings, tung oil, antimony, silk, tea, wool, hides, straw braid, and fireworks, [10] while difficult to estimate, could not by any assessment be regarded as more than a tiny proportion of traditional production.

But in their role as beachheads of an alien system,[11] the treaty ports revealed the ineffectiveness of the national political order. It was unable to prevent their incursive nibblings at Chinese sovereignty or to shield individual Chinese from bitter humiliation. Arrogance, high-handedness, and gunboat diplomacy also accompanied the missionary effort. The foreigners were frustrated in their dreams of trade and modernization, but they cut a sore wound in the Chinese psyche. Their technology too, though it failed for the most part to spread let alone transform the country, was ideologically important in its revelation of China's backwardness; it hurt China more psychologically than it helped her economically.

The political center was politically and ideologically powerless. Great China was humbled, and one result was the rise of a regionalism which, whatever its real meaning, was ultimately read, and resented by Chinese nationalists, as a sign of weakness and national disintegration. For much of this, nationalists argued, the treaty ports were to blame. It was they and the system they represented which had assaulted and emasculated the center, had helped to prevent its overthrow by the Taipings and the regeneration which might have followed. It was they who had kept the Ch'ing in office as a client regime, profiting from its growing weakness, bleeding it through unequal treaties, imposed tariff levels, customs revenues, and indemnities, while they manipulated it to yield more and more concessions. In such a context, and from the post-1949 vantage point, those Chinese who collaborated with foreigners, who lived in and made a good thing out of the treaty ports—perhaps especially those who adopted foreign techniques and attitudes (the modernizers, the apostles of Western-style progress)—were by abundant definition simply traitors, as the treaty ports themselves were cancers on the Chinese body. In the perspective of the 1970s, the Chinese response to the West appears more rather than less effective than the Indian response. Singlemindedness, ideological fervor, and xenophobia—the major legacies of the treaty ports—unite, organize, and invigorate more effectively than compromise or cosmopolitanism.

The foreign presence in China was almost exclusively urban,[12] as was the kind of modernization they tried to promote. And although the treaty ports were not in the main new cities but only adjuncts to existing Chinese cities, they were obvious symbols of an alien intrusion under the unequal treaties. Chinese nationalists saw them not as spark plugs or vital centers but as malignant tumors, excrescences unrelated to the real China except in their efforts to subvert and exploit it. The strangers at the gate, in Frederic Wakeman's phrase, stirred up far more negative than positive response, as Wakeman's absorbing picture of Kwangtung in the 1840s and 1850s makes clear.[13] The Western model of development was not softened by adaptation to indigenous tradition in China as it was in India. As a result, contemporary China is far more integrated than India, mobilized in the denigration of foreignism, the elevation of Chineseness (self-reliance), and the drive for technological development to demonstrate that China does not need the West and that technology is not culture bound, that the Western package can be rejected while China pursues its own, better road to wealth and power.

The anti-urban theme is directed primarily against the former treaty ports (which with the single exception of Peking include all of the largest cities), but it involves by association all cities. It has roots earlier than the treaty ports, in peasant risings against cities as landlord strongholds, and in Confucian gentry attitudes, but its focus shifted by the twentieth century to the very different and more nationalist target of the treaty ports. From the first beginnings of the Chinese Communist Party, and before Mao took up the idea, Li Ta-chao and Tai Chi-t'ao castigated both the decadence and the parasitism of cities, using the specific example of the treaty ports.[14]

> Tai's attitude toward Shanghai was the prime catalyst of his commit-ment to social revolution. For Tai and for the entire spectrum of Chinese revolutionaries as well, she was a bitch-goddess who gnawed at their souls, scarring them brutally and indelibly. Life in the Concessions was comparatively safe, for example, but the very security which Tai enjoyed there galled and tormented him at the same time. He, a Chinese, was being protected from fellow Chinese by the grace and scientific superiority of Westerners. His asylum rapidly crystallized into a personal confrontation with the entire legacy of China's humiliations at the hands of the West. . . . [The countryside] represented idyllic, uncontaminated China for Tai. There he saw Chinese living in a natural economy. . . . Thus while the workers of Shanghai were in hell, the handicraft worker-peasants of Hu-chou were in heaven. . . . He expressed grief that 'old' Hu-chou, no doubt, would soon be forced to enter the modern world under the impact of European civilization.[15]

Li Ta-chao, the principal founder of the Party, urged his student followers "to leave the 'corrupting life' of the cities and universities and 'go to the villages' . . . in the 'wholly human life' of the countryside."[16] By 1927, Mao's famous Hunan Report identifies the peasantry as the revolutionary army and foreshadows the downgrading and ultimate con-frontation of the cities, the home of Westernized intellectuals and degen-erate cosmopolitanism, of collaborators and revisionists, and of a prole-tariat whose revolutionary will could not be counted on, subverted and demoralized as they were by their environment. The countryside by comparison is pure, Chinese, untainted by Western influences through the treaty ports, and ready to strike against oppression, to purge China of its treaty-port-brewed poison. Subsequent experience hardened these atti-tudes, as efforts to organize the workers and to seize power in the cities (the treaty ports) failed. The treaty ports were the strongholds of the Kuomintang as well as of the foreigners; they were evil, and they must be purged. China's rural-based revolution, taking the treaty ports as its target, became a model for world revolution in explicitly anti-urban terms:

> To rely on the peasants, build rural base areas, and use the country-side to encircle and finally capture the cities—such was the way to victory in the Chinese revolution. Comrade Mao Tse-tung pointed

out the importance of building revolutionary base areas: "Since China's key cities have long been occupied by the powerful imperialists and their reactionary Chinese allies, it is imperative for the revolutionary ranks to turn the backward villages into advanced consolidated base areas, into great military, political, economic, and cultural bastions of the revolution from which to fight their vicious enemies who are using the cities for attacks on the rural districts, and in this way gradually to achieve the complete victory of the revolution through protracted fighting." The imperialists usually begin by seizing the big cities and the main lines of communication, but they are unable to bring the vast countryside completely under their control. . . . The countryside and the countryside alone can provide the revolutionary bases from which the revolutionaries can go forward to final victory. . . . The contemporary world revolution also presents a picture of the encirclement of cities by the rural areas.[17]

Admittedly, Chinese Communist anti-urbanism has not always been entirely consistent, and its contradiction with pro-industrialism makes it incompletely consistent even during the Cultural Revolution. But the revolutionary pattern for the road to power in Chinese Communist strategy in the 1920s was aimed *at* the cities, in the expectation that the oppression which they created would breed revolution. "City" meant and still largely means treaty port, and hence was seen as evil, suppurating with revolutionary potential. It took the failure of uprisings and attacks in Canton, Changsha, and Wuhan and the Kuomintang coup of 1927 in Shanghai to persuade the Communists that the cities were not ripe for their purposes, and to convince them of the rottenness, moral corruption, and counterrevolutionary character of cities which has since dominated the Maoist view. Such a view arises equally understandably from the role which all large cities (treaty ports) in China played, and which made them and their inhabitants evil. There were of course other reasons, primarily nationalist, why China reacted negatively to the treaty ports. But the violence of the reaction was also fueled by the economic character of these cities. The treaty ports have indeed influenced the new China; far more than they ever succeeded in realizing their own goals, their legacy has helped to create the Maoist blueprint for the Chinese world which excluded them.

Those former imperialist bastions must also be remade, to serve the people, and their exploitative and degrading influences on the rest of the country eradicated. Shanghai was the chief stronghold of treaty port land, and it is still a symbol of potential evil to be controlled, to be rechanneled into good. All the old foreign buildings remain; physically Shanghai still looks strangely as it did when foreigners controlled it; the Shanghai Club, which once boasted of "the longest bar in the world," still stands. Perhaps this shows the confidence of China's new rulers that the inward reality, which has been transformed, is what counts. As if to symbolize such a conviction, the Westminster chimes of the clock on the old Maritime Customs building on the Bund, by which Shanghai-landers set their foreign watches in the old days, were replaced early in the Cultural Revolution (in August of 1966) by a new set of chimes which play "The East is Red":

> Over a century ago, the western colonialist robbers crashed the gates of China. By controlling China's Maritime Customs they drained away the blood of the Chinese working people. The heavy church-like chimes of the big clock on the customs building . . . were a constant reminder of this imperialist exploitation. Control of the Maritime Customs was taken back by the Chinese people in 1949 when Shanghai was liberated, but the imperialist chimes stayed on. Then came China's great cultural revolution . . . clearing away the remnant traces of filth left over from the old Shanghai.[18]

But potential threat to Maoist values remains and may even be newly generated in these urban centers whose history is so tainted. Although the former treaty ports, especially Shanghai, are the worst, the treaty port legacy has shaped a Maoist vision of all cities as potentially corrupt and corrupting, latent centers of revisionism, unnatural environments where even workers can be dragged down into the moral rottenness of "economism"—Mao's version of creeping capitalism—in which people are seduced into elevating personal material gain above the needs of society. Economism, elitism, parasitism, bureaucratism, and status-quoism, the cardinal sins of contemporary China, are no doubt associated with urbanism, in China as elsewhere. The derivation of the word "bourgeoisie" is no accident. The *hsia-fang* (down to the countryside) movement put this attitude into sharp perspective. No one, it seems, can hope to remain ideologically or behavioristically pure in the foul environment of a city, and must periodically be sent to the untainted countryside for self-redeeming, purging labor in order to recoup his socialist, *Chinese* revolutionary, vision.

Austerity and nativism are familiar themes in revolutions, and China is here consistent with earlier revolutionary experiences in Russia, France, and Cromwellian England. But by historical circumstance, cities became the *targets* of the Chinese revolution rather than its breeding grounds or power bases, and the association of cities with colonialism in the Chinese context has further sharpened anti-urbanism. The treaty ports tried to be the vanguard of China's transformation, from the outside in, from their marginal bases on the coast and as beachheads of an all-powerful but foreign Western system. In South and Southeast Asia, the same essential formula did indeed produce transformation. The colonial port cities set the pace and the pattern for the remaking of each national unit in a willing hybridization of Western and indigenous strands. Calcutta, Bombay, New (but not Old) Delhi, Colombo, Rangoon, Bangkok, Singapore, Saigon and Hanoi, Batavia (Djakarta), Surabaja, Manila, all foreign bases and most of them foreign founded, became the predominant centers of the national life of each country, as they still are, not merely in size or industrial production or as transport and communications nuclei but as the easily acknowledged pinnacles and shapers of the new national life. The treaty port Indian, Ceylonese, Burmese, Thai, Annamese, Javanese, and Filipino became the dominant postindependence figures in each country. In China, transformation of this sort was bitterly resisted. China in the end transformed itself, in an indigenous, negating response to the treaty port goad, a wave which was generated in the still largely inviolate inland rural areas to overwhelm and purge the alien cities. What was not indigenous— Marxism-Leninism, and the new conversion to modern technology—was purged of its connections with the Western model and used as a weapon against the West, as means to build a *Chinese* answer to the Western challenge.

But though China was never conquered by the imperialists, it is ideologically driven still by its semicolonial past to a degree not found elsewhere in Asia, where the foreigners had it all their own way. Because the treaty ports failed to make a significant material impact, and failed to produce the kind of blending which took place in the rest of Asia, the Chinese could continue to regard them as alien, could resent and reject them, and with them, they thought, all of Western-style urbanism. Where India is ruled, with no sense of its being inappropriate, from the Edwardian monument of Luytens's and Bakers's Viceregal Secretariat in the imperialist-planned colonial city of New Delhi, China can be ruled only from untaintedly, traditionally Chinese Peking, the one major city which was never a treaty port, where the T'ien An Men remains the chief monumental symbol of the state, as it was long before the Westerners arrived. But although China remained unconquered, the semicolonial interlude may, because of its very ineffectiveness, have made a deeper impact on the Chinese mind, and in the longer run thus helped to put greater forces in train than all the imperial achievements of the West in the rest of the world east of Suez.

The outsiders finally made their mark on China. For the present it seems a largely negative or counter mark. But as a postrevolutionary China continues to confront hard but ineluctable choices in its drive for industrialization in a country which its leaders recognize has become relatively poor and technologically backward by comparison with the modern West, the negative aspects of the Western impact may come to seem less prominent. Marxism-Leninism, and even Maoism, embrace the industrial-technological path to development as fervently as ever did the modern West. For Maoism this implies a contradiction, one suspects an ultimately antagonistic contradiction, with the rural-based anti-urban ideals of the early revolution. Cities are growing rapidly, as industrialization progresses. This includes big cities as well as the smaller ones officially favored; there were only nine million-class cities according to the 1953 census; by the mid-1970s there were over twenty. Manufacturing still centers heavily, though now with pride, in the former treaty ports, which remain the biggest cities of all. Although the consequent emergence of urban and technological-managerial elites is seen as a problem to be perennially corrected, and although rural commune-based industrialization offers an exciting (if still relatively limited) alternative to Western-style urban concentration of industrial functions, China in another generation may appear to be following a course less directly counter to the original Western model. By the same time, the nativist reactions in India described in chapter 5 may have reshaped in more distinctively indigenous terms what now appears to be so heavily a Western-colonial legacy.

China's bulk and inertia were harder to move, but transformation has now acquired momentum. It is following in critical respects an originally Western path. The Chinese way will certainly remain distinctive and will long carry a profound revolutionary and Maoist imprint. But it is unlikely to remain permanently based on total rejection of what was once the treaty port model of the road to wealth and power. As the association of industrialization, urbanism, and modern technology with foreign imperialism recedes farther into the past, and as China develops pride in its own independent achievements in all these respects, it may come to travel, in its own way, along the same road which the Western colonialists first urged and demonstrated in their efforts to transform the Middle Kingdom.

Notes

Chapter 1

1. R. H. Tawney, *Land and Labour in China* (London, 1932), p. 13.
2. An Anglo-Indian corruption of the Arabic word *sarraf*, a banker.
3. J. R. Levenson, *Confucian China and Its Modern Fate: The Problem of Intellectual Continuity* (Berkeley, 1958), p. 87.
4. Translation by E. L. Farmer of an Imperial Edict of 1759 from the *Ta Ch'ing li-ch'ao shih-lu*, in E. L. Farmer, "James Flint versus the Canton Interest, 1755–1760," *Papers on China*, vol. 17 (Cambridge, Mass., 1963), pp. 38–66.

Chapter 2

1. On traditional Asian shipping, and on the da Gama story, see R. G. Gravenstein, ed., *Journal of the First Voyage of Vasco da Gama* (London, 1898); J. L. Duyvendak, *China's Discovery of Africa* (London, 1949); Joseph Needham, *Science and Civilization in China*, vol. 4 (Cambridge, 1971), Nautical Technology, pp. 379–699; W. H. Moreland, "The Ships of the Arabian Sea About A.D. 1500," *Journal of the Royal Asiatic Society* (April 1939), pp. 174–75; C. N. Parkinson, *Trade in the Eastern Seas* (Cambridge, 1937); R. K. Mookerjee, *Indian Shipping* (London, 1912); R. J. Aston, "The Merchant Shipping Activity of South China, 1644–1847" (Ph.D. diss., University of Hawaii, 1964); M. A. P. Meilink-Roelofsz, *Asian Trade and European Influence in the Indonesian Archipelago* (The Hague, 1962). The European side is dealt with in several general accounts: C. M. Cipolla, *Guns, Sails, and Empires: Technological Innovations and the Early Phase of European Expansion, 1400–1700* (London, 1965); J. H. Parry, *The Age of Reconnaissance* (London, 1963), see especially the sources referred to in the notes for chapters 3, 4, 7, and 8; idem, *The Discovery of the Sea* (London, 1975); idem, *The Establishment of the European Hegemony, 1415–1715* (New York, 1961); idem, *Trade and Exploration in the Age of the Renaissance* (New York, 1961); C. R.

Boxer, *Four Centuries of Portuguese Expansion* (Johannesburg, 1961); idem, *The Dutch Seaborne Empire* (London, 1965).

2. The best single account of the first century of such encounters, centered in detail on the early Portuguese presence in Gujerat, is contained in M. N. Pearson, "Commerce and Compulsion: Gujerati Merchants and the Portuguese System in Western India, 1500–1600" (Ph.D. diss., University of Michigan, 1971). His extensive notes and bibliography list a variety of relevant Portuguese, English, and Indian-Persian sources.

3. O. K. Nambiar, *Portuguese Pirates and Indian Seamen* (Mysore, 1955), and Grace Fox, *British Admirals and Chinese Pirates* (London, 1940), provide two accounts.

4. Hsieh Kuo-chen, "Ch'ing-ch'u tung-nan yen-hai ch'ien" [Evacuation of the southeast coast in early Ch'ing], *Kuo-hsüeh chi-k'an* 2 (December 1930): 797–826. On Japanese piracy during the Ming more generally, see Ch'en Mao-heng, "Ming-tai wo-k'ou k'ao-lueh" [Japanese pirate attacks during the Ming], *Yen-ching Hsüeh-pao*, Monograph Series, no. 6 (Peking, 1934).

5. Parkinson, *Trade in the Eastern Seas*, pp. 320 ff.

6. The best known statement is of course K. M. Panikkar, *Asia and Western Dominance* (London, 1953).

7. Rhoads Murphey, "Traditionalism and Colonialism: Changing Urban Roles in Asia," *Journal of Asian Studies* 29 (November 1969): 67–84; and idem, "The City in the Swamp: Aspects of the Site and Early Growth of Calcutta," *The Geographical Journal* 130 (June 1964): 241–56.

8. Murphey, "Traditionalism and Colonialism," p. 70.

9. For more detail on this problem and on solutions to it, see R. Murphey, "Colonialism in Asia and the Role of the Port Cities," *East Lakes Geographer* 5 (1969): 24–49, and sources cited there.

10. Reproduced from Murphey, "Traditionalism and Colonialism" but originally prepared in fact for this book, as was the research on which the map and notes are based. My major focus here is the high tide of the West in Asia, after about 1800, specifically in China after 1842.

11. With the qualified exception of Japan. See below, p. 24.

12. Quoted in George Lanning, *A History of Shanghai* (Shanghai, 1923), p. 134.

13. The pattern of interaction between center and periphery has common features in many historical settings; transformation of the center through change initiated at the periphery, and often of alien origin, has in fact been widespread in many parts of the world, as many scholars have noted. See, for example, Eric Wolf, "Understanding Civilizations: A Review Article," *Comparative Studies in Society and History* 9 (1967): 446–65, and the several studies cited therein.

14. This question is pursued in the Indian context by J. H. Broomfield in "The Regional Elites: A Theory of Modern Indian History," *The Indian Economic and Social History Review* 3 (September 1966): 279–91, and at book length in idem, *Elite Conflict in a Plural Society: Twentieth Century Bengal* (Berkeley, 1968).

15. Population statistics for the countries and cities concerned, now or at any time in the past, vary widely in reliability. Urban figures are also ambiguous in terms of the extent of the conurbation covered, and are seldom reliably comparable within any one country or between different census periods, let alone between different countries. Multiple (and often conflicting) figures exist for all the cities concerned, but they can be used with any confidence in so few cases, especially on a comparative basis, that they have not been used here except as general guides to orders of magnitude. Urban size ranking within each country, especially from about 1870 to the 1950s, is however reasonably clear for at least the larger cities.

16. On Bangkok see D. G. E. Hall, *A History of Southeast Asia* (London, 1955), pp. 389–402; on Rangoon, see B. R. Pearn, *A History of Rangoon* (Rangoon, 1939).

17. *The Statistical Abstract of India,* an annual publication, lists total trade values and shipping tonnages for all important ports from 1909. Earlier all-India figures refer only to states or presidencies and do not distinguish individual ports, although they do suggest a similar pattern.

18. Hong Kong and Canton are best regarded for trade statistical purposes from 1860 to 1941 as a single unit.

19. Sample studies include Anil Seal, *The Emergence of Indian Nationalism: Competition and Collaboration in the Later Nineteenth Century* (New York, 1968); David Kopf, *British Orientalism and the Bengal Renaissance: The Dynamics of Indian Modernization, 1773–1835* (Berkeley, 1969); Benjamin Schwartz, *In Search of Wealth and Power: Yen Fu and the West* (Harvard, 1964); Chow Tse-tsung, *The May Fourth Movement: Intellectual Revolution in Modern China* (Cambridge, Mass., 1960); Paul Cohen, "Wang T'ao's Perspective on a Changing World," in *Approaches to Modern Chinese History*, ed. Albert Feuerwerker, Rhoads Murphey, and Mary Wright (Berkeley, 1967); and Mary Backus Rankin, *Early Chinese Revolutionaries: Radical Intellectuals in Shanghai and Chekiang, 1902–1911* (Cambridge, Mass., 1971).

20. For Latin America the best guide is a long review of recent research by Richard Morse, "Trends and Issues in Latin American Urban Research," *Latin American Research Review* 6, no. 1 (1971): 3–34, and 6, no. 2 (1971): 19–75. Sample studies of African urbanization include M. Crowder, *West Africa Under Colonial Rule* (Evanston,

1969); H. Kuper, *Urbanization and Migration in West Africa* (Berkeley, 1965); and H. Miner, ed., *The City in Modern Africa* (New York, 1968).

21. The phrase was coined by O. H. K. Spate, "Factors in the Development of Capital Cities," *The Geographical Review* 32 (1942): 622–31.

22. Similar stories could doubtless be told of rural Nigeria or Mexico, but the staying power of traditional African and pre-Columbian Amerind cultures in competition with or conflict with the West was and is very much less than that of traditional Asian cultures.

23. On this point, and for a brilliant essay on aspects of the larger themes touched on, see M. Singer, "Beyond Tradition and Modernity in Madras," *Comparative Studies in Society and History* 13 (1971): 160–95.

24. Let me refer to some sample studies, and some critiques, of the "modernization" theme. Joseph Levenson has beautifully elaborated the importance of the distinction between "modern" and "Western" in his *Confucian China and Its Modern Fate: The Problem of Intellectual Continuity* (Berkeley, 1958), esp. pp. 117 ff. The dimensions, Protean meanings, and evolution of "modernization" in a number of actual contexts have been examined in several standard studies, including C. E. Black, *The Dynamics of Modernization: A Study of Comparative History* (New York, 1966); M. J. Levy, *Modernization and the Structure of Societies: A Setting for International Affairs,* 2 vols. (Princeton, 1966); David Apter, *The Politics of Modernization* (Chicago, 1965); Myron Weiner, ed., *Modernization: The Dynamics of Growth* (New York, 1966); and in specific Asian settings, M. B. Jansen, ed., *Changing Japanese Attitudes Toward Modernization* (Princeton, 1965); M. Singer, *When a Great Tradition Modernizes* (New York, 1972); and L. I. and S. H. Rudolph, *The Modernity of Tradition: Political Development in India* (Chicago, 1967). Useful critiques include, as samples from a wide range of periodical and other material, Singer, "Beyond Tradition and Modernity in Madras," pp. 160–95; D. C. Tripp, "Modernization Theory and the Comparative Study of Societies," *Comparative Studies in Society and History* 15 (1973): 199–225; L. E. Shiner, "Tradition/Modernity: An Ideal Type Gone Astray," *Comparative Studies in Society and History* 17 (1975): 245–52; R. P. Dore, "On the Possibility and Desirability of a Theory of Modernization" in Report from the International Conference on the Problems of Modernization, Asian Research Centre (Seoul, 1968), reprinted in C. C. A. S. Newsletter, no. 3, March 1969, pp. 59–64; M. Gasster, "Reform and Revolution in China's Political Modernization," in *China in Revolution,* ed. M. C. Wright (New Haven, 1968), pp. 67–96; M. Gasster, *China's Struggle to Modernize* (New York, 1972) where the modernization-Westernization contrast is further explored;

James O'Connell, "The Concept of Modernization," *South Atlantic Quarterly* 64 (1965): 549–64; and B. I. Schwartz, "The Limits of Tradition Versus Modernity," *Daedalus* 101 (Spring 1972): 71–88.

25. Bayard Taylor, *A Visit to India, China, and Japan, in the Year 1853* (New York, 1855).

26. See notes 27 and 28.

27. On Asian conceptions of time, including historical time, see W. N. Brown, *Man in the Universe: Some Cultural Continuities in Indian Thought* (Berkeley, 1966); Joseph Needham, *Time and Eastern Man* (London, 1965); J. T. Marcus, "Time and the Sense of History: West and East," *Comparative Studies in Society and History* 2 (1960): 123–29; N. Sivin, "Chinese Concepts of Time," *Earlham Review* 1 (1966): 82–92.

28. The lines are quoted, with Tennyson's explanation, in J. B. Bury, *The Idea of Progress: An Inquiry Into Its Origin and Growth* (London, 1920), which also provides a useful general discussion of the evolution of the concept of progress in the Western mind.

29. For a discussion of the traditional Asian view of man's relation to the natural world, see Rhoads Murphey, "Man and Nature in China," *Modern Asian Studies* 1 (1967): 313–33, and idem, "City and Countryside as Ideological Issues: India and China," *Comparative Studies in Society and History* 14 (June 1972): 250–67.

30. Richard Cobden, *The Political Writings of Richard Cobden,* 2d ed., 2 vols. (New York, 1868), vol. 1, p. 45.

31. Quoted in J. K. Fairbank, *Trade and Diplomacy on the China Coast: The Opening of the Treaty Ports, 1842–1854,* 1 vol. ed. (Cambridge, Mass., 1964), p. 173, from articles by Alcock, "The Chinese Empire and Its Destinies," *The Bombay Quarterly Review* 4 (October 1855) and 6 (April 1856).

32. Quoted in J. K. Fairbank, *Trade and Diplomacy,* p. 173.

Chapter 3

1. The following discussion is based extensively on four articles by John Irwin, "Indian Textile Trade in the Seventeenth Century," *Journal of Indian Textile History* 1 (1955): 113–27; 2 (1956): 24–42; 3 (1957): 59–72; and 4 (1959): 57–64; and in J. Irwin and P. R. Schwartz, *Studies in Indo-European Textile History* (Ahmadabad, 1966), pp. 5–33. The Indonesian archipelago remained from the beginning the chief source of most spices reaching Europe, originally carried to Indian ports by a variety of Asian traders and there, after 1498, bought by the Portuguese. After the Portuguese, and later the Dutch, established their own bases in Southeast Asia they carried these spices

directly to Europe. The development of fodder crops (especially turnips) in Europe after the seventeenth century made it possible to carry more livestock over the winter instead of slaughtering most of them each fall and hence decreased the need for spices as a preservative or as an additive to disguise the taste of tainted meat.

2. Part of the problem was the small economic margin of most Indian consumers which, as in China later, restricted effective demand, especially for imported goods.

3. The story is repeated in many places, including Robert Orme, *Historical Fragments of the Mughal Empire* (London, 1782), p. 409. Orme also stresses Bengal's productivity, as had so many earlier observers, and adds: "It is difficult to find a village in Bengal in which every man, woman, or child is not employed in making a piece of cloth." One should add, however, that productivity per worker was low, partly because for many it was a parttime occupation; contemporary Europeans complained chronically about the slow rate of output and could never obtain as much cloth as they wanted for export.

4. Saltpeter is a curious commodity, a naturally occurring form of potassium nitrate, which is highly soluble and hence rarely found in nature except in deserts, such as the Atacama in Chile. It forms where organic nitrogenous materials decay in contact with potassium salts, and thus is often found in association with the lime and plaster of old buildings where sewage effluents have percolated. In Europe, manure and brushwood heaps were artifically built and covered with ashes or lime to yield saltpeter. In India, and especially in Bengal (at that time including what is now Bihar), conditions were far more favorable: a dense and cattle-keeping population using wood and dung as fuel and in a situation of high temperatures and humidity which prompted rapid organic decay. Efflorescences containing saltpeter grew on walls, refuse heaps, house floors, deserted village sites, and around existing villages. The discovery of the Atacama deposits in Chile and of a process to convert these to sodium nitrate as a basis for explosives instead of potassium nitrate destroyed the market for saltpeter by the last decades of the nineteenth century, although it is still used locally as fertilizer. Earlier, the high quality of Bengali-Bihari saltpeter, and the post-1760 practical English monopoly of export trade in it, was said to have been a factor in English military success against the French in India, North America, and Europe, and to have contributed something to the outcome of Trafalgar and Waterloo. For more detail on saltpeter, see J. C. Brown and A. K. Dey, *India's Mineral Wealth*, 3d ed. (Oxford, 1955), pp. 467 ff.

5. Quoted in J. N. das Gupta, *India in the Seventeenth Century* (Calcutta, 1916), p. 212.

6. The major published primary sources on which this and the following

summary accounts are based are documentary collections by Charles Fawcett, ed., *The English Factories in India*, 4 vols., particularly vol. 4, *The East Coast and Bengal* (Oxford, 1952); William Foster, ed., *The English Factories in India, 1618–1621*, 3 vols. (Oxford, 1906–27); Charles R. Wilson, ed., *Early Annals of the English in Bengal*, 3 vols. (Calcutta, 1895–1917); S. A. Khan, ed., *The East India Trade in the Seventeenth Century* (London, 1923). Of the many secondary accounts, two of the best are Sukumar Bhattacharya, *The East India Company and the Economy of Bengal* (London, 1954); and Tappan Raychaudhuri, *Bengal under Akbar and Jahangir* (Calcutta, 1953). On the Portuguese, see J. J. Campos, *History of the Portuguese in Bengal* (Calcutta, 1919), and F. C. Danvers, *The Portuguese in India*, 2 vols. (London, 1894).

7. Other choices elsewhere involved open roadsteads, or similarly limited creeks or silted river mouths. Madras remained without an adequate harbor until 1881, when two breakwaters were finally built. Until then ships had to anchor offshore and to load and unload by surfboat or lighter, as at Tientsin, but even this was not possible for at least two months during the worst of the northeast monsoon (October 15 to December 15). The 1881 breakwaters were destroyed by a storm in less than a year and were not rebuilt permanently until 1896.

8. The history of Madras has been surprisingly little studied, although primary materials are reasonably well preserved and have been published in the documentary collections mentioned in note 6 above. The best of the very few secondary accounts is Glyn Barlow, *The Story of Madras* (Oxford, 1921). On the Dutch, see T. Raychaudhuri, *Jan Company in Coromandel, 1605–1690* (The Hague, 1962).

9. From a memorandum from the Company Directors at Madras dated September 11, 1689, quoted in C. R. Wilson, ed., *Old Fort William in Bengal*, 2 vols. (Calcutta, 1906), vol. 1, p. 5.

10. James Methwold, as quoted in R. Mukerjee, *The Changing Face of Bengal* (Calcutta, 1938), p. 381.

11. Memorandum from the Company Directors at Madras of September 11, 1689, reproduced in C. R. Wilson, *Old Fort William*, vol. 1, p. 5.

12. The basic sources on the origins of Calcutta and the English experience in Bengal are the voluminous East India Company records, selectively reproduced with commentary in Fawcett, *The English Factories*, Foster, *The English Factories*, and in C. R. Wilson, *Early Annals of the English in Bengal* and *Old Fort William*. It is a much-told tale in a variety of secondary accounts, including those cited earlier. Some of this material is presented in greater detail in R. Murphey, "The City in the Swamp: Aspects of the Site and Early Growth of Calcutta," *The Geographical Journal* 130 (June 1964): 241–56.

13. On the history and growth of this aspect of Bombay, see A. R. Wadia, *The Bombay Dockyard and the Wadia Master Builders,* 2d ed. (Bombay, 1957).

14. Quoted in S. N. Edwardes, *The Rise of Bombay* (Bombay, 1902), pp, 170–71.

15. The English factory records, as published in the collections already referred to, are the chief sources for all of this summary material on Bombay and the west coast. Additional secondary accounts include H. G. Rawlinson, *British Beginnings in Western India, 1579–1675* (Oxford, 1920); P. B. M. Malibari, *Bombay in the Making: 1661–1726* (London, 1910); A. R. Ingram, *The Gateway to India: The Story of Methwold and Bombay* (London, 1938); Holden Furber, *Bombay Presidency in the Mid-Eighteenth Century* (London, 1965), and other sources cited in all the above.

16. There is a relatively large secondary literature on various aspects of Mughal India, of varying quality but including some excellent studies ranging from the magistral sweep of W. H. Moreland's now classic surveys, *India at the Death of Akbar* (London, 1920), and *From Akbar to Aurangzeb: A Study in Indian Economic History* (London, 1923), to the more recent proliferation of detailed monographic studies by Indian scholars. Several of these are cited in what follows, or have been cited above, but the discussion here owes a particular debt to M. D. Morris, a friend and colleague of many years from whom, in and out of print, I have learned much of what I know about India. He has provided a masterful summary in an article titled "Trends and Tendencies in Indian Economic History," *The Indian Economic and Social History Review* 5, no. 4 (December 1968): 319–88, in the form of a reply to a series of Indian critics and commentators on an essay of his on the same subject, "Towards a Reinterpretation of Nineteenth Century Indian Economic History," originally published in the *Journal of Economic History* 23 (December 1963): 606–18, and reprinted, with commentaries by Toru Matsui, Bipan Chandra, and Tappan Raychaudhuri in *The Indian Economic and Social History Review* 5 (March 1968): 1–100.

Chapter 4

1. In addition to the variety of contemporary Western travelers' accounts, there is a growing secondary literature on the economy at this period. To mention only a few not previously cited, the several studies of B. G. Gokhale, including "Capital Accumulation in Seventeenth Century Western India," *Journal of the Asiatic Society of Bombay* 39–40 (1964–65): 51–60; idem, "Ahmadabad in the Seventeenth Century," *Journal of the Economic and Social History of the*

Orient 12 (1969): 187–97; idem, "Burhanpur: Notes on the History of an Indian City in the XVIIth Century," *Journal of the Economic and Social History of the Orient* 15 (1972): 316–23; and H. K. Naqvi, *Urban Centers and Industrialization in Upper India, 1556–1803* (Bombay, 1968), and idem, *Urbanization and Urban Centers Under the Great Mughals* (Simla, 1971). These and other studies tend to stress, perhaps to overplay even for western India, the scale and relative economic importance of trade, merchants, and commercial urban bases, as other scholars, including Pearson and Morris in the works already referred to, have suggested. I am inclined to agree with this criticism, but would point out also that Gokhale, Naqvi, and other proponents of the importance of the commercial sector in Mughal times make clear in their work the destructive impact of imperial and bureaucratic power on merchants, and the grossly disrupting effects of chronic warfare and disorder.

2. Morris, "Trends and Tendencies," p. 344.
3. Village *panchayats* ("councils") managed the bulk of local affairs in the noneconomic spheres, and typified the essentially atomistic nature of the sociocultural and political landscape.
4. The most detailed effort to establish a time series of Indian agricultural yields is George Blyn, *Agricultural Trends in India, 1891–1947* (Philadelphia, 1966).
5. Even at what appears to have been the height of north Indian commercial prosperity, in the seventeenth century, the major Gujerat city and trade center of Ahmadabad suffered severe famine at least ten times between 1631 and 1695. See Irfan Habib, *The Agrarian System of Mughal India* (Bombay, 1963), pp. 106–7.
6. Such an estimate, although it seems implausibly high when viewed as a percentage of gross national product (GNP) or compared with the tax revenues of modern let alone premodern states, is confirmed by most historians of Mughal India, to which a convenient single guide is Percival Spear's *India: A Modern History,* 2d ed. (Ann Arbor, 1972). See his discussion and his own estimate of one-third on pp. 153 ff., as well as the sources he refers to, including W. H. Moreland's *India at the Death of Akbar* and *From Akbar to Aurangzeb.* Irfan Habib, *The Agrarian System of Mughal India,* is an excellent study of the land administration and revenue collection. The area controlled by the Mughals well enough to permit collection of revenue varied widely from period to period, but during most of the sixteenth and seventeenth centuries included well over half of what is now India and Pakistan, and most of the areas or centers of high productivity and trade except for the southern third of the peninsula.
7. François Bernier, *Travels in the Mogul Empire,* trans. I. Broch, 2 vols. (London, 1826), vol. 1, p. 259.
8. For an analysis of the Chinese village as moving along the spectrum

between open and closed, in response to changing perceptions of order-disorder and of the overall impact of outside forces on village welfare, see G. W. Skinner, "Chinese Peasants and the Closed Community: An Open and Shut Case," *Comparative Studies in Society and History* 13 (1971): 270–81.

9. The best account of this and other aspects of the Mughal system of administration and revenue collection is Irfan Habib, *The Agrarian System of Mughal India.* Habib suggests (pp. 271–72) that except for a very few years under Akbar, four-fifths of the supposed imperial lands was assigned to jagirdars.

10. Morris, "Trends and Tendencies," provides an excellent summary discussion of all these problems; see especially section 4, pp. 352–65, where Morris also refers to additional sources.

11. Spear, *India: A Modern History,* p. 156.

12. Bernier, *Travels,* p. 155.

13. Nicolo Manucci, *Storia de Mogor,* trans. W. Irvine, Indian Text Series (London, 1908), vol. 2, p. 452, a seventeenth-century travel account, quoted in B. K. Gupta, "Indian Response to Early Western Contacts in Bengal, 1650–1756," *Studies on Asia* (University of Nebraska) 1 (1960): 9–19.

14. Père Calmette, *Lettres edifiantes et curieuses* (Paris, 1730), pp. xxi, 3–4, quoted in B. K. Gupta, "Indian Response," p. 11.

15. Basic documents are provided in C. R. Wilson, *Early Annals of the English in Bengal,* vol. 2, pt. 2 (Calcutta, 1911).

16. Most conveniently presented in C. R. Wilson, *Early Annals of the English in Bengal.*

17. An indeterminate but excessive number of the English defenders were forced to spend a hot July night as prisoners in a dungeon in their own fort—the notorious "Black Hole." The literature on this incident is reviewed and assessed by B. K. Gupta in "The Black Hole Incident," *Journal of Asian Studies* 19 (November 1959): 53–63.

18. Such a collaborationist gesture is suggested in B. B. Misra, *The Indian Middle Classes* (London, 1961), pp. 78 ff., and in N. K. Sinha, *The Economic History of Bengal,* vol. 1 (Calcutta, 1956), pp. 6 ff.

19. European troops also came to be distinguished in their own minds by the fact that they fired on command, in regular volleys, with obviously greater effectiveness than the often haphazard shooting and uncoordinated sallies of their Asian opponents.

20. Misra, *Indian Middle Classes,* p. 9.

21. On merchant-state relations in Mughal Gujerat, see M. N. Pearson, "Merchants and Rulers in Mughal Gujerat" (Paper, 1973). A similar theme is pursued for the following century by Ashin Das Gupta, "Trade and Politics in Eighteenth Century Asia," in *Islam in the Trade of Asia,* ed. F. J. Richards (Philadelphia, 1970), 181–214; Das Gupta's

earlier study, *Malabar in Asia Trade, 1740–1800* (Cambridge, 1967), gives a picture of another regional center of traditional commerce as it was acted on by and responded to Western pressures and gives additional detail on indigenous merchants; see also Das Gupta's "The Crisis at Surat, 1730–32," *Bengal Past and Present,* Diamond Jubilee Number, 1967, pp. 148–62.

22. Literacy rates in general in India remained very low, by comparison with Europe or with China and Japan; this further retarded economic and technological growth—see the brief discussion in M. D. Morris, "Private Industrial Investment on the Indian Sub-Continent, 1900–1939: Some Methodological Considerations," *Modern Asian Studies* 8 (1974): 550–51. There was nothing in India resembling the widespread system of academies plus charity schools in Ming and Ch'ing China, nor the established social and political order which made them possible. Literacy in late traditional China was much higher than has often been assumed, as the current research and forthcoming study by Evelyn Rawski will show.

23. Letter from Patna to the Council at Madras dated July 6, 1678, quoted as part of the "Documentary Memoirs of Job Charnock" in *The Diary of William Hedges,* ed. H. Yule, 3 vols. (London, 1887), vol. 2, p. xlvi.

24. The name is preserved even in contemporary American slang, as in mug, mugging.

25. Reproduced in C. R. Wilson, ed., *Old Fort William,* vol. 1, pp. 32–33.

26. Letter from the Council at Madras to those at Fort William, dated in July of 1709, reproduced in C. R. Wilson, *Old Fort William,* vol. 1, p. 76.

27. From the *Diary of Streynsham Master,* entry dated December 20, 1676, reproduced in *The Diary of William Hedges,* ed. H. Yule, vol. 2, p. ccxxxvii.

28. From a 1678 account by William Clavell of the trade of Hughly, reproduced in *The Diary of William Hedges,* ed. H. Yule, pp. ccxxxix–x.

29. A. Tripathi, *Trade and Finance in the Bengal Presidency, 1793–1833* (Calcutta, 1956), p. 259.

30. From an account of about 1800, reprinted in *Selections from the Records of the Bombay Government,* vol. 39, N.S. (Bombay, 1856), p. 21, and quoted in Howard Spodek, "Rulers, Merchants, and Other Elites in the City-States of Saurashtra, India" (Paper prepared for the South Asia Regional Studies Seminar, University of Pennsylvania, March, 1973), p. 5.

31. Spodek, "Rulers," p. 5.

32. Quoted in Spodek, "Rulers," p. 5, from *Selections from the Records of the Bombay Government,* vol. 16 (Bombay, 1855), p. ix.

33. Spodek, "Rulers," pp. 9–10.
34. Quoted in Spodek, "Rulers," p. 10, from G. L. Jacob, *Western India Before and During the Mutinies* (London, 1872), p. 121.
35. Quoted in Habib, *The Agrarian System,* p. 325, and also in Ashin Das Gupta, "Trade and Politics," p. 186.
36. K. L. Gillion, *Ahmedabad: A Study in Indian Urban History* (Berkeley, 1969), deals with one of the most successful of these, an old center of trade and manufacturing which "adapted to the new age."

Chapter 5

1. Benoy Ghosh, "Some Old Family Founders in Eighteenth Century Calcutta," *Bengal Past and Present* 79 (1960): 26–41.
2. For an analysis of this process, see Broomfield, "The Regional Elites," and idem, *Elite Conflict.*
3. Blair Kling, *The Blue Mutiny: The Indigo Disturbances in Bengal, 1859–1862* (Philadelphia, 1966), gives an excellent account of the exploitative impact of the system of indigo production, centered in the Ganges valley.
4. This matter is most helpfully pursued by M. B. McAlpin, "The Effects of Expansion of Markets on Rural Income Distribution in 19th Century India." (Paper presented at the 26th Annual Meeting, Association for Asian Studies, Boston, 1974). Her analysis includes a convincing attempt to show that even rural income distribution improved rather than worsened, because of the relative labor shortage which developed as a result of expanded cultivation, responding to a widened market. This made it possible even for landless laborers to share in new economic opportunity and rising incomes. The issue of what was really happening to peasant material welfare during this period is still, however, far from settled. For a different and valuable perspective, see Ira Klein, "Population and Agriculture in Northern India, 1872–1921," *Modern Asian Studies* 8 (April 1974): 191–216, which argues that although there probably was a small net increase in overall or average peasant incomes and consumption there was also disastrously high mortality, principally as the result of disease flourishing in newly crowded and substandard living conditions and aggravated by new irrigation; "welfare" refers only to the survivors.
5. Angus Maddison, *Class Structure and Economic Growth: India and Pakistan Since the Mughals* (New York, 1972), attempts to do this, in the absence of adequate data, and provides a stimulating and often persuasive evaluation of the Mughal and British impact, but without claiming to pin down definitively what was quantitatively happening to mass or average welfare under British rule.

6. Literature on "The Drain" and more generally on the economic consequences of British rule is extensive. Sound guides on this question, including their bibliographic references, are Morris, "Trends and Tendencies," and his "Towards a Reinterpretation of Nineteenth Century Indian Economic History," *Journal of Economic History* 23 (December 1963): 606—18; and idem, "Values as an Obstacle to Economic Growth in South Asia: An Historical Survey," *Journal of Economic History* 27 (December 1967): 588—607.

7. In this they paralleled both the Marxist and the imperialist view that the British presence and their agency were necessary to stir up toward productive change an India which was itself unable any longer to generate change.

8. Ranade and his career are examined in the context of late nineteenth-century India in an excellent interpretive study by Richard Tucker, *Ranade and the Roots of Indian Nationalism* (Chicago, 1972).

9. For a summary of Deshmukh's writings, see M. L. Apte, "Lokahita-vadi and V. K. Chiplunkar: Spokesmen of Change in Nineteenth Century Maharashtra," *Modern Asian Studies* 7 (April 1973): 193—208.

10. All these men were Brahmins from Maharashtra, educated and active in Poona and then in the heady atmosphere of nineteenth-century Bombay. For more detail on the views and actions of this new national focus on the part of the many regional elites, see Seal, *The Emergence of Indian Nationalism.*

11. Quoted in M. L. Apte, "Lokahitavadi," p. 203.

12. Seal, *The Emergence of Indian Nationalism,* pp. 14—15.

13. Unfortunately and rather surprisingly, there is no adequate book-length account of Dwarkanath Tagore, and no adequate periodical literature, although as a colorful and distinguished figure he is mentioned in a number of primary and secondary accounts; the only biography, by K. Mittra, was published in Calcutta in 1870. I have therefore drawn especially heavily here on an unpublished paper of 1968 by Dilip Basu, "Dwarkanath Tagore: Citizen-landlord and Entrepreneur"; the notes list a variety of fragmentary references to Tagore, and other sources in Bengali and English. I am grateful to Professor Basu for making his manuscript available to me.

14. The Minute is reprinted in *Macaulay, Prose and Poetry* ed. G. M. Young (London, 1952), pp. 719—30.

15. The best survey is B. T. McCully, *English Education and the Origins of Indian Nationalism* (New York, 1940). See also the excellent study of the interaction between nineteenth-century British thought and the Indian scene by Eric Stokes, *The English Utilitarians and India* (Oxford, 1959). Christian missionary activity was also important, first in Bengal, through education, publishing, translation, and reformist movements. For two recent studies see M. A. Laird, *Missionaries and*

Education in Bengal, 1793–1837 (Oxford, 1972); and K. P. S. Gupta, *The Christian Missionaries in Bengal, 1793–1833* (Calcutta, 1971). "Official" education in Bengal is dealt with by D. P. Sinha, *The Educational Policy of the East India Company in Bengal* (Calcutta, 1964).

16. Seal, *The Emergence of Indian Nationalism*, pp. 195–96.

17. For a Marxist-oriented discussion of this matter, see T. W. Weisskopf, "Dependence and Imperialism in India," in *Imperialism in Asia*, eds. Edward Friedman and Mark Selden (New York, 1973).

18. For a discussion of these issues see Rhoads Murphey, "City and Countryside as Ideological Issues: India and China," *Comparative Studies in Society and History* 14 (June 1972): 250–67.

Chapter 6

1. For a recent study of the Dutch effort, see John E. Wills, *Pepper, Guns, and Parleys: The Dutch East India Company and China, 1662–1681* (Cambridge, Mass., 1974).

2. From a letter-report from Robert Douglas to Governor Thomas Pitt in Madras dated 1702, in *The Diary of William Hedges*, ed. H. Yule, vol. 2, p. cxxvi.

3. *The Diary of William Hedges*, ed. H. Yule, vol. 2, p. cccxxviii ff.

4. On this and the end of the Catchpoole story, see Alexander Hamilton, *A New Account of the East Indies*, ed. William Foster (Originally published 1727; London, 1930), vol. 2, p. 48.

5. Figures cited in Michael Greenberg, *British Trade and the Opening of China, 1800–1842* (Cambridge, 1951), p. 79.

6. The standard treatment of opium is still David Owen, *British Opium Policy in India and China* (New Haven, 1934); basic documentation is provided in H. B. Morse, *The Chronicles of the East Indian Company Trading to China, 1635–1834*, 5 vols. (Oxford, 1926–29); Holden Furber, *John Company at Work* (Cambridge, Mass., 1948), gives a lively general account.

7. On the mechanics and details of the country trade, see Morse, *Chronicles*, Furber, *John Company*, and Parkinson, *Trade in the Eastern Seas*.

8. This persistent goal was stated as early as 1589 by Richard Hakluyt in the dedication of volume 2 of the second edition of *The Principall Navigations*, as follows: "Because our chief desire is to find ample vent of our woolen cloth . . . the fittest places are the manifold islands of Japan and the northern parts of China."—quoted in William Foster, *England's Quest of Eastern Trade* (London, 1933), p. 6. Foster's general account is full of references to successive, as well as earlier,

statements stressing the wealth of China and the primary importance of establishing full and direct trade with it.

9. Flint's effort on behalf of the Company to conduct trade at Ningpo is recounted most conveniently in E. L. Farmer's, "James Flint versus the Canton Interest, 1755–1760," *Papers on China*, vol. 17 (Cambridge, Mass., 1963), pp. 38–66. Flint was jailed and then deported; the Emperor ordered execution for the Chinese who had prepared the Chinese language version of Flint's petition to the representative of the Salt Commission at Tientsin. The Flint case provided the ultimate cause for the official restriction of all Western traders to Canton in 1759.

10. The chief source is Dalrymple *A Plan for Extending the Commerce of This Kingdom and of the East India Company* (London, 1769), which still makes exciting and persuasive reading. It has been extensively used, summarized, and commented on in V. T. Harlow, *The Founding of the Second British Empire*, 2 vols. (London, 1952), especially vol. 1, chap. 3. H. T. Fry, *Alexander Dalrymple (1737–1808) and the Expansion of British Trade* (Toronto, 1970), gives a somewhat more detailed account of Dalrymple's career as a whole and of his project at Balambangan.

11. The best account of this and the later development of the British position in Malaya, including the founding of Penang and Singapore, is K. C. Tregonning, *The British in Malaya*, Monograph 18 of the Association for Asian Studies (Tucson, 1965).

12. For a detailed account, see Tregonning, *The British in Malaya*, pp. 15–20.

13. Morse, *The Chronicles of the East India Company*, vol. 2, pp. 114–17.

14. For an account of this venture, see C. R. Markham, *Narratives of the Mission of George Bogle to Tibet, and the Journey of Thomas Manning to Lhasa* (London, 1876); a brief general account is also given in Tregonning, *The British in Malaya*, p. 29.

15. These figures, and a detailed account of the early history of Penang, are given in Tregonning, *The British in Malaya*, chap. 4 and p. 57.

16. For a detailed account, see Greenberg, *British Trade*, pp. 86 ff.

17. For more detail on this, see H. J. Marks, *The First Contest for Singapore, 1819–1824* (The Hague, 1959), pp. 143–48; and Tregonning, *The British in Malaya*, p. 155.

Chapter 7

1. Morse, *Chronicles of the East India Company*, vol. 2, chap. 42.

2. Greenberg, *British Trade*, Appendix 1, D.

3. As perhaps the principal theme and argument of my approach, and of

the contrast between China and India, this point is explored in detail later in this chapter and in chapters 9 and 10, from both Chinese and Western data and observations. The present chapter aims to provide a more general overview of the Western effort in China and its consequences.

4. Over a hundred of these were officially established between 1843 and 1930; they included nearly all of the major cities (except for Peking) and many lesser centers (see the back endpaper map); many were inland marts rather than ports; some were merely "ports of call," and the Maritime Customs Service operated in less than half of them. Foreigners were permitted to reside permanently and to own property in sixty-nine of these treaty ports, but there were actual areal concessions in only a few of the largest, while many others were without foreign residents or were resided in by one or a few missionaries (see chap. 11). Yen Chung-p'ing, *Chung-kuo chin-tai ching-chi shih t'ung-chi tzu-liao hsüan-chi* [Selected statistical materials on China's modern economic history] (Peking, 1955), pp. 41–48 (table 1) lists 105 treaty ports opened from 1843 to 1930, by years, giving data on the circumstances of each opening, the foreign demands, the name of the treaty or agreement, and the cases where treaty ports were nominally opened voluntarily by the Chinese government, in response to or in anticipation of foreign demands. Yen also lists (pp. 49–53) the foreign concessions granted in sixteen of these ports, by location, date, and grantee.

5. British Chamber of Commerce, Tientsin, "The Present State of British Trade in North China," Tientsin, 1930, pp. 10, 14.

6. The standard Western-language study of the compradores is Hao Yen-p'ing, *The Comprador in Nineteenth Century China: Bridge Between East and West* (Cambridge, Mass., 1970), but see also Liu Kwang-ching, "T'ang T'ing-shu chih mai-pan shih-tai" [Tong King-sing's compradore years], *Ch'ing-hua hsüeh-pao* [Tsing Hua Journal of Chinese Studies], June 1961, pp. 143–83; and for a good description of the compradore and his functions late in the history of the treaty ports, see Carl Crow's reminiscences of treaty port life, especially *Foreign Devils in the Flowery Kingdom* (New York, 1940), pp. 32–46.

7. At least in commercial terms, Hong Kong and Canton are best regarded as closely integrated parts of a single city in which Hong Kong acted as the wholesaling and shipping center. The circulation pattern of goods and individuals between the two (see for example the continuous shuttle basis of the steamer schedules after about 1880) reveals the closeness of their integration.

8. Literally, official supervision, merchant management, a label applied

to the joint government-merchant industrial enterprises which formed part of the self-strengthening movement in the last third of the nineteenth century. Nearly all of these enterprises failed, for a variety of reasons; the merchant managers never had a free hand, and the official side drained off scarce operating capital. The best guide is Albert Feuerwerker, *China's Early Industrialization: Sheng Hsuan-huai and Mandarin Enterprise* (Cambridge, Mass., 1958).

9. Seal, *The Emergence of Indian Nationalism.*

10. See H. D. Fong (Fang Hsien-ting), *Industrial Capital in China* (Tientsin, 1936).

11. See Paul Cohen, "Wang T'ao's Perspective on a Changing World," in *Approaches to Modern Chinese History,* ed. Feuerwerker, Murphey, and Wright (Berkeley, 1967), pp. 133–62; Leong Sow-cheng, "Wang T'ao and the Movement for Self-Strengthening and Reform in the Late Ch'ing Period," *Papers on China,* vol. 17, mimeographed (Cambridge, Mass., 1963), pp. 101–30; Paul Cohen, "Wang Tao and Incipient Chinese Nationalism," *Journal of Asian Studies* 26 (1967): 559–74; and P. Cohen, *Between Tradition and Modernity: Wang T'ao and Reform in Late Ch'ing China* (Cambridge, Mass., 1974).

12. K'ang's experience in Hong Kong and Shanghai led him to admire the strength and vigor of the West, and particularly to appreciate the virtues of Western government and law, which made an important contribution to his later efforts at radical reform; see Chien Po-tsan, ed., *Wu-hsu pien-fa* [The reform movement of 1898], 4 vols. (Shanghai, 1957), vol. 4, pp. 115–16.

13. Reformist and revolutionary ideas were current well before the first rumblings began at the center, and were being voiced by Chinese who had experienced the treaty ports. See for example Lloyd Eastman, "Political Reformism in China Before the Sino-Japanese War," *Journal of Asian Studies* 27 (1968): 695–710.

14. Karl Marx, "The Future Results of British Rule in India," *New York Herald Tribune,* August 8, 1853.

15. J. Nehru, *Toward Freedom* (New York, 1941), pp. 431–32.

16. See for example the brief run of railway figures published by the Kuomintang government, which show a very low level of operation especially in terms of kilometer/tons hauled—*Statistics of the Chinese National Railways, 1915–1929* (Nanking, 1931). Much of what the railways did carry was troops and military supplies. These figures are further analyzed in Murphey, "China's Transport Problem and Communist Planning," *Economic Geography* 32 (1956): 17–28.

17. Indian figures from M. D. Morris and C. B. Dudley, "Selected Railway Statistics for the Indian Subcontinent and Burma, 1853–1946/7," (Paper based on a variety of official railway and government sources

listed therein); China figures from Yen Chung-p'ing, *Selected Statistical Materials*, pp. 207–8, which I have converted from kilometers to miles; Yen uses 1912 as the base year for index number purposes.

18. Vera Anstey, *The Economic Development of India*, 2d ed. (London, 1942), p. 144.

19. John Hurd, "Railways and the Expansion of Markets in India, 1861–1921," (Paper presented at the Association for Asian Studies Annual Meeting, Washington, 1971), and in *Explorations in Economic History* (forthcoming).

20. M. B. McAlpin, "The Impact of Railways on Agriculture in India, 1860–1900" (Ph.D. diss., University of Wisconsin, 1973); idem, "Railroads, Prices, and Peasant Rationality: India, 1860–1900," *Journal of Economic History* 24 (1971): 662–84.

21. P. J. Marshall, "Economic and Political Expansion: The Case of Oudh." *Modern Asian Studies* 9 (1975): 465–82.

22. C. A. Bayly, "Town Building in North India, 1790–1830," *Modern Asian Studies* 9 (1975): 483–504.

23. Liu Ta-chung and Yeh Kung-chia, *The Economy of the Chinese Mainland: National Income and Economic Development, 1933–1959* (Princeton, 1965); M. Mukherjee, *National Income of India: Trends and Structure* (Calcutta, 1969).

24. From Liu-Yeh, *The Economy of the Chinese Mainland* p. 94, table 8, for China in 1933 (I have converted their value figures into percentages for easier comparison); from Mukherjee, *National Income of India*, p. 130, table A 3.2 for India in 1946. Depression and war occupied the intervening years, not a period of significant growth or change in either economy. Both sets of figures may reasonably be ·taken as representative of each economy at or toward the end of the period of foreign dominance. The categories in both sources which cover the remainder of the total are not comparable and hence are not given here.

25. These are multitudinous, not easy to use, and frequently ambiguous, but they suggest, at least impressionistically, a volume of internal trade and a prominence of merchants which does not agree with traditional-official stereotypes. One effort to analyze the commercial economy of an important area, based largely on gazetteer materials, is Fu I-ling, *Ming-tai Chiang-nan shih min ching-chi shih tan* [A study of the economy of the urban population of Kiangnan in Ming times] (Shanghai, 1957). Sung Ying-hsing, *T'ien Kung K'ai Wu*, trans. E. T. Z. Sun and S. C. Sun (University Park, Pa., 1966), discusses technology, commodities, production, and transport in the seventeenth century. The efforts to assess the size of interprovincial trade in Dwight Perkins, *Agricultural Development in China* (Chicago, 1969), pp. 345–65, are useful but highly speculative and are largely limited

to the post-1870 period. The Ch'ing administrative system, including those parts of it which dealt with the economy: commerce and finance, agrarian policy, living conditions, crop yields, manufactures, grain transport, water routes, the salt trade, currency, etc., is pictured in detailed handbook-form in the massive multiauthor collection of documents, *Huang-ch'ao ching-shih Wen-pien*, assembled between 1821 and 1902 and published in a somewhat shortened eight-volume edition by World Book Company in 1964—see the short descriptive article on this edition by Frederic Wakeman in *Ch'ing Shih Wen T'i* 1, no. 10 (1969): 8–22. It draws on selected gazetteer accounts and since it is arranged according to topics provides a convenient means of approach to the seemingly endless morass of gazetteer materials.

26. A recent study based on Ch'ing rice price data and official reports and memorials emphasizes the sophistication of eighteenth-century market mechanisms and transport systems, as of the operations of both merchants and government (through price stabilization programs). These qualities were evident in the remarkable success in providing stable amounts of rice and at relatively stable prices for the support of large urban populations, and in the impressive scale of long-distance trade even in so bulky a commodity as rice—Han-sheng Chuan and R. A. Kraus, *Mid-Ch'ing Rice Markets and Trade* (Cambridge, Mass., 1975).

27. The report appears in "Ch'ing kuo mien hua mien pu chi mien ssu shu ju ching k'uang" (Shinkoku menka mempu oyobi menshi yunyū keikyō) [The outlook for imports of raw cotton, cotton, cloth, and cotton thread in China], published by Dai Nippon menshi bōseki dōgyō rengōkai hōkoku [Report of the United Association of Japanese Cotton Spinners] (Tokyo, 1898), but included in Hatano Yoshihiro, "The Organization of Production in the Cotton Cloth Industry in China after the Opium War," *Chūgoku kindai kōgyō-shi no kenkyū* [Studies in China's early industrialization] (Kyoto: Tōyōshi-Kenkyū-kai, 1961) pp. 523 ff. I have, however, used Hatano only in a summary English translation by Mark Elvin, as part of the series prepared and edited by him titled Michigan Abstracts of Chinese and Japanese Works on Chinese History, Center for Chinese Studies, University of Michigan.

28. Hatano, "The Organization of Production," pp. 529–30.

29. Nakahara Teruo, "The Mercantilization of the Tribute Grain Under the Ch'ing Dynasty," *Shigaku Kenkyū* 70 (1965): 46; and Nakahara Teruo, "The Flow of Commodities on Grain Transport Ships During the Ch'ing Dynasty," *Shigaku Kenkyū* 64 (1959): 67. I have used these articles only in a rough-summary English translation by Mark Elvin, to whom I am deeply grateful.

30. Hoshi Ayao, *Mindai sōun no kenkyū* [A study of the transport system

of the grain tribute during Ming] (Tokyo, 1963). Again I have been dependent on Mark Elvin's summary English translation, now published as *The Ming Tribute Grain System,* Michigan Abstracts of Chinese and Japanese Works on Chinese History, no. 1 (Ann Arbor, 1970), pp. 30 ff. The same practices and orders of magnitude continued in the Ch'ing and are further described and estimated in Nakahara, "Mercantilization," p. 46.

31. This is the main point of Nakahara, "Mercantilization," for which the article provides ample documentation.
32. Ibid., p. 46.
33. Ibid., pp. 46–50.
34. Ibid., p. 49.
35. Nakahara, "The Flow of Commodities," pp. 69–70.
36. Nakahara, "Mercantilization," pp. 53–55.
37. Nakahara, "The Flow of Commodities," p. 77.
38. Ibid., pp. 69–70.
39. Ibid., pp. 96 ff.
40. Andrew Watson, trans., *Transport in Transition: The Evolution of Traditional Shipping in China,* Michigan Abstracts of Chinese and Japanese Works on Chinese History, no. 3 (Ann Arbor, 1972), p. iv.
41. See especially, in Watson, *Transport in Transition,* his abstract of the article by Koizumi Teizo, "The Operation of Chinese Junks," pp. 1–13.
42. Saeki Tomi, *Shindaiense no kenkyu* [A study of the Ch'ing dynasty salt monopoly] (Kyoto, 1956).
43. Ibid., and Thomas Metzger, "T'ao Chu's Reform of the Huaipei Salt Monopoly," *Papers on China,* vol. 16, mimeographed (Cambridge, Mass., 1962), pp. 1–39. Metzger draws on Saeki's earlier work and on a great variety of other sources. See also Metzger's "The Organizational Capabilities of the Ch'ing State in the Field of Commerce: The Liang-huai Salt Monopoly, 1740–1840," in *Economic Organization in Chinese Society* ed. W. E. Wilmott (Stanford, 1972), pp. 9–45.
44. Metzger, "T'ao Chu's Reform," p. 4.
45. Ibid.
46. Ibid., pp. 30–31. See also Metzger's *The Internal Organization of the Ch'ing Bureaucracy* (Cambridge, Mass., 1974), which similarly suggests that bureaucratic norms tended toward rational and flexible official responses to many problems.
47. Mark Elvin, *The Pattern of the Chinese Past* (London and Stanford, 1973), esp. chap. 17; idem, "The High-Level Equilibrium Trap: The Causes of the Decline of Invention in the Traditional Chinese Textile Industries," in *Economic Organization,* ed. W. E. Wilmott, pp. 137–72; Albert Feuerwerker, *The Chinese Economy, 1870–1911,* Michigan

Papers in Chinese Studies, (Center for Chinese Studies, no. 5, Ann Arbor, Mich., 1968); and idem, *The Chinese Economy 1912–1949*, Michigan Papers in Chinese Studies (Center for Chinese Studies, no 1, Ann Arbor, Mich., 1969).

48. For brief but provocative remarks on this matter, see Thomas Metzger, "Ch'ing Commercial Policy," *Ch'ing shih Wen t'i* 1, no.3 (February 1966): 4–10. L. S. Yang, "Government Control of Urban Merchants," *Tsing Hua Journal of Chinese Studies* 8, nos. 1 and 2 (1970), provides a valuable survey of varied data on the role and status of merchants, especially in late Ming and Ch'ing times. These data demonstrate merchant success in entering the gentry group via examination and purchase, the relatively light level of regulation and taxation or exaction, and the genuine concern of the state not to ruin or even seriously to impede merchant activity. Yang further stresses the nonrebellious character of merchants as a whole and the infrequency of any merchant-led uprisings or even of protests during the Ch'ing, suggesting that they had their own vested interest in the existing system which protected and rewarded them. P. T. Ho, *The Ladder of Success in Imperial China; Aspects of Social Mobility, 1388–1911* (New York, 1962), pp. 53–91, esp. 83–84, describes merchant success through the examination system, the purchase of degrees, and the more general upward mobility of merchants in the surprisingly fluid social system of late traditional China. More conventional, or perhaps literal, readings of official policy and actions with respect to merchants may be found in Jean Escarra, *Le droit Chinois* (Paris, 1936), and T. Jernignan, *China in Law and Commerce* (New York, 1905). F. L. Dawson, "Law and the Merchant in Traditional China," *Papers on China*, vol. 2 (Cambridge, Mass., 1948), pp. 55–92, takes for the most part a similar view, but does point to the relative operational strength of the guilds as semi-independent merchant groups, and also to the effectiveness of official connections in protecting and nourishing individual merchants and collective commercial enterprises.

49. See Gilbert Rozman, *Urban Networks in Ch'ing China and Tokugawa Japan* (Princeton, 1973), for a comparative study by a sociologist.

50. Adam Smith, *The Wealth of Nations*, Everyman, vol. 2, bk. 5, chap. 1, p. 217.

51. Ibid., vol. 1, bk. 1, chap. 3, pp. 16–19; chap. 2, pp. 188; vol. 2, bk. 4, chap. 9, pp. 174.

52. "Report on British Trade with China," Blue Book of 1857–59.

53. Maritime Customs, *Report on Trade for 1866*, Report for Tientsin, pp. 88–90.

54. Ibid., p. 93. The transit pass system was provided for by the Treaty of Tientsin in 1858; foreign imports might pay half the tariff duty after landing at a treaty port, which would then free them from the

payment of any inland transit dues once they left the treaty port en route to internal markets.

55. See for example, M. D. Morris, "Towards a Reinterpretation of Nineteenth Century Indian Economic History," *Journal of Economic History* 23 (1963): 606–18.

56. H. D. Fong, *The Cotton Industry and Trade in China,* 2 vols. (Tientsin, 1932), vol. 2. p. 230.

57. For more details, see H. D. Fong, "Rural Weaving and the Merchant Employers in a North China District," *Nankai Social and Economic Quarterly* 8, no. 1 (1934): 75–120; and 8, no. 2 (1934): 274–308.

58. Fong, *The Cotton Industry.*

59. Hatano, "Organization of Production," trans. M. Elvin. See note 27.

60. Ibid., pp. 5, 6, and 11. See also Bruce Reynolds, "Weft: The Technological Sanctuary of Chinese Handspun Yarn," *Ch'ing-shih wen-t'i* 3, no. 2 (1974): 1–19, and the larger treatment in Reynolds, "The Impact of Trade and Foreign Investment on Industrialization: Chinese Textiles, 1875–1931" (Ph.D. diss., University of Michigan, 1974).

61. Ch'en Shih-chi, "Chia wu chien ch'ien Chung-kuo nung ts'un shou kung yeh ti pien hua ho tzu pen chu i sheng ch'an ti ch'eng chang" [Rural household hand cloth making and the rise of capitalist production before the Sino-Japanese war], *Li shih Yen chiu* 2 (1959): 17–38.

62. P'eng chih-i, ed., *Chung-kuo chin tai shou kung yeh shih tzu liao* [Materials on the history of modern China's handicraft industries], vol. 11 (Peking, 1957), pp. 189 ff. Albert Feuerwerker's "Handicraft and Manufactured Cotton Textiles in China, 1871–1910," *Journal of Economic History* 30 (1970): 338–78, confirms and provides additional detailed evidence for the general propositions advanced here and gives estimates for the respective shares of imported, Chinese machine-manufactured, and handicraft cloth and yarn.

63. For detail on this experience, see Lillian Li, "Kiangnan and the Silk Export Trade, 1842–1937," (Paper presented at the Association for Asian Studies Annual Meeting, Chicago, 1973), an early version of one chapter in Li's Ph.D. dissertation (Harvard University, forthcoming).

64. Yen Chung-p'ing, *Chung-kuo mien-fang chih shih-kao* [History of the Chinese textile industry] (Peking, 1955), p. 311; A. Feuerwerker, "Handicraft and Manufactured Cotton Textiles," p. 377; Feuerwerker cites Yen's estimate of 61 percent but points out that this is in square yards, while if the output were measured simply in yards of varying width the handwoven share would be 73 percent.

65. Yen Chung-p'ing, *Chung-kuo mien-fang,* p. 315.

66. S. G. Checkland, "An English Merchant House in China After 1842," *Bulletin of the Business Historical Society* 27 (1953): 162–63.

67. Ibid., pp. 162–63, 168, 170, 181.

68. Wang Ching-yü, "Shih chiu shih chi wai kuo ch'in hua chih yeh chung ti hua shang tu ku shou tung" [The rise of Chinese merchants as investors in foreign controlled enterprises in the late nineteenth century], *Li shih Yen chiu* 4 (1965): 39–74. It is worth noting in this connection, however, that it was common practice for Chinese investors and managers not to disclose more than a fraction of the full amount of their investment or capitalization, in an effort to minimize taxation and other exactions and, in the case of industrial establishments, to avoid restrictions on factory conditions. This was common knowledge, but by its nature hard to document. The same applies to the widespread use by Chinese of foreigners as fronts under whose name ownership of enterprises was listed; this brought a great many advantages and was correspondingly common. It seems probable that the true total of Chinese investment in "modern" as well as traditional enterprises was significantly greater than any surveys or even estimates suggest. I am grateful to my colleague Cheng Chu-yuan for reminding me of these points.

69. See K. C. Liu, *Anglo-Chinese Steamship Rivalry in China, 1862–1874* (Cambridge, Mass., 1962).

70. Detail on the role of Chinese investors in these activities is provided in Wang Ching-yü, ed., *Chung-kuo chin tai kung yeh shih tzu liao chi yao: ti erh chi* [Materials on the history of modern industry in China, second series], 2 vols. (Peking, 1960).

71. Ibid., vol. 1, pp. 68–69.

72. Chang Chung-li, *The Income of the Chinese Gentry* (Seattle, 1962), pp. 139 ff., argues that by the 1880s the profit returns from trade had become substantially greater than the financial rewards of landholding, especially as land prices rose. See also P'eng Chih-i, "Shih chiu shih chi hou ch'i Chung-kuo ch'eng shih shou kung yeh shang yeh hsing hui ti chung chien ho tso yung" [The importance and function of urban handicraft and trade organizations in the late nineteenth century], *Li shih yen chiu* 1 (1965): 81–90, on the changing profitability of alternate uses of investment capital.

73. The best treatment of the experience and problems of the government-managed enterprises after 1870 is Feuerwerker, *China's Early Industrialization.* For an analysis of a single undertaking which manifested many of these problems, especially the shortage of both investment and operating capital, see his "China's Nineteenth Century Industrialization: The Case of the Hanyehping Coal and Iron Company, Limited," in *The Economic Development of China and Japan,* ed. C. D. Cowan (London, 1964), pp. 79–110. Feuerwerker has also examined a different case, that of a privately owned Chinese firm (although it profited from official connections) whose striking success was due at least in part to its ability to obtain ample capital, depen-

dent in turn on its success in maintaining a consistent and reasonably secure high rate of return to investors: A. Feuerwerker, "Industrial Enterprise in Twentieth Century China: The Chee Hsin Cement Co.," in *Approaches to Modern Chinese History,* ed. A. Feuerwerker, R. Murphey, and M. Wright, pp. 304—41.

74. Similar figures and estimates on this are given in many sources, of which the most convenient are C. F. Remer, *The Foreign Trade of China* (Shanghai, 1926); Cheng Yu-kuei, *Foreign Trade and Industrial Development of China* (Washington, 1956); and John Chang, *Industrial Development in Pre-Communist China* (Chicago, 1969).

75. Cheng Yu-kuei, *Foreign Trade,* p. 40.

76. Feuerwerker, *The Chinese Economy, 1912—1949,* pp. 8—10.

77. See Watson, *Transport in Transition,* and the Liu-Yeh figures on transport cited above in the table on p. 112.

78. See for example H. K. Naqvi, "The Progress of Urbanization in the United Provinces, 1550—1800," *Journal of the Economic and Social History of the Orient* 10 (1967): 81—99; in my opinion, Naqvi overestimates Indian city populations for this period and over-stresses their commercial functions. Habib, *The Agrarian System of Mughal India,* and idem, "Potentialities of Capitalistic Development in the Economy of Mughal India—An Enquiry." (Manuscript for the International Economic History Congress, 1968), also represents seventeenth-century India as highly productive, commercialized, monetized, and well ordered.

79. Habib, "Potentialities of Capitalistic Development," p. 69; see also his more general remarks on the drastic deterioration of mass economic welfare after the seventeenth century on p. 17.

80. The most convenient treatment of these matters is Hou Chi-ming, *Foreign Investment and Economic Development in China, 1840—1937* (Cambridge, Mass., 1965); but see also Robert Dernberger, "The Role of the Foreigner in China's Economic Development, 1840—1949," in *China's Modern Economy in Historical Perspective,* ed. Dwight Perkins (Stanford, 1975), pp. 19—47.

81. Remer, *Foreign Trade,* p. 73. Manchuria after 1905 and especially after 1931 was a separate system divorced from China particularly in economic terms; see chap. 11 for a discussion of Manchuria's separateness.

82. Dernberger, "Role of the Foreigner," p. 45.

83. The best single sample, though with extensive references to other works, is probably R. H. Myers, *The Chinese Peasant Economy; Agricultural Development in Hopei and Shantung, 1890—1949* (Cambridge, Mass., 1970); although Myers does not generalize for China as a whole he does imply, if only in his title, that his local data are appropriate at least to eastern north China and that this may be suggestive for the rest of the rural economy.

Chapter 8

1. From Imperial Commissioner Lin Tse-hsu's "moral advice" to Queen Victoria in a letter of 1839, on the eve of the Opium War which he attempted to avert, translated in S. Y. Teng and J. K. Fairbank, *China's Response to the West: A Documentary Survey, 1839–1923*, Atheneum edition (New York, 1963), pp. 24–26.
2. J. K. Fairbank, "The Early Treaty System in the Chinese World Order," in *The Chinese World Order*, ed. J. K. Fairbank (Cambridge, Mass., 1968), pp. 257–75.
3. The Manchurian ports, except for Newchwang, were a separate and later development under what amounted to Japanese colonial control after 1905. Hong Kong is of course a similarly separate and wholly colonial matter.
4. There was more urban change in parts of eastern north China served by railways, especially after 1900, than elsewhere; but even there, despite the rapid growth of cities such as Chinan (Tsinan) or Shih-chiachuang, the overall rank order was little altered, nor did these new centers displace older cities functionally to any major extent. In the south, where steamshipping became more important, some urban places served by the new carriers grew, and others without such access declined, as for example in the Canton delta—see Winston Hsieh, "Peasant Insurrection and the Marketing Hierarchy," in *The Chinese City Between Two Worlds*, ed. M. Elvin and G. W. Skinner (Stanford, 1974), pp. 119–41. But there too the major urban patterns were little changed.
5. Some missions negotiated semiperpetual leases of small amounts of land for mission buildings; the late and brief German concessions in Shantung were a further minor exception.
6. As the European historian Philip Guedalla put it, "The people of China are Chinese, a singular fact which seems to have escaped the attention of European diplomats." His statement is quoted in an interesting little book by a foreign resident of Tientsin, O. D. Rasmussen, *What's Right With China* (Shanghai, 1927), p. 248. Rasmussen's book was a direct reply to one published by another Old China hand, Rodney Gilbert, *What's Wrong With China* (London, 1926).
7. Archibald Little, *Gleanings from Fifty Years in China*, (London, n.d., ca. 1910); the essay quoted from pp. 29–37 was written in 1898; Little died in 1908, and *Gleanings* was edited by his wife.
8. Little, *Gleanings from Fifty Years in China*, p. 88.
9. G. W. Cooke, *China: Being the Times Special Correspondence from China in the Years 1857–58* (London, 1858), p. v.
10. J. H. Wilson, *China: Travels and Investigations in the Middle Kingdom* (New York, 1887), pp. 21–22.
11. A. S. Krause, *China in Decay* (London, 1898), pp. 3–46.

12. From "A Chinese Tract of the Mid-Nineteenth Century," translated by W. H. Medhurst and quoted in E. P. Boardman, *Christian Influence on the Ideology of the Taiping Rebellion, 1851–1864* (Madison, 1952), p. 129.

13. George Smith, *Narrative of an Exploratory Visit to the Consular Cities of China, on Behalf of the Church Missionary Society, in the Years 1844, 1845, and 1846* (London, 1847), pp. 66–67.

14. Account and translation printed in *Accounts and Papers: Commercial Reports from H.M. Consuls in China* 65 (London, 1870), pp. 113–15. Report by Consul Swinhoe of his Special Mission up the River Yangtze-kiang [*sic*] dated Hankow, June 5, 1869.

15. Robert Fortune, *A Residence Among the Chinese* (London, 1857), pp. 267, 351.

16. H. G. Woodhead, *The Yangtze and Its Problems* (Shanghai, 1931).

17. Ibid., p. 58.

18. Ibid., p. 101.

19. Ibid., p. 105

20. Ibid., p. 106.

21. Ibid., p. 125.

22. Ibid., p. 132.

23. Ibid., p. 143, 146–48.

24. Ibid., p. 150.

25. Maritime Customs, *Decennial Reports for 1902–1911,* Report for Canton, pp. 140–41.

26. J. R. Levenson, *Revolution and Cosmopolitanism: The Western Stage and the Chinese Stages,* ed. Frederic Wakeman (Berkeley, 1971).

27. R. H. Graves, *Forty Years in China* (Baltimore, 1895), p. 37. Graves appears to have been more willing than most missionaries to see some virtue in Chinese as compared with Christian or Western morality, however, and makes a particularly striking comment in this connection: "We say, 'Is it right?' The Chinese say, 'Is it kindly?' " (p. 37).

28. I am indebted to B. H. Farmer for this expressive phrase; see his "The Social Basis of Nationalism in Ceylon," *Journal of Asian Studies* 24 (1965): 431–39.

29. Erwin Baelz, *Awakening Japan: The Diary of a German Doctor,* trans. Eden Paul and Odar Paul (New York, 1932), p. 17, quoted in W. W. Lockwood, "Japan's Response to the West," *World Politics* 9 (1956): 37–54.

30. I have drawn extensively in what follows here from an outstanding paper by Warren Gunderson, "Modernization and Cultural Change: The Self-Image and World View of the Bengali Intelligentsia as found in the Writings of the Mid-Nineteenth Century, 1830–1870," in *Bengal Literature and History,* ed. E. C. Dimock (Asian Studies Center, Michigan State University, 1967), pp. 127–77.

31. B. Chandra, *Travels of a Hindoo* (London, 1869), vol. 1, pp. 162, 170, as quoted in Gunderson, "Modernization and Cultural Change," p. 133.
32. R. Mitra, *Speeches,* ed. J. Mitra, (Calcutta, 1892), p. 65, quoted in Gunderson, "Modernization and Cultural Change," p. 133.
33. K. Mitra, "On the Progress of Education in Bengal," Transactions of the Bengal Social Science Association, 1 (1867), p. 54, quoted in Gunderson, "Modernization and Cultural Change," pp. 133–34.
34. *Selections from the Writings of G. C. Ghose,* ed. M. Ghose (Calcutta, 1912), pp. 122, 127, quoted in Gunderson, "Modernization and Cultural Change," p. 134.
35. Ibid., p. 6, quoted in Gunderson, "Modernization and Cultural Change," p. 130.
36. K. Mitra, "On the Progress of Education in Bengal," Appendix, p. xi, quoted in Gunderson, "Modernization and Cultural Change," p. 130.
37. K. C. Mitra, *Memoirs of Dwarkanath Tagore* (Calcutta, 1870), pp. 60 and 94, quoted in Gunderson, "Modernization and Cultural Change," pp. 130–31–the words are Tagore's.
38. Keshub Chunder Sen, *Keshub Chunder Sen in England,* 3d ed. (Calcutta, 1938), p. 90, quoted in Gunderson, "Modernization and Cultural Change," p. 131–the passage cited here was however written in 1870.
39. There was bitter resentment of English racism, discrimination, arrogance, and patronizing, and of course of cultural prejudice. By the end of the nineteenth century a nationalist Indian reaction had begun, gathering force toward independence. But the British model, minus these disfiguring warts, was praised and followed by the majority of politically conscious Indians even in the twentieth century.
40. Krishna Bandyopadhyay, in *Minutes for 1866–67,* University of Calcutta Senate (Calcutta, 1867), p. 53, quoted in Gunderson, "Modernization and Cultural Change," p. 139.
41. Rajendralal Mitra, *Speeches,* ed. J. Mitra, p. 17, quoted in Gunderson, "Modernization and Cultural Change," p. 139–the speech was delivered in 1868.
42. I am indebted in a general but significant way in much of the following to Joseph Levenson's many treatments of the Chinese identity problem, *Confucian China and its Modern Fate: The Problem of Intellectual Continuity* (Berkeley, 1958); *The Problem of Monarchial Decay* (Berkeley, 1964); and *The Problem of Historical Significance* (Berkeley, 1965); *Liang Ch'i-ch'ao and the Mind of Modern China* (Cambridge, Mass., 1953); and a number of shorter works, for a complete listing of which see R. Murphey and M. Meisner, *The Mozartian Historian* (Berkeley, 1976), Appendix 1.
43. The phrase is Bill Bradley's, the All-American basketballer; see John McPhee, *A Sense of Where You Are* (New York, 1965).

44. I am grateful to Peter Van Ness for suggesting this point in a stimulating personal discussion.
45. See note 42 above.
46. G. W. Skinner, "Marketing and Social Structure in Rural China." *Journal of Asian Studies* 24 (1964–65), pt. 1 (November 1964), pt. 2 (February 1965), pt. 3 (May 1965).
47. E. O. Reischauer ed., trans., *Ennin's Travels in T'ang China* (New York, 1955).
48. J. Gernet, *Daily Life in China on the Eve of the Mongol Invasion,* trans. E. M. Wright (New York, 1962).
49. L. J. Gallagher, trans., *China in the Sixteenth Century: The Journals of Matthew Ricci, 1583–1610* (New York, 1953).
50. Personal communication from Lui Kui-on, a native of the village in question and subsequently a graduate student of mine at Michigan, plus his unpublished summary of his grandfather's recollections and his conversations with other former residents of the village now living in Hong Kong.
51. Marion Levy, *Family Revolution in Modern China* (Cambridge, Mass., 1949), and idem, "Contrasting Factors in the Modernization of China and Japan," *Economic Development and Cultural Change* 2 (1953): 161–97. See also B. I. Schwartz, "Modernization and the Maoist Vision: Some Reflections on Chinese Communist Goals," *The China Quarterly* no. 21 (1965), pp. 3–19.

Chapter 9

1. See for example, F. H. King, *Farmers of Forty Centuries* (London and New York, 1928).
2. Perkins, *Agricultural Development in China, 1368–1968,* which gives a detailed picture of the system and its modern evolution, goes so far as to suggest that even in the 1950s per capita availability and consumption of grain were far above subsistence levels (pp. 33–35), remained "quite high by world standards" (p. 297), and that this was so throughout Ming and Ch'ing, including the nineteenth century.
3. Ramon Myers, *The Chinese Peasant Economy: Agricultural Development in Hopei and Shantung, 1890–1949* (Cambridge, Mass., 1970). For perhaps the best of many critical reviews, see that by Thomas Wiens in *Modern Asian Studies* 9, pt. 2 (1975): 279–88.
4. The volume edited by Dwight Perkins, *China's Modern Economy in Historical Perspective* (Stanford, 1975), appeared as this book was in press. Several of the articles which it contains address in detail the questions of productivity and welfare levels in the half century or so before 1949. They, and the volume as a whole, lend further support

to the general statements made here. Carl Riskin's article in the Perkins volume (pp. 49–84) titled "Surplus and Stagnation in Modern China" maintains that the late traditional economy continued to produce a large surplus even into the 1930s, and estimates that over one-third of total product was potential surplus above the level of mass consumption. The article by Perkins himself, "Growth and Changing Structure of China's Economy" (pp. 115–65) suggests that both Gross Domestic Product and per capita incomes were not falling in the period 1900–1949, and that he finds no evidence even for a worsening of income distribution, no increased numbers of the very poor, no rise in tenancy rates, and that the sufferings attendant on the floods and famines in north China in the 1920s were probably less than during the similar catastrophes in the same areas in the late 1870s. The article by Kang Chao, "The Growth of a Modern Cotton Textile Industry and the Competition with Handicrafts" (pp. 167–201), argues that handicraft production survived partly because it used family labor and was often a sideline. This also tended to preserve a good deal of hand spinning of cotton by young girls and older women who had little alternative occupation and could in effect afford to spin cotton for a very low return. Kang maintains that handicraft cloth production remained vigorous and even dominant within the Chinese market into the 1930s, and was hurt by the loss of Manchuria and by other domestic disasters rather than by imports or by factory-based competition.

5. Joseph Needham, *Science and Civilization in China,* vol. 4 (Cambridge, 1971), p. 11; roadbuilding (pp. 145–210); waterworks and canals (pp. 211–378); nautical technology (pp. 379–699).

6. Wassily Petrov, *Triple Commission* (London, 1968), p. 117.

7. *Accounts and Papers,* 63, Commercial Reports from H.M. Consuls in China for the Year 1862, Report for Tientsin, p. 446.

8. See for example L. Oliphant, *Narrative of the Earl of Elgin's Mission to China and Japan* (New York, 1860), pp. 267 ff; ibid., p. 259, Oliphant records that the local inhabitants told him that Tientsin "had been decaying both in opulence and population since the overflowing of the Yellow River" [i.e., in 1852] . . . had broken down the banks of the Grand Canal"; "The Diary of S. Wells Williams," ed. F. W. Williams in *Journal North China Branch Royal Asiatic Society* 42 (1911): 1–232 (hereafter cited *JNCBRAS*). (The elder Williams was secretary and interpreter for the American Embassy to China during the expedition to Tientsin and Peking in 1848–59.)

9. These accounts are of course very numerous—most Westerners who went to China, it would seem, wrote books about it. I list here only a few of the more important examples: the various accounts of the Macartney mission and its inland journey from Peking to Canton;

G. T. Staunton's account of the Amherst mission, *Notes of Proceedings and Occurrences During the British Embassy to Peking in 1816* (London, 1824); John Phipps, *A Practical Treatise on China and the Eastern Trade* (London, 1836); J. F. Davis, *The Chinese: A General Description of China and Its Inhabitants*, 1st ed., 2 vols. (London, 1836), final and 4th ed., 3 vols (London, 1851); H. H. Lindsay and K. Gutzlaff, *Report of Proceedings on a Voyage to the Northern Ports of China* (London, 1834); Karl Gutzlaff, *China Opened*, 2 vols. (London, 1838); David Abeel, *Journal of a Residence in China and Neighboring Countries* (New York, 1835); W. H. Medhurst, *China* (London, 1838); the several accounts of Robert Fortune: *Three Years' Wanderings in the Northern Provinces of China* (London, 1847), *A Journey to the Tea Countries of China and India* (London, 1852); *Two Visits to the Tea Countries of China and the British Plantations in the Himalaya* (London, 1853), *The Tea Districts of China and India*, 2 vols. (London, 1853), *A Residence Among the Chinese* (London, 1857), and *Yedo and Peking* (London, 1863); L. Oliphant, *Narrative of the Earl of Elgin's Mission to China and Japan* (New York, 1860); F. W. Williams, ed., "The Diary of S. Wells Williams," *JNCBRAS* 42 (1911): 1–232; Abbé Huc, *The Chinese Empire*, trans. (London, 1859); W. Dickinson, "Narrative of an Overland Trip through Hunan from Canton to Hankow," *JNCBRAS* 1 (1864): 159–73; A. S. Bickmore, "Sketch of a Journey from Canton to Hankow," *JNCBRAS* 4 (1868): 1–20.

10. Fortune succeeded in this mission, kept tea cuttings alive in tubs through a journey around the Cape of Good Hope to London, established a growing stock at Kew Gardens, and shipped healthy plants back to Ceylon. Ironically, the Indian and Ceylonese tea industry was ultimately based not on these transplants but on a slightly different native tea shrub found growing in the Assam hills, which proved more vigorous and high-yielding in the Indian climate.

11. Fortune, *Three Years' Wanderings*, p. 196. The same statement is left unchanged in a later edition published in 1853, which Fortune in his introduction to it indicated he had "corrected by later experience"— *The Tea Districts of China and India*, vol. 1, p. 96.

12. Fortune, *A Residence Among the Chinese*, pp. vi–viii, 38, 63, 99.

13. F. E. Forbes, *Five Years in China, 1842–1847* (London, 1848), pp. 5–6.

14. Ibid., p. 73.

15. Ibid., pp. 84, 92.

16. J. R. Ross, "Journal of a Trip Overland from Hainan to Canton in 1819," *The Chinese Repository* 18 (May 1849): 230.

17. H. H. Lindsay and Karl Gutzlaff, *Report on Proceedings*. Lindsay and Gutzlaff were sent by the East India Company in the ship Lord

Amherst on an exploratory mission to ports north of Canton, seeking permission to trade in an effort to break out of the Canton system. They were turned away by officials at Amoy, Foochow, and Ningpo, but were given an audience by the Shanghai tao-tai (intendant of circuit) and spent a month in the city before being obliged to leave empty handed.

18. A weekly average of 550 ships averaging 158 tons entered the port of London between 1840 and 1842—*Tables of the Revenue, Population, Commerce, etc., of the United Kingdom and its Dependencies* (London, 1840, 1841, 1842). Such an assessment is not necessarily inconsistent with categorizations of Shanghai above as a second-rank regional town. In the 1840s, estimates of its population place it far below the other lower Yangtze cities of Soochow, Hangchow, Nanking, and Ningpo, let along Peking, Canton, Tientsin, Wuhan, and other major centers—for estimates, see R. Murphey, *Shanghai: Key to Modern China* (Cambridge, Mass., 1953), p. 66.

19. L. Oliphant, *Narrative*, pp. 559–65.

20. Ibid., p. 561.

21. Ibid., p. 601.

22. A. S. Bickmore, "Sketch of a Journey from Canton to Hankow," *Journal North China Branch Royal Asiatic Society* 4 (1868): 1–20. A very similar account, of a trip through the same area in 1861 by W. Dickson, appeared in the same journal, 1 (1864): 159–73.

23. Fortune, *The Tea Districts of China and India*, vol. 1, p. 12.

24. Fortune, *A Residence Among the Chinese*, p. 342.

25. Fortune, *The Tea Districts of China and India*, vol. 2, pp. 17–20.

26. John Davis, *The Chinese: A General Description of China and Its Inhabitants* (London, 1836) first appeared in two volumes; it was revised and augmented in successive editions after the war, drawing on his later experiences. Davis was the first widely read English interpreter of China, and was able to draw on a twenty-year residence, beginning in 1813 when he joined the Canton factory staff of the old Company at age eighteen. In 1816 he accompanied the ill-fated Amherst mission to Peking and thus saw something of the interior on the trip back to Canton by inland waterways. In 1834 he was appointed second superintendent of trade at Canton under Lord Napier, and succeeded him as superintendent for a year on Napier's death at Macao shortly thereafter. Davis had studied Chinese from his first arrival at Canton and had long experience in the dealings of the Company and the Crown with Chinese officialdom. His career in China concluded with a term as governor of Hong Kong (1844–48), in which office he also had general responsibility for the British position in the five mainland ports.

27. Davis, *The Chinese: A General Description of China and Its Inhabi-*

tants, 4th ed., 3 vols (London, 1857), vol. 1, pp. 195 ff, 200. Davis was doubtless right to attribute a large part of the prosperity to the existence of a peaceful civil order, although this surely worked both ways.

28. Ibid., vol. 1, p. 202.
29. Ibid., vol. 2, p. 67.
30. Ibid., vol. 2, p. 119 (italics in original).
31. Ibid., vol. 2, p. 27.
32. Ibid., vol. 2, pp. 29–30.
33. Ibid., vol. 2, p. 103.
34. Ibid., vol. 2, p. 90.
35. Abbé Huc, *The Chinese Empire,* trans. (London, 1859), pp. 332–65. In this description, Huc's estimate of "nearly eight millions of inhabitants" was mainly responsible for numerous charges that Huc was at best a teller of tall stories, at worst a liar who wove his entire story out of whole cloth and had never even seen Wuhan—see for example the well-known account edited by N. B. Denys, *The Treaty Ports of China and Japan* (London, 1867), p. 440. The controversy over the validity and accuracy of Huc's remarks was much later settled definitively by Paul Pelliot in his carefully detailed critical introduction to the Broadway Travellers' edition of Huc and Gabet's *Travels in Tartary, Tibet, and China,* trans. W. Hazlitt, vol. 1 (London, 1928), pp. v–xx, which draws on and adds to Pelliot's earlier article, "Le voyage de M. M. Gabet et Huc," *T'oung Pao* (1925–26): 133–78. Pelliot concludes that Huc "had a somewhat ardent imagination" but did not intentionally falsify or mislead. He spoke excellent Chinese, although he could read only simple texts. "He invented nothing, but he transposed his material in order to please, and he succeeded." (Huc and Gabet, *Travels,* p. xxxv). As Pelliot suggests, Huc's account should not be depended on in specific details, and certainly not for its estimate of the population of Wuhan in 1850–51, but in general his description may be accepted as valid.
36. Huc, *The Chinese Empire,* trans. (London, 1859), pp. 332–65.
37. Ibid.
38. Ibid.
39. These include most importantly Jean Baptiste du Halde, *Description of the Empire of China,* trans. (London, 1738); Grosier, *General Description of China* (London, 1795); Winterbotham, *Historical and Geographical View of the Chinese Empire* (London, 1795); and Murray, *China* (Edinburgh, 1843). Accounts of the journeys of the Macartney and Amherst missions are important exceptions, and are discussed immediately below. John Phipps, *A Practical Treatise on China and the Eastern Trade* (London, 1836), includes a statement on page 23 which may be compared with those cited above: "I do not

think they are exceeded by the natives of any country as a commercial people, including European countries. The Chinese, *if left by their rulers to themselves* (my emphasis) would be perhaps the most industrious and commercial people in the world." Huc, Fortune, and Davis would certainly have agreed, but it is interesting to see the backhanded reference to the negative role of what was even by the 1830s a parasitic rather than helpful central government, as well as the implication that the local economy and its entrepreneurs were in vigorous health despite official political decline.

40. George T. Staunton, *Notes of Proceedings and Occurrences During the British Embassy to Peking in 1816* (London, 1924), pp. 40–42.
41. Ibid., p. 54.
42. Ibid., p. 153.
43. The struggle to maintain Tientsin's water connections will be dealt with as part of my projected study of Tientsin's growth and role as a treaty port; for a brief secondary account from the early 1930s, see M. Hitch, "The Port of Tientsin and its Problems," *The Geographical Review* 25 (1935).
44. Staunton, *Notes,* p. 153.
45. Ibid., p. 205.
46. Ibid., pp. 201–2.
47. Ibid., p. 186.
48. Ibid., p. 225.
49. W. S. and E. S. Woytinsky, *World Population and Production* (New York, 1953), table 14, p. 34.
50. See P. T. Ho, *Studies on the Population of China, 1368–1953* (Cambridge, Mass., 1959).

Chapter 10

1. W. B. Dunlop, "The Key of Western China," *Asiatic Quarterly Review* 7 (1889): pp. 317–18.
2. Maritime Customs, *Decennial Reports, 1892–1901,* Report for Kiukiang, p. 326.
3. See chapter 11 for a discussion of Manchuria's separateness and its significance.
4. See Marie-Claire Bergère, *Une crise financière à Shanghai à la fin de l'Ancien Regime* (Paris, 1964); Andrea McElderry, "The Shanghai Ch'ien-chuang in the Nineteenth and Twentieth Centuries." (Ph.D. diss., University of Michigan, 1975).
5. Chang Kuo-hui, "Shih-chiu shih-chi hou-pan ch'i Chung-kuo ch'ien-chuang ti mai-pan hua" [The Chinese native banks as compradores in the latter half of the nineteenth century], *Li-shih Yen-chiu* 6 (1963):

85–98; Ch'in Jun-ching, "Shang-hai chih ch'ien-chuang shih yeh" [A study of native banking in Shanghai], *Ch'ien-yeh Yüeh-pao* 6, no. 10 (November 19, 1926): 22–40; Kuo Hsiao-hsien, "Shang-hai ti ch'ien-chuang" [Native banks in Shanghai], *Shang-hai shih t'ung-chih kuan ch'i-k'an* 3 (1933): 803–57; S. M. Jones, "Finance in Ningpo: The Ch'ien-Chuang, 1750–1880," in *Economic Organization in Chinese Society,* ed. W. E. Wilmott (Stanford, 1972), pp. 47–77; McElderry, "The Shanghai Ch'ien-chuang."

6. Jones, "Finance in Ningpo," p. 72. Foreign loans to the central government did greatly increase foreign control and influence, but for the most part only at that level; they provided little leverage for manipulation of the rest of the economy.

7. N. B. Dennys, ed., *The Treaty Ports of China and Japan* (London, 1867), pp. 450–52.

8. Ibid., p. 476.

9. *Accounts and Papers,* 60, Commercial Reports from H.M. Consuls in China for the Years 1868 and 1869, Report on Canton 1869; the Consul worded his comment in this way because of the incompleteness and misleading aspect of the Customs trade figures, which did not include Hong Kong, in fact the major external trade center for Canton. The Consul's Report for 1869 continues a few sentences later: "Hong Kong is the depot of this port, and the Returns of the foreign Customs House do not represent the true trade of the port." The great bulk of the shuttle trade between these two parts of what was in effect a single city in commercial terms was entirely Chinese owned and managed.

10. Maritime Customs, *Reports on Trade for 1869,* Report for Hankow, p. 28.

11. Archibald Little, *Gleanings from Fifty Years in China,* p. 205.

12. A. J. Sargent, *Anglo-Chinese Trade and Diplomacy* (Oxford, 1907), pp. 269, 225.

13. Elvin, *The Pattern of the Chinese Past,* p. 277.

14. See for example P'eng Chih-i, "Shih chiu shih chi hou ch'i Chung-kuo ch'eng shih shou kung-yeh shang-yeh hsing hui ti chung chien ho tso yung" [The importance and function of urban handicraft and commercial organization in the late nineteenth century], *Li-shih Yen-chiu* 1 (1965): 81–90.

15. The first story on the case appeared in the *North China Herald* (*NCH*), September 9, 1879, p. 255, and was picked up in a number of subsequent issues including editorials in the issues dated September 23 and November 7, 1879, and March 25, 1880.

16. *NCH,* September 23, 1879, p. 299.

17. *NCH,* September 23, 1879, p. 290. Likin was of course required even for foreign shipments of opium beyond the treaty ports.

18. *NCH,* September 23, 1879, p. 308.

19. *NCH*, April 10, 1880, p. 320.
20. See for example Ou Chi-luan, *Kuang-chou chih yin-yeh* [Traditional banking in Canton] (Canton, 1932), pp. 209 ff.; and Wu Ch'eng-hsi, *Chung-kuo ti yin-hang* [Chinese banks] (Shanghai, 1934). Chu counts 540 "native" banks in Canton in the early 1930s–p. 237.
21. Wu Ch'eng-hsi, *Chinese Banks*, pp. 70 ff.
22. On the modern Chinese banks, see also L. G. Ting, "The Chinese Banks and the Financing of Government and Industry," *Nankai Social and Economic Quarterly* no. 8 (1935): 578–616; he counts 146 such banks in China as a whole (excluding Manchuria) in 1932, and "over 300" foreign and Sino-foreign banks, whose total assets were considerably greater. The article also distinguishes three types of native banks, but stresses their interlocking connections throughout the China market and their practice of making loans on personal credit. Frank Tamagna, *Banking and Finance in China* (New York, 1942), includes a brief survey of the development of native banks, the decline of the Shansi banks, and the rise of modern banking.
23. The pioneer study of the diffusion of innovation is Torsten Hagerstrand, *The Propagation of Innovation Waves* (Lund, 1952); his larger study of 1953, translated by A. Pred as *Innovation Diffusion as a Spatial Process,* was published by the University of Chicago Press in 1968. I am, however, indebted to Professor Hagerstrand for calling this point to my attention in personal conversation.
24. Whatever the Marxist connotations of the term "semicolonial," it fits China's circumstances from 1842 to 1949, when foreign powers extracted privileges which no fully sovereign modern government would freely have granted.
25. See their application to the China case in M. J. Levy, *The Rise of the Modern Chinese Business Class*, pt. 1, Institute of Pacific Relations, mimeographed (New York, 1949). The point however is primarily the exclusiveness of the kin-based network through which Chinese merchants worked, a phenomenon observed and commented on by foreigners in China at every period.
26. Two recent Japanese studies of late-traditional Chinese merchant operations, conveniently summarized by Ramon Myers in a review article in *Ch'ing-shih wen-t'i* 3, no. 2 (1974): 77–95, deserve mention in this connection as providing pictures of a smoothly functioning system fully able to resist foreign competition, in an overall Chinese context, including its official component, which nourished and rewarded merchant activity in a mutually beneficial association: Yokoyama Suguru, *Chūkoku kindaika no keizai kōzō* [The modernization of China's economic structure] (Tokyo, 1972), and Terada Takanobu, *Sansei chōnin no kenkyu* [A study of Shansi merchants] (Kyoto, 1972).
27. See K. C. Liu, *Anglo-American Steamship Rivalry in China, 1862–*

1874 (Cambridge, Mass., 1962), and idem, "Steamship Enterprise in Nineteenth Century China," *Journal of Asian Studies* 18 (1959): 435–56.

28. See Shih Kuo-heng, *The Early Development of the Modern Chinese Business Class*, pt. 2, Institute of Pacific Relations, mimeographed (New York, 1949), p. 38. A foreign observer noted in 1876 that "there is much private capital seeking an outlet, but all outlet is denied by the fear that when the undertaking to which it is intended is gotten into working order, the myrmidons of government will pounce down upon it to the ruin of its promoters . . . their subscriptions would be regarded as a measure of their capacity to contribute to official coffers." (*NCH,* September 23, 1876). Here is further evidence, incidentally, that the economy was still producing surpluses for investment, but the same point was made even more explicitly two years later: "There are hundreds of intelligent men in China possessed of large wealth. This money they are only too eager to employ in mines, telegraphs, and in all public works which would enrich them and benefit the country, but they are absolutely obliged to hide their wealth and pretend to be poor, lest the mandarins should rob them of every last cash." (*NCH,* October 3, 1878).

29. Yen Chung-p'ing, *Chung-kuo mien fang-chih shih-kao* [Draft history of the Chinese cotton industry] (Peking, 1955), p. 122. Hao Yen-p'ing, *The Comprador,* shows an even earlier spurt of industrial and business investment by compradores and ex-compradores, but accelerating after about 1900–chap. 6, pp. 127–32.

30. Yen, *Draft History,* p. 158.

31. Sources of financing for Chinese mills, and interest rates paid, are given in ibid., pp. 182–85 and 233–37.

32. Charles K. Moser, *The Cotton Textile Industry of Far Eastern Countries* (Boston, 1930), p. 68.

33. See L. G. Ting, *Recent Developments in China's Cotton Industry,* China Institute of Pacific Relations (Shanghai, 1936); Hou Chi-ming, *Foreign Investment and Economic Development in China: 1840–1937* (Cambridge, Mass., 1965), pp. 153 ff.

34. As recorded in the Maritime Customs *Annual Returns of Trade.*

35. Carl Crow includes an amusing description of this contrast even in Shanghai in his *Four Hundred Million Customers* (New York, 1937), pp. 56 ff.

36. H. B. Morse, *The Gilds of China,* 2d ed. (London, 1932), p. 33.

37. Ibid., pp. 53–54.

38. Ibid., p. 169.

39. *Accounts and Papers,* 68, Commercial Reports from H.M. Consuls in China for the Years 1865 and 1866, Report for Canton for 1866, pp. 393–94.

40. Ibid., Report for Tientsin for 1866, p. 433.
41. Ibid., Report for Chinkiang for 1865, p. 328.
42. Ibid., 60, Report for Canton for 1868, p. 504.
43. Ibid., Report for Swatow for 1868, p. 517.
44. Ibid., 91, Report for Hankow for 1880, pp. 462–63.
45. Ibid., 65, Report of the Delegates of the Shanghai General Chamber of Commerce on the Trade of the Upper Yangtze, by A. Michie and R. Francis (London, 1870), pp. 151–52, 158, 170–71.
46. Henri Cordier, "Un Voyage à Yunnansen," *La Chine* 53 (1923): 21–24. *La Chine* was published only briefly in Tientsin, as a "Franco-Chinese bi-monthly report review" in the early 1920s. The passage quoted here refers to the city of A-Mi, in southern Yunnan, but applies equally well to the major treaty ports, where similar foreign descriptions and attitudes have already been cited above.
47. *Report of the Mission to China of the Blackburn Chamber of Commerce, 1896–97* (Blackburn, 1898), F. S. A. Bourne's section, pp. 53–55.
48. Smith, *The Wealth of Nations*, p. 605.
49. N. B. Dennys, ed., *The Treaty Ports of China and Japan* (London, 1867), pp. 396–97.
50. One should perhaps note that the world depression, and especially the silver crisis of 1933–34 in China, sent shock waves via the treaty ports into those parts of the rural hinterland which had become involved in the production or handling of export goods, causing considerable economic distress.

Chapter 11

1. For a detailed account, see J. K. Fairbank, "The Provisional System at Shanghai in 1853–54," *Chinese Social and Political Science Review* 18 (1935): 455–504; 19 (1936): 469–514; and 20 (1936): 42–100.
2. See S. F. Wright, *Hart and the Chinese Customs* (Belfast, 1950).
3. The Customs figures are conveniently presented as a series, with brief commentary and some adjustments, in Hsiao Liang-lin, *China's Foreign Trade Statistics, 1864–1949* (Cambridge, Mass., 1974). See also Franklin L. Ho, *Index Numbers of the Quantities and Prices of Imports and Exports and of the Barter Terms of Trade in China, 1867–1928* (Tientsin, 1930).
4. *Accounts and Papers*, 53, Report on Foreign Trade at the Port of Canton for the Year 1863, p. 76.
5. A treaty port by definition provided for permanent foreign residence and ownership of land and for the establishment of a Maritime Customs station. Some 11 of the total of 69 were however specially

designated "trade marts" opened "voluntarily" by the Chinese government where foreigners could only lease premises for fixed periods. In addition, there were a varying number of "ports of call" along the Yangtze and West Rivers where foreign steamers were permitted to take on and discharge freight and passengers. Between 1842 and 1930, a total of 105 "open ports" were established, 73 by treaties or conventions between China and foreign governments (virtually all of whom had most-favored-nation agreements with China) and 32 unilaterally by the Chinese government. Some of the treaty ports (Kashgar, Tengyüeh) were far from any navigable water, and some of them remained treaty ports in name only as the foreigners chose not to pursue their option to establish residence, consulates, or Customs stations there.

6. *Accounts and Papers,* 92, Report on the Trade of Newchwang for 1898, by Mr. Consul Hosie, pp. 531–32.

7. Ibid., Report on the Trade of Hangchow for 1898, by Acting Consul Werner, p. 546.

8. The tael was originally a unit weight of silver of specified fineness, although it varied somewhat from region to region; Customs statistics were based on the Haikuan (Customs) tael, which was uniform but whose exchange value with currencies of course fluctuated and in those terms declined steadily after 1870.

9. Manchurian trade figures are taken from the Maritime Customs series, as assembled for comparison in *The Manchukuo Yearbook,* Tao keizai Chosakyoku [East Asiatic Economic Investigation Bureau] (Tokyo, 1934), table 4, pp. 579–80.

10. The likin revenue statistics offer a rough but grossly incomplete indication of internal trade movements. I am inclined to feel that Perkins, *Agricultural Development,* pp. 345–57, attempts to extract more meaning and validity from them in this connection than they possess, but his discussion does lend support to the point made here about statistical illusions created by the expanding coverage of the Customs figures.

11. The comparisons here are based on figures provided in *Memorandum on International Trade and Balances of Payments, 1912–1926,* League of Nations (Geneva, 1927–28), vols. 1 and 2, and in *Yearbook of International Trade Statistics,* published by the United Nations. Both publications attempt, in spite of the difficulties involved, to make trade data internationally comparable, although comparability can never be perfect. The United Nations figures, which cover the 1930s, are based on "new" United States dollars, i.e., dollars of the gold content fixed in 1934, and on the rates used by each national authority responsible for external trade statistics to convert national currency into foreign currency values.

12. See the similar guesses made by Feuerwerker, *The Chinese Economy,*

1912–1949, Michigan Papers in Chinese Studies, no. 1, 1968, p. 69. Feuerwerker includes as table 21 values and index numbers of foreign trade from 1912 to 1935, based on Li Choh-ming and Cheng Yu-kwei.

13. George Masselman, *The Cradle of Colonialism* (New Haven, 1963), p. 224. The same point is made by J. C. Van Leur, *Indonesian Trade and Society* (The Hague, 1955), pp. 162 ff. and 170 ff.; and by M. A. F. Meilink-Roelofez, *Asian Trade and European Influence in the Indonesian Archipelago* (The Hague, 1962), pp. 134 ff. and 178 ff.

14. Letter dated January 12, 1864, to Bruce's sister, Lady Augusta Stanley, discovered by Jack Gerson in the Elgin-Bruce archive in Broomhall, Scotland, and printed in *Ch'ing-shih wen-t'i* 5 (April 1967): 11–14.

15. *Accounts and Papers*, 60, Report for Tientsin in 1868.

16. Maritime Customs, *Reports on Trade for 1879*, Report for Tientsin, p. 263.

17. Ibid., p. 271.

18. *Accounts and Papers*, 60, Report for Tientsin in 1879, p. 714. This represented an increase of 30 percent over 1876.

19. Maritime Customs, *Reports on Trade for 1890 and 1891*, Report for Tientsin.

20. Maritime Customs, *Reports on Trade for 1899*, Report for Tientsin.

21. Maritime Customs, *Reports on Trade for 1920*, Report for Tientsin.

22. O. D. Rasmussen, *Tientsin: An Illustrated Outline History* (Tientsin, 1925), p. 295.

23. Maritime Customs, *Reports on Trade for 1928*, Report for Tientsin, p. 231.

24. Maritime Customs, *Decennial Reports, 1922–1931*, Report for Tientsin, p. 412.

25. Ibid., pp. 337–39.

26. Ibid., p. 413

27. Ibid.

28. Ibid., p. 340.

29. Ibid.

30. These quotes are taken from pp. 5 and 6 of The British Chamber of Commerce, *The Present State of British Trade in North China*, which was published at Tientsin in 1930.

31. Ibid., p. 10.

32. Ibid., p. 12.

33. Maritime Customs, *Decennial Reports, 1922–1931*, Report for Tientsin, p. 341.

34. Ibid., p. 344.

35. Ibid.

36. *The Present State of British Trade in North China*, p. 3. On the transit trade of Shanghai and its relative scale, see R. Murphey, *Shanghai: Key to Modern China* (Cambridge, Mass., 1953), pp. 116–32.

37. Maritime Customs, *Decennial Reports, 1922–1931,* Tientsin, pp. 376–77.
38. *The Present State of British Trade in North China,* p. 22.
39. These may seem extravagant statements; my findings surprise me too, and it may be that further research into the commodity trading patterns for specific goods would suggest a different picture. Such research has not to my knowledge been done for any of the treaty ports or their commercial hinterlands, at least not in a way which could throw light on this sort of question. However, for the results of disaggregation in the case of Tientsin, see p. 219.
40. The parallel is incomplete since the chief form of natural disaster in the Hankow area was flooding, which interrupted the water transport on which the port was almost wholly dependent, as Tientsin was not. Hankow's trade thus tended to decline during periods of flooding and to recover once the waterways became usable again, carrying in that case a large backlog held back while water transport was inoperable. The impact of civil disorder more nearly parallels the Tientsin case, as summarized below, and there was the same pattern of heavy refugee movement into Hankow at such times. Hankow was also unusual in showing a steady increase in tea exports while Chinese tea generally was losing its share of world markets, from 1864 to 1940. This was the result of the Russian choice of Hankow as their chief base for tea purchases in central China and their construction of a steam-powered factory there to press brick tea, which was shipped to Russia overland and by rail and river via Shanghai and/or Tientsin. The Russian market developed a taste for brick tea made from inferior or rejected leaf, broken bits, and stems and stuck to its original Chinese and Hankow source relatively unaffected by shifts in world market preferences and price changes for higher quality teas.
41. Maritime Customs, *Decennial Reports, 1922–1931,* Report for Hankow, pp. 560 ff.
42. *Accounts and Papers,* 93, Report from Hankow for 1913, p. 465.
43. Maritime Customs, *Reports on Trade for 1920,* Report for Canton.
44. See Murphey, *Shanghai,* pp. 19–24, 10.
45. Ibid., p. 22.
46. Maritime Customs, *Decennial Reports, 1922–1931,* Report for Hankow, pp. 581–82.
47. Ibid., Tientsin, p. 411.
48. Maritime Customs, *Reports on Trade for 1910,* Report for Canton.

Chapter 12

1. *The Journal of Lord Macartney During His Embassy to China,* entry for January 2–7, 1794, at Canton, as published in J. L. Cranmer-Byng, ed., *An Embassy to China* (London, 1962), pp. 212–13.

2. See K. C. Liu, *Anglo-American Steamship Rivalry;* idem, "Steamship Enterprise"; and Ellsworth Carlson, *The Kaiping Mines* (Cambridge, Mass., 1957).

3. Liu and Yeh, *The Economy of the Chinese Mainland,* pp. 66, 69, 89, tables 8, 11, and 21.

4. Quoted in N. A. Pelcovits, *Old China Hands and the Foreign Office* (New York, 1948), p. 101.

5. This is discussed by Lucien Bianco in two manuscripts of 1973, "The Economic Plight of the Chinese Peasant in the 1920's and 1930's," and "The Land Tax in Republican China Until 1937." Perkins, *Agricultural Development,* pp. 94 ff., also suggests, following J. L. Buck, that the rate of return from landholding was falling, especially after about 1890, and that it was not more than 5 per cent on most land; this was far lower than the return from most alternative investments. See also Yuji Muramatsu, "A Documentary Study of Chinese Landlordism in Late Ch'ing and Early Republican Kiangnan," *Bulletin of the School of Oriental and African Studies* 29 (1966): 566–99.

6. Arnold Wright, ed., *Twentieth Century Impressions of Hong Kong, Shanghai, and Other Treaty Ports of China: Their History, People, Commerce, Industries, and Resources* (London, 1908), pp. 525 ff., includes an account of the leading compradores of Shanghai at the turn of the century, their activities and investments, and their purchase of rank. He indicates that in 1900, fifteen of the forty compradores he enumerates in the Shanghai area were expectant taotai, while most of the others had or planned to purchase titles.

7. See for example the account of two compradores, "Choping" and Ho Tung, as prominant philanthropists in the *North China Herald,* November 29, 1870, p. 395. Ho also made large gifts to Hong Kong University, among other institutions—see Brian Harrison, ed., *University of Hong Kong: The First Fifty Years, 1911–1961* (Hong Kong, 1962), p. 154. Two other compradores, Hsü Jun and Cheng Kuan-ying, were typical of many who organized, led, and helped to finance local relief operations at times of flood and famine—see the references to these activities in the well-known tract by Cheng Kuan-ying, *Sheng-shih wei-yen hou-p'ien* [Warnings to the seemingly prosperous age, part 2], 15 chüan (Shanghai, 1920): 14:22–23.

8. An account of Yeh Ch'eng-chung's foundation of his school in Shanghai is given in *Shang-hai hsien hsü-chih* [Gazeteer of Shanghai County], 30 chüan (Shanghai, 1918): 10–14. On the compradore role in the Red Cross and the Shanghai Rescue Society, see A. Wright, *Twentieth Century,* p. 538. Wright also (on p. 413) mentions the role of compradores at Shanghai in organizing and funding a merchant militia which in 1907 merged with the Shanghai Volunteer Corps. Much of this and other material on the traditional-style activities of the compradores, including their prominent role in merchant guilds, is

presented in greater detail in Hao Yen-p'ing, "New Class in China's Treaty Ports: The Rise of the Compradore-Merchants, 1842–1911," Manuscript. See also Huang I-feng, "Kuan-yü chiu Chung-kuo mai-pan chieh-chi ti yen-chiu" [A study of the compradore group in old China], *Li-shih Yen-chiu* 7 (1964): 89–116, which includes information on the important compradore role in the Chinese Chamber of Commerce at Shanghai, based on that Chamber's archives.

9. These were based however, as pointed out in chapter 10, on the traditional guilds and were often dominated numerically by guild representatives. Most Chinese merchants belonged to both, but the Chambers of Commerce were in any case formed to *resist* foreign commercial competition and influence. On the Chambers as a response to the foreign example, see Shirley Garrett, "The Chambers of Commerce and the Y.M.C.A.," in *The Chinese City Between Two Worlds,* ed. M. Elvin and G. W. Skinner (Stanford, 1974), pp. 213–38.

10. These were the most important export commodities by value (although not in order of importance, which varied from period to period), between 1870 and 1936, the last "normal" trade year before the outbreak of war with Japan, for China exclusive of Manchuria.

11. Webster defines beachhead as "any initial advance position or foothold to be used as vantage ground for exploitation."

12. Even the missionaries had for the most part close links with urban bases, without which they could not have functioned; this included the periodic intervention of the treaty port system in the form of gunboats or political pressures on the center and the provinces, as well as the more regular streams of supply.

13. Frederic Wakeman, *Strangers at the Gate: Social Disorder in South China, 1839–1861* (Berkeley, 1966), esp. pp. 45–46 and 50–51.

14. See Maurice Meisner, "Leninism and Maoism: Some Populist Perspectives on Marxism-Leninism in China," *The China Quarterly,* no. 45 (1971), pp. 2–36, and Herman Mast, "Tai Chi-t'ao, Sunism and Marxism During the May Fourth Movement in Shanghai," *Modern Asian Studies* 5 (1971): 227–50.

15. Mast, "Tai Chi-t'ao," pp. 229, 247.

16. Meisner, "Leninism," p. 17.

17. Lin Piao, "Long Live the Victory of Peoples' War," as published in *Peking Review,* no. 36 (September 3, 1965), pp. 9–30. Lin is here quoting from Mao's "The Chinese Revolution and the Chinese Communist Party," written in 1939.

18. Quoted from the account published in *China Reconstructs* 16 (February, 1967): 10.

Works Cited

Abeel, David. *Journal of a Residence in China and Neighboring Countries.* New York: Leavitt and Co., 1834.

Accounts and Papers. 63. Commercial Reports from H.M. Consuls in China for the Year 1862, Report for Tientsin for 1862. London, 1864.

Accounts and Papers, 53, Commercial Reports from H.M. Consuls in China for the Year 1863, Report for Canton for the Year 1863. London, 1865.

Accounts and Papers, 68. Commercial Reports from H.M. Consuls in China for the Years 1865 and 1866. Report for Canton for 1866. London, 1867.

Accounts and Papers, 68. Commercial Reports from H.M. Consuls in China for the Years 1865 and 1866, Report for Tientsin for 1866. London, 1867.

Accounts and Papers, 68. Commercial Reports from H.M. Consuls in China for the Years 1865 and 1866, Report for Chinkiang for 1865. London, 1867.

Accounts and Papers, 60. Commercial Reports from H.M. Consuls in China for the Years 1868 and 1869, Report for Canton for 1868. London, 1870.

Accounts and Papers, 60. Commercial Reports from H.M. Consuls in China for the Years 1868 and 1869, Report for Swatow for 1868. London, 1870.

Accounts and Papers, 60. Commercial Reports from H.M. Consuls in China for the Years 1868 and 1869, Report for Tientsin for 1868. London, 1870.

Accounts and Papers, 65. Commercial Reports from H.M. Consuls in China for the Year 1866. London, 1870.

Accounts and Papers, 71. Commercial Reports from H.M. Consuls in China for the Year 1879, Report for Tientsin for 1879. London, 1880.

Accounts and Papers, 91. Commercial Reports from H.M. Consuls in China for the Year 1880, Report for Hankow for 1880. London, 1881.

Accounts and Papers, 134. Commercial Reports from H.M. Consuls in China for the Year 1913, Report for Hankow for 1913. London, 1914.

Anstey, Vera. *The Economic Development of India.* Rev. ed. London: Longmans, Green and Co., 1942.

Apte, M. L. "Lokahitavadi and V. K. Chiplunkar: Spokesmen of Change in Nineteenth Century Maharashtra." *Modern Asian Studies* 7 (April 1973): 193–208.

Apter, Davis. *The Politics of Modernization.* Chicago: University of Chicago Press, 1965.

Aston, R. J. "The Merchant Shipping Activity of South China, 1644–1847." Ph.D. dissertation, University of Hawaii, 1964.

Barlow, Glyn. *The Story of Madras.* London: H. Milford, Oxford University Press, 1921.

Basu, Dilip. "Dwarkanath Tagore: Citizen-landlord and Entrepreneur." Manuscript, University of California at Santa Cruz, 1968.

Bayly, C. A. "Town Building in North India, 1790–1830." *Modern Asian Studies* 9 (1975): 483–504.

Bergère, Marie-Claire. *Une crise financière à Shanghai à la fin de l'ancien régime.* Paris: Mouton, 1964.

Bernier, Francois. *Travels in the Mogul Empire.* Translated by I. Broch, 2 vols. London: W. Pickering, 1826.

Bhattacharya, Sukumar. *The East India Company and the Economy of Bengal from 1704 to 1740.* London: Luzac, 1954.

Bianco, Lucien. "The Economic Plight of the Chinese Peasant in the 1920s and 1930s." Manuscript, University of Paris, n.d.

——. "The Land Tax in Republican China Until 1937." Manuscript, University of Paris, n.d.

Bickmore, A. S. "Sketch of a Journey from Canton to Hankow." *Journal of the North China Branch Royal Asiatic Society (JNCBRAS)* 4 (1868): 1–20.

Black, Cyril E. *The Dynamics of Modernization: A Study of Comparative History.* New York: Harper and Row, 1966.

Blyn, George. *Agricultural Trends in India, 1891–1947.* Philadelphia: University of Pennsylvania Press, 1966.

Boardman, Eugene P. *Christian Influence on the Ideology of the Taiping Rebellion, 1851–1864.* Madison: University of Wisconsin Press, 1952.

Boxer, Charles R. *The Dutch Seaborne Empire, 1600–1800.* London: Knopf, 1965.

——. *Four Centuries of Portuguese Expansion, 1415–1825: A Succinct Survey.* Johannesburg: Witwatersrand University Press, 1961.

Broomfield, J. H. *Elite Conflict in a Plural Society: Twentieth Century Bengal.* Berkeley: University of California Press, 1968.

——. "The Regional Elites: A Theory of Modern Indian History." *The Indian Economic and Social History Review* 3 (September 1966): 279–91.

Brown, J. Coggin, and Dey, A. K. *India's Mineral Wealth.* 3d ed. London: Oxford University Press, 1955.

Brown, W. N. *Man in the Universe: Some Cultural Continuities in Indian*

Thought (Rabindranath Tagore Memorial Lectures). Berkeley: University of California Press, 1966.

Bury, J. B. *The Idea of Progress: An Inquiry Into its Origin and Growth.* London: Macmillan and Co., Limited, 1920.

Campos, J. J. *History of the Portuguese in Bengal.* Calcutta: Butterworth and Co., 1919.

Carlson, Ellsworth. *The Kaiping Mines (1877–1912).* Chinese Economic and Political Studies. Cambridge: Harvard University Press, 1957.

Chandra, Bholanatha. *Travels of a Hindoo to Various Parts of Bengal and Upper India.* London: N. Trübner and Co., 1869.

Chang Chung-li. *The Income of the Chinese Gentry.* Seattle: University of Washington Press, 1962.

Chang, John. *Industrial Development in Pre-Communist China: A Quantitative Analysis.* Committee on the Economy of China Monographs. Chicago: Aldine, 1969.

Chang Kuo-hui. "Shih-chiu shih-chi hou-pan ch'i Chung-kuo ch'ien-chuang ti mai-pan hua" [The Chinese native banks as compradores in the latter half of the nineteenth century]. *Li-shih Yen-chiu* 6 (1963): 85–98.

Checkland, S. G. "An English Merchant House in China After 1842." *Bulletin of the Business Historical Society* 27 (1953): 161–81.

Ch'en Mao-heng. "Ming-tai wo-k'ou k'ao-lueh" [Japanese pirate attacks during the Ming]. *Yen-ching Hsüeh-pao.* Monograph series, No. 6. Peking, 1934.

Ch'en Shih-chi. "Chia wu chien ch'ien Chung-kuo nung ts'un shou kung yeh ti pien hua ho tzu pen chu i sheng ch'an ti ch'eng chang" [Rural household hand cloth making and the rise of capitalist production before the Sino-Japanese war]. *Li shih Yen chiu* 2 (1959): 17–38.

Cheng Kuan-ying. *Sheng-shih wei-yen hou-p'ien* [Warnings to the seemingly prosperous age, part 2]. 15 chüan (Shanghai: 1920) 14: 22–23.

Cheng Yu-kuei. *Foreign Trade and Industrial Development of China.* Washington: University Press of Washington, D.C., 1956.

Chien Po-tsan, ed. *Wu-hsu pien-fa* [The reform movement of 1898]. 4 vols. Shanghai, 1957.

Ch'in Jun-ching. "Shang-hai chih ch'ien-chuang shih yeh" [A study of native banking in Shanghai]. *Ch'ien-yeh Yüeh-pao* 6, no. 10 (November 19, 1926): 22–40.

China Reconstructs. Vol. 16. Peking: Foreign Language Press, February, 1967.

"Ch'ing kuo mien hua mien pu chi mien ssu shu ju ching k'uang" (Shinkoku menka mempu oyobi menshi yunyū keikyō) [The outlook for imports of raw cotton, cotton cloth, and cotton thread in China]. Published by Dai Nippon menshi bōseki dōgyō rengōkai hōkoku [Report of the United Association of Japanese Cotton Spinners]. Tokyo, 1898. In Hatano Yoshihiro. "The Organization of Production in the

Cotton Cloth Industry in China after the Opium War." *Chūgoku kindai kōgyō-shi no kenkyū* [Studies in China's early industrialization]. Kyoto: Tōyōshi-kenkyū-kai, 1961.

Chow Tse-tsung. *The May Fourth Movement: Intellectual Revolution in Modern China.* Cambridge: Harvard University Press, 1960.

Cipolla, Carlo M. *Guns, Sails and Empires: Technological Innovations and the Early Phases of European Expansion.* London: Pantheon Books, 1965.

Cobden, Richard. *The Political Writings of Richard Cobden.* 2d ed. 2 vols. New York: D. Appleton and Co., 1868.

Cohen, Paul. *Between Tradition and Modernity: Wang T'ao and Reform in Late Ch'ing China.* Cambridge: Harvard University Press, 1974.

_____. "Wang T'ao and Incipient Chinese Nationalism." *Journal of Asian Studies* 26 (1967): 559–74.

_____. "Wang T'ao's Perspective on a Changing World." In *Approaches to Modern Chinese History,* edited by Albert Feuerwerker, Rhoads Murphey, and Mary Wright, pp. 133–62. Berkeley: University of California Press, 1967.

Cooke, G. W. *China: Being the Times Special Correspondence from China in the Years 1857–58.* London: G. Routledge and Co., 1858.

Cordier, Henri. "Un Voyage à Yunnansen." *La Chine* 53 (1923): 21–24.

Cowan, C. D., ed. *The Economic Development of China and Japan.* London: G. Allen and Unwin, 1964.

Cranmer-Byng, J. L., ed. *An Embassy to China.* London: Paragon, 1962.

Crow, Carl. *Foreign Devils in the Flowery Kingdom.* New York: Harper and Brothers, 1940.

_____. *Four Hundred Million Customers.* 3d ed. New York: Harper, 1937.

Crowder, M. *West Africa Under Colonial Rule.* Evanston: Northwestern University Press, 1969.

Dalrymple, Alexander. *A Plan for Extending the Commerce of This Kingdom and of the East India Company.* London: J. Nourse and T. Payne, 1769.

Danvers, F. C. *The Portuguese in India.* 2 vols. London: W. H. Allen and Co., Limited, 1894.

Darwin, Charles. *The Origin of Species.* 2 vols. London: R. West, 1914.

Das Gupta, Ashin. "The Crisis at Surat, 1730–32." *Bengal Past and Present* Diamond Jubilee Number (1967): 148–62.

_____. *Malabar in Asia Trade, 1740–1800.* Cambridge: Harvard University Press, 1967.

_____. "Trade and Politics in Eighteenth Century Asia." In *Islam in the Trade of Asia,* edited by F. J. Richards, pp. 181–214. Philadelphia: University of Pennsylvania Press, 1970.

Das Gupta, J. N. *India in the Seventeenth Century.* Calcutta: University of Calcutta, 1916.

Davis, John F. *The Chinese: A General Description of the Empire of China and Its Inhabitants*. 1st ed. 2 vols. London: C. Knight, 1836; 4th ed. 3 vols. London: J. Murray, 1857.

Dawson, F. L. "Law and the Merchant in Traditional China." *Papers on China*, vol. 2. Cambridge: East Asian Research Center, Harvard University, 1948.

Dennys, N. B., ed. *The Treaty Ports of China and Japan*. London: Trübner and Co., 1867.

Dernberger, Robert. "The Role of the Foreigner in China's Economic Development, 1840–1949." In *China's Modern Economy in Historical Perspective*, edited by Dwight Perkins, pp. 19–47. Stanford: Stanford University Press, 1975.

Dickinson, W. "Narrative of an Overland Trip Through Hunan from Canton to Hankow." *Journal of the North China Branch Royal Asiatic Society* 1 (1864): 159–73.

Dimock, E. C., ed. *Bengal Literature and History*. Asian Studies Center. East Lansing, Mich.: Michigan State University Press, 1967.

Dore, R. P. "On the Possibility and Desirability of a Theory of Modernization." In Report from the International Conference on the Problems of Modernization. Asian Research Centre. Seoul, 1968. Reprinted in Committee of Concerned Asian Scholars, *Newsletter*, no. 3 (March 1969), pp. 59–64.

du Halde, Jean Baptiste. *Description of the Empire of China*. Translation. London: E. Cave, 1738.

Dunlop, W. B. "The Key of Western China." *Asiatic Quarterly Review* 7 (1889): 290–320.

Duyvendak, J. L. *China's Discovery of Africa*. London: A. Probsthain, 1949.

Eastman, Lloyd. "Political Reformism in China Before the Sino-Japanese War." *Journal of Asian Studies* 27 (1968): 695–710.

Edwardes, S. N. *The Rise of Bombay*. Bombay, 1902.

Elvin, Mark. "The High-Level Equilibrium Trap: The Causes of the Decline of Invention in the Traditional Chinese Textile Industries." In *Economic Organization in China Society*, edited by W. E. Wilmott, pp. 121–48. Stanford: Stanford University Press, 1972.

_____. *The Pattern of the Chinese Past*. London and Stanford: Stanford University Press, 1973.

Elvin, Mark, and Skinner, G. W., eds. *The Chinese City Between Two Worlds*. Stanford: Stanford University Press, 1974.

Escarra, Jean. *Le droit Chinois*. Paris: Librairie du Recueil Sirey, 1936.

Fairbank, John K. "The Early Treaty System in the Chinese World Order." In *The Chinese World Order*, edited by J. K. Fairbank, pp. 257–75. Cambridge: Harvard University Press, 1968.

_____. "The Provisional System at Shanghai in 1853–54." *Chinese Social* and *Political Science Review* 18 (1935): 455–504; 19 (1936): 469–514; 20 (1936): 42–100.

———. *Trade and Diplomacy on the China Coast: The Opening of the Treaty Ports, 1842–1854.* 1953. Cambridge: Harvard University Press, 1964.

Fairbank, John K., ed. *The Chinese World Order.* Cambridge: Harvard University Press, 1968.

Farmer, B. H. "The Social Basis of Nationalism in Ceylon." *Journal of Asian Studies* 24 (1965): 431–39.

Farmer, E. L. "James Flint versus the Canton Interest, 1755–1760." *Papers on China,* vol. 17. Cambridge: East Asian Research Center, Harvard University, 1963.

Fawcett, Charles, ed. *The English Factories in India.* 4 vols. Oxford, Clarendon Press, 1952.

Feuerwerker, Albert. *China's Early Industrialization: Sheng-Hsuan-huai (1844–1916) and Mandarin Enterprise.* Cambridge: Harvard University Press, 1958.

———. "China's Nineteenth Century Industrialization: The Case of the Hanyehping Coal and Iron Company, Limited." In *The Economic Development of China and Japan,* edited by C. D. Cowan, pp. 79–110. London: G. Allen and Unwin, 1964.

———. *The Chinese Economy, 1870–1911.* Michigan Papers in Chinese Studies, Center for Chinese Studies, no. 5. Ann Arbor: University of Michigan, 1968.

———. *The Chinese Economy, 1912–1949.* Michigan Papers in Chinese Studies, Center for Chinese Studies, no. 1. Ann Arbor: University of Michigan, 1969.

———. "Handicraft and Manufactured Cotton Textiles in China, 1871–1910." *Journal of Economic History* 30 (1970): 338–78.

———. "Industrial Enterprise in Twentieth Century China: The Chee Hsin Cement Co." In *Approaches to Modern Chinese History,* edited by Albert Feuerwerker, Rhoads Murphey, and Mary Wright, pp, 304–41. Berkeley: University of California Press, 1967.

Feuerwerker, Albert, Murphey, Rhoads, and Wright, Mary. *Approaches to Modern Chinese History.* Berkeley: University of California Press, 1967.

Fitch, Ralph. *Journal of Ralph Fitch, 1583–1591.* In *Early Travels in India,* edited by William Foster, pp. 41–42. London: H. Milford, Oxford University Press, 1921.

Fong, H. D. *The Cotton Industry and Trade in China.* 2 vols. Tientsin: The Chihli Press, 1932.

———. *Industrial Capital in China.* Tientsin: The Chihli Press, 1936.

———. "Rural Weaving and the Merchant Employers in a North China District." *Nankai Social and Economic Quarterly* 8, no. 1 (1934): 75–120; no. 2: 274–308.

Forbes, Frederick E. *Five Years in China. 1842–1847.* London: R. Bentley, 1848.

Fortune, Robert. *A Journey to the Tea Countries of China and India.* London: J. Murray, 1852.

———. *A Residence Among the Chinese.* London: J. Murray, 1857.

———. *The Tea Districts of China and India.* 2 vols. London: J. Murray, 1853.

———. *Three Years' Wanderings in the Northern Provinces of China.* 2d ed. London: J. Murray, 1847.

———. *Two Visits to the Tea Countries of China and the British Plantations in the Himalaya.* London: J. Murray, 1853.

———. *Yedo and Peking.* London: J. Murray, 1863.

Foster, William. *England's Quest of Eastern Trade.* London: A. & C. Black, Ltd., 1933.

Foster, William, ed. *Early Travels in India, 1583–1619.* London: H. Milford, Oxford University Press, 1921.

———. *The English Factories in India, 1618–1621.* 3 vols. Oxford: The Clarendon Press, 1906–27.

Fox, Grace. *British Admirals and Chinese Pirates, 1832–1869.* London: K. Paul, Trench, Trübner and Co., Ltd., 1940.

Friedman, Edward, and Selden, Mark, eds. *Imperialism in Asia.* New York: Paragon, 1973.

Fry, H. T. *Alexander Dalrymple (1737–1808) and the Expansion of British Trade.* Toronto: University of Toronto Press, 1970.

Fu I-ling. *Ming-tai Chiang-nan shih min ching-chi shih tan* [A study of the economy of the urban population of Kiangnan in Ming times]. Shanghai, 1957.

Furber, Holden. *Bombay Presidency in the Mid-Eighteenth Century.* New York and London: Asia Publishing House, 1965.

———. *John Company at Work.* Cambridge: Harvard University Press, 1948.

Gallagher, L. J., trans. *China in the Sixteenth Century: The Journals of Matthew Ricci, 1583–1610.* New York: Random House, 1953.

Garrett, Shirley. "The Chambers of Commerce and the Y.M.C.A." In *The Chinese City Between Two Worlds,* edited by Mark Elvin and G. W. Skinner, pp. 213–38. Stanford: Stanford University Press, 1974.

Gasster, Michael. *China's Struggle to Modernize.* New York: Knopf, 1972.

———. "Reform and Revolution in China's Political Modernization." In *China in Revolution,* edited by M. C. Wright, pp. 67–96. New Haven: Yale University Press, 1968.

Gernet, J. *Daily Life in China, on the Eve of the Mongol Invasion, 1250–1276.* Translated by H. M. Wright. New York: Macmillan, 1962.

Ghosh, Benoy. "Some Old Family Founders in Eighteenth Century Calcutta." *Bengal Past and Present* 79 (1960): 26–41.

Gilbert, Rodney. *What's Wrong with China.* London: J. Murray, 1926.

Gillion, K. L. *Ahmedabad: A Study in Indian Urban History.* Berkeley: University of California Press, 1968.

Gokhale, B. G. "Ahmadabad in the Seventeenth Century." *Journal of the Economic and Social History of the Orient* 12 (1969): 187–97.

——. "Burhanpur: Notes on the History of an Indian City in the XVIIth Century." *Journal of the Economic and Social History of the Orient* 15 (1972): 316–23.

——. "Capital Accumulation in Seventeenth Century Western India." *Journal of the Asiatic Society of Bombay* 39–40 (1964–65): 51–60.

Gravenstein, R. G., ed. *Journal of the First Voyage of Vasco da Gama.* London, 1898.

Graves, Rosewell H. *Forty Years in China.* Baltimore: R. H. Woodward Co., 1895.

Greenberg, Michael. *British Trade and the Opening of China, 1800–1842.* Cambridge: At the University Press, 1951.

Grosier, Jean Baptiste G. A. *General Description of China.* Translated by Abbé Grosier. London: G. G. and J. Robinson, 1795.

Gunderson, Warren. "Modernization and Cultural Change: The Self-Image and World View of the Bengali Intelligentsia as Found in the Writings of the Mid-Nineteenth Century, 1830–1870." In *Bengal Literature and History,* edited by E. C. Dimock, pp. 127–77. Asian Studies Center. East Lansing, Mich.: Michigan State University Press, 1967.

Gupta, B. K. "The Black Hole Incident." *Journal of Asian Studies* 19 (November 1959): 53–63.

——. "Indian Response to Early Western Contacts in Bengal, 1650–1756." *Studies on Asia* (University of Nebraska) 1 (1960): 9–19.

Gutzlaff, Karl. *China Opened.* 2 vols. London: Smith, Elder and Co., 1838.

Habib, Irfan. *The Agrarian System of Mughal India, 1556–1707.* Bombay: Asia Publishing House, 1963.

——. "Potentialities of Capitalistic Development in the Economy of Mughal India—An Inquiry." Paper read at the International Economic History Conference, 1968.

Hagerstrand, Torsten. *Innovation Diffusion as a Spatial Process.* Translated by Allan Pred. Chicago: University of Chicago Press, 1968.

——. *The Propagation of Innovation Waves.* Lund: Royal University of Lund, 1952.

Hakluyt, Richard. *The Principall Navigations.* London: George Bishop and Ralph Newberie, 1589.

Hall, Daniel G. E. *A History of Southeast Asia.* London: Macmillan, 1955.

Hamilton, Alexander. *A New Account of the East Indies.* Edited by William Foster. London: The Argonaut Press, 1930. Originally published in 1727.

Han-sheng Chuan and R. A. Kraus. *Mid-Ch'ing Rice Markets and Trade.* Cambridge: Harvard University Press, 1975.

Hao Yen-p'ing. *The Comprador in Nineteenth Century China: Bridge Between East and West.* East Asian Series, no. 45. Cambridge: Harvard University Press, 1970.

————. "New Class in China's Treaty Ports: The Rise of the Compradore-Merchants, 1842–1911." Manuscript.

Harlow, V. T. *The Founding of the Second British Empire.* 2 vols. London: Longmans, Green, 1952.

Harrison, Brian, ed. *University of Hong Kong: The First Fifty Years, 1911–1961.* Hong Kong: Hong Kong University Press, 1962.

Hatano Yoshihiro. "The Organization of Production in the Cotton Cloth Industry in China after the Opium War." *Chūgoku kindai kōgyō-shi no kenkyū* [Studies in China's early industrialization]. Kyoto: Toyoshi-Kenkyū-kai, 1961.

Hitch, M. "The Port of Tientsin and Its Problems." *The Geographical Review* 25 (1935): 367–81.

Ho, Franklin L. *Index Numbers of the Quantities and Prices of Imports and Exports and of the Barter Terms of Trade in China, 1867–1928.* Tientsin: The Chihli Press, 1930.

Ho, P. T. *The Ladder of Success in Imperial China: Aspects of Social Mobility, 1388–1911.* New York: Columbia University Press, 1962.

————. *Studies on the Population of China, 1368–1953.* East Asia Series, no. 4. Cambridge: Harvard University Press, 1959.

Hoshi Ayao. *Mindai soun no kenkyu* [A study of the transport system of the grain tribute during Ming]. Tokyo, 1963. English translation *The Ming Tribute Grain System.* Translated by Mark Elvin. Michigan Abstracts of Chinese and Japanese Works on Chinese History, no. 1. Ann Arbor: Center for Chinese Studies, University of Michigan, 1970.

Hou Chi-ming. *Foreign Investment and Economic Development in China: 1840–1937.* Cambridge: Harvard University Press, 1965.

Hsiao Liang-lin. *China's Foreign Trade Statistics, 1864–1949.* Cambridge: Harvard University Press, 1974.

Hsieh Kuo-chen. "Ch'ing-ch'u tung-nan yen-hai ch'ien" [Evacuation of the southeast coast in early Ch'ing]. *Kuo-hsüeh chi-k'an* 2 (December 1930): 797–826.

Hsieh, Winston. "Peasant Insurrection and the Marketing Hierarchy." In *The Chinese City Between Two Worlds,* edited by Mark Elvin and G. W. Skinner, pp. 119–41. Stanford: Stanford University Press, 1974.

Huang I-feng. "Kuan-yü chiu Chung-kuo mai-pan chieh-chi ti yen-chiu" [A study of the compradore group in old China]. *Li-shih Yen-chiu* 7 (1964): 89–116.

Huc, Evariste R. *The Chinese Empire.* 2 vols. Translated from the French. London: Longman, Brown, Green, Longmans, and Roberts, 1859.

Huc, Evariste R., and Gabet, Jean. *Travels in Tartary, Tibet and China.* Translated by W. Hazlitt. Vol. 1. London: Harper and Brothers, 1928.

Hurd, John. "Railways and the Expansion of Markets in India, 1861–1921." Paper read at the Association for Asian Studies Annual Meeting, Washington, D.C., 1971.

Ingram, Alexander R. *The Gateway to India: The Story of Methwold and Bombay.* London: Oxford University Press, 1938.

Irwin, John. "Indian Textile Trade in the Seventeenth Century." *Journal of Indian Textile History* 1 (1955): 5–33; 2 (1956): 24–42; 3 (1957): 59–72; 4 (1959): 57–64.

Irwin, John, and Schwartz, P. R. *Studies in Indo-European Textile History.* Ahmadabad: Calico Museum of Textiles, 1966.

Jacob, G. L. *Western India Before and During the Mutinies.* 3d ed. London: H. S. King, 1872.

Jansen, Marius B., ed. *Changing Japanese Attitudes Toward Modernization.* Princeton: Princeton University Press, 1965.

Jernignan, Thomas R. *China in Law and Commerce.* New York: The Macmillan Company, 1905.

Jones, S. M. "Finance in Ningpo: The Ch'ien-Chuang, 1750–1880." In *Economic Organization in Chinese Society,* edited by W. E. Wilmott, pp. 47–77. Stanford: Stanford University Press, 1972.

Khan, Shafaat A., ed. *The East India Trade in the Seventeenth Century.* London: H. Milford, 1923.

King, Franklin H. *Farmers of Forty Centuries.* New York and London: J. Cape Limited, 1928.

Klein, Ira. "Population and Agriculture in Northern India, 1872–1921." *Modern Asian Studies* 8 (April 1974): 191–216.

Kling, Blair. *The Blue Mutiny: The Indigo Disturbances in Bengal, 1859–1862.* Philadelphia: University of Pennsylvania Press, 1966.

Koizumi Teizo. "The Operation of Chinese Junks." In *Transport in Transition: The Evolution of Traditional Shipping in China,* edited by Andrew Watson, pp. 1–13. Michigan Abstracts of Chinese and Japanese Works on Chinese History, no. 3. Ann Arbor: Center for Chinese Studies, University of Michigan, 1972.

Kopf, David. *British Orientalism and the Bengal Renaissance: The Dynamics of Indian Modernization, 1773–1835.* Berkeley: University of California Press, 1969.

Krause, A. S. *China in Decay.* London: H. S. King, 1898.

Kuo Hsiao-hsien. "Shang-hai ti ch'ien-chuang" [Native banks in Shanghai]. *Shang-hai shih t'ung-chih kuan ch'i-k'an* 3 (1933): 803–57.

Kuper, Hilda, ed. *Urbanization and Migration in West Africa.* Berkeley: University of California Press, 1965.

Laird, M. A. *Missionaries and Education in Bengal, 1793–1837.* Oxford: Oxford University Press. 1972.

Lanning, George. *A History of Shanghai.* Shanghai: Kelly and Walsh, Ltd., 1923.

Leong Sow-cheng. "Wang T'ao and the Movement for Self-Strengthening and Reform in the Late Ch'ing Period." *Papers on China,* vol. 17. Mimeographed. Cambridge: East Asian Research Center, Harvard University, 1963.

Levenson, Joseph. *Confucian China and its Modern Fate: The Problem of Intellectual Continuity.* Berkeley: University of California Press, 1958.

_____. *Liang Ch'i-ch'ao and the Mind of Modern China.* Harvard Historical Monographs, no. 26. Cambridge: Harvard University Press, 1953.

_____. *The Problem of Historical Significance.* Berkeley: University of California Press, 1965.

_____. *The Problem of Monarchial Decay.* Berkeley: University of California Press, 1964.

_____. *Revolution and Cosmopolitanism: The Western Stage and the Chinese Stages.* Edited by Frederic Wakeman. Berkeley: University of California Press, 1971.

Levy, Marion. "Contrasting Factors in the Modernization of China and Japan." *Economic Development and Cultural Change* 2 (1953): 161–97.

_____. *Family Revolution in Modern China.* Cambridge: Harvard University Press, 1949.

_____. *Modernization and the Structure of Societies: A Setting for International Affairs.* 2 vols. Princeton: Princeton University Press, 1966.

_____. *The Rise of the Modern Chinese Business Class.* Part I. Mimeographed. New York: Institute of Pacific Relations, 1949.

Li, Lillian, "Kiangnan and the Silk Export Trade, 1842–1937." Paper read at the Association for Asian Studies Annual Meeting, Chicago, 1973.

Lin Piao. "Long Live the Victory of Peoples' War." *Peking Review,* no. 36 (September 3, 1965): 9–30.

Lindsay, H. H., and Gutzlaff, K. *Report of Proceedings on a Voyage to the Northern Ports of China.* 2d ed. London: B. Fellowes, 1834.

Little, Archibald. *Gleanings from Fifty Years in China.* London: S. Low, Marston and Co., Ltd., 1910.

Liu, K. C. *Anglo-Chinese Steamship Rivalry in China, 1862–1874.* East Asian Series, no. 8. Cambridge: Harvard University Press, 1962.

_____. "Steamship Enterprise in Nineteenth Century China." *Journal of Asian Studies* 18 (1959): 435–56.

_____. "T'ang T'ing-shu chih mai-pan shih tai" [Tong king-sing's compradore years]. *Ch'ing-hua hsüeh-pao* [Tsing Hua Journal of Chinese Studies]. June 1961, pp. 143–83.

Liu Ta-chung, and Yeh Kung-chia. *The Economy of the Chinese Mainland: National Income and Economic Development, 1933–1959.* Rand Corporation Research Studies. Princeton: Princeton University Press, 1965.

Lockwood, W. W. "Japan's Response to the West." *World Politics* 9 (1956): 37–54.

McAlpin, M. B. "The Effects of Expansion of Markets on Rural Income Distribution in 19th Century India." Paper read at the 26th Annual Meeting of the Association for Asian Studies. Boston, 1974.

———. "The Impact of Railways on Agriculture in India, 1860–1900." Ph.D. dissertation, University of Wisconsin, 1973.

———. "Railroads, Prices, and Peasant Rationality: India, 1860–1900." *Journal of Economic History* 24 (1971): 662–84.

Macartney, Viscount James. *The Journal of Lord Macartney During His Embassy to China.* In *An Embassy to China,* edited by J. L. Cranmer-Byng, pp. 212–13. London: Paragon, 1962.

McElderry, Andrea. "The Shanghai Ch'ien-chuang in the Nineteenth and Twentieth Centuries." Ph.D. dissertation, University of Michigan, 1975.

McGully, B. T. *English Education and the Origins of Indian Nationalism.* New York: Columbia University Press, 1940.

McPhee, John. *A Sense of Where You Are: A Profile of William Warren Bradley.* New York: Farrarr, Straus, and Giroux, 1965.

Maddison, Angus. *Class Structure and Economic Growth: India and Pakistan Since the Mughals.* New York: Norton, 1972.

Malibari, P. B. M. *Bombay in the Making: 1661–1726.* London, 1910.

Manchukuo Yearbook. Tao Keizai Chosakyoku [East Asiatic Economic Investigation Bureau]. Toyko, 1934.

Manucci, Niccolo. *Storia de Mogor.* Translated by W. Irvine. Indian Text Series, vol. 2. London: J. Murray, 1907–8.

Marcus, J. T. "Time and the Sense of History: West and East." *Comparative Studies in Society and History* 2 (1960): 123–29.

Markham, Clements R., ed. *Narratives of the Mission of George Bogle to Tibet, and of the Journal of Thomas Manning to Lhasa.* London: Trübner and Co., 1876.

Marks, H. J. *The First Contest for Singapore, 1819–1824.* The Hague: M. Nijhoff, 1959.

Marshall, P. J. "Economic and Political Expansion: The Case of Oudh." *Modern Asian Studies* 9 (1975): 465–82.

Marx, Karl. "The Future Results of British Rule in India." *New York Herald Tribune,* August 8, 1853.

Masselman, George. *The Cradle of Colonialism.* New Haven: Yale University Press, 1963.

Mast, Herman. "Tai Chi-t'ao, Sunism, and Marxism During the May Fourth Movement in Shanghai." *Modern Asian Studies* 5 (1971): 227–50.

Medhurst, Walter Henry. *China.* Boston: Crocker and Brewster, 1838. Reprint, London: J. Snow, 1842.

Meilink-Roelofez, M. A. F. *Asian Trade and European Influence in the Indonesian Archipelago.* The Hague: M. Nijhoff, 1962.

Meisner, Maurice. "Leninism and Maoism: Some Populist Perspectives on Marxism-Leninism in China." *The China Quarterly* 45 (1971): 2–36.

Memorandum on International Trade and Balances of Payments, 1912–1926. Vols. 1 and 2. Geneva: League of Nations, 1927–28.

Metzger, Thomas. "Ch'ing Commercial Policy." *Ch'ing Shih Wen t'i* 1 (February 1966): 4–10.

_____. *The Internal Organization of Ch'ing Bureaucracy: Legal, Normative and Communication Aspects.* Cambridge: Harvard University Press, 1973.

_____. "The Organizational Capabilities of the Ch'ing State in the Field of Commerce: The Liang-huai Salt Monopoly, 1740–1840." In *Economic Organization in Chinese Society,* edited by W. E. Wilmott, pp. 9–45. Stanford: Stanford University Press, 1972.

_____. T'ao Chu's Reform of the Huaipei Salt Monopoly." *Papers on China,* vol. 16. Mimeographed. Cambridge: East Asian Research Center, Harvard University, 1962.

Michie, A., and Francis, R. *Accounts and Papers,* 65. Report of the Delegates of the Shanghai General Chamber of Commerce on the Trade of the Upper Yangtze. London, 1870.

Miner, Horace M., ed. *The City in Modern Africa.* New York: Praeger, 1967.

Misra, B. B. *The Indian Middle Classes.* London: Oxford University Press, 1961.

Mookerjee, R. K. *Indian Shipping.* London: Longmans, Green and Co., 1912.

Moreland, William H. *From Akbar to Aurangzeb: A Study in Indian Economic History.* London: Macmillan and Co., Ltd., 1923.

_____. *India at the Death of Akbar.* London: Macmillan and Co., Ltd., 1920.

_____. "The Ships of the Arabian Sea about A.D. 1500." *Journal of the Royal Asiatic Society,* April 1939, pp. 174–75.

Morris, M. D. "Private Industrial Investment on the Indian Sub-Continent, 1900–1939: Some Methodological Considerations." *Modern Asian Studies* 8 (1974): 535–55.

_____. "Towards a Reinterpretation of Nineteenth Century Indian Economic History." *Journal of Economic History* 23 (December 1963): 606–18. Reprinted, with commentaries in *The Indian Economic and Social History Review* 5 (March 1968): 1–100.

_____. "Trends and Tendencies in Indian Economic History." *The Indian Economic and Social History Review* 5 (December 1968): 319–88.

_____. "Values as an Obstacle to Economic Growth in South Asia: An Historical Survey." *Journal of Economic History* 27 (December 1967): 588–607.

Morris, M. D., and Dudley, C. B. "Selected Railway Statistics for the Indian Sub-continent and Burma, 1853–1946/47." Paper.

Morse, Hosea B. *The Chronicles of the East India Company Trading to China, 1635–1834.* 5 vols. Oxford: The Clarendon Press, 1926–29.

_____. *The Gilds of China.* 2d ed. London: Longmans, Green and Co., 1932.

Morse, Richard. "Trends and Issues in Latin American Urban Research." *Latin American Research Review* 1 (1971): 3–34; 2 (1971): 19–75.

Moser, Charles K. *The Cotton Textile Industry of Far Eastern Countries.* Boston: Peperell Manufacturing Co., 1930.

Mukherjee, M. *National Income of India: Trends and Structure.* Calcutta, 1969.

Mukherjee, Radhakamal. *The Changing Face of Bengal.* Calcutta: The University of Calcutta, 1938.

Murphey, Rhoads. "China's Transport Problem and Communist Planning." *Economic Geography* 32 (1956): 17–28.

_____. "City and Countryside as Ideological Issues: India and China." *Comparative Studies in Society and History* 14 (June 1972): 250–67.

_____. "The City in the Swamp: Aspects of the Site and Early Growth of Calcutta." *The Geographical Journal* 130 (June 1964): 241–56.

_____. "Colonialism in Asia and the Role of the Port Cities." *East Lakes Geographer* 5 (1969): 24–49.

_____. "Man and Nature in China." *Modern Asian Studies* 1 (1967): 313–33.

_____. *Shanghai: Key to Modern China.* Cambridge: Harvard University Press, 1953.

_____. "Traditionalism and Colonialism: Changing Urban Roles in Asia." *Journal of Asian Studies* 29 (November 1969): 67–84.

_____. *The Treaty Ports and China's Modernization: What Went Wrong?* Michigan Papers in Chinese Studies, no. 7. Ann Arbor: Center for Chinese Studies, University of Michigan, 1970.

Murphey, Rhoads, and Meisner, M. *The Mozartian Historian.* Berkeley: University of California Press, 1976.

Murray, W. H. *China.* Edinburgh, 1843.

Myers, Ramon H. *The Chinese Peasant Economy: Agricultural Development in Hopei and Shantung, 1890–1949.* East Asian Series, no. 47. Cambridge: Harvard University Press, 1970.

Nakahara Teruo. "The Flow of Commodities on Grain Transport Ships During the Ch'ing Dynasty." *Shigaku Kenkyū* 64 (1959).

_____. "The Mercantilization of the Tribute Grain Under the Ch'ing Dynasty." *Shigaku Kenkyū* 70 (1965).

Nambiar, O. K. *Portuguese Pirates and Indian Seamen.* Mysore: M. Bhaktavatsalam, 1955.

Naqvi, H. K. "The Progress of Urbanization in the United Provinces, 1550–1800." *Journal of the Economic and Social History of the Orient* 10 (1967): 81–99.

_____. *Urban Centers and Industrialization in Upper India, 1556–1803.* Bombay: Asia Publishing House, 1968.

_____. *Urbanization and Urban Centers Under the Great Mughals, 1556–1707.* Simla: International Publishing Service, 1971.

Needham, Joseph. *Science and Civilization in China.* Vol. 4. Cambridge: Cambridge University Press, 1971.

_____. *Time and Eastern Man.* London: Oxford University Press, 1965.

Nehru, Jawaharlal. *Toward Freedom.* New York: The John Day Company, 1941.

O'Connel, James. "The Concept of Modernization." *South Atlantic Quarterly* 64 (1965): 549–64.

Oliphant, Lawrence. *Narrative of the Earl of Elgin's Mission to China and Japan in the Years 1857, 1858, and 1859.* New York: Harper and Brothers, 1860.

Orme, Robert. *Historical Fragments of the Mughal Empire.* London: C. Nourse, 1782.

Ou Chi-luan. *Kuang-chou chih yin-yeh* [Traditional banking in Canton]. Canton, 1932.

Owen, David. *British Opium Policy in India and China.* New Haven: Yale University Press, 1934.

Pannikkar, Kavalam M. *Asia and Western Dominance.* London: Allen and Unwin, 1953.

Parkinson, C. N. *Trade in the Eastern Seas, 1793–1813.* Cambridge: The University Press, 1937.

Parry, John H. *The Age of Reconnaissance.* London: New American Library, 1963.

_____. *The Discovery of the Sea.* London: Weidenfeld and Nicolson, 1975.

_____. *Trade and Exploration in the Age of Renaissance.* New York: Harper and Row, 1961.

Parry, John H., ed. *The Establishment of the European Hegemony, 1415–1715.* New York: Harper and Row, 1961.

Pearn, B. R. *A History of Rangoon.* Rangoon: American Baptist Mission Press, 1939.

Pearson, M. N. "Merchants and Rulers in Mughal Gujerat." Paper, 1973.

_____. "Commerce and Compulsion: Gujerati Merchants and the Portuguese System in Western India, 1500–1600." Ph.D. dissertation, University of Michigan, 1971.

Pelcovits, Nathan A. *Old China Hands and the Foreign Office.* New York: King's Crown Press, 1948.

Pelliot, Paul. "Le voyage de M. M. Gabet et Huc." *T'oung Pao,* 1925–26, pp. 133–78.

P'eng chih-i, ed. *Chung-kuo chin tai shou kung yeh shih tzu liao* [Materials on the history of modern China's handicraft industries]. vol. 11. Peking, 1957.

_____. "Shih chiu shih chi hou ch'i Chung-kuo ch'eng shih shou kung-yeh shang-yeh hsing hui ti chung chien ho tso yung" [The importance and function of urban handicraft and commercial organization in the late nineteenth century]. *Li-shih Yen-chiu* 1 (1965): 81–90.

Perkins, Dwight. *Agricultural Development in China, 1368–1968.* Committee on the Economy of China Monographs. Chicago: Aldine, 1969.

Perkins, Dwight, ed. *China's Modern Economy in Historical Perspective.* Stanford: Stanford University Press, 1975.

Petrov, Wassily. *Triple Commission.* London: Eyre, Methuen, 1968.

Phipps, John. *A Practical Treatise on China and the Eastern Trade.* London, 1836.

Rankin, Mary Backus. *Early Chinese Revolutionaries: Radical Intellectuals in Shanghai and Chekiang, 1902–1911.* East Asian Series, no. 50. Cambridge: Harvard University Press, 1971.

Rasmussen, O. D. *Tientsin: An Illustrated Outline History.* Tientsin: The Tientsin Press, Ltd., 1925.

_____. *What's Right with China.* Shanghai: The Commercial Press, Ltd., 1927.

Rawlinson, H. G. *British Beginnings in Western India, 1579–1675.* Oxford: The Clarendon Press, 1920.

Raychaudhuri, Tappan. *Bengal under Akbar and Jahangir.* Calcutta: A. Mukherjee, 1953.

_____. *Jan Company in Coromandel, 1605–1690.* The Hague: M. Nijhoff, 1962.

Reischauer, E. O., ed. and trans. *Ennin's Travels in T'ang China.* New York: Ronald Press Company, 1955.

Remer, Charles F. *The Foreign Trade of China.* Shanghai: The Commercial Press, Ltd., 1926.

Report of the Mission to China of the Blackburn Chamber of Commerce, 1896–97. Blackburn, 1898.

Reynolds, Bruce. "The Impact of Trade and Foreign Investment on Industrialization: Chinese Textiles, 1875–1931." Ph.D. dissertation, University of Michigan, 1974.

_____. "Weft: The Technological Sanctuary of Chinese Handspun Yarn." *Ch'ing-shih wen-t'i* 3 (1974): 1–19.

Richards, F. J., ed. *Islam in the Trade of Asia.* Philadelphia: University of Pennsylvania Press, 1970.

Ross, J. R. "Journal of a Trip Overland from Hainan to Canton in 1819." *The Chinese Repository* 18 (May 1849): 228–35.

Rozman, Gilbert. *Urban Networks in Ch'ing China and Tokugawa Japan.* Princeton: Princeton University Press, 1973.

Rudolph, L. I., and Rudolph, S. H. *The Modernity of Tradition: Political Development in India.* Chicago: University of Chicago Press, 1967.

Saeki Tomi. *Shindai ensei no kenkyū* [A study of the Ch'ing dynasty salt monopoly]. Kyoto: Toyōshi Kenkyūkai, 1956.

Sargent, Arthur J. *Anglo-Chinese Trade and Diplomacy.* Oxford: The Clarendon Press, 1907.

Schwartz, Benjamin. *In Search of Wealth and Power: Yen Fu and the West.* East Asian Series, no. 16. Cambridge: Harvard University Press, 1964.

_____. "The Limits of 'Tradition versus Modernity.'" *Daedalus* 101 (Spring 1972): 71–88.

_____. "Modernization and the Maoist Vision: Some Reflections on Chinese Communist Goals." *The China Quarterly* 21 (1965): 3–19.

Seal, Anil. *The Emergence of Indian Nationalism: Competition and Collaboration in the Later Nineteenth Century.* Cambridge and New York: Cambridge University Press, 1968.

Sen Gupta, K. P. *The Christian Missionaries in Bengal, 1793–1833.* 1st ed. Calcutta: Firma K. L. Mukhopadhyay, 1971.

Shih Kuo-heng. *The Early Development of the Modern Chinese Business Class.* Part 2. Mimeographed. New York: Institute of Pacific Relations, 1949.

Shiner, L. E. "Tradition/Modernity: An Ideal Type Gone Astray." *Comparative Studies in Society and History* 17 (1975): 245–52.

Singer, Martin. "Beyond Tradition and Modernity in Madras." *Comparative Studies in Society and History* 13 (1971): 160–95.

_____. *When a Great Tradition Modernizes.* New York: Praeger, 1972.

Sinha, Devi P. *The Educational Policy of the East India Company in Bengal to 1854.* Calcutta: Verry, 1964.

Sinha, Nandalal K. *The Economic History of Bengal.* Calcutta: Verry, 1956.

Sivin, N. "Chinese Concepts in Time." *Earlham Review* 1 (1966): 82–92.

Skinner, G. W. "Chinese Peasants and the Closed Community: An Open and Shut Case." *Comparative Studies in Society and History* 13 (1971): 270–81.

_____. "Marketing and Social Structure in Rural China." *Journal of Asian Studies* 24 (1964–65): 3–43, 195–224, 363–99.

Smith, Adam. *The Wealth of Nations.* London, 1776.

Smith, George. *Narrative of an Exploratory Visit to the Consular Cities of China, on Behalf of the Church Missionary Society, in the Years 1844, 1845 and 1846.* London: Seeley, Burnside and Seeley, 1848.

Spate, O. H. K. "Factors in the Development of Capital Cities." *The Geographical Review* 32 (1942): 622–31.

Spear, Percival. *India: A Modern History.* 2d ed. History of the Modern World Series. Ann Arbor: University of Michigan Press, 1972.

Spodek, Howard. "Rulers, Merchants and Other Elites in the City-States of Saurashtra, India." Paper read at the South Asia Regional Studies Seminar, at the University of Pennsylvania, March 1973.

Statistical Abstract of India. Delhi, Government of India. Annual publication from 1909.

Statistics of the Chinese National Railways, 1915–1929. Nanking: Kuomintang Government, 1931.

Staunton, G. T. *Notes of Proceedings and Occurences During the British Embassy to Peking in 1816.* London: J. Murray, 1824.

Stokes, Eric. *The English Utilitarians and India.* Oxford: Oxford University Press, 1959.

Sung Ying-hsing. *T'ien Kung K'ai Wu.* Translated by E. T. Z. Sun and S. C. Sun. University Park, Pa.: Pennsylvania State University Press, 1966.

Tables of the Revenue, Population, Commerce, etc., of the United Kingdom and Its Dependencies. London, 1840, 1841, and 1842.

Tamagna, Frank. *Banking and Finance in China.* New York: Institute of Pacific Relations, 1942.

Tawney, Richard H. *Land and Labour in China.* London: G. Allen and Unwin, Ltd., 1932.

Taylor, Bayard. *A Visit to India, China and Japan in the Year 1853.* New York: G. P. Putnam's Sons, 1855, 1869.

Teng Ssu-yu, and Fairbank, John K. *China's Response to the West: A Documentary Survey, 1839–1923.* New York: Atheneum, 1963.

Terada Takanobu. *Sansei chōnin no kenkyū* [A study of Shansi merchants]. Kyoto, 1972.

Ting, L. G. "The Chinese Banks and the Financing of Government and Industry." *Nankai Social and Economic Quarterly* 8 (1935): 578–616.

———. *Recent Developments in China's Cotton Industry.* Shanghai: China Institute of Pacific Relations, 1936.

Tregonning, Kennedy C. *The British in Malaya.* Association for Asian Studies, monograph 18. Tucson: University of Arizona Press, 1965.

Tripathi, A. *Trade and Finance in the Bengal Presidency, 1793–1833.* Calcutta: Verry, 1956.

Tripp, D. C. "Modernization Theory and the Comparative Study of Societies." *Comparative Studies in Society and History* 15 (1973): 199–225.

Tucker, Richard. *Ranade and the Roots of Indian Nationalism.* Chicago: University of Chicago Press, 1972.

Van Leur, J. C. *Indonesian Trade and Society.* The Hague: M. Nijhoff, 1955.

Wadia, Ardeshir R. *The Bombay Dockyard and the Wadia Master Builders.* 2d ed. Bombay, 1957.

Wakeman, Frederic. "Huang-ch'ao ching-shih Wen-pien." *Ch'ing Shih Wen T'i* 1, no. 10 (1969): 8–22.

———. *Strangers at the Gate: Social Disorder in South China, 1839–1861.* Berkeley: University of California Press, 1966.

Wang Ching-yü, ed. *Chung-kuo chin tai kung yeh shih tzu liao chi yao: ti erh chi* [Materials on the history of modern industry in China, second series]. 2 vols. Peking, 1960.

———. "Shih chiu shih chi wai kuo ch'in hua chih yeh chung ti hua shang fu ku shou tung" [The rise of Chinese merchants as investors in foreign-controlled enterprises in the late nineteenth century]. *Li shih Yen chiu* 4 (1965): 39–74.

Watson, Andrew, trans. *Transport in Transition: The Evolution of Traditional Shipping in China.* Michigan Abstracts of Chinese and Japanese Works on Chinese History, no. 3. Ann Arbor: Center for Chinese Studies, University of Michigan, 1970.

Weiner, Myron, ed. *Modernization: The Dynamics of Growth.* New York: Basic, 1966.

Weisskopf, T. W. "Dependence and Imperialism in India." In *Imperialism in Asia,* edited by Edward Friedman and Mark Selden. New York: Paragon, 1973.

Williams, F. W., ed. "The Diary of S. Wells Williams." *Journal of the North China Branch Royal Asiatic Society* 42 (1911): 1–232.

Wills, John E. *Pepper, Guns, and Parleys: The Dutch East India Company and China, 1662–1681.* East Asian Series. Cambridge: Harvard University Press, 1974.

Wilmott, W. E., ed. *Economic Organization in Chinese Society.* Stanford: Stanford University Press, 1972.

Wilson, Charles R., ed. *Early Annals of the English in Bengal.* 3 vols. Calcutta, 1895–1917.

———. *Old Fort William in Bengal.* 2 vols. Calcutta, 1906.

Wilson, James H. *China: Travels and Investigations in the Middle Kingdom.* New York: D. Appleton and Company, 1887.

Winterbotham, William. *Historical and Geographical View of the Chinese Empire.* London, 1795. Printed in Philadelphia: Dunning, Hyer and Palmer Printers, 1796.

Wolf, Eric. "Understanding Civilizations: A Review Article." *Comparative Studies in Society and History* 9 (1967): 446–65.

Woytinsky, Wladimir S., and Woytinsky, Emma S. *World Population and Production.* New York: Twentieth Century Fund, 1953.

Wright, Arnold, ed. *Twentieth Century Impressions of Hong Kong, Shanghai, and other Treaty Ports of China: Their History, People, Commerce, Industries and Resources.* London, 1908.

Wright, Mary Clabaugh, ed. *China in Revolution: The First Phase, 1900–1913.* New Haven: Yale University Press, 1968.

Wright, S. F. *Hart and the Chinese Customs.* Belfast: W. Mullan, 1950.

Wu Ch'eng-hsi. *Chung-kuo ti yin-hang* [Chinese banks]. Shanghai, 1934.

Yang, L. S. "Government Control of Urban Merchants." *Tsing Hua Journal of Chinese Studies* 8 (1970): nos. 1 and 2.

Yearbook of International Trade Statistics. New York: United Nations, 1934.

Yeh Ch'eng-chung. *Shang-hai hsien hsü-chih* [Gazeteer of Shanghai county]. 30 chüan (Shanghai 1918): 10–14.

Yen Chung-p'ing. *Chung-kuo chin-tai ching-chi shih t'ung-chi tzu-liao hsüan-chi* [Selected statistical materials on China's modern economic history]. Peking, 1955.

————. *Chung-kuo mien fang-chih shih-kao* [Draft history of the Chinese cotton industry]. Peking, 1955.

Yokoyama Suguru. *Chūkoko kindaika no keizai kōzō* [The modernization of China's economic structure]. Tokyo, 1972.

Young, G. M., ed. *Macaulay, Prose and Poetry.* London: R. Hart-Davis, 1952.

Yuji Muramatsu. "A Documentary Study of Chinese Landlordism in Late Ch'ing and Early Republican Kiangnan." *Bulletin of the School of Oriental and African Studies* 29 (1966): 566–99.

Yule, Henry, ed. *The Diary of William Hedges.* 3 vols. London, 1887.

Index